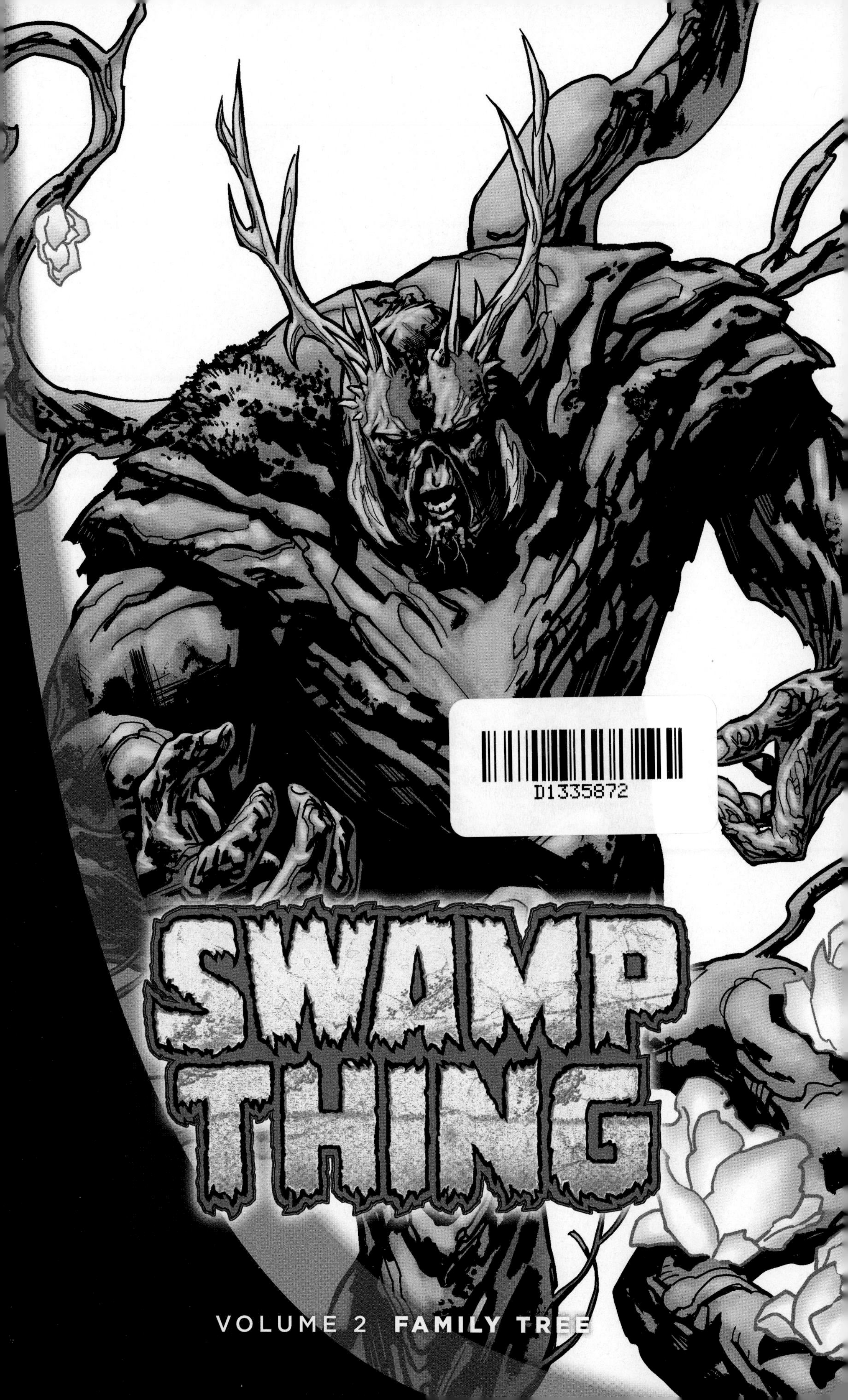
SWAMP
THING
VOLUME 2 FAMILY TREE

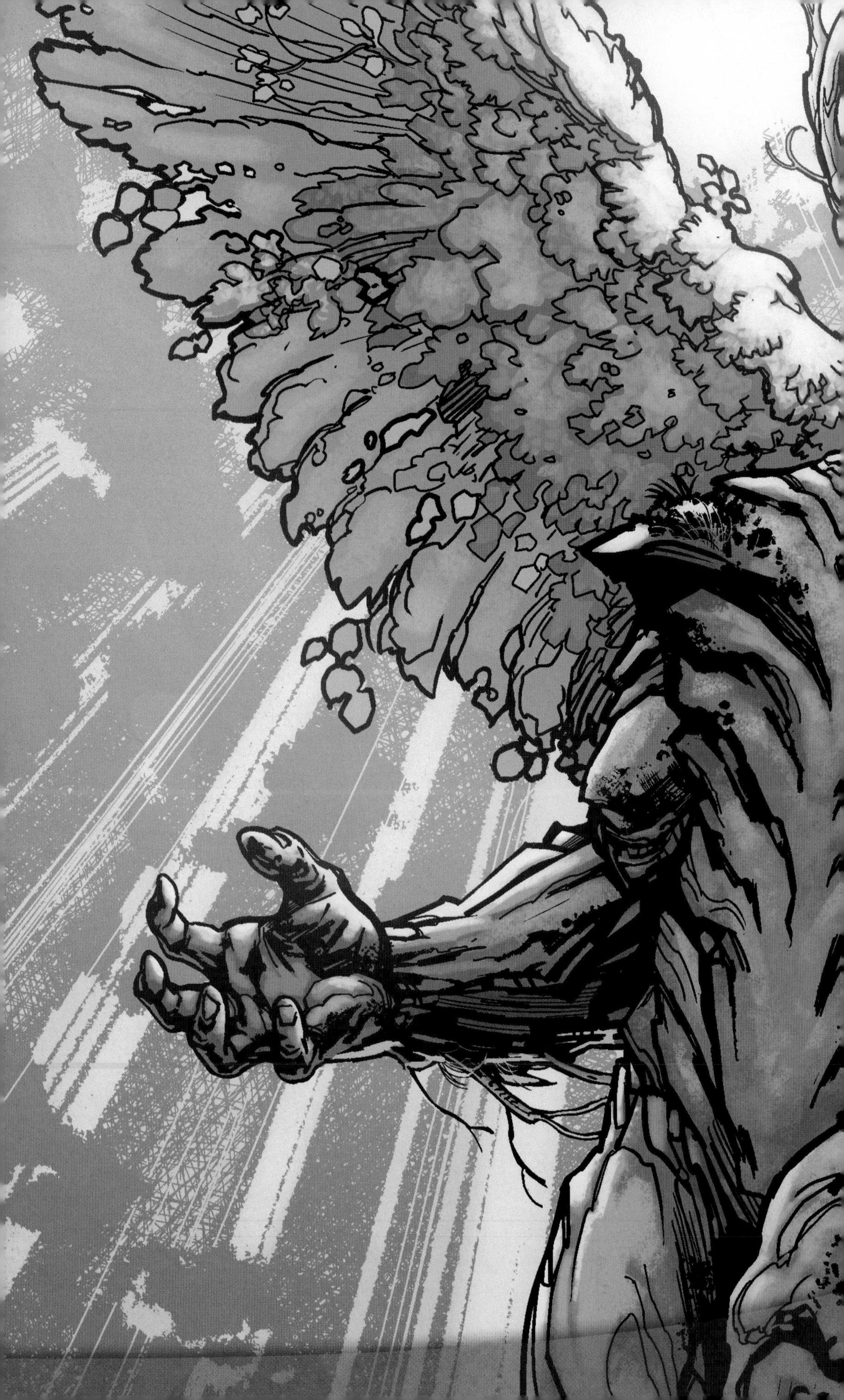

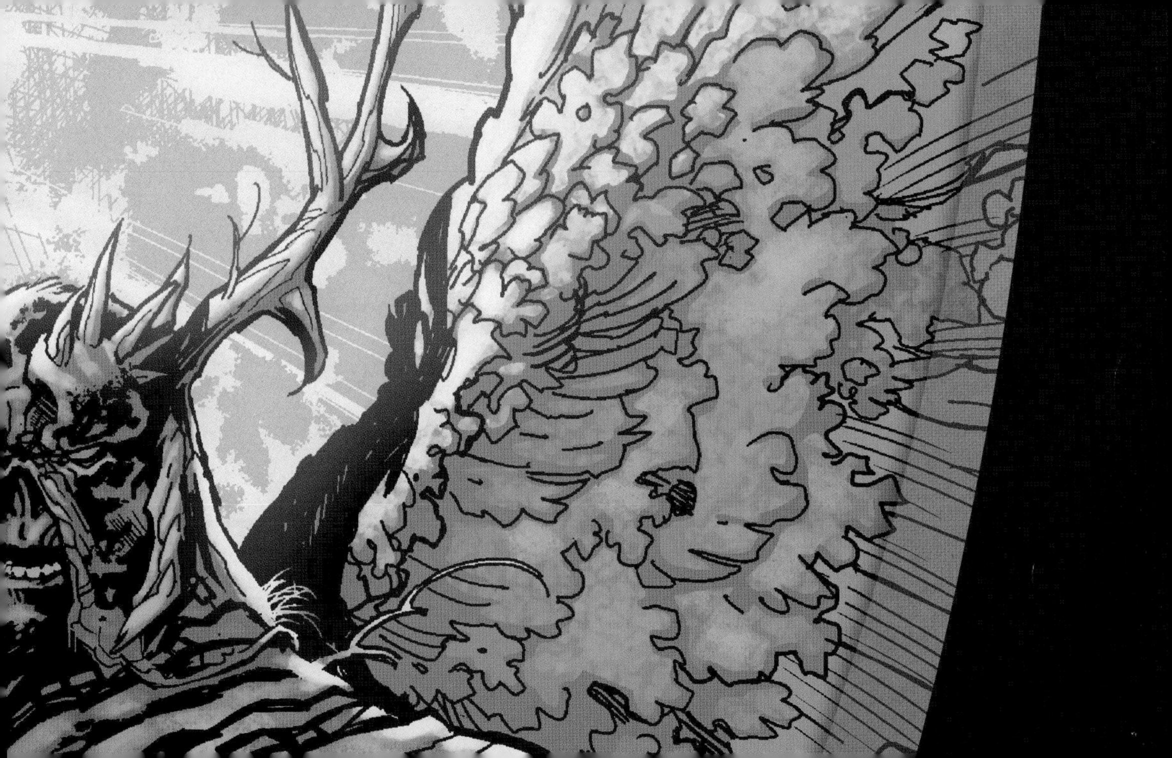

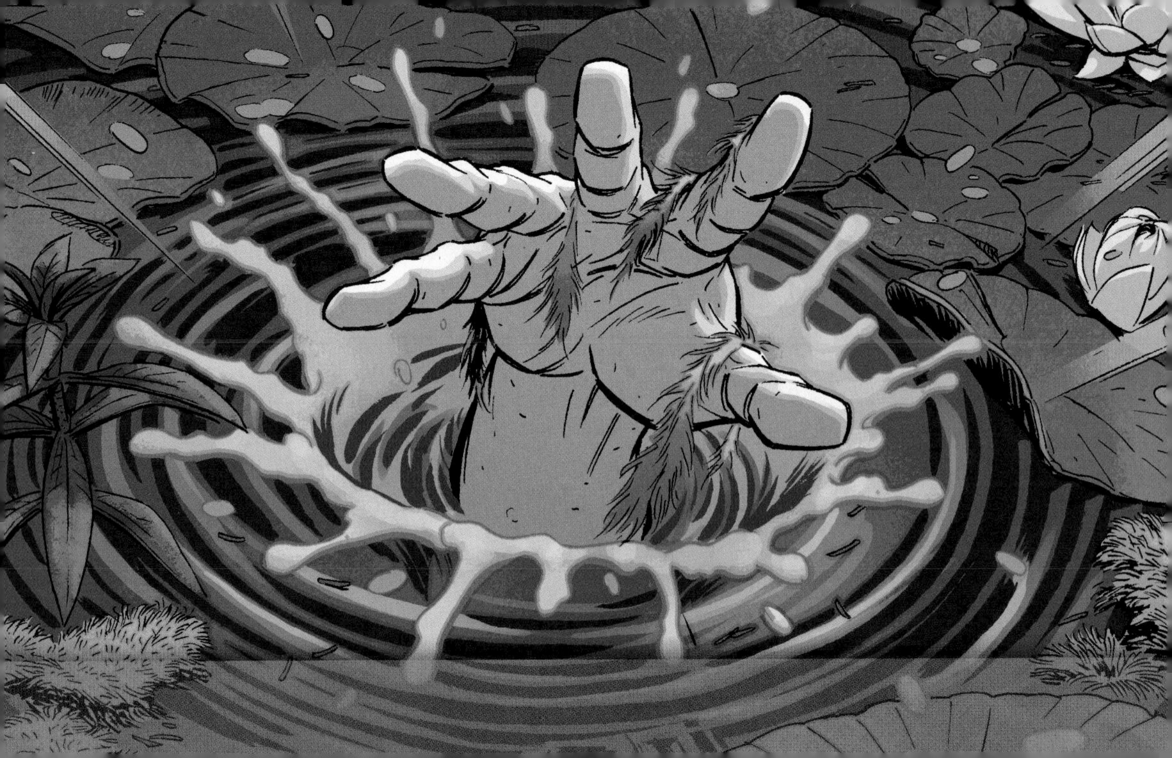

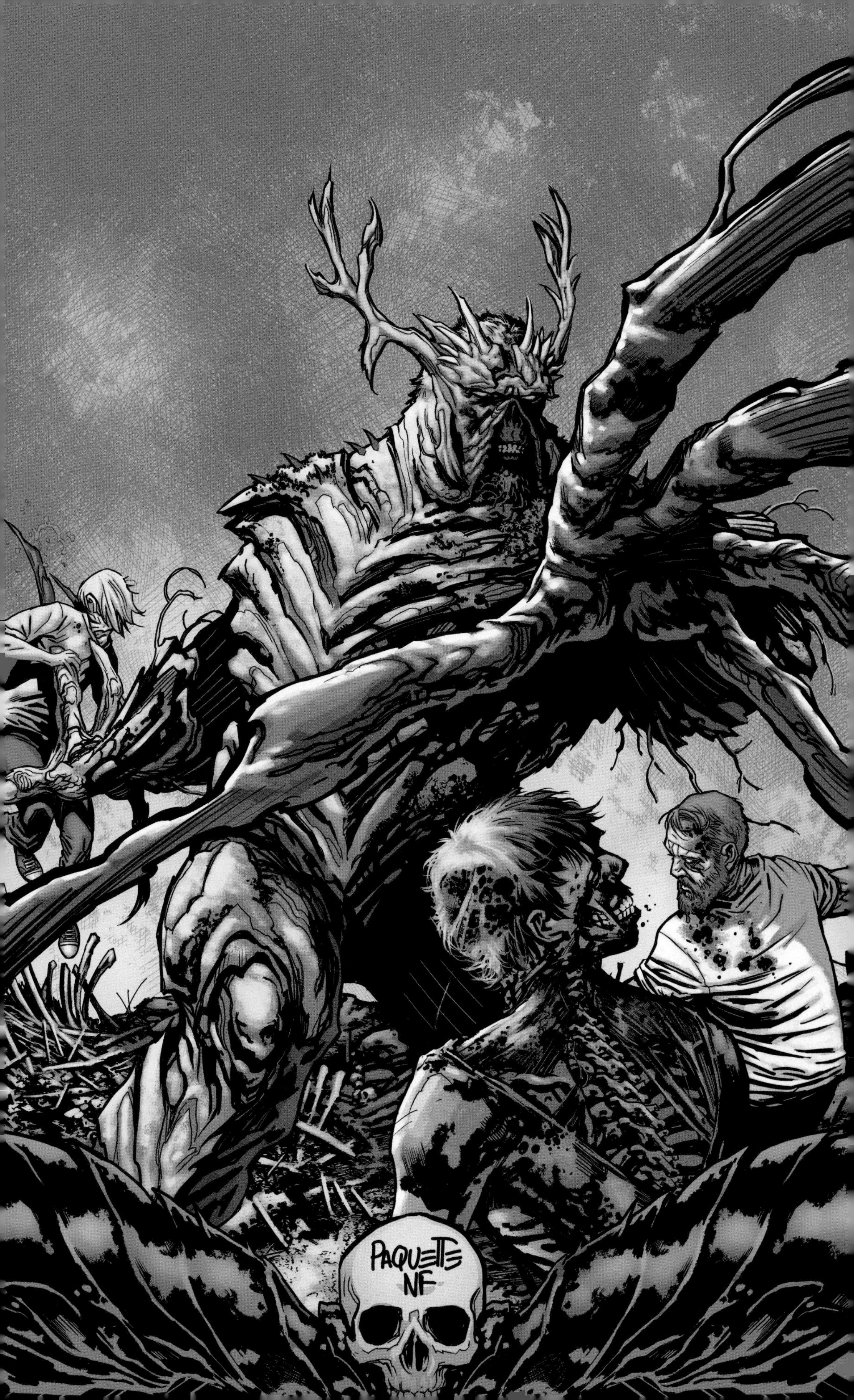
PAQUETTE
NF

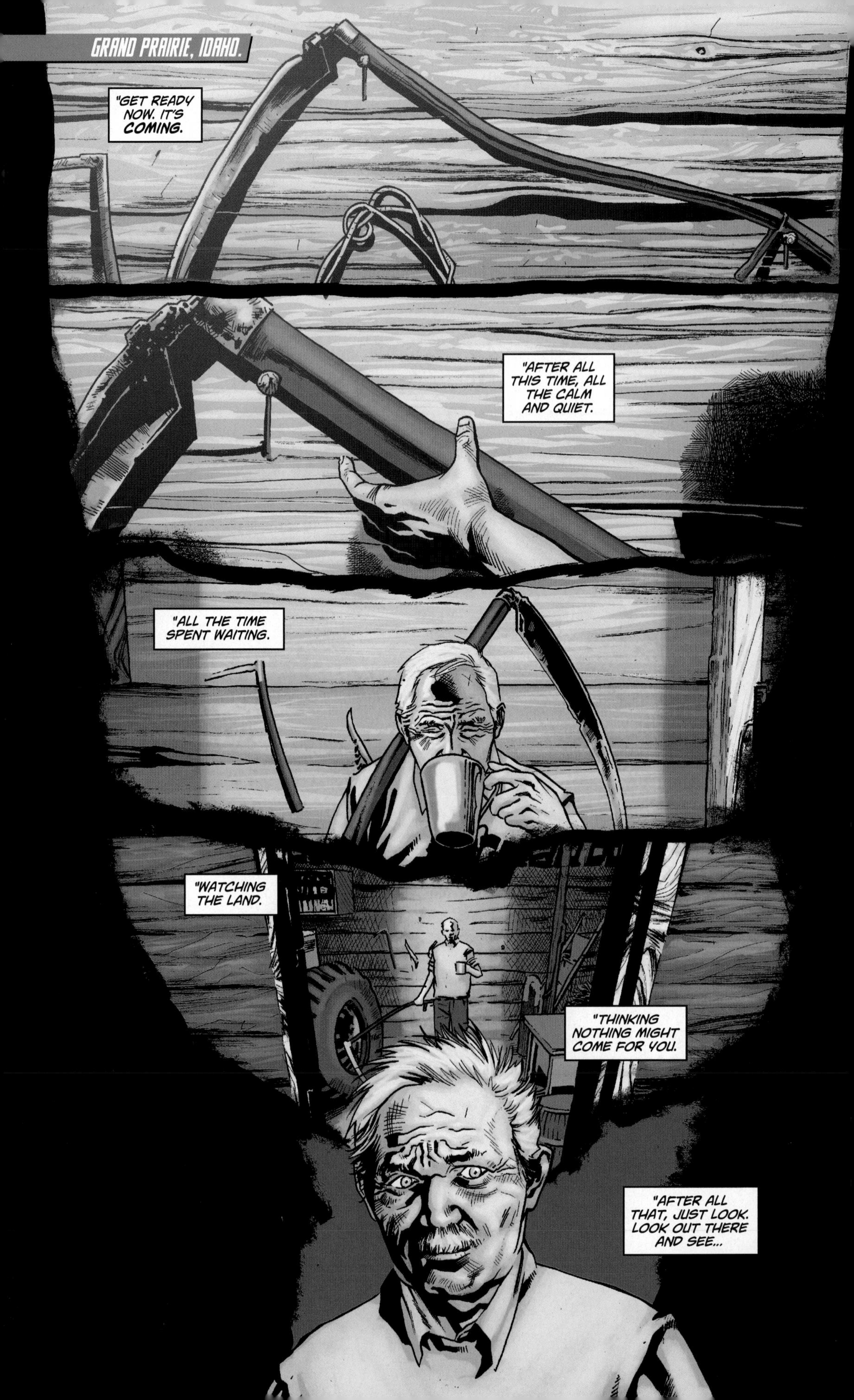
GRAND PRAIRIE, IDAHO.
"GET READY NOW. IT'S COMING.
"AFTER ALL THIS TIME, ALL THE CALM AND QUIET.
"ALL THE TIME SPENT WAITING.
"WATCHING THE LAND.
"THINKING NOTHING MIGHT COME FOR YOU.
"AFTER ALL THAT, JUST LOOK. LOOK OUT THERE AND SEE...

writer: SCOTT SNYDER artists: MARCO RUDY (pgs 1–9) & YANICK PAQUETTE (pgs 10–20)
olors: NATHAN FAIRBAIRN letters: TRAVIS LANHAM cover: YANICK PAQUETTE & NATHAN FAIRBAIRN

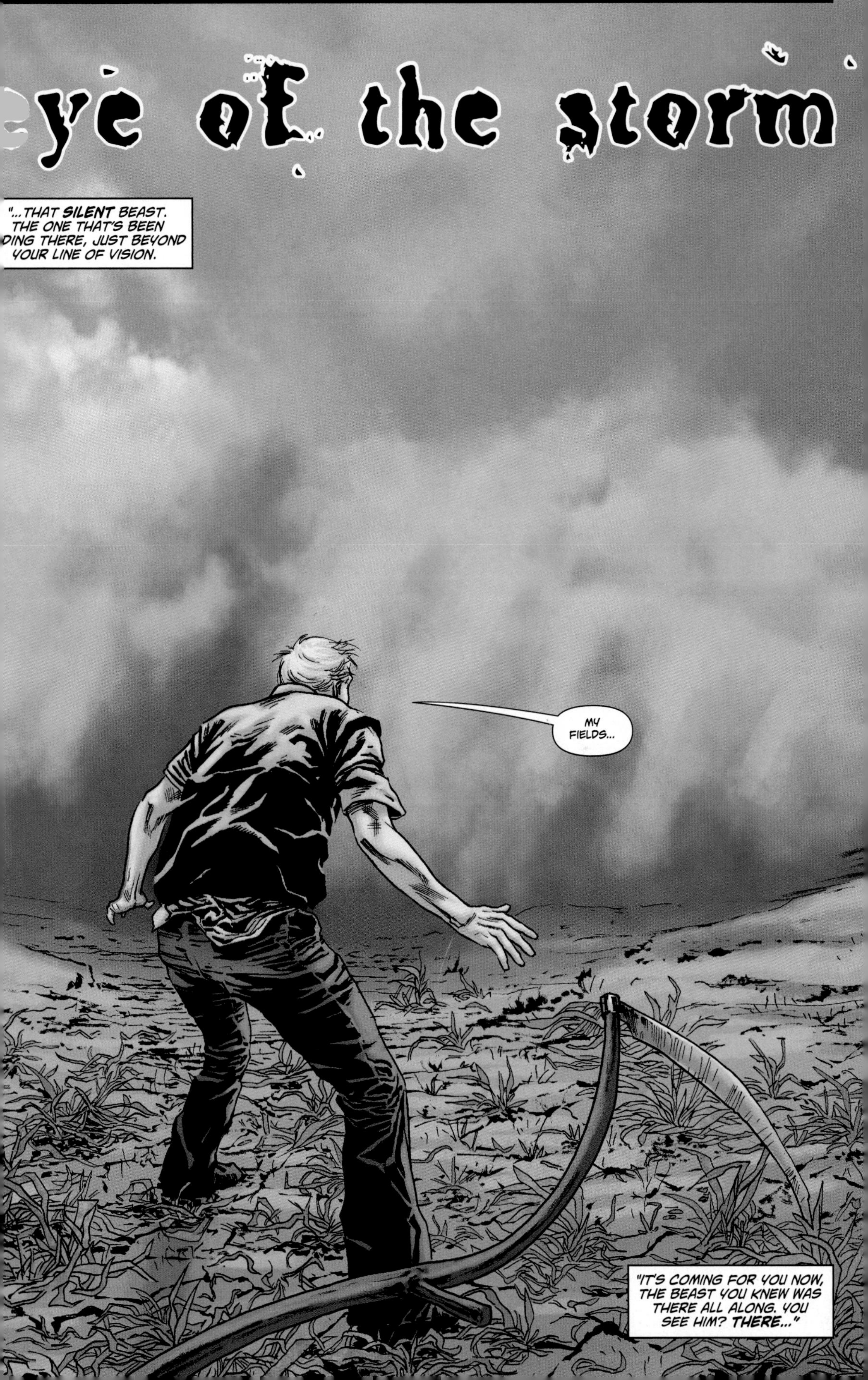
ye of the storm
"...THAT **SILENT** BEAST. THE ONE THAT'S BEEN DING THERE, JUST BEYOND YOUR LINE OF VISION.
MY FIELDS...
"IT'S COMING FOR YOU NOW, THE BEAST YOU KNEW WAS THERE ALL ALONG. YOU SEE HIM? **THERE...**"

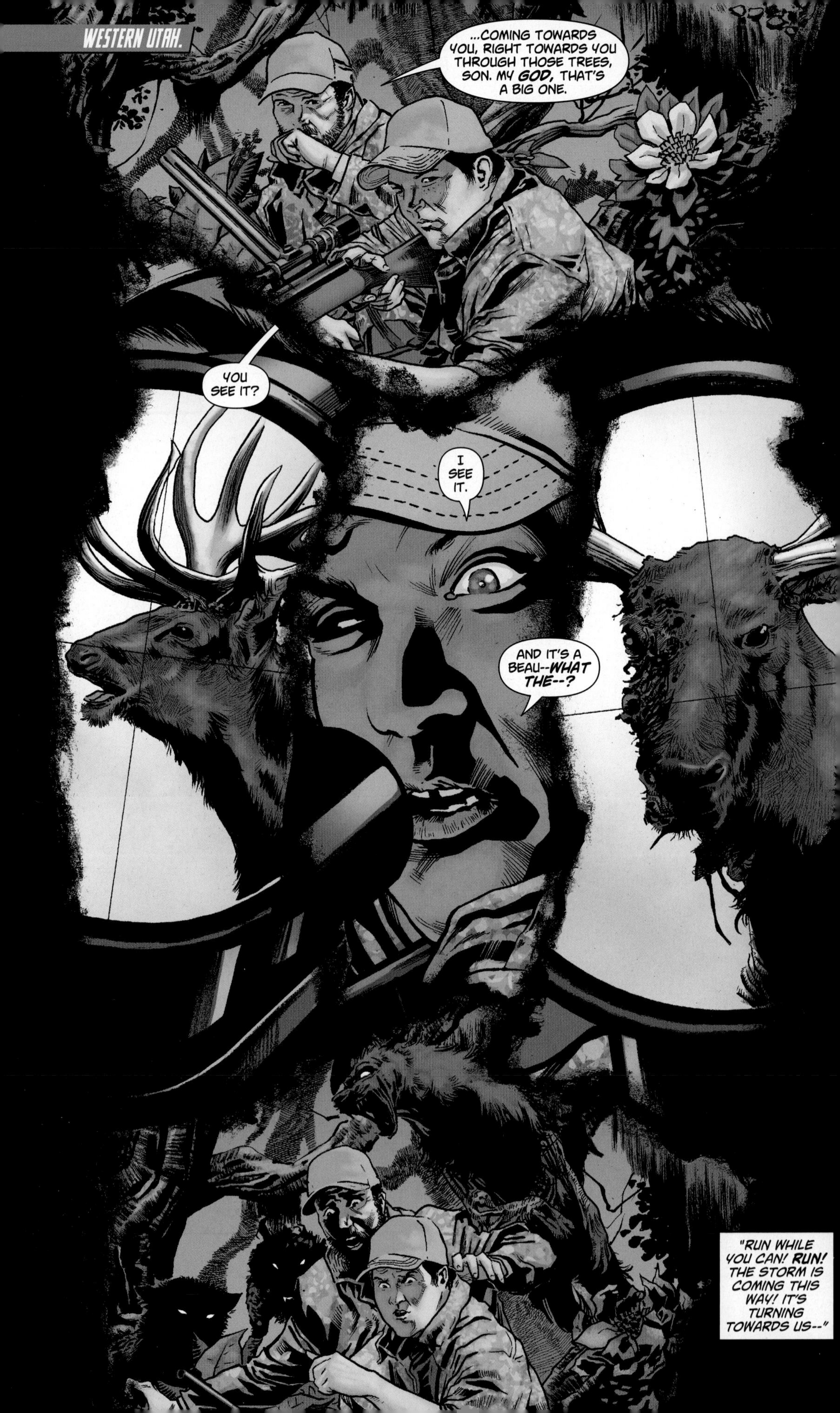
WESTERN UTAH.
...COMING TOWARDS YOU, RIGHT TOWARDS YOU THROUGH THOSE TREES, SON. MY GOD, THAT'S A BIG ONE.
YOU SEE IT?
I SEE IT.
AND IT'S A BEAU--WHAT THE--?
"RUN WHILE YOU CAN! RUN! THE STORM IS COMING THIS WAY! IT'S TURNING TOWARDS US--"

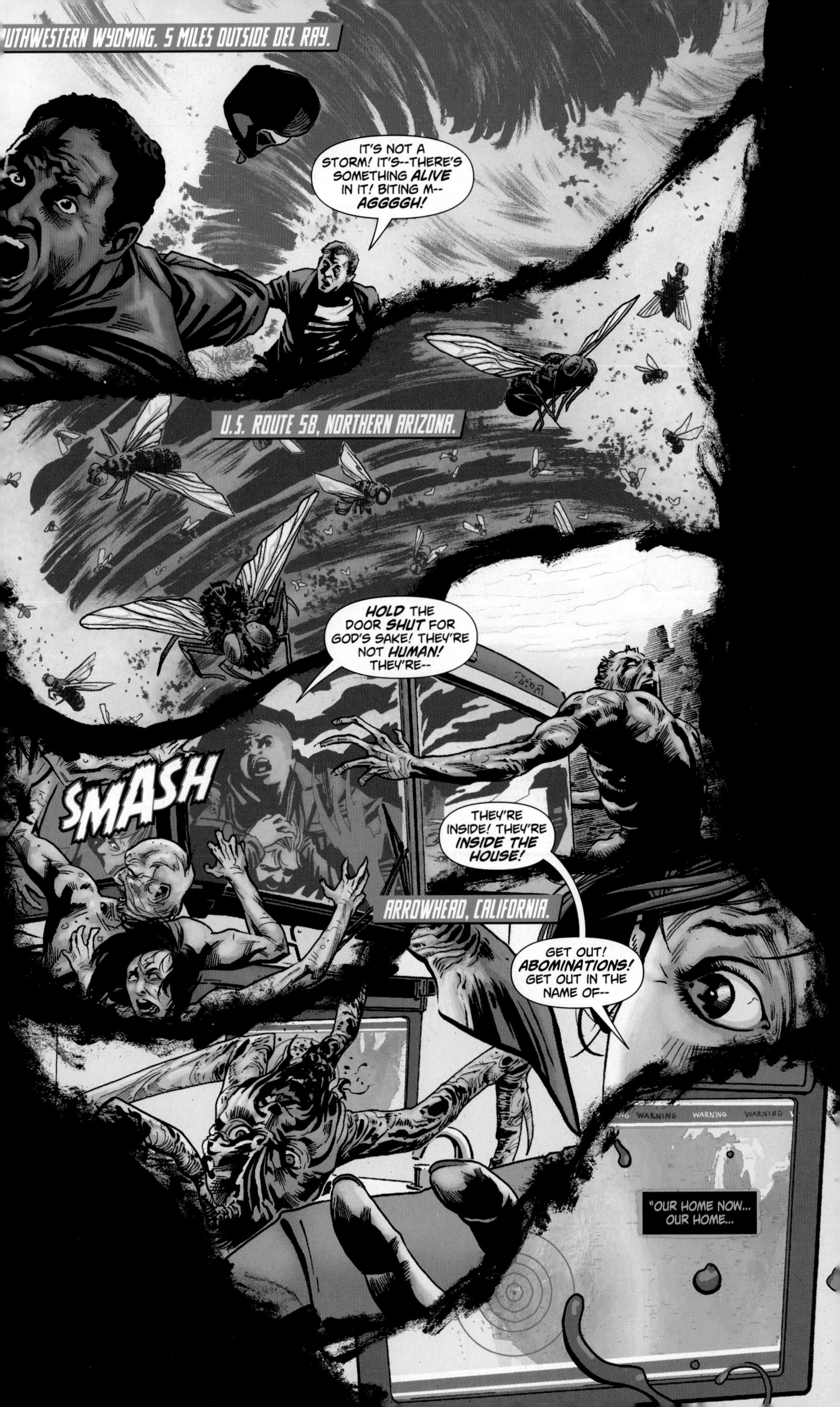
UTHWESTERN WYOMING. 5 MILES OUTSIDE DEL RAY.
IT'S NOT A STORM! IT'S--THERE'S SOMETHING ALIVE IN IT! BITING M-- AGGGGH!
U.S. ROUTE 58, NORTHERN ARIZONA.
HOLD THE DOOR SHUT FOR GOD'S SAKE! THEY'RE NOT HUMAN! THEY'RE--
SMASH
THEY'RE INSIDE! THEY'RE INSIDE THE HOUSE!
ARROWHEAD, CALIFORNIA.
GET OUT! ABOMINATIONS! GET OUT IN THE NAME OF--
WARNING WARNING WARNING
"OUR HOME NOW... OUR HOME...

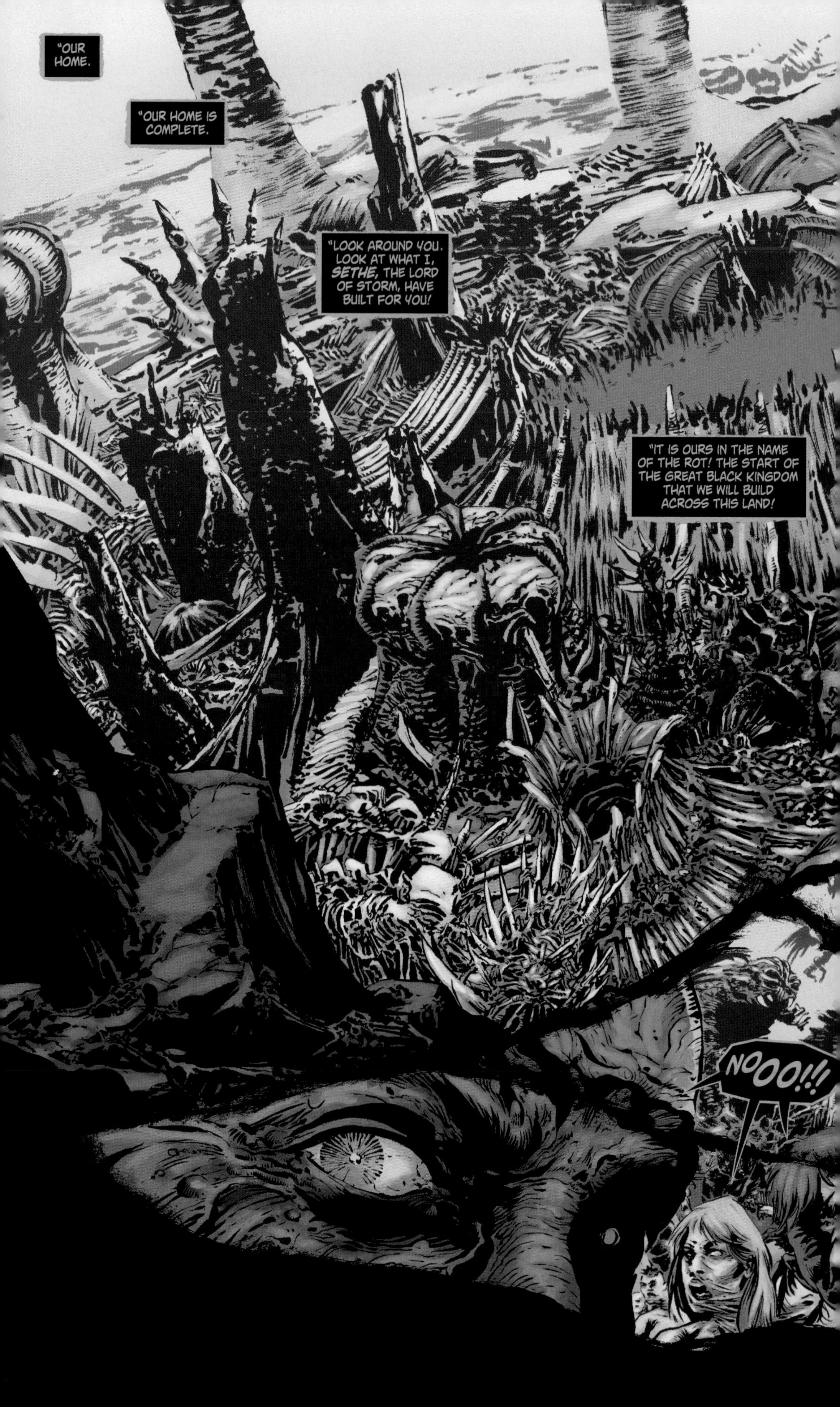
"OUR HOME.
"OUR HOME IS COMPLETE.
"LOOK AROUND YOU. LOOK AT WHAT I, SETHE, THE LORD OF STORM, HAVE BUILT FOR YOU!
"IT IS OURS IN THE NAME OF THE ROT! THE START OF THE GREAT BLACK KINGDOM THAT WE WILL BUILD ACROSS THIS LAND!
NOOO!!!

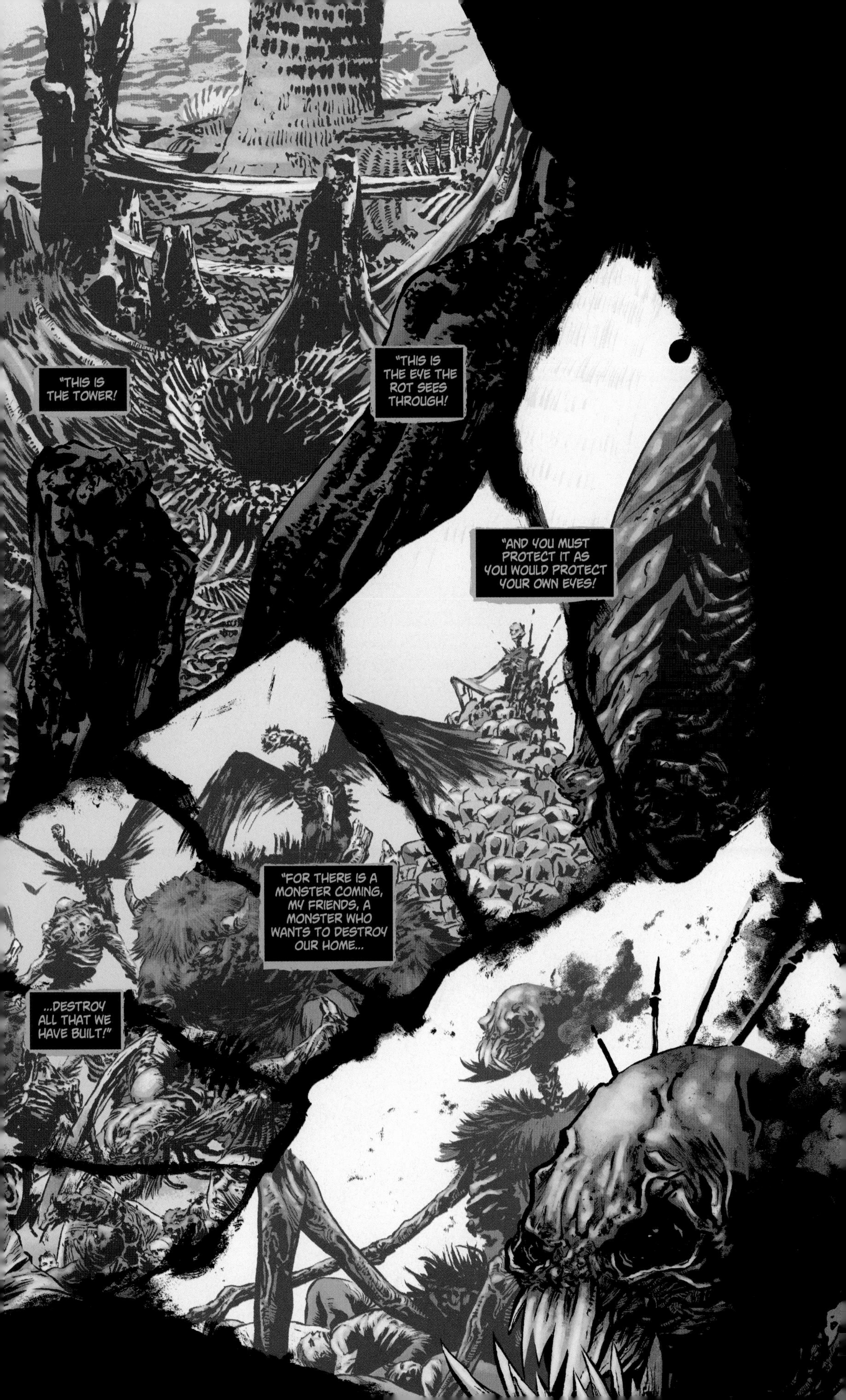
"THIS IS THE TOWER!
"THIS IS THE EYE THE ROT SEES THROUGH!
"AND YOU MUST PROTECT IT AS YOU WOULD PROTECT YOUR OWN EYES!
"FOR THERE IS A MONSTER COMING, MY FRIENDS, A MONSTER WHO WANTS TO DESTROY OUR HOME...
...DESTROY ALL THAT WE HAVE BUILT!"

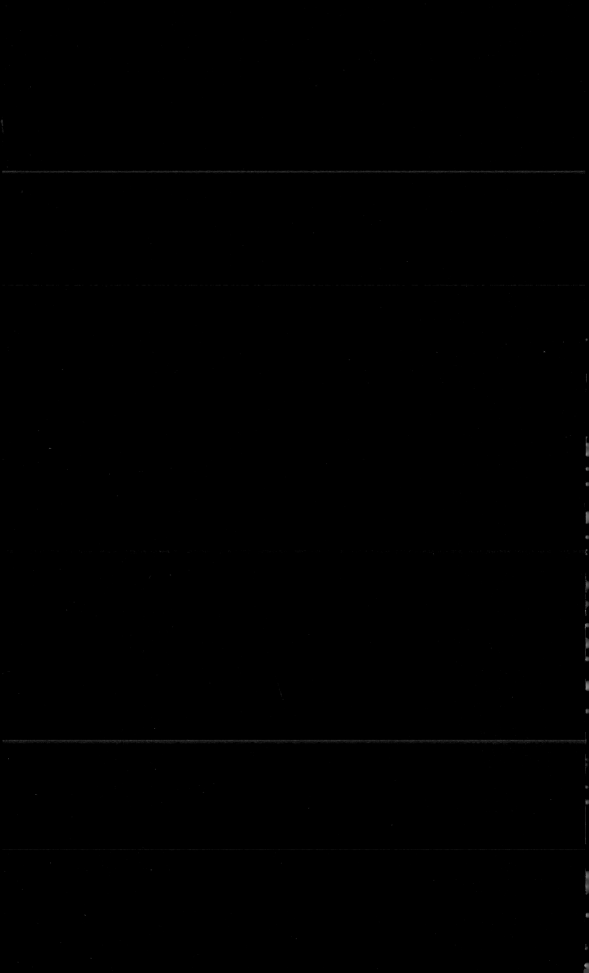

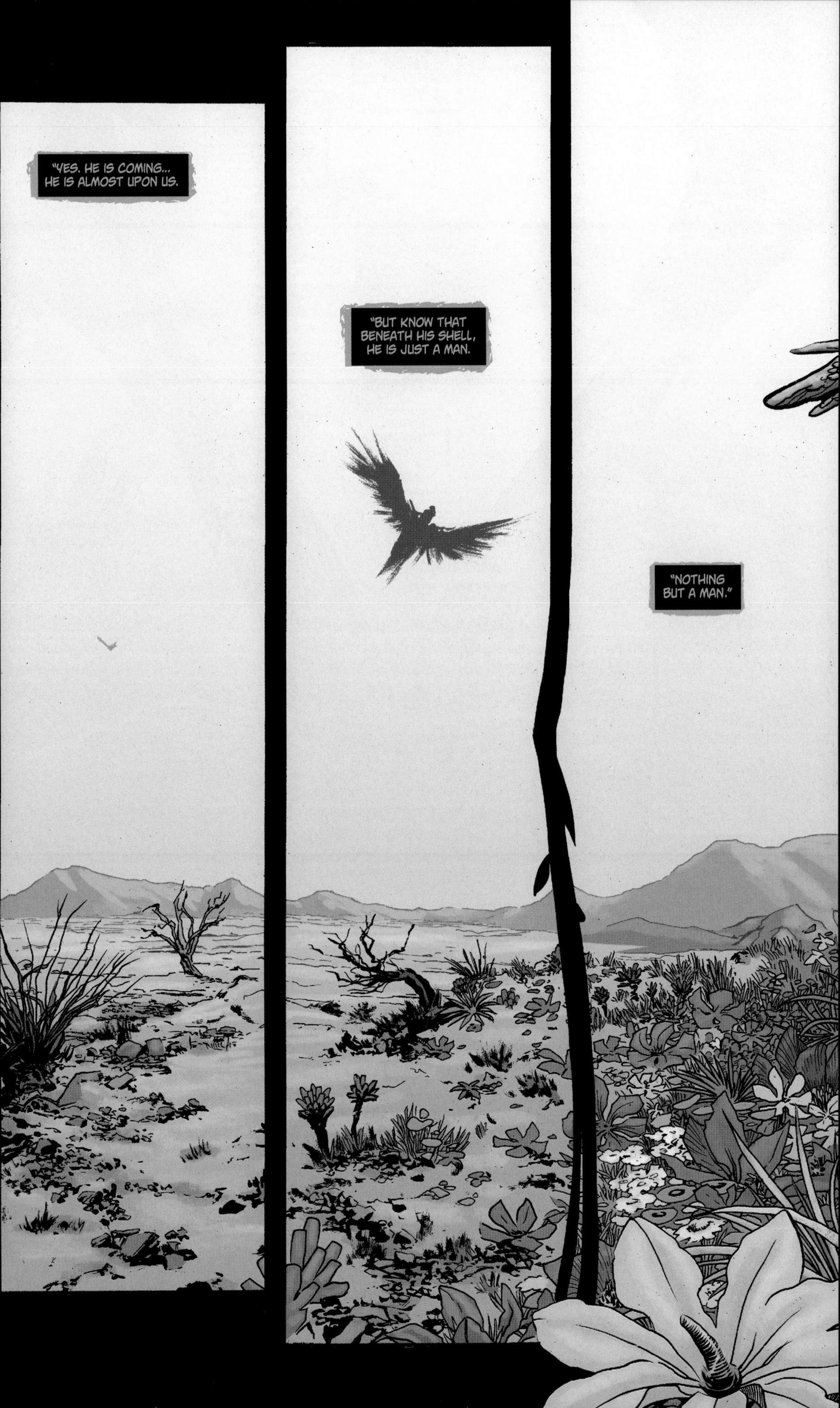
"YES. HE IS COMING... HE IS ALMOST UPON US.
"BUT KNOW THAT BENEATH HIS SHELL, HE IS JUST A MAN.
"NOTHING BUT A MAN."

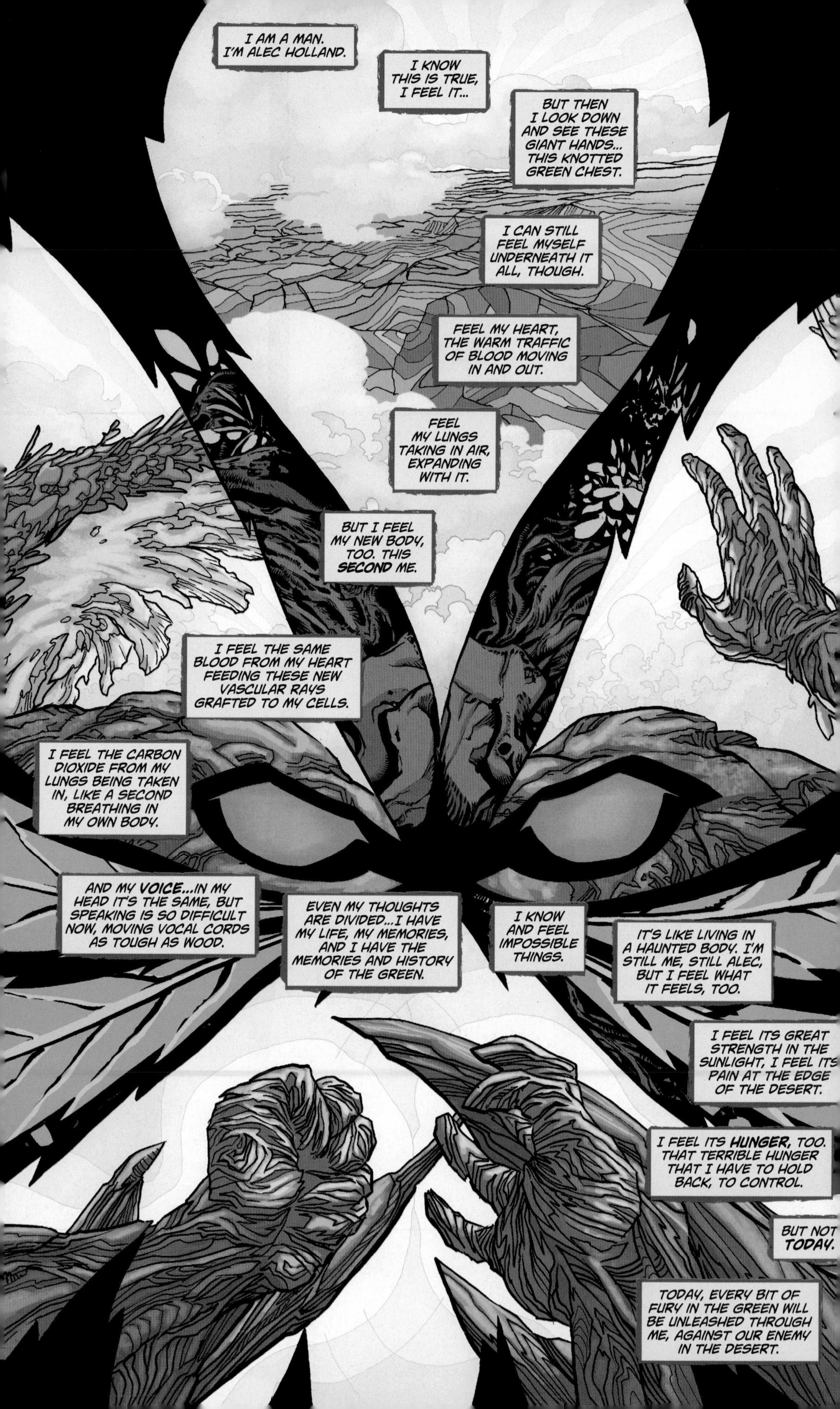
I AM A MAN. I'M ALEC HOLLAND.
I KNOW THIS IS TRUE, I FEEL IT...
BUT THEN I LOOK DOWN AND SEE THESE GIANT HANDS... THIS KNOTTED GREEN CHEST.
I CAN STILL FEEL MYSELF UNDERNEATH IT ALL, THOUGH.
FEEL MY HEART, THE WARM TRAFFIC OF BLOOD MOVING IN AND OUT.
FEEL MY LUNGS TAKING IN AIR, EXPANDING WITH IT.
BUT I FEEL MY NEW BODY, TOO. THIS SECOND ME.
I FEEL THE SAME BLOOD FROM MY HEART FEEDING THESE NEW VASCULAR RAYS GRAFTED TO MY CELLS.
I FEEL THE CARBON DIOXIDE FROM MY LUNGS BEING TAKEN IN, LIKE A SECOND BREATHING IN MY OWN BODY.
AND MY VOICE...IN MY HEAD IT'S THE SAME, BUT SPEAKING IS SO DIFFICULT NOW, MOVING VOCAL CORDS AS TOUGH AS WOOD.
EVEN MY THOUGHTS ARE DIVIDED...I HAVE MY LIFE, MY MEMORIES, AND I HAVE THE MEMORIES AND HISTORY OF THE GREEN.
I KNOW AND FEEL IMPOSSIBLE THINGS.
IT'S LIKE LIVING IN A HAUNTED BODY. I'M STILL ME, STILL ALEC, BUT I FEEL WHAT IT FEELS, TOO.
I FEEL ITS GREAT STRENGTH IN THE SUNLIGHT, I FEEL ITS PAIN AT THE EDGE OF THE DESERT.
I FEEL ITS HUNGER, TOO. THAT TERRIBLE HUNGER THAT I HAVE TO HOLD BACK, TO CONTROL.
BUT NOT TODAY.
TODAY, EVERY BIT OF FURY IN THE GREEN WILL BE UNLEASHED THROUGH ME, AGAINST OUR ENEMY IN THE DESERT.

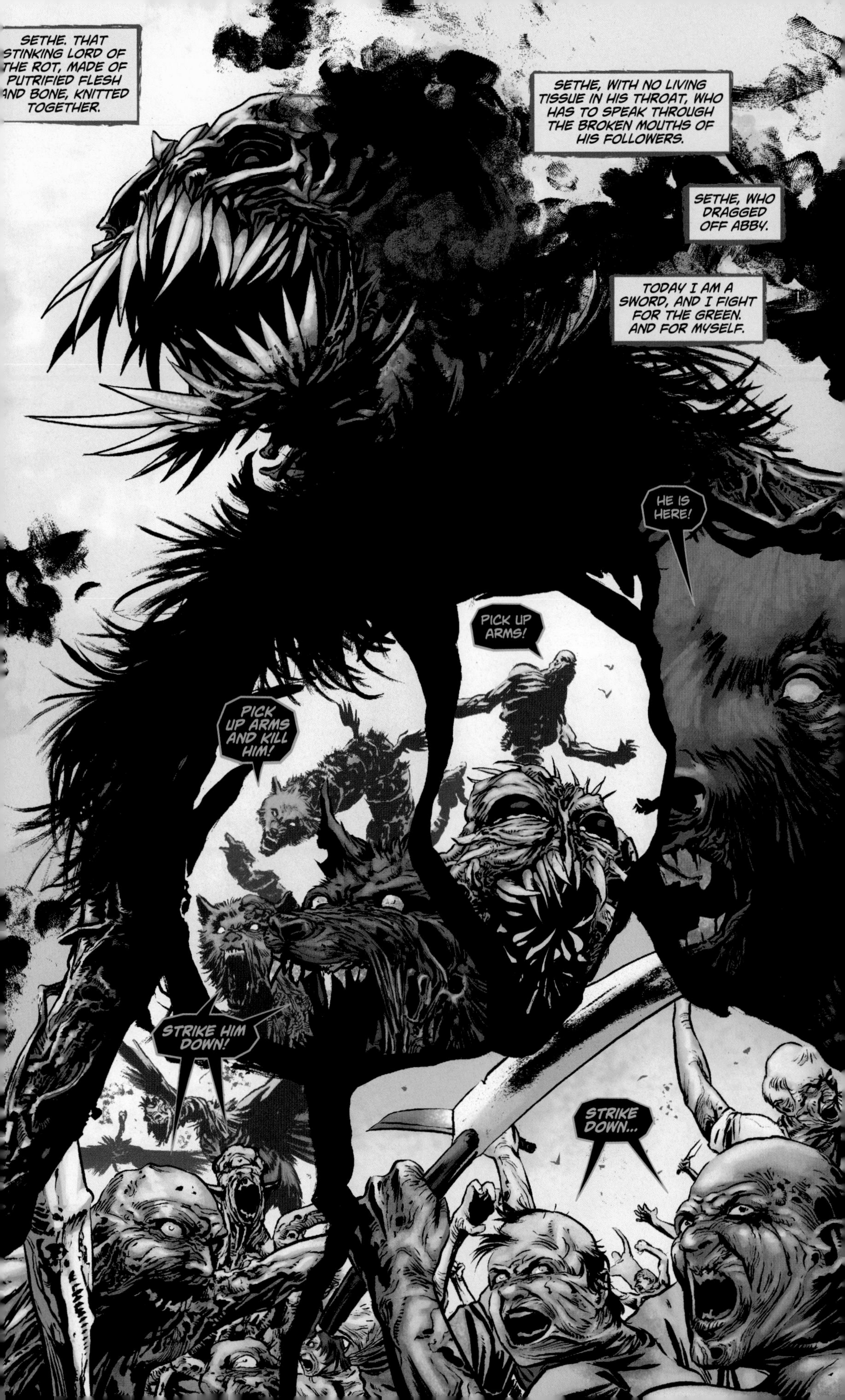
SETHE. THAT STINKING LORD OF THE ROT, MADE OF PUTRIFIED FLESH AND BONE, KNITTED TOGETHER.
SETHE, WITH NO LIVING TISSUE IN HIS THROAT, WHO HAS TO SPEAK THROUGH THE BROKEN MOUTHS OF HIS FOLLOWERS.
SETHE, WHO DRAGGED OFF ABBY.
TODAY I AM A SWORD, AND I FIGHT FOR THE GREEN. AND FOR MYSELF.
HE IS HERE!
PICK UP ARMS!
PICK UP ARMS AND KILL HIM!
STRIKE HIM DOWN!
STRIKE DOWN...

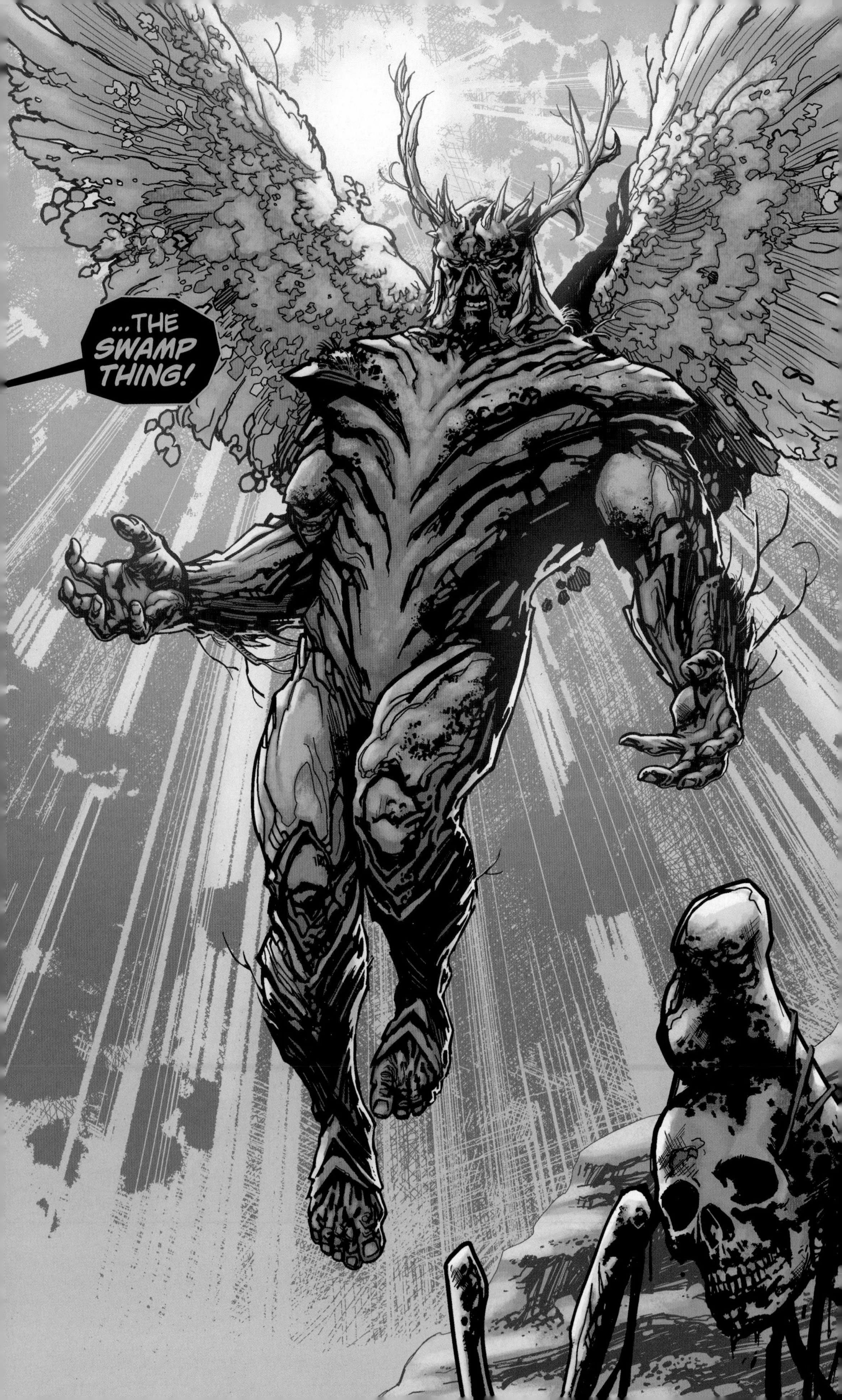
...THE SWAMP THING!

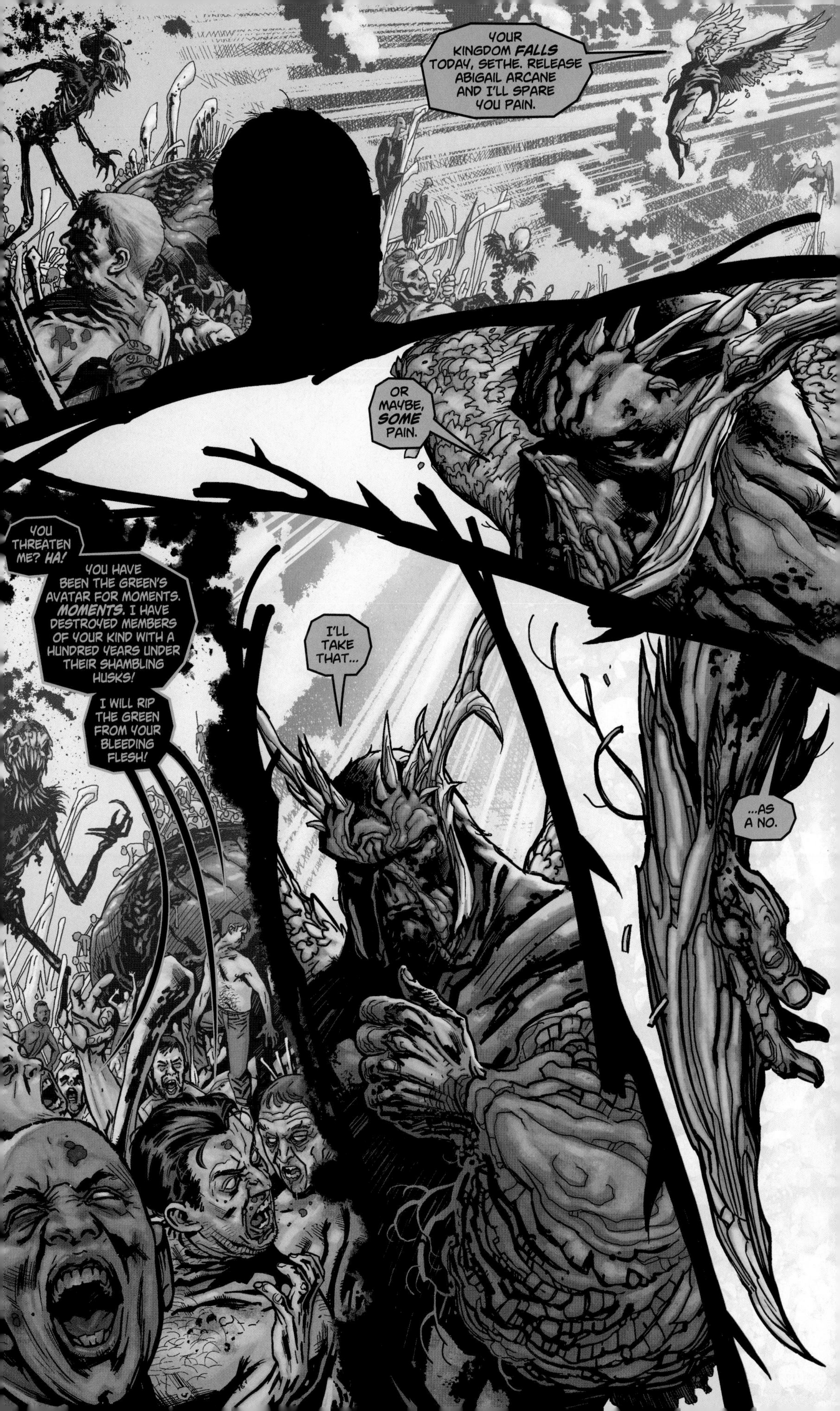
YOUR KINGDOM **FALLS** TODAY, SETHE. RELEASE ABIGAIL ARCANE AND I'LL SPARE YOU PAIN.
OR MAYBE, **SOME** PAIN.
YOU THREATEN ME? **HA!**
YOU HAVE BEEN THE GREEN'S AVATAR FOR MOMENTS. **MOMENTS.** I HAVE DESTROYED MEMBERS OF YOUR KIND WITH A HUNDRED YEARS UNDER THEIR SHAMBLING HUSKS!
I WILL RIP THE GREEN FROM YOUR BLEEDING FLESH!
I'LL TAKE THAT...
...AS A NO.

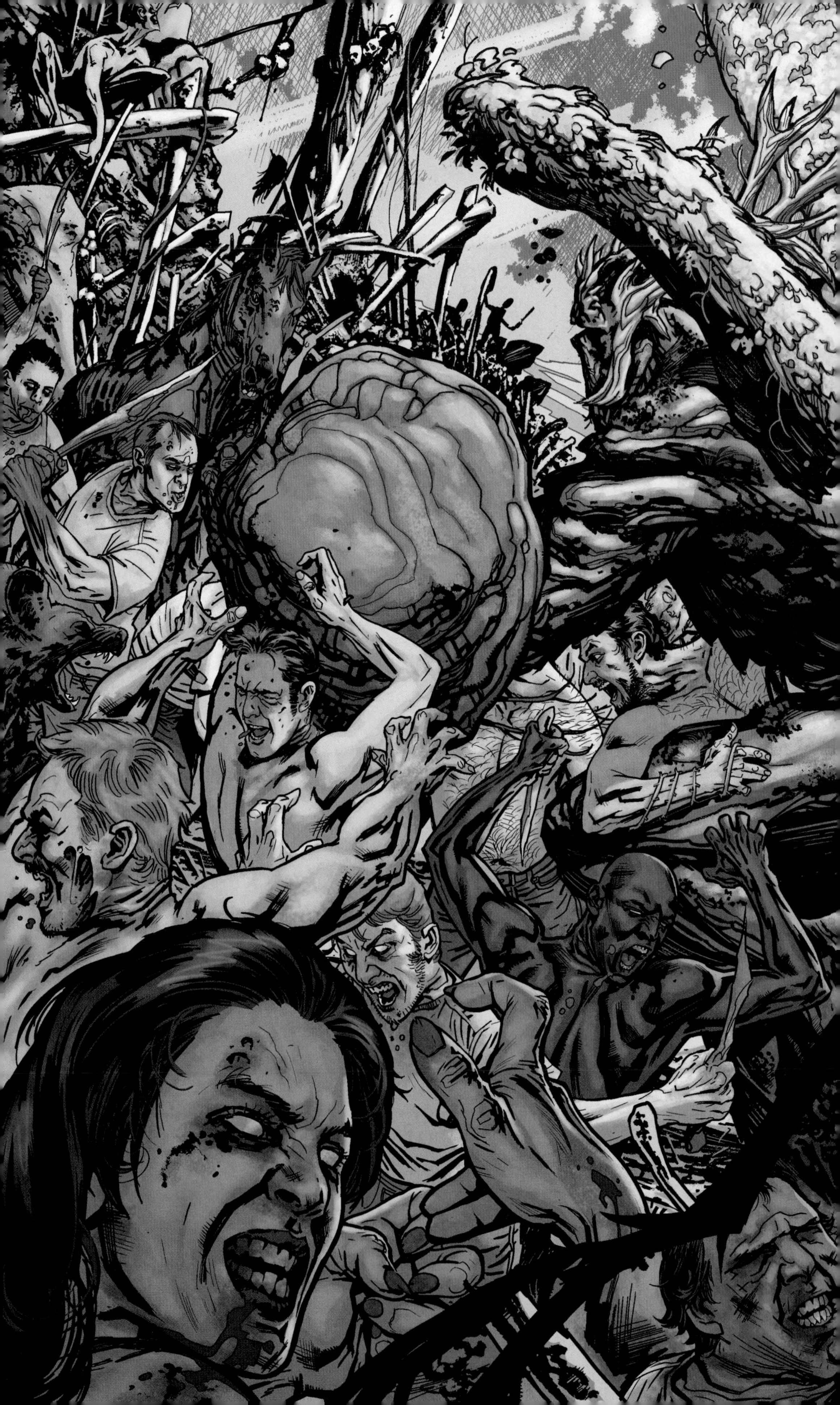

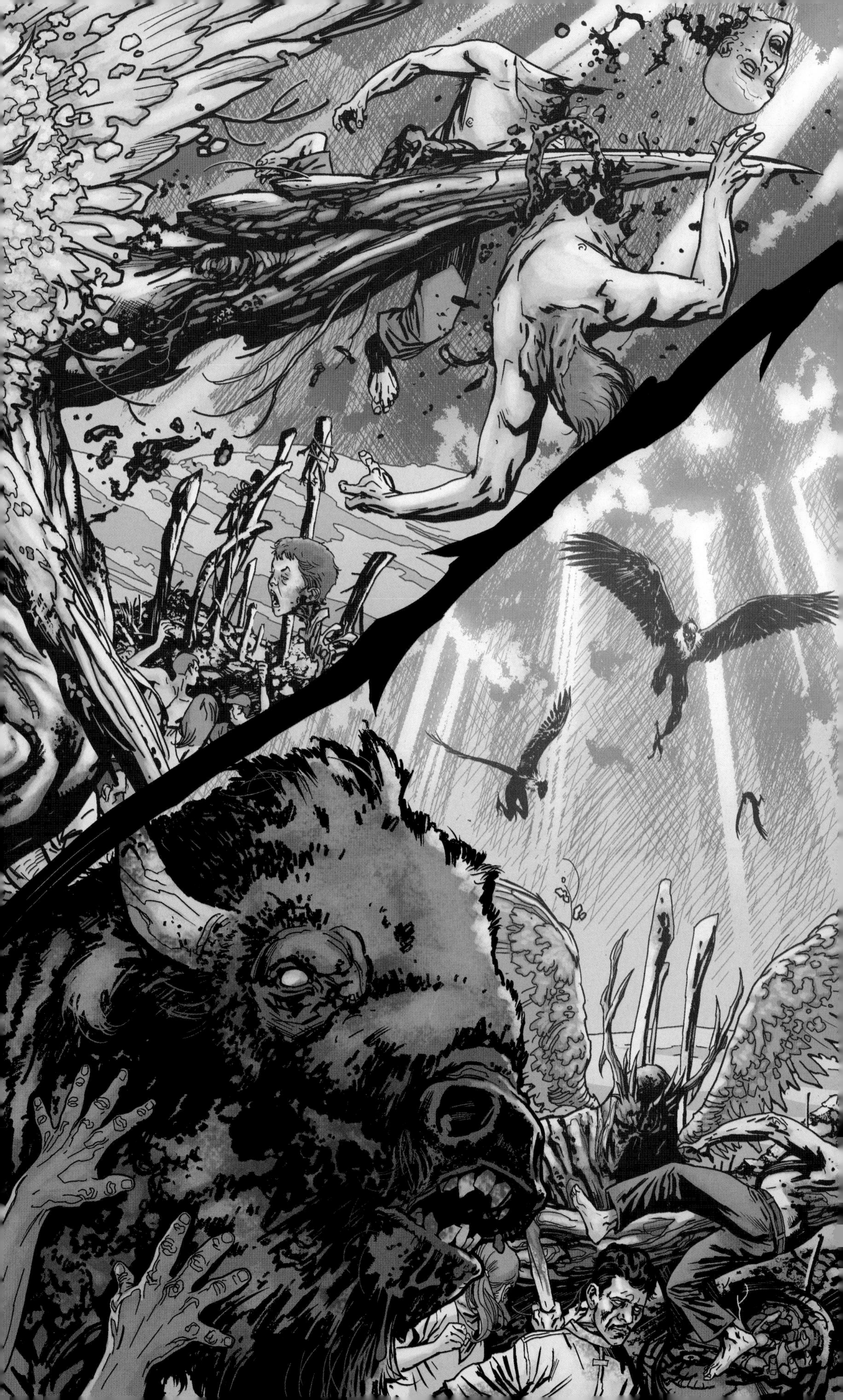

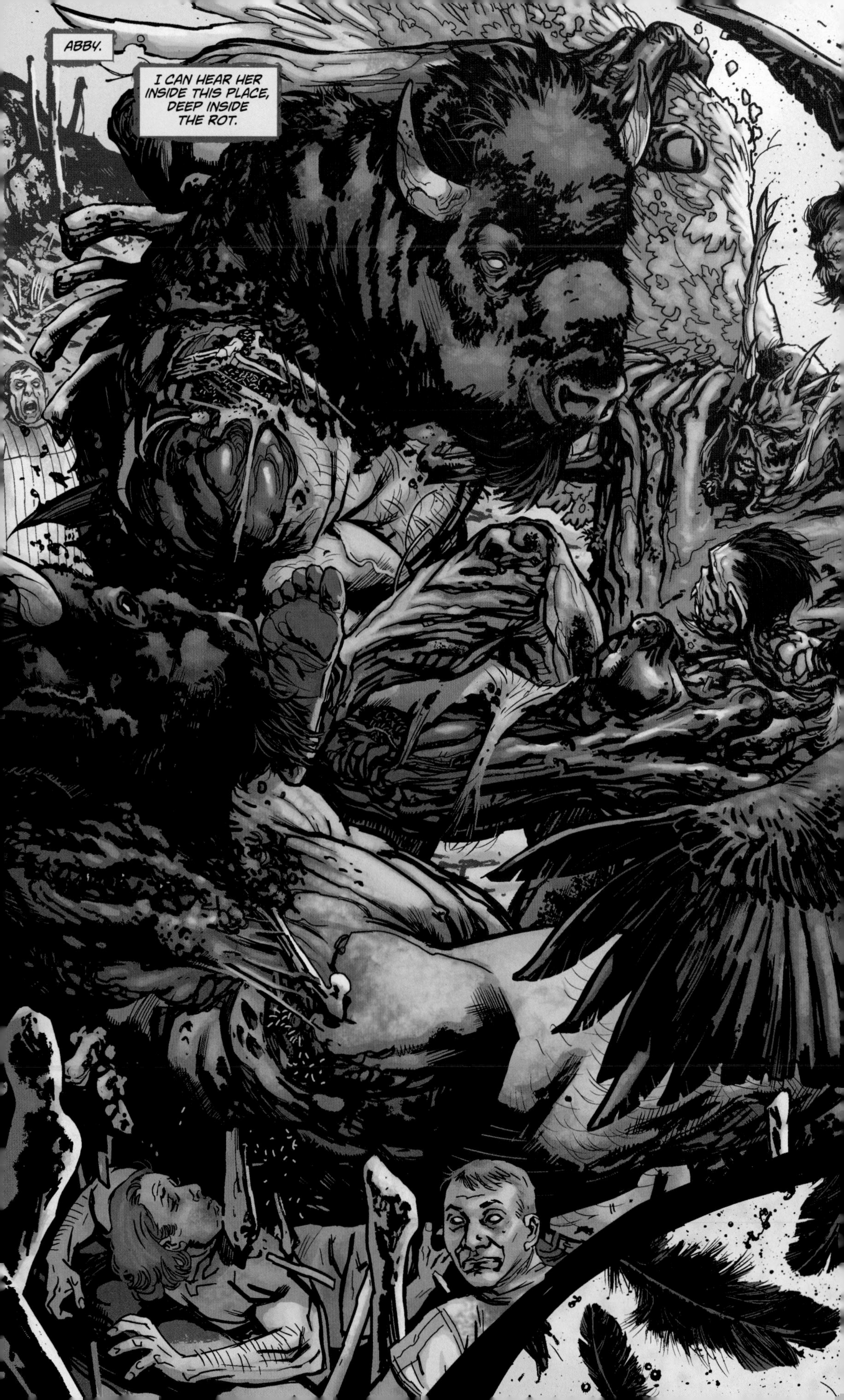
ABBY.
I CAN HEAR HER INSIDE THIS PLACE, DEEP INSIDE THE ROT.

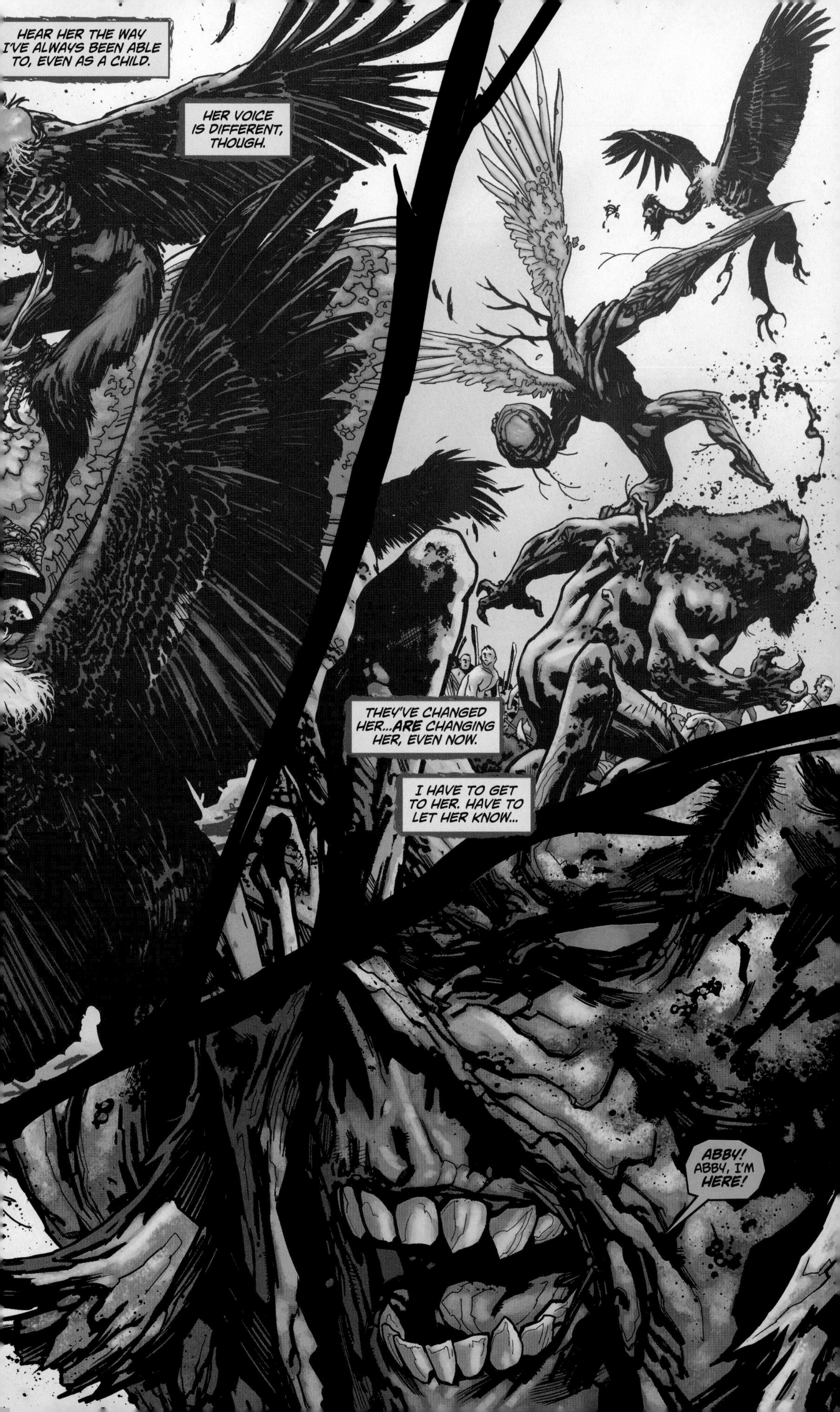
HEAR HER THE WAY I'VE ALWAYS BEEN ABLE TO, EVEN AS A CHILD.
HER VOICE IS DIFFERENT, THOUGH.
THEY'VE CHANGED HER...**ARE** CHANGING HER, EVEN NOW.
I HAVE TO GET TO HER. HAVE TO LET HER KNOW...
ABBY! ABBY, I'M **HERE!**

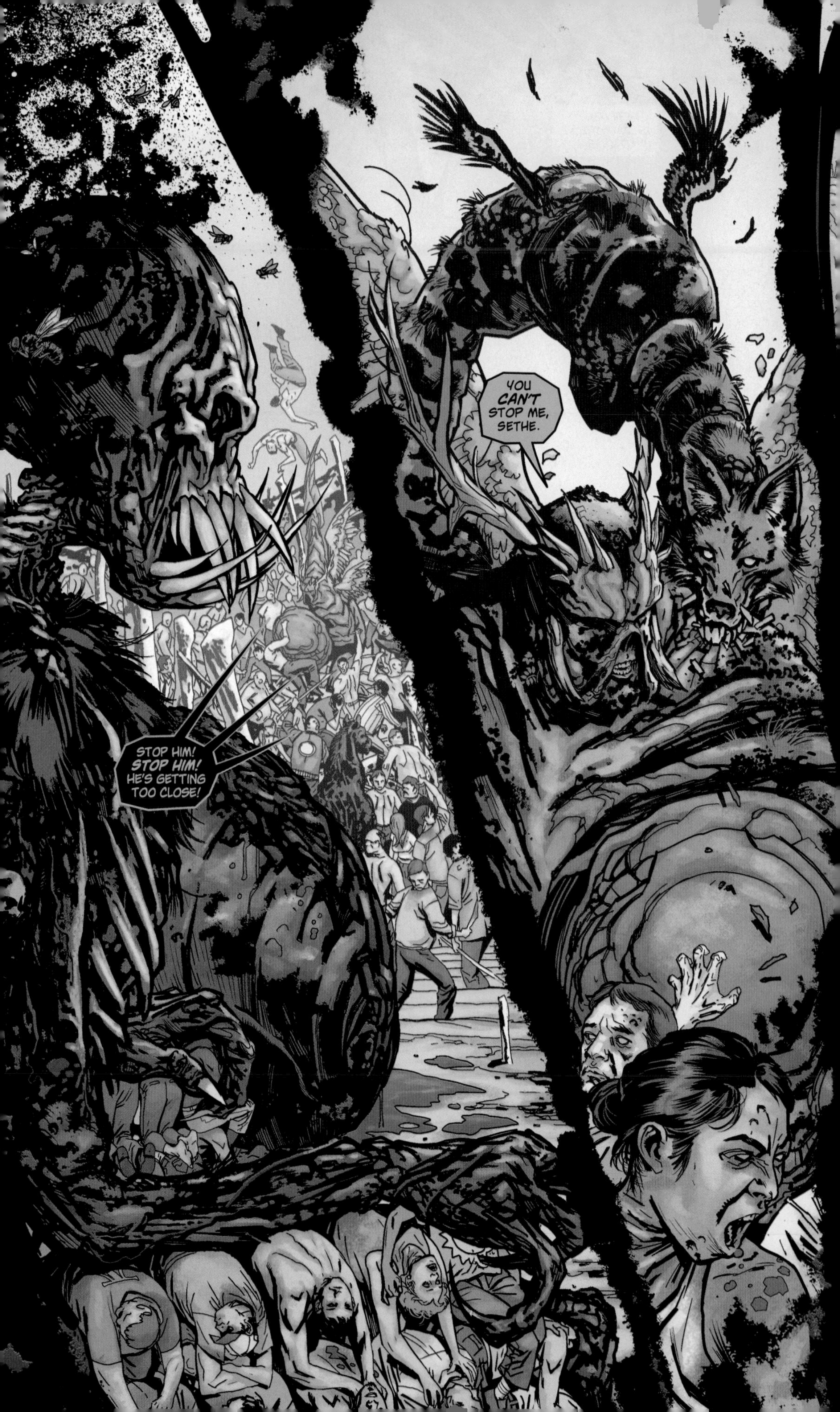
YOU CAN'T STOP ME, SETHE.
STOP HIM! STOP HIM! HE'S GETTING TOO CLOSE!

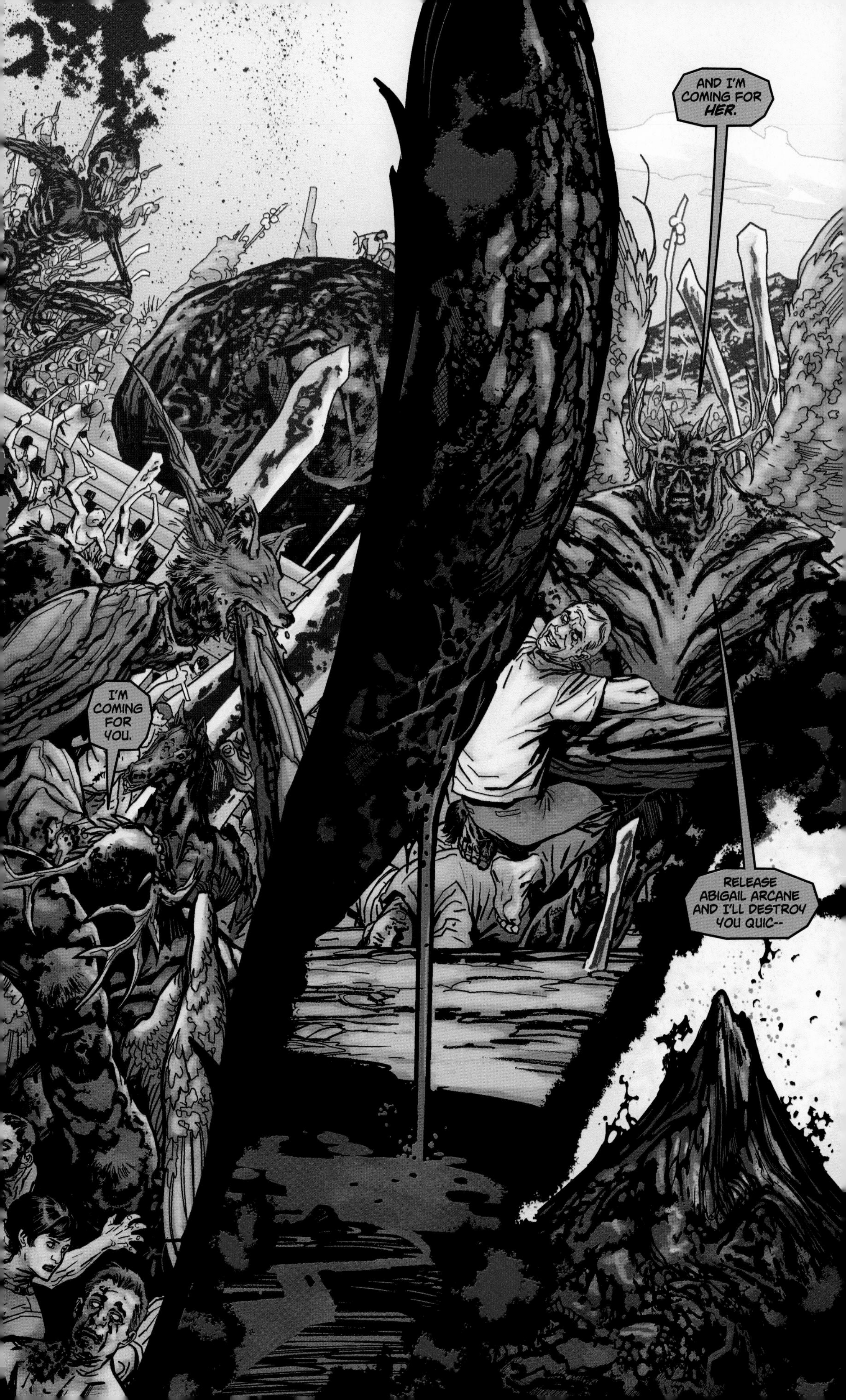
AND I'M COMING FOR HER.
I'M COMING FOR YOU.
RELEASE ABIGAIL ARCANE AND I'LL DESTROY YOU QUIC--

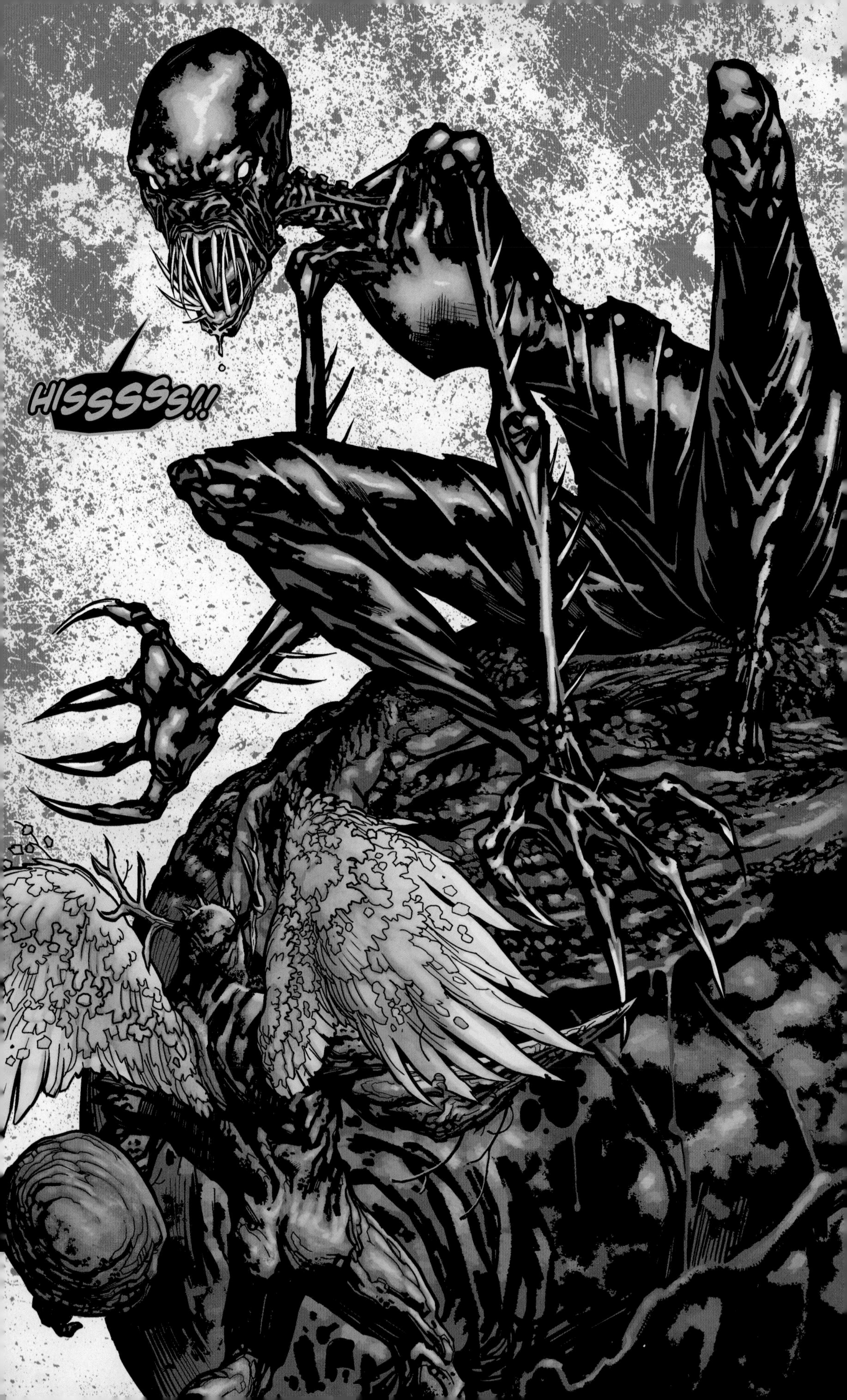
HISSSSSs!!

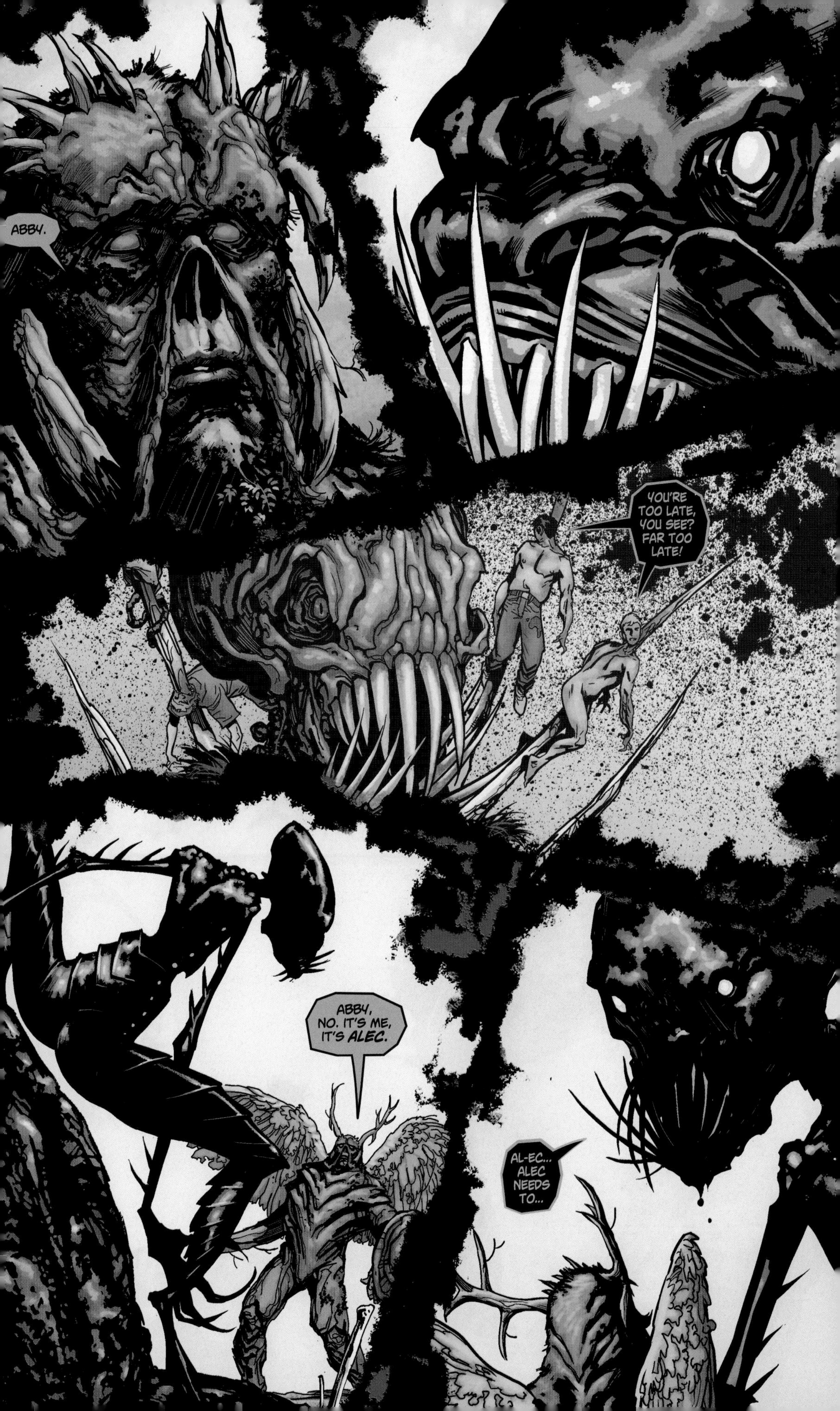
ABBY.
YOU'RE TOO LATE, YOU SEE? FAR TOO LATE!
ABBY, NO. IT'S ME, IT'S ALEC.
AL-EC... ALEC NEEDS TO...

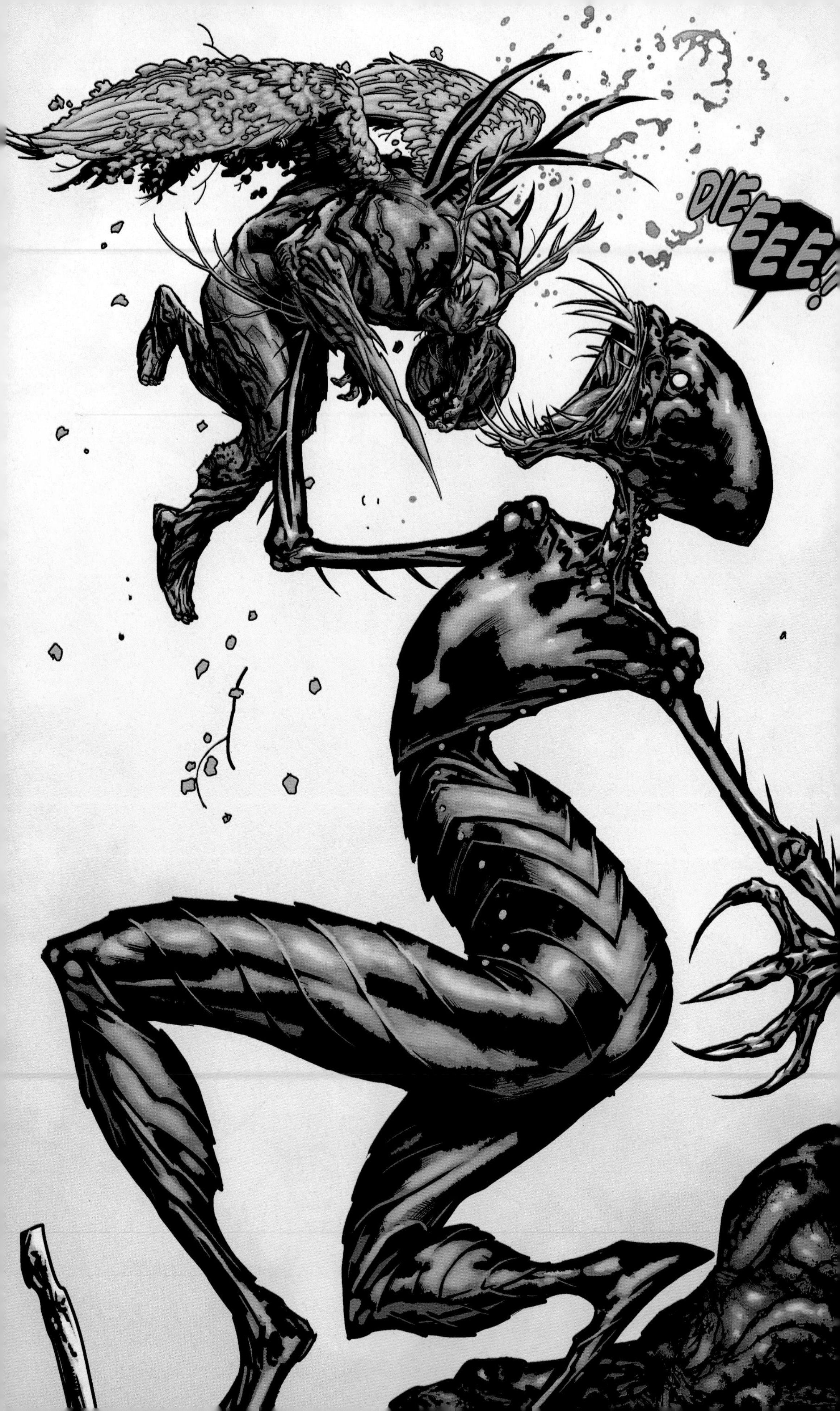
DIEEEE!!

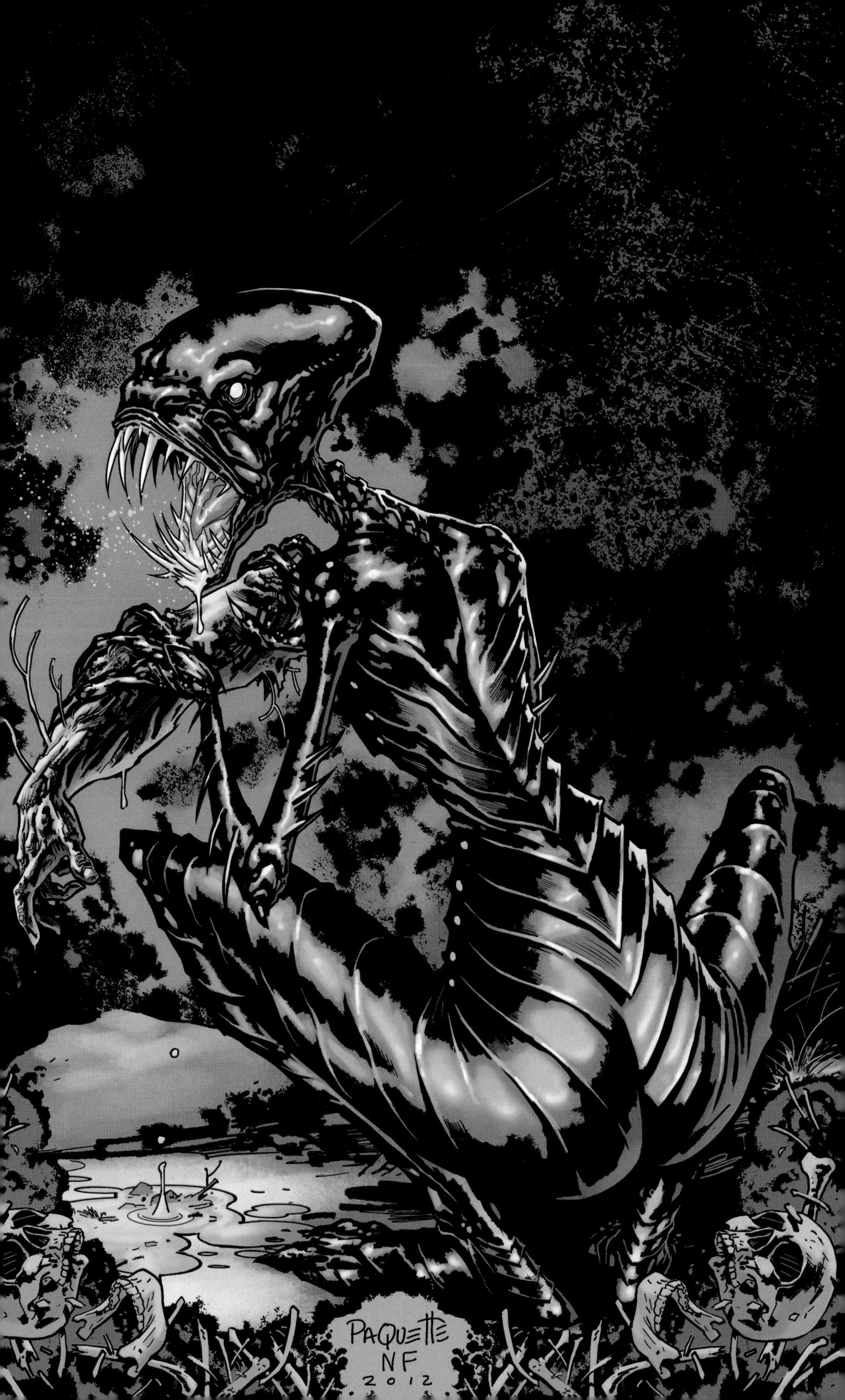
PAQUETTE
NF
2012

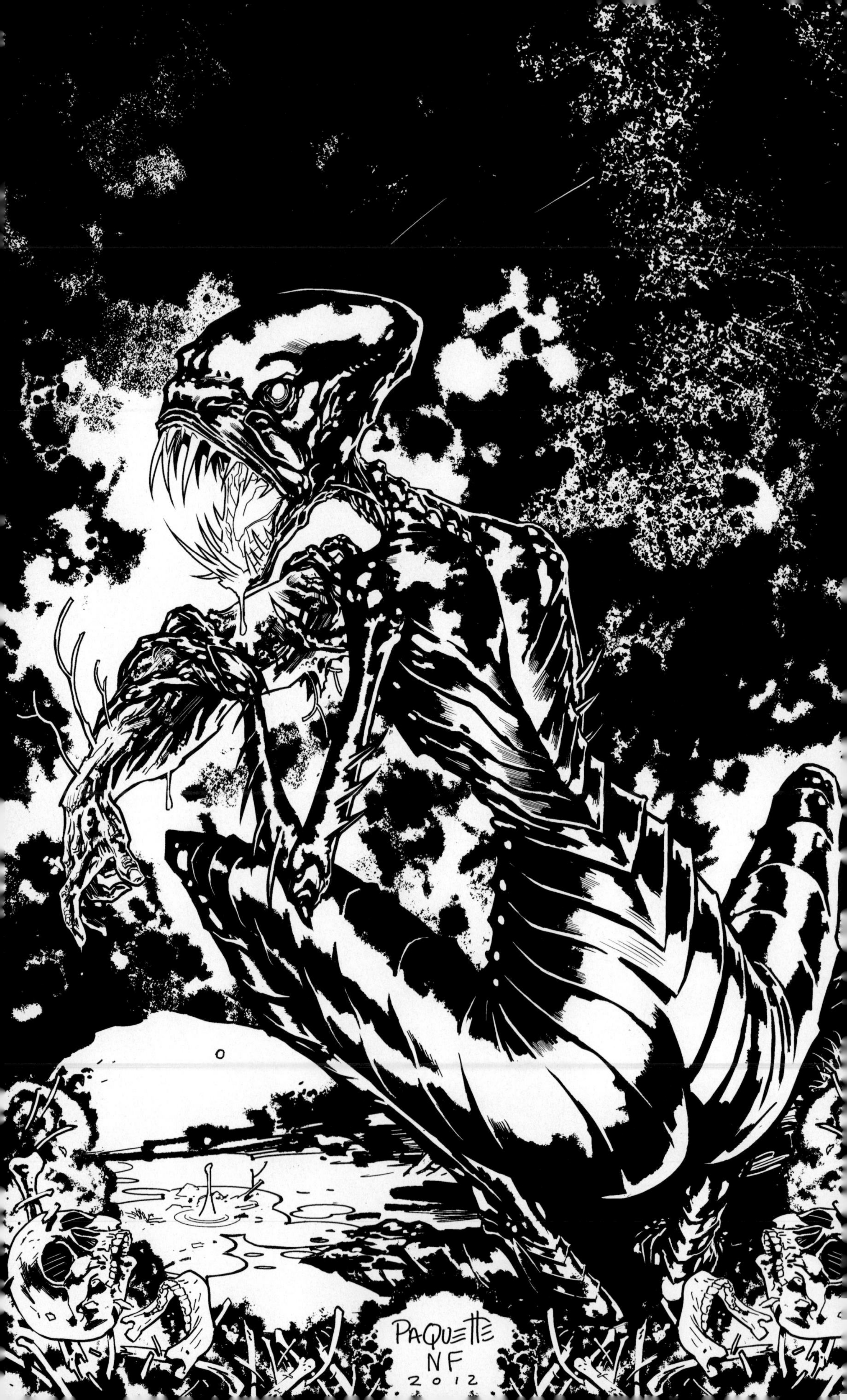
PAQUETTE
NF
2012

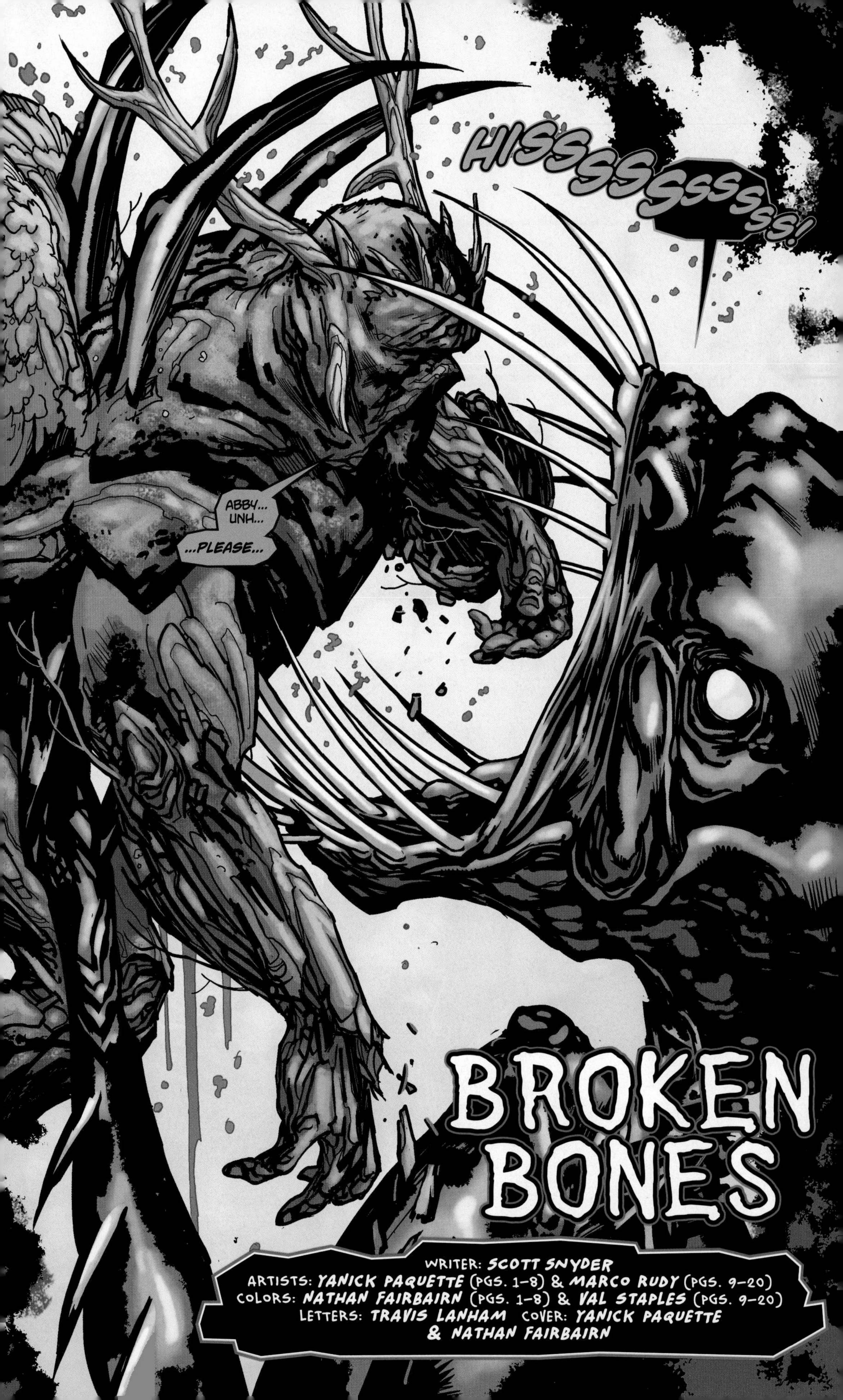
HISSSSSSSSSS!
ABBY... UNH...
...PLEASE...
BROKEN BONES
WRITER: SCOTT SNYDER
ARTISTS: YANICK PAQUETTE (PGS. 1-8) & MARCO RUDY (PGS. 9-20)
COLORS: NATHAN FAIRBAIRN (PGS. 1-8) & VAL STAPLES (PGS. 9-20)
LETTERS: TRAVIS LANHAM COVER: YANICK PAQUETTE & NATHAN FAIRBAIRN

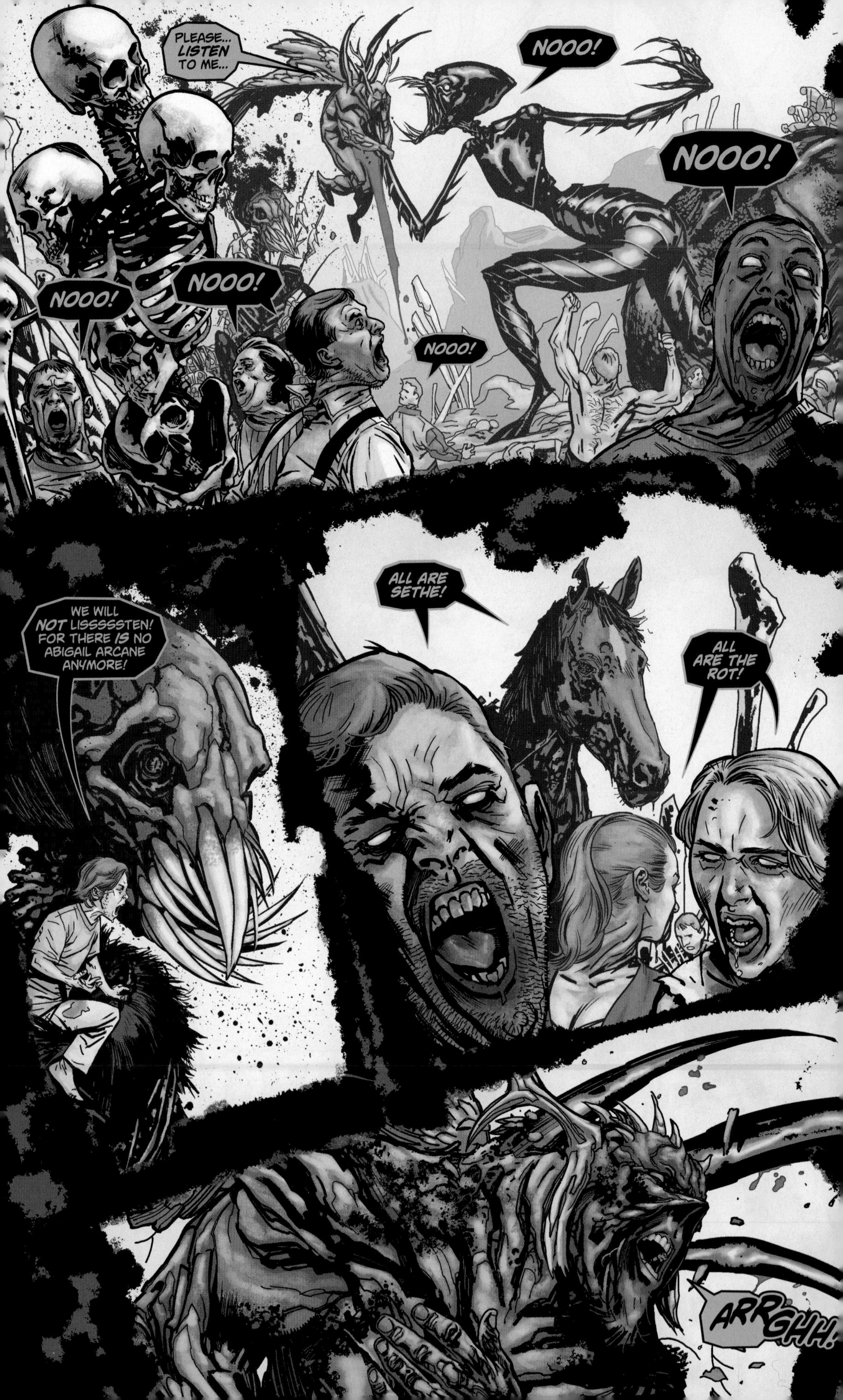

PLEASE... LISTEN TO ME...
NOOO!
NOOO!
NOOO!
NOOO!
NOOO!
WE WILL NOT LISSSSSTEN! FOR THERE IS NO ABIGAIL ARCANE ANYMORE!
ALL ARE SETHE!
ALL ARE THE ROT!
ARRGHH!

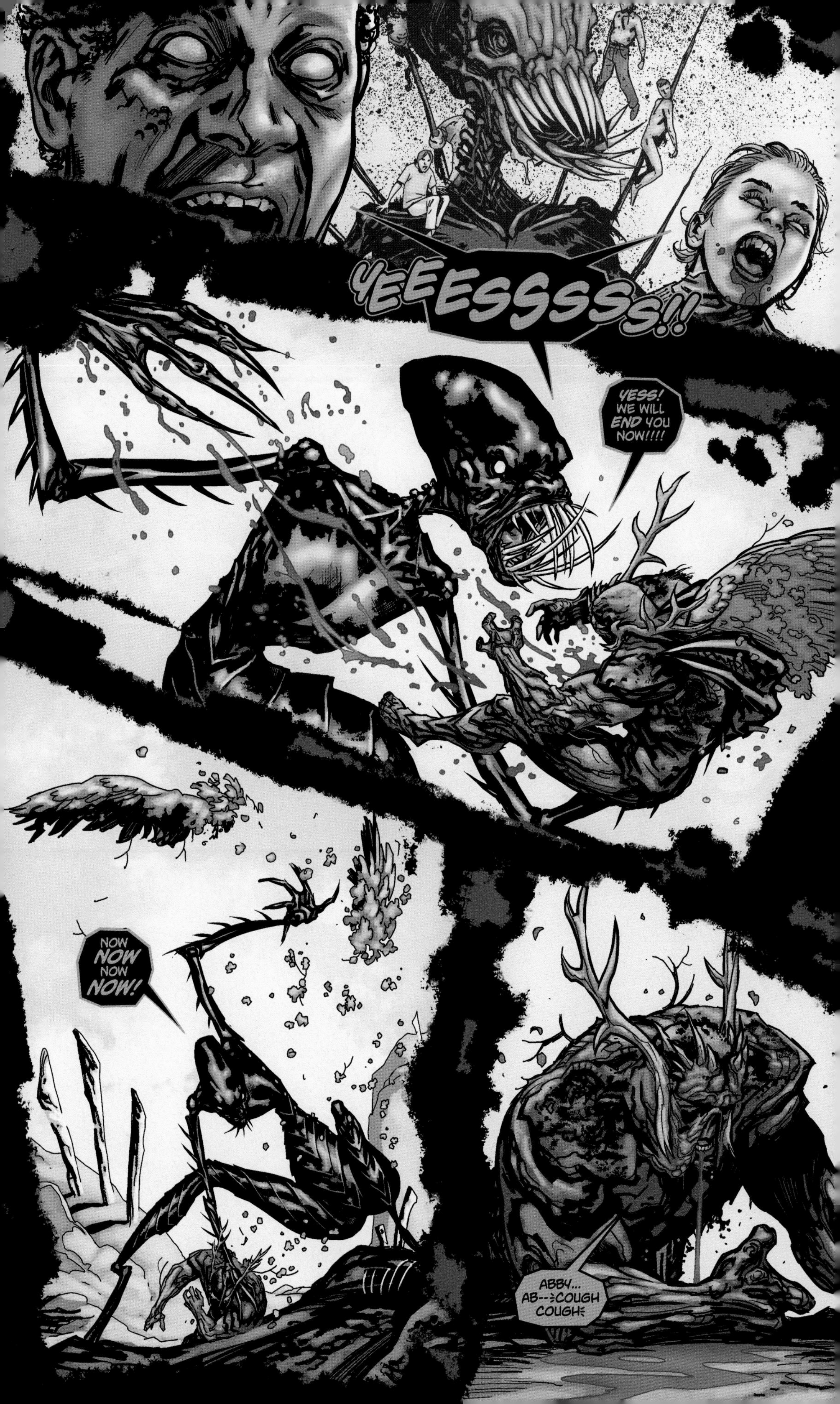
YEEESSSSSS!!
YESS! WE WILL END YOU NOW!!!!
NOW NOW NOW NOW!
ABBY... AB--COUGH COUGH

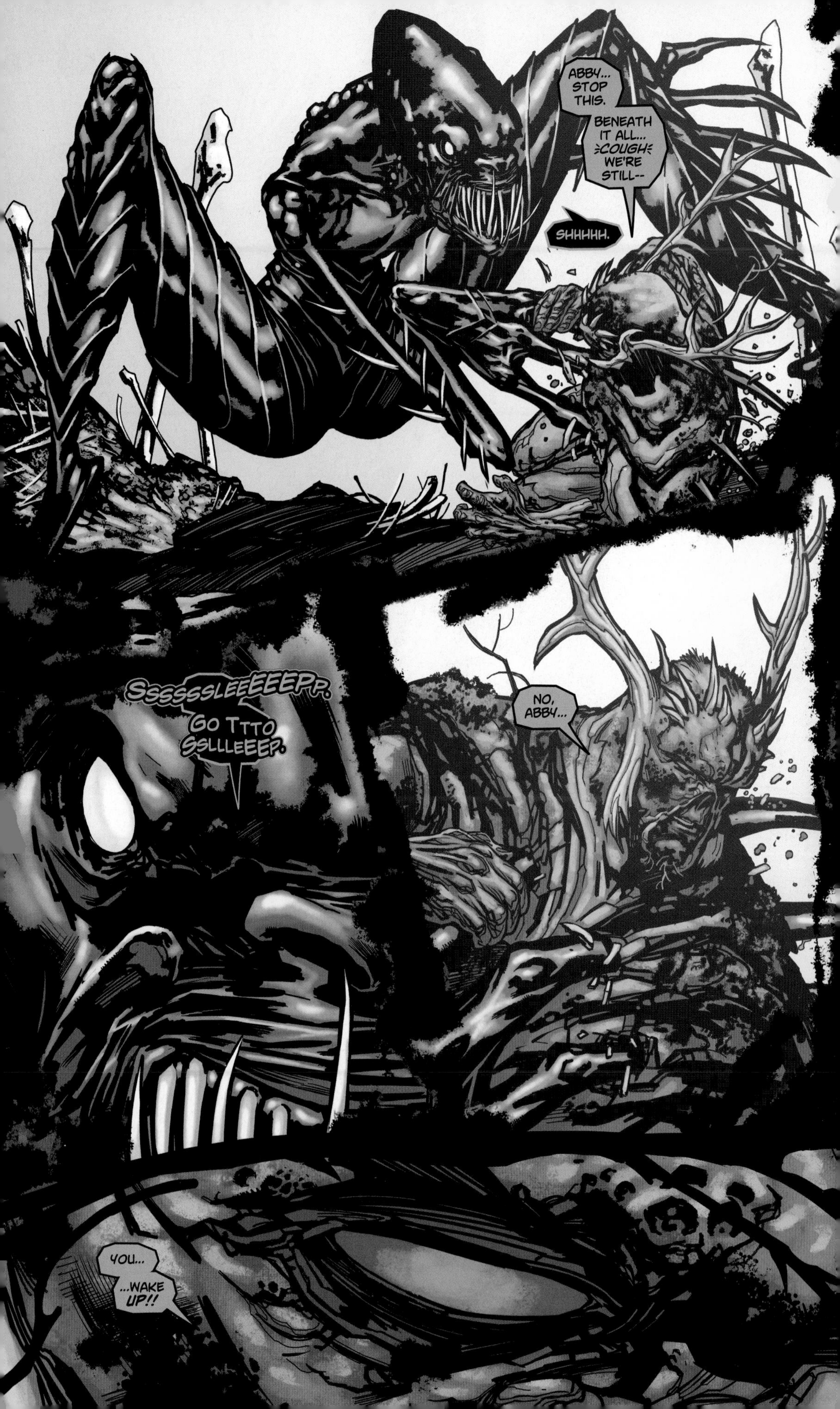

ABBY... STOP THIS.
BENEATH IT ALL... *COUGH* WE'RE STILL--
SHHHHH.
SssssssleeEEEPp.
GO TTTO SSLLLEEEP.
NO, ABBY...
YOU...
...WAKE UP!!

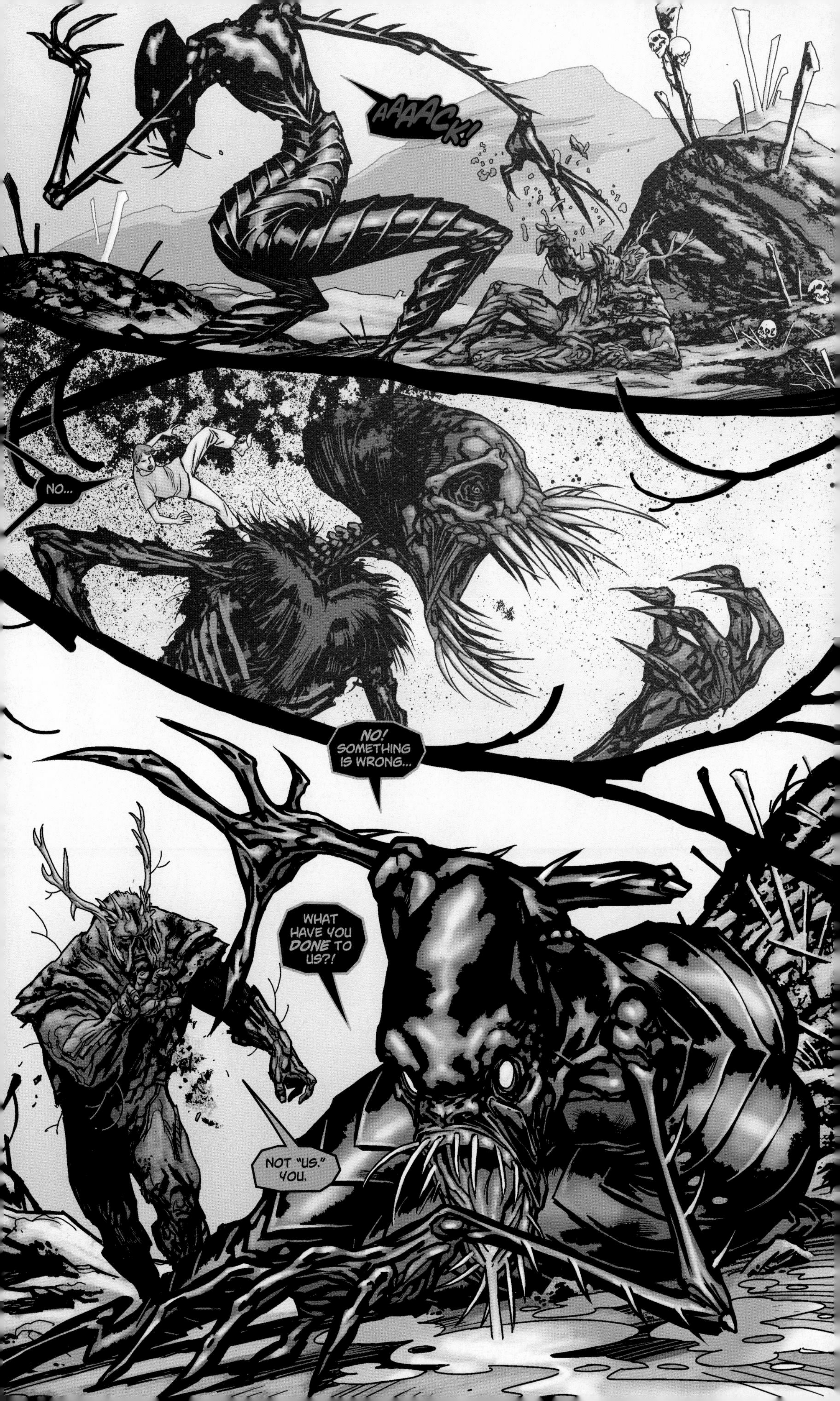
AAAACK!
NO...
NO! SOMETHING IS WRONG...
WHAT HAVE YOU DONE TO US?!
NOT "US." YOU.

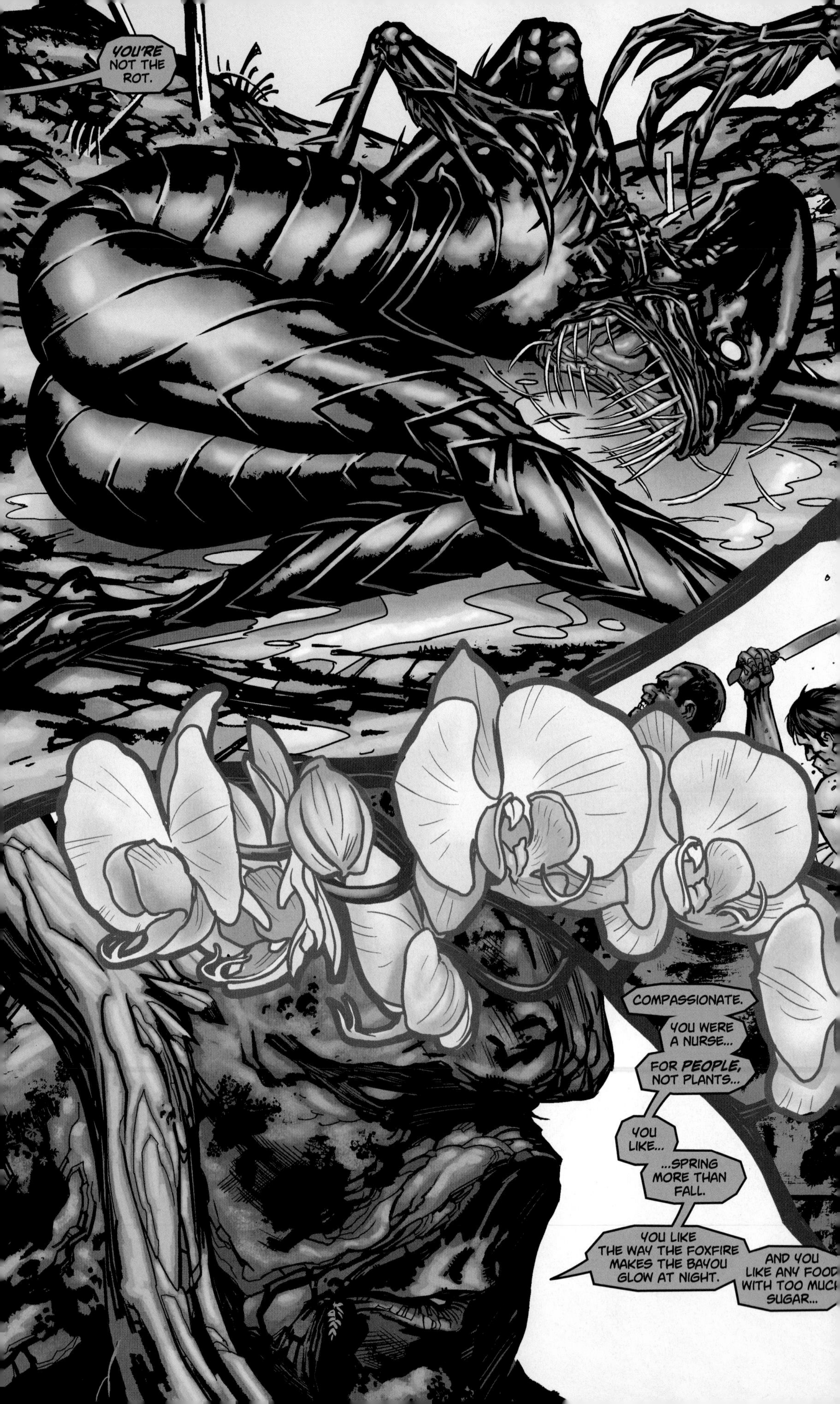
YOU'RE NOT THE ROT.
COMPASSIONATE.
YOU WERE A NURSE...
FOR PEOPLE, NOT PLANTS...
YOU LIKE...
...SPRING MORE THAN FALL.
YOU LIKE THE WAY THE FOXFIRE MAKES THE BAYOU GLOW AT NIGHT.
AND YOU LIKE ANY FOOD WITH TOO MUCH SUGAR...

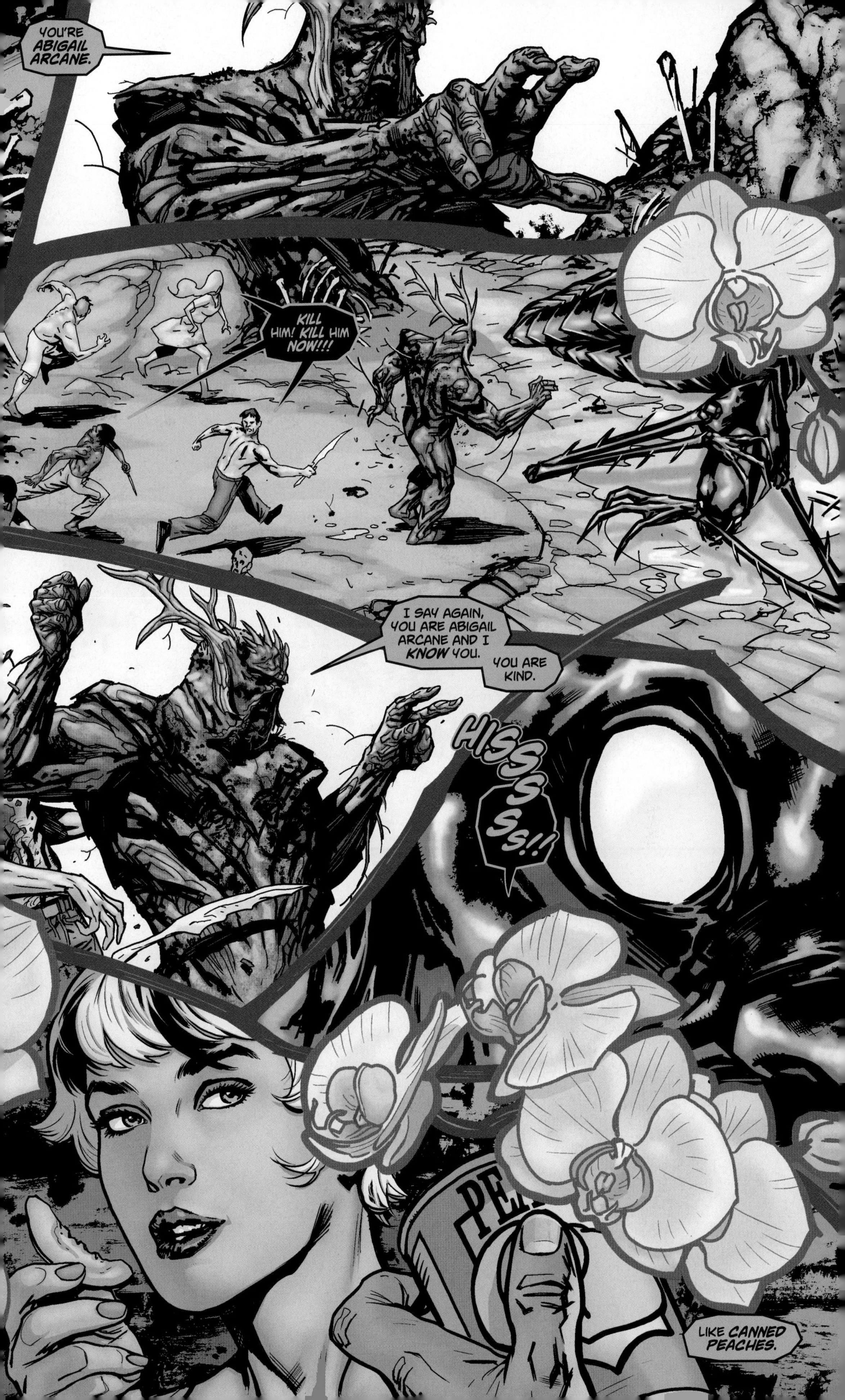
YOU'RE ABIGAIL ARCANE.
KILL HIM! KILL HIM NOW!!!
I SAY AGAIN, YOU ARE ABIGAIL ARCANE AND I KNOW YOU.
YOU ARE KIND.
HISSSSSs!!
LIKE CANNED PEACHES.

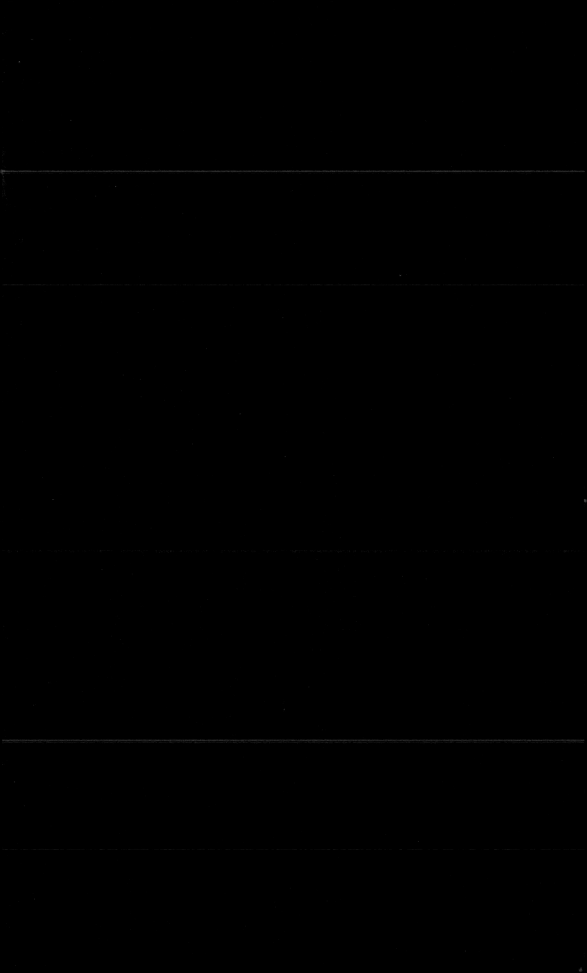

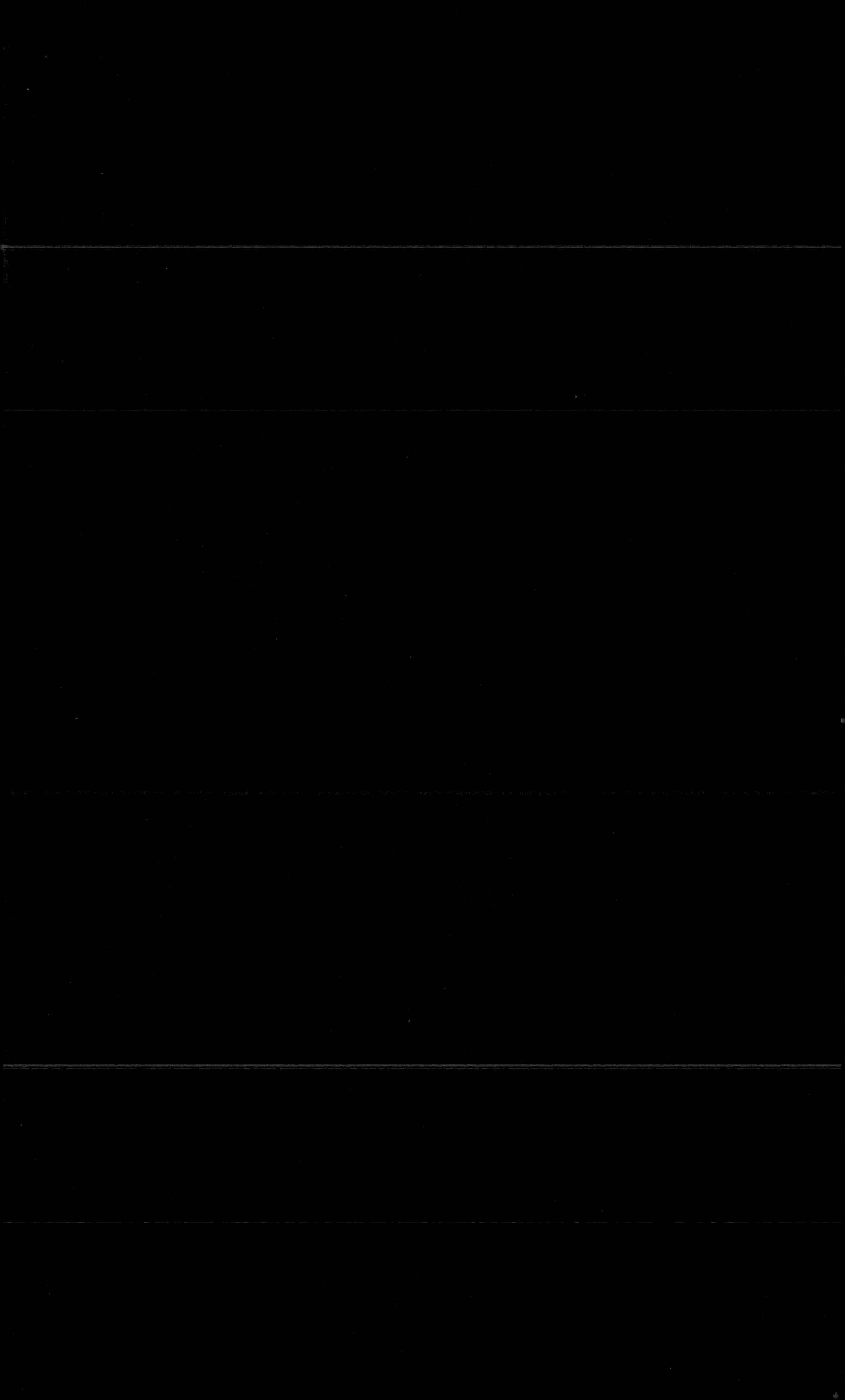

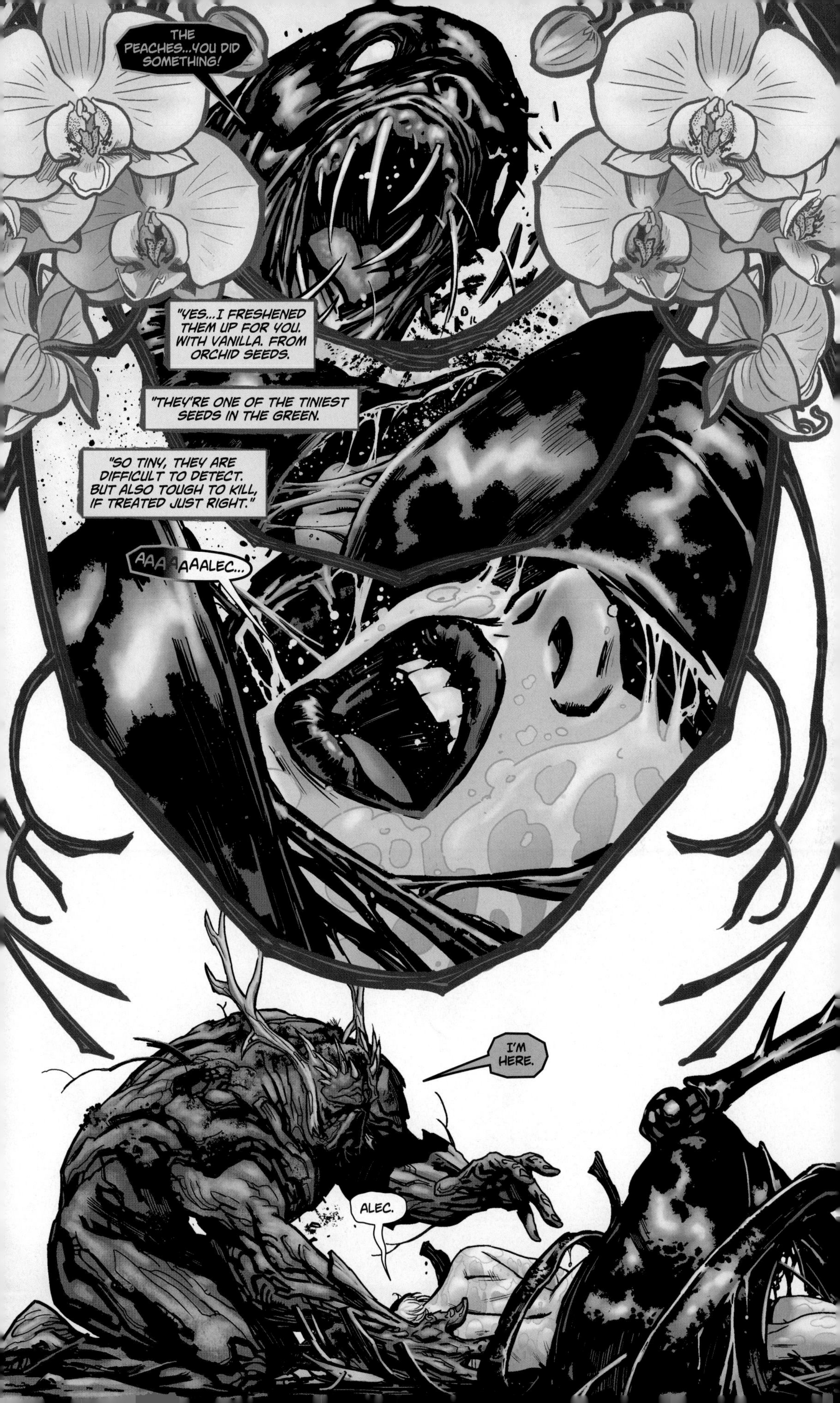
THE PEACHES...YOU DID SOMETHING!
"YES...I FRESHENED THEM UP FOR YOU. WITH VANILLA. FROM ORCHID SEEDS.
"THEY'RE ONE OF THE TINIEST SEEDS IN THE GREEN.
"SO TINY, THEY ARE DIFFICULT TO DETECT. BUT ALSO TOUGH TO KILL, IF TREATED JUST RIGHT."
AAAAAAALEC...
I'M HERE.
ALEC.

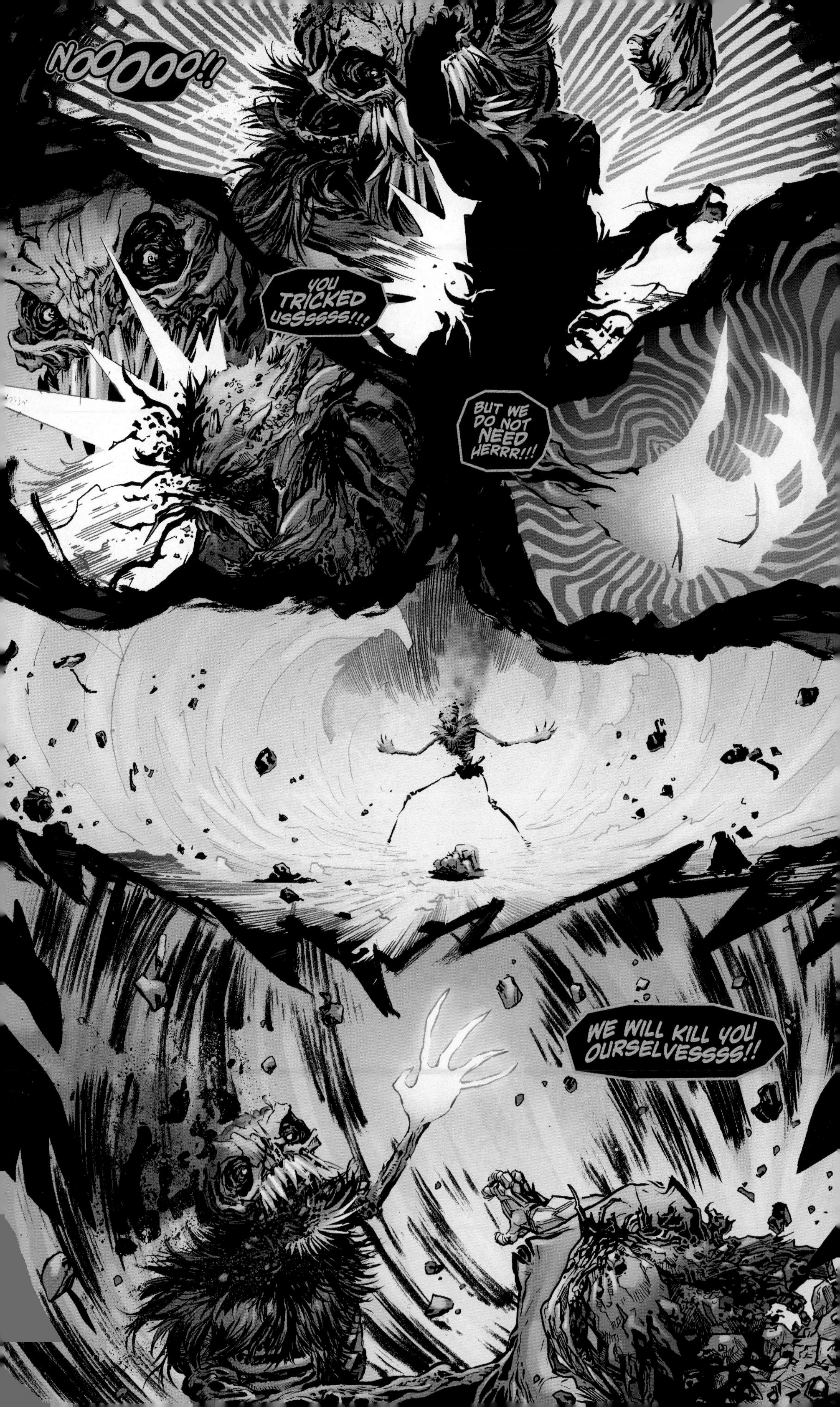
NOOOOO!!
YOU TRICKED USSSSS!!!
BUT WE DO NOT NEED HERRR!!!
WE WILL KILL YOU OURSELVESSSS!!

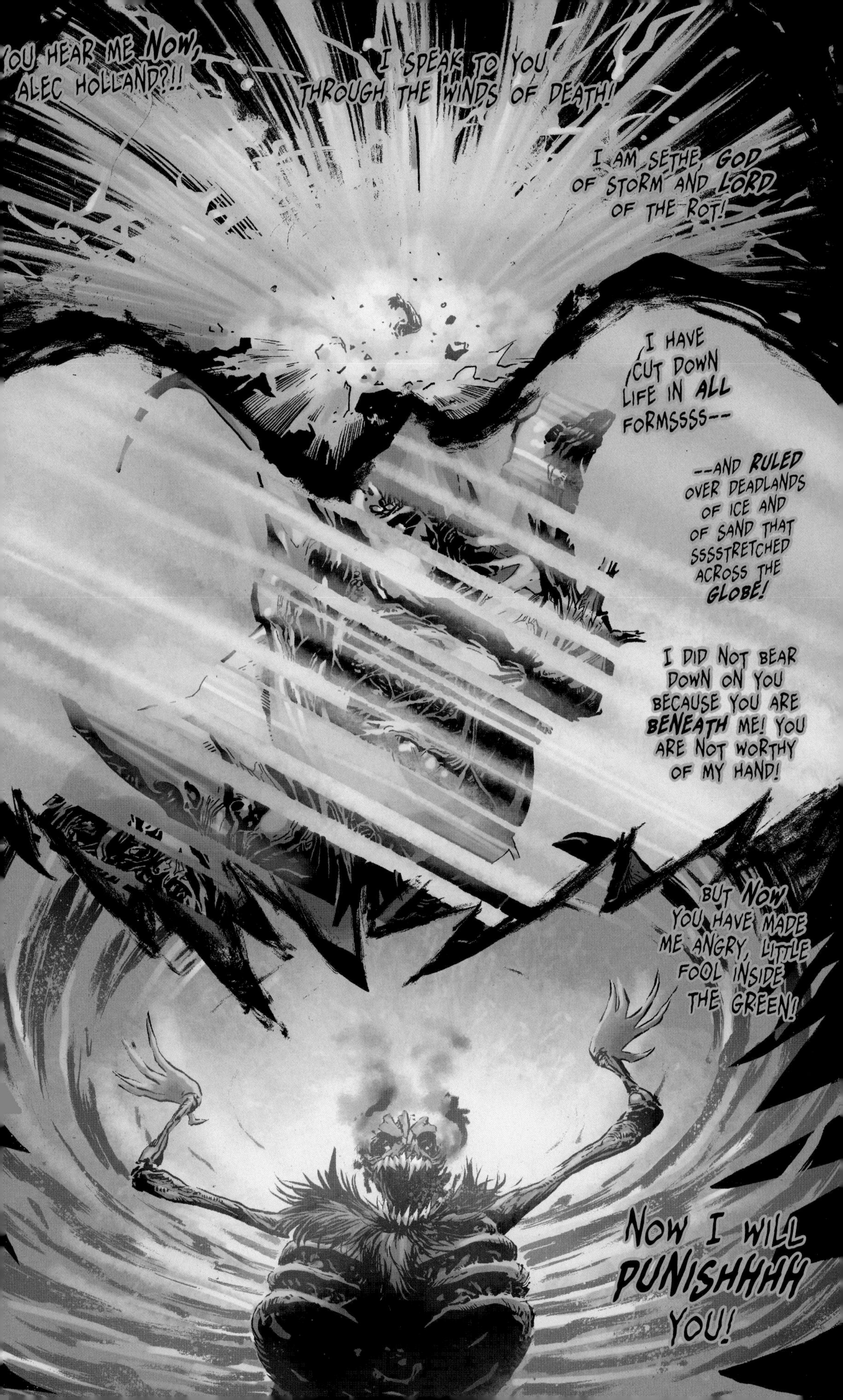
YOU HEAR ME NOW, ALEC HOLLAND?!!
I SPEAK TO YOU THROUGH THE WINDS OF DEATH!
I AM SETHE, GOD OF STORM AND LORD OF THE ROT!
I HAVE CUT DOWN LIFE IN ALL FORMSSSS--
--AND RULED OVER DEADLANDS OF ICE AND OF SAND THAT SSSSTRETCHED ACROSS THE GLOBE!
I DID NOT BEAR DOWN ON YOU BECAUSE YOU ARE BENEATH ME! YOU ARE NOT WORTHY OF MY HAND!
BUT NOW YOU HAVE MADE ME ANGRY, LITTLE FOOL INSIDE THE GREEN!
NOW I WILL PUNISHHHH YOU!

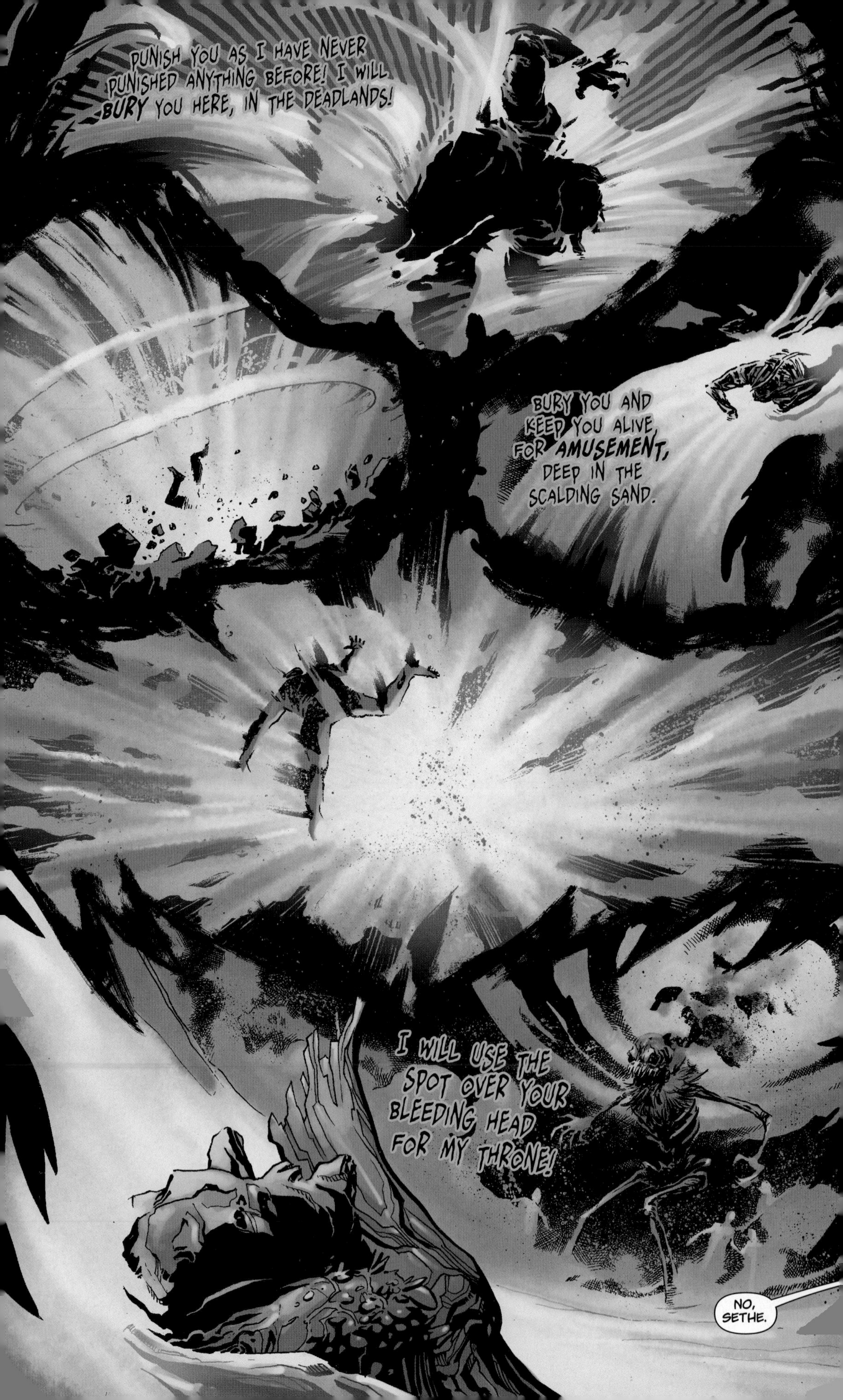
PUNISH YOU AS I HAVE NEVER PUNISHED ANYTHING BEFORE! I WILL BURY YOU HERE, IN THE DEADLANDS!
BURY YOU AND KEEP YOU ALIVE FOR AMUSEMENT, DEEP IN THE SCALDING SAND.
I WILL USE THE SPOT OVER YOUR BLEEDING HEAD FOR MY THRONE!
NO, SETHE.

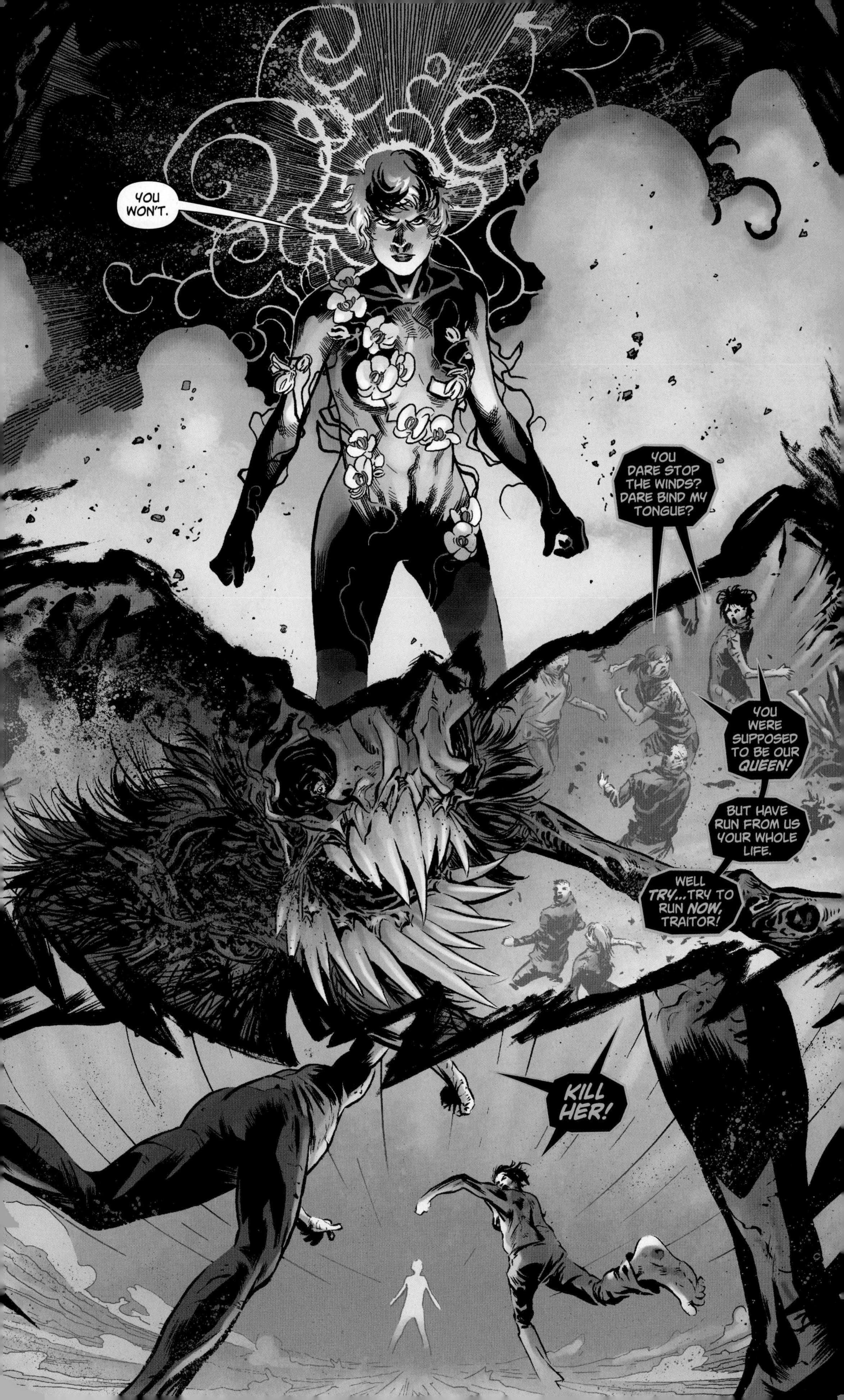
YOU WON'T.
YOU DARE STOP THE WINDS? DARE BIND MY TONGUE?
YOU WERE SUPPOSED TO BE OUR QUEEN!
BUT HAVE RUN FROM US YOUR WHOLE LIFE.
WELL TRY... TRY TO RUN NOW, TRAITOR!
KILL HER!

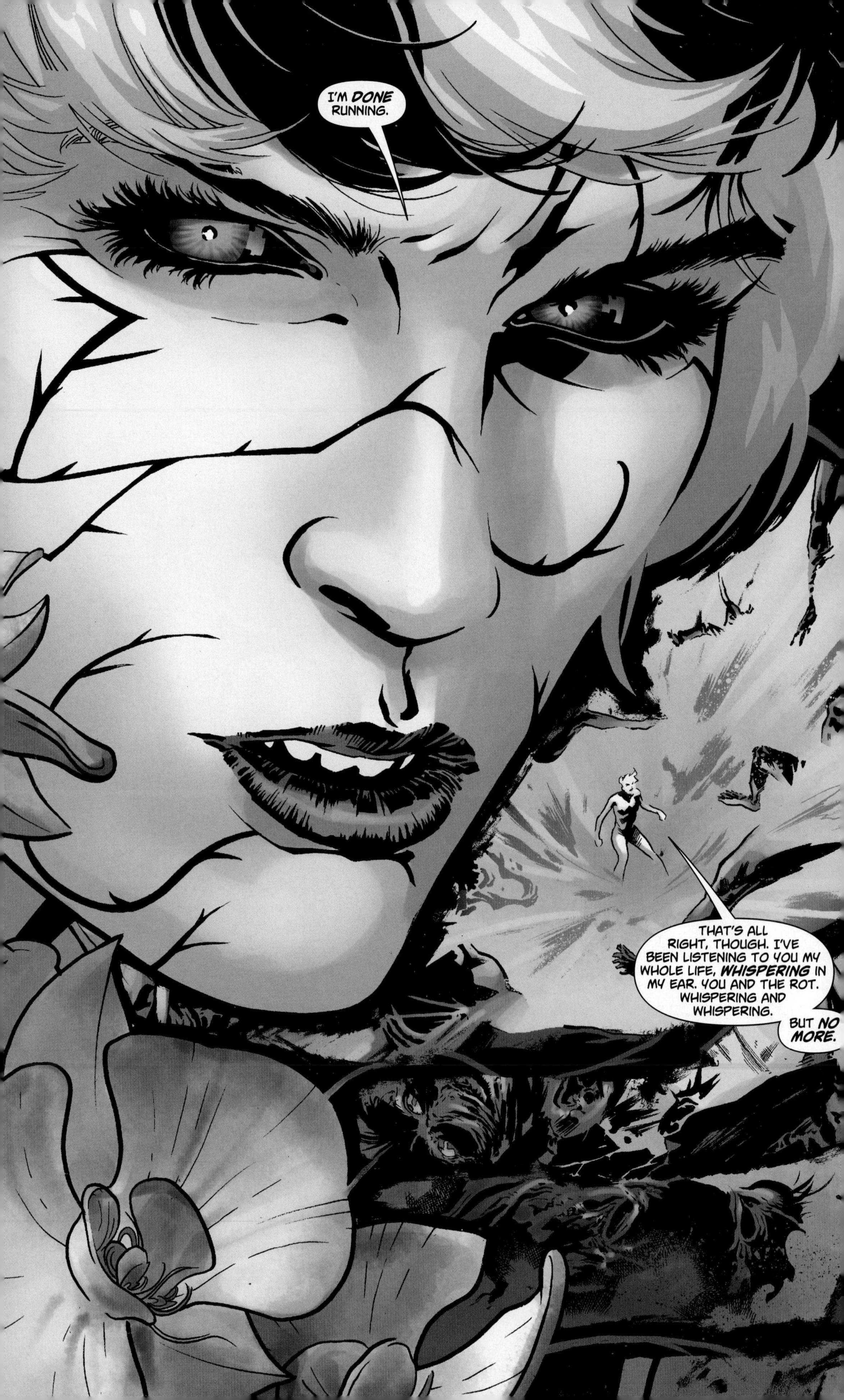
I'M *DONE* RUNNING.
THAT'S ALL RIGHT, THOUGH. I'VE BEEN LISTENING TO YOU MY WHOLE LIFE, *WHISPERING* IN MY EAR. YOU AND THE ROT. WHISPERING AND WHISPERING.
BUT *NO MORE.*

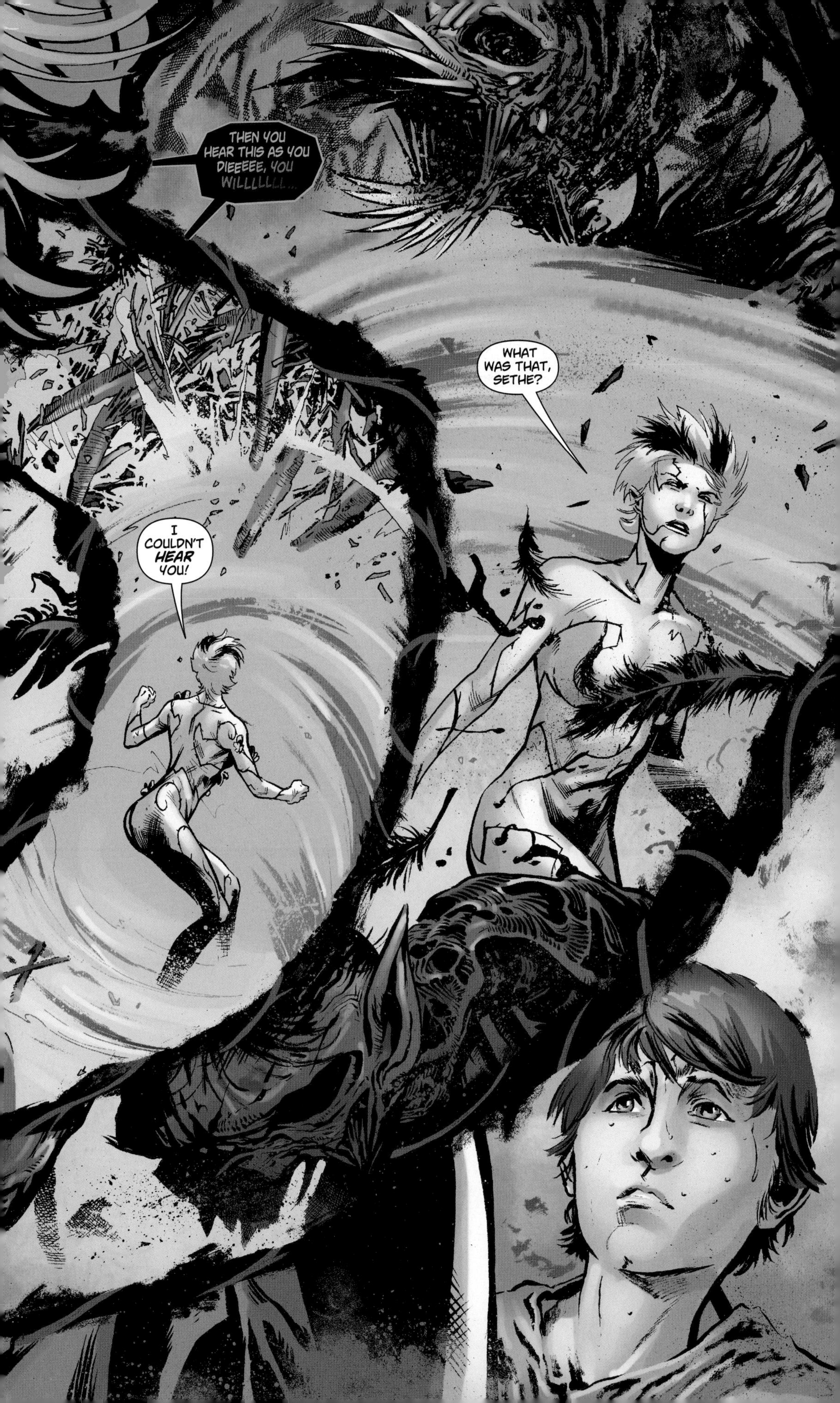
THEN YOU HEAR THIS AS YOU DIEEEEE, YOU WILLLLLLL...
WHAT WAS THAT, SETHE?
I COULDN'T HEAR YOU!

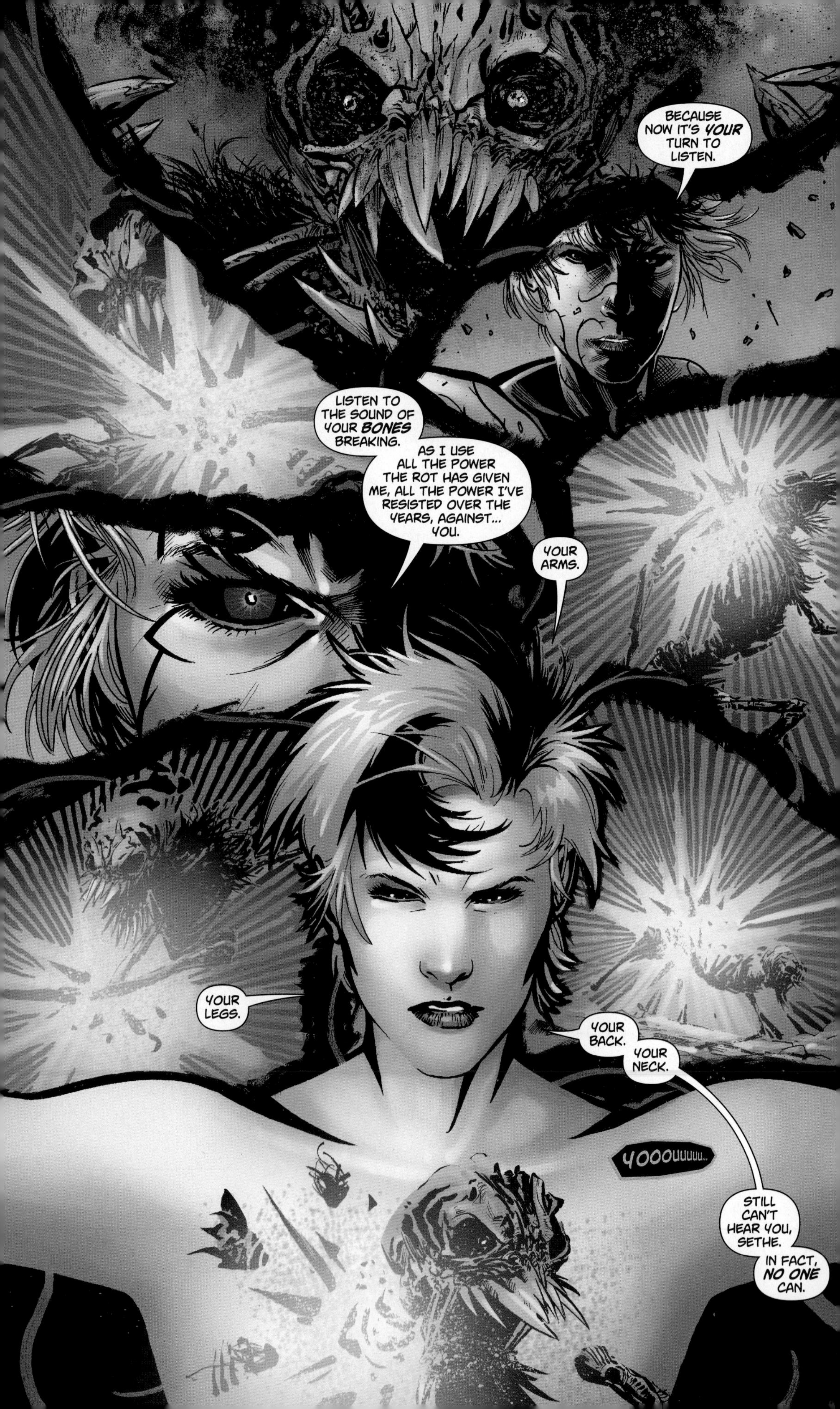
BECAUSE NOW IT'S YOUR TURN TO LISTEN.
LISTEN TO THE SOUND OF YOUR BONES BREAKING.
AS I USE ALL THE POWER THE ROT HAS GIVEN ME, ALL THE POWER I'VE RESISTED OVER THE YEARS, AGAINST... YOU.
YOUR ARMS.
YOUR LEGS.
YOUR BACK.
YOUR NECK.
YOOOUUUUU...
STILL CAN'T HEAR YOU, SETHE.
IN FACT, NO ONE CAN.

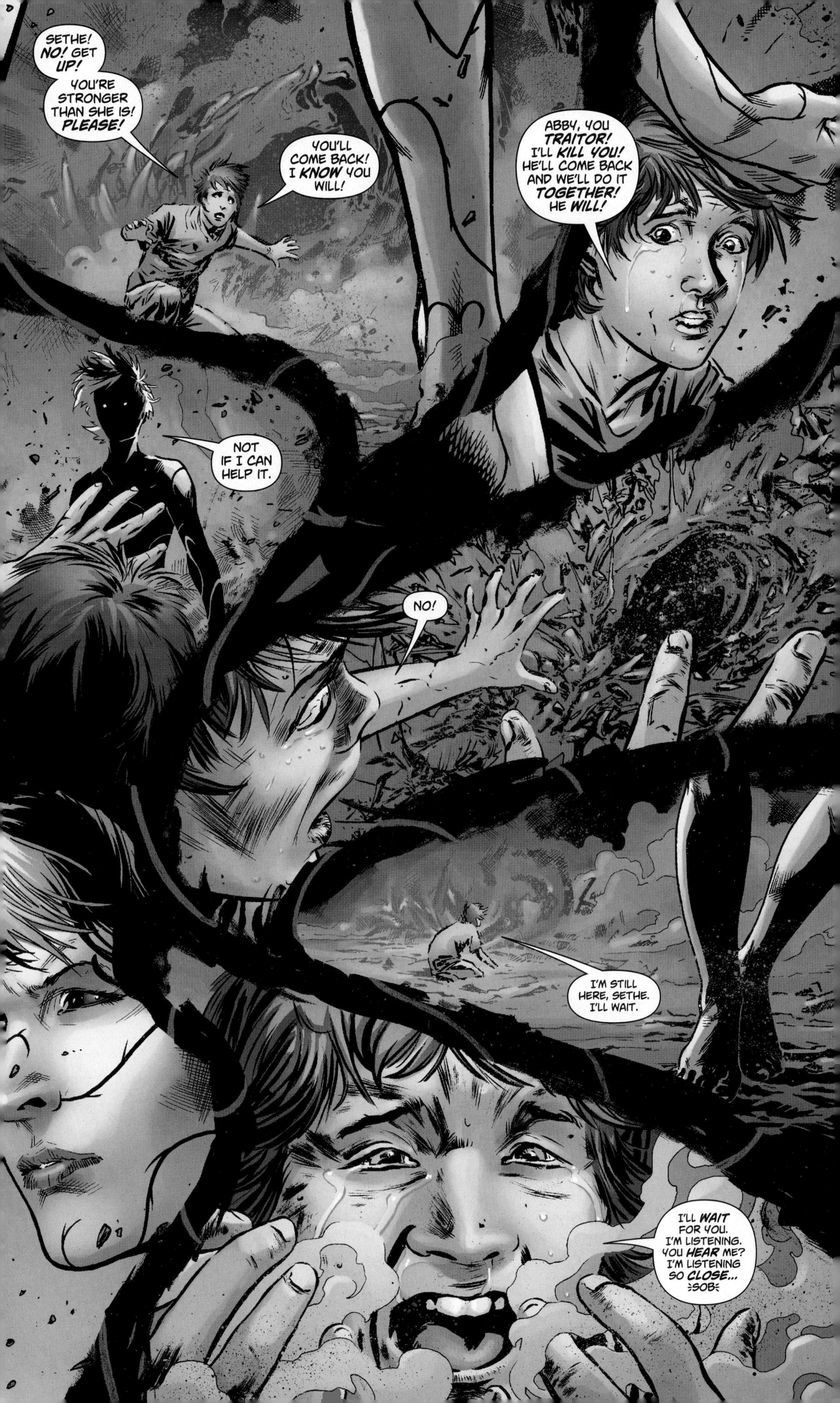

SETHE! NO! GET UP!
YOU'RE STRONGER THAN SHE IS! PLEASE!
YOU'LL COME BACK! I KNOW YOU WILL!
ABBY, YOU TRAITOR! I'LL KILL YOU! HE'LL COME BACK AND WE'LL DO IT TOGETHER! HE WILL!
NOT IF I CAN HELP IT.
NO!
I'M STILL HERE, SETHE. I'LL WAIT.
I'LL WAIT FOR YOU. I'M LISTENING. YOU HEAR ME? I'M LISTENING SO CLOSE...
SOB

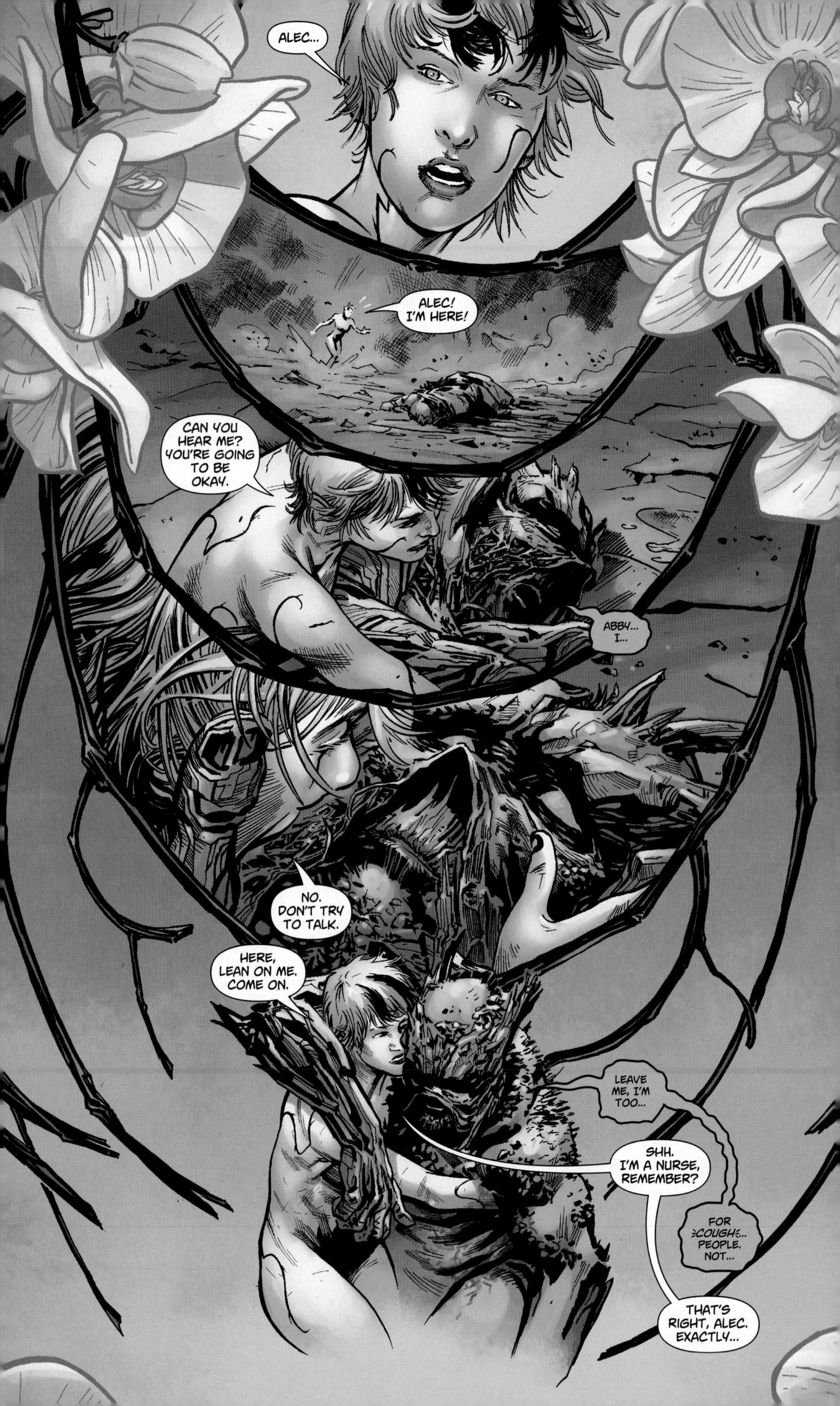
ALEC...
ALEC! I'M HERE!
CAN YOU HEAR ME? YOU'RE GOING TO BE OKAY.
ABBY... I...
NO. DON'T TRY TO TALK.
HERE, LEAN ON ME. COME ON.
LEAVE ME, I'M TOO...
SHH. I'M A NURSE, REMEMBER?
FOR *COUGH*... PEOPLE. NOT...
THAT'S RIGHT, ALEC. EXACTLY...

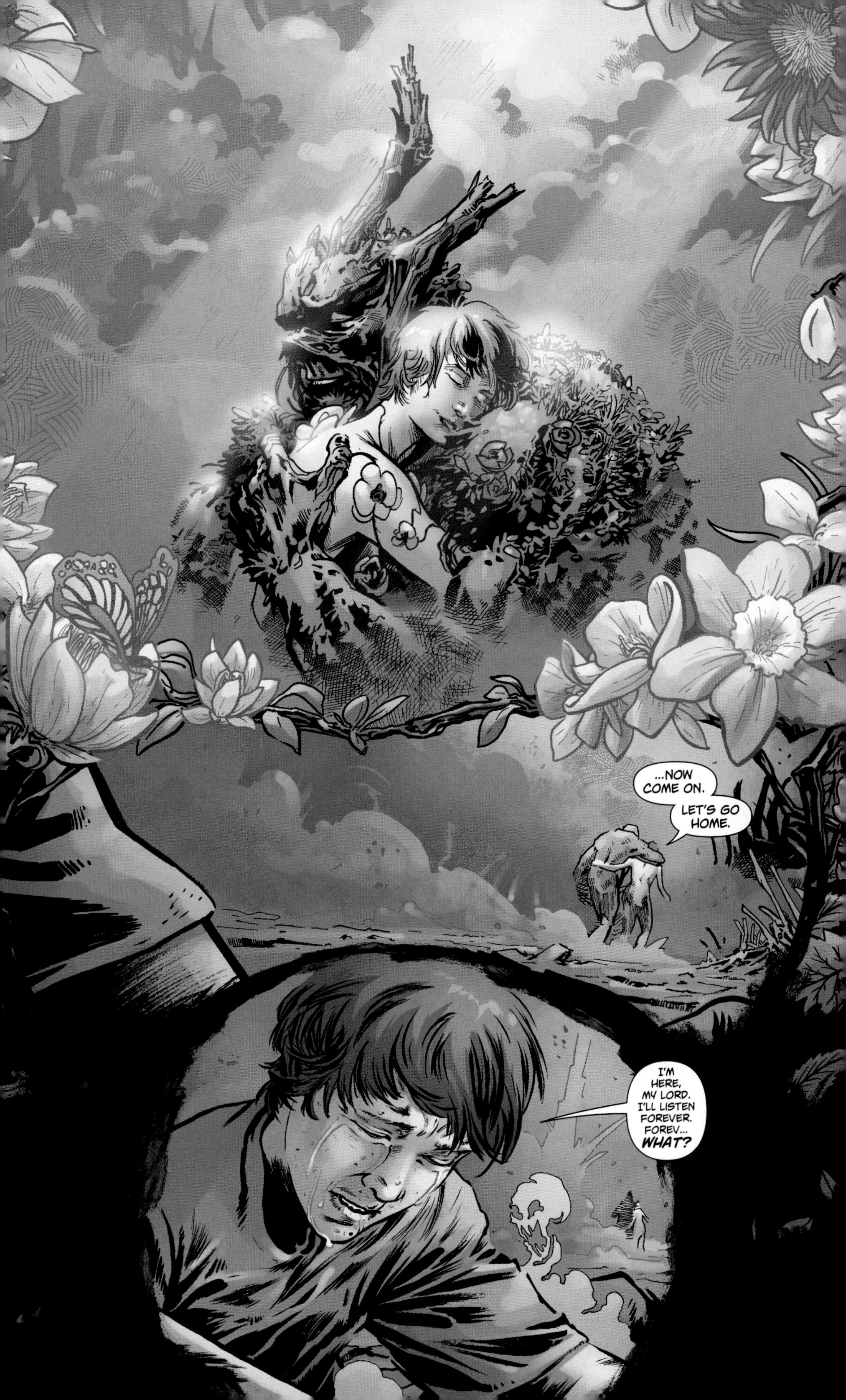
...NOW COME ON.
LET'S GO HOME.
I'M HERE, MY LORD. I'LL LISTEN FOREVER. FOREV... WHAT?

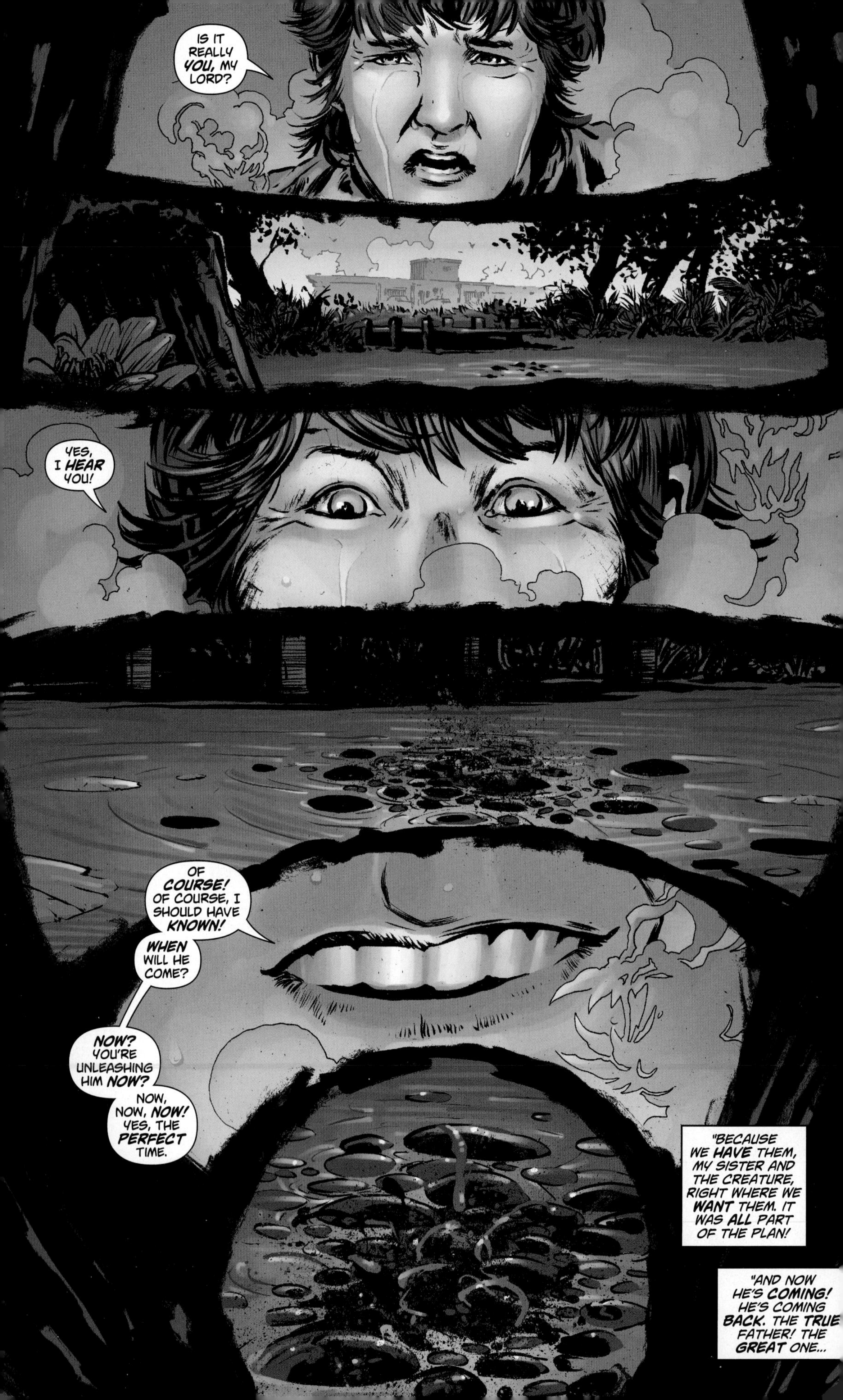
IS IT REALLY YOU, MY LORD?
YES, I HEAR YOU!
OF COURSE! OF COURSE, I SHOULD HAVE KNOWN!
WHEN WILL HE COME?
NOW? YOU'RE UNLEASHING HIM NOW?
NOW, NOW, NOW! YES, THE PERFECT TIME.
"BECAUSE WE HAVE THEM, MY SISTER AND THE CREATURE, RIGHT WHERE WE WANT THEM. IT WAS ALL PART OF THE PLAN!
"AND NOW HE'S COMING! HE'S COMING BACK. THE TRUE FATHER! THE GREAT ONE...

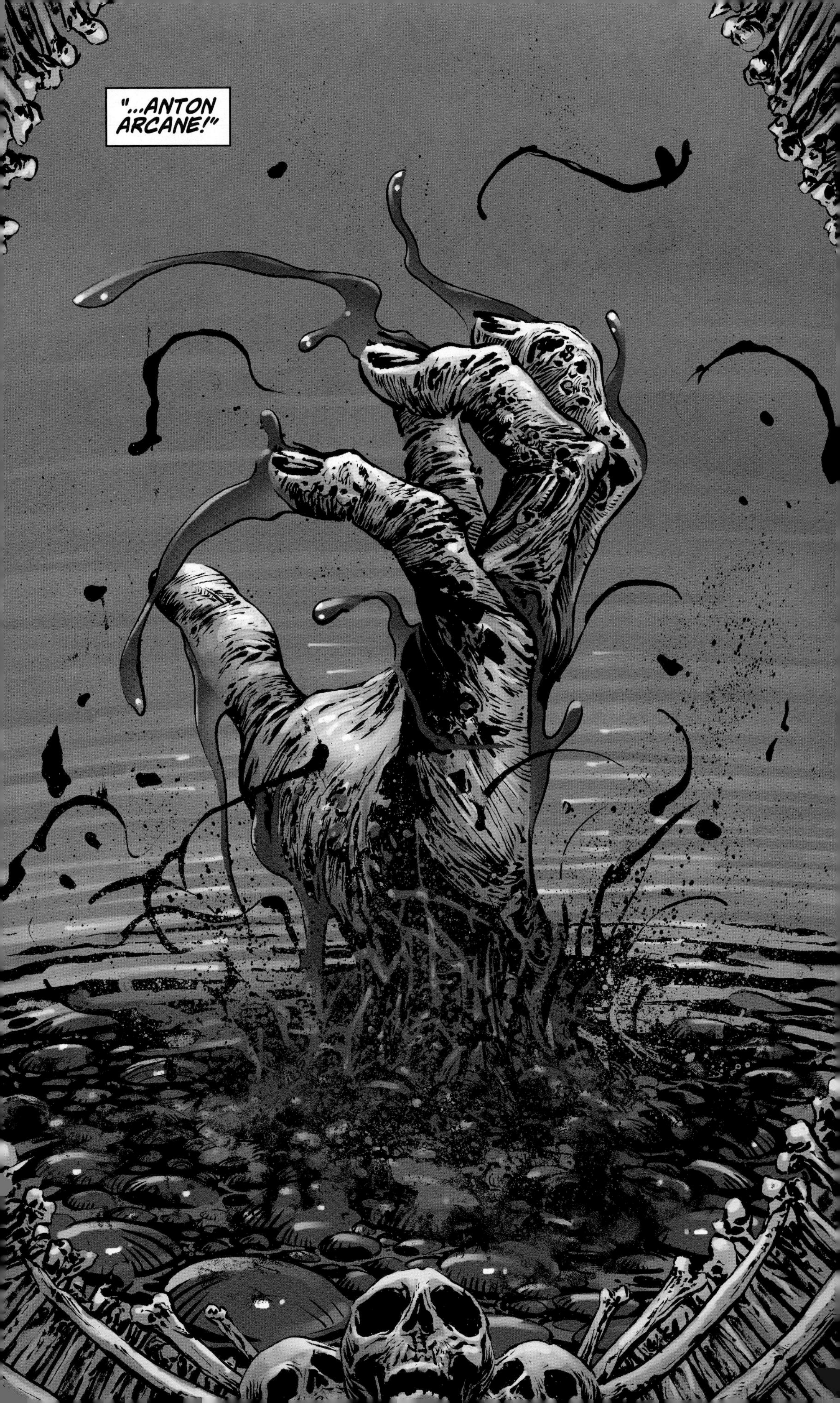
"...ANTON ARCANE!"

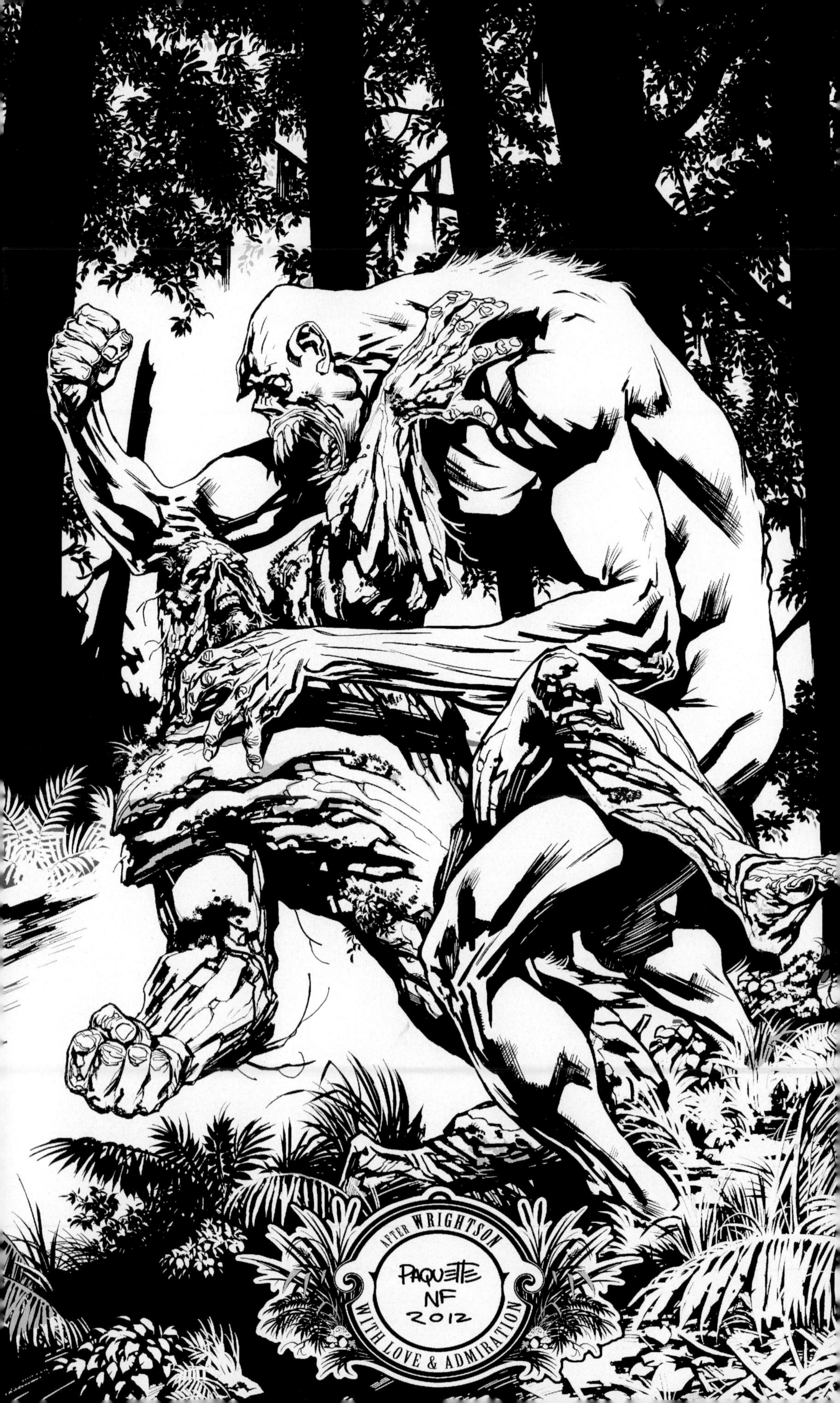
AFTER WRIGHTSON
PAQUETTE
NF
2012
WITH LOVE & ADMIRATION

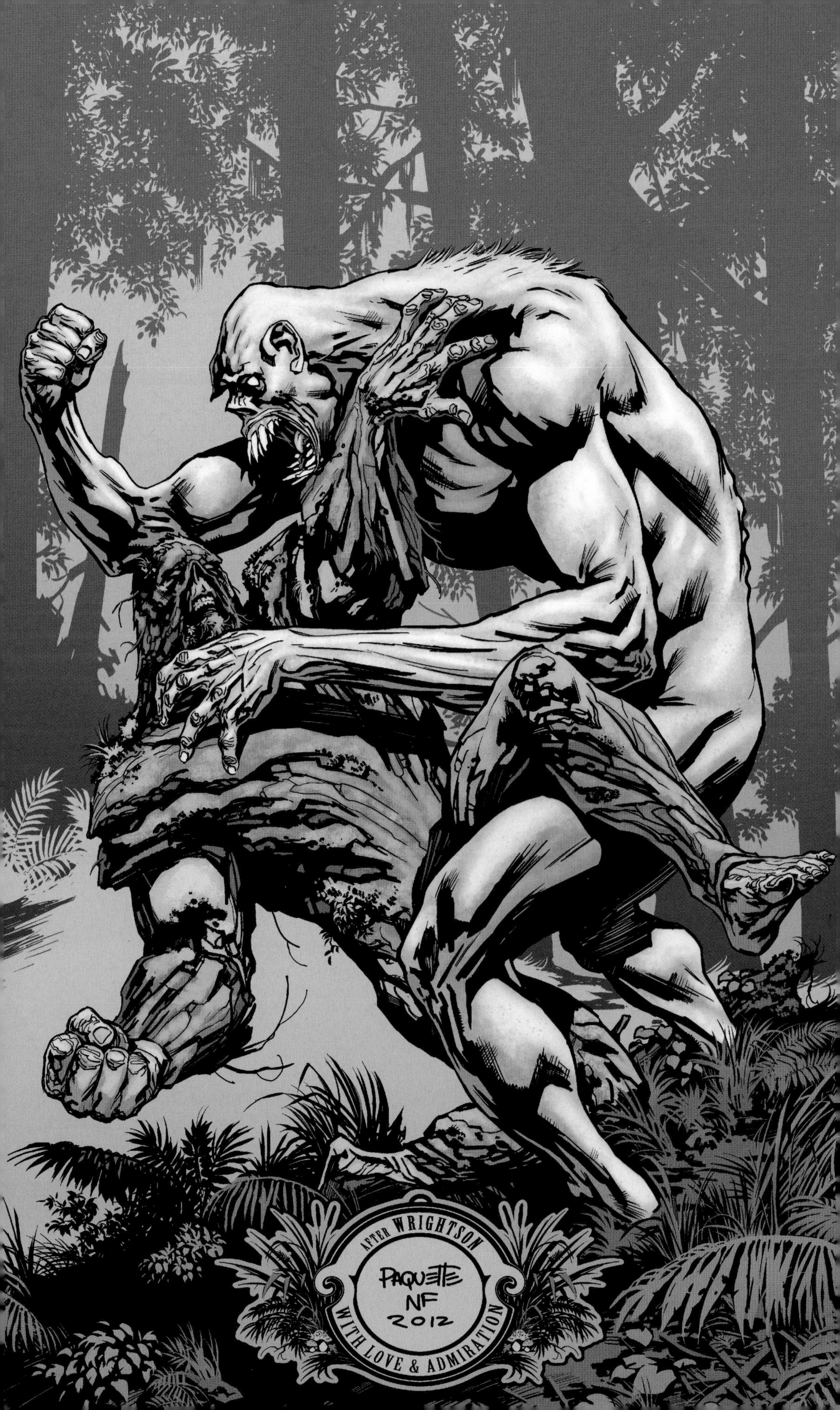
AFTER WRIGHTSON
PAQUETTE
NF
2012
WITH LOVE & ADMIRATION

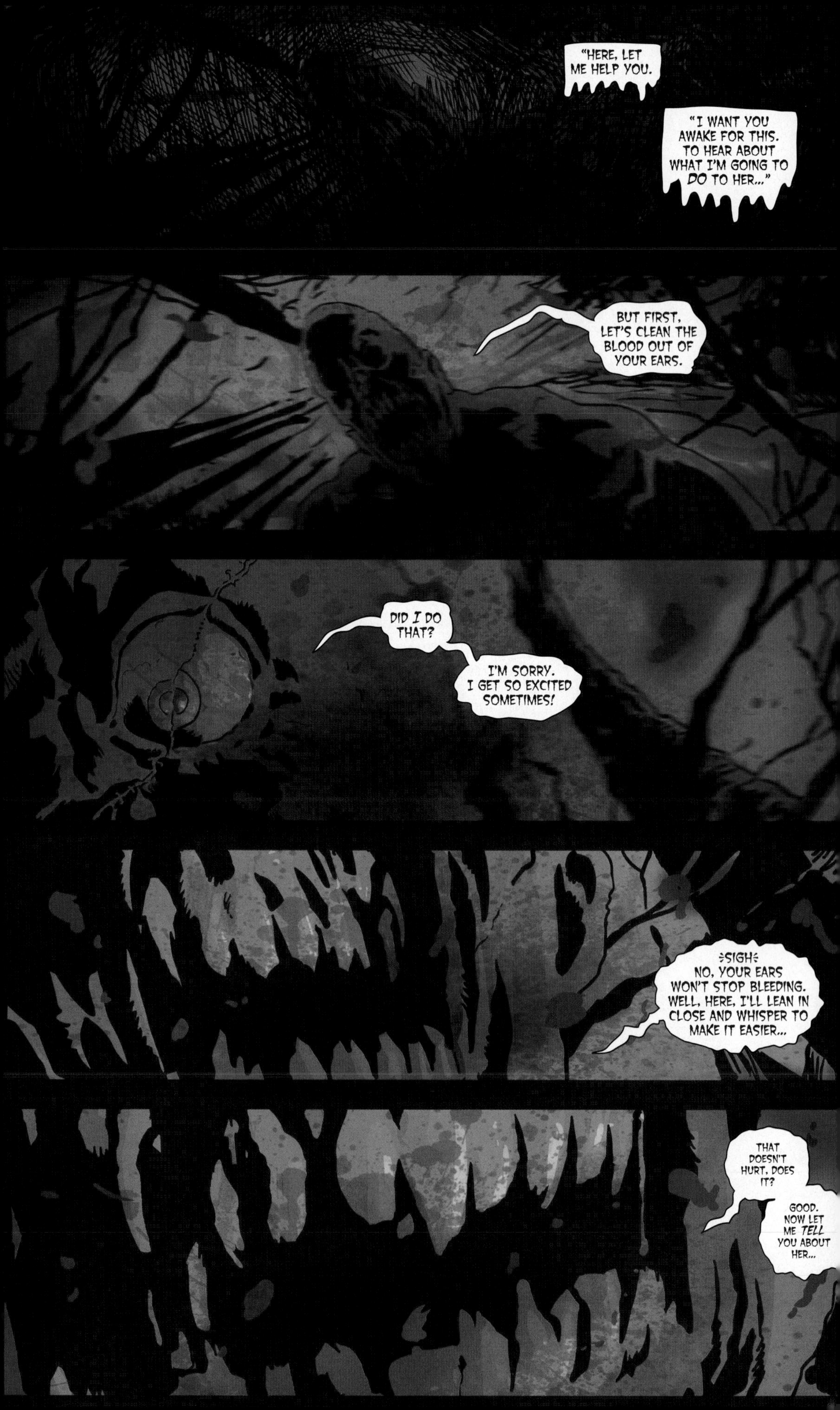
"HERE, LET ME HELP YOU.
"I WANT YOU AWAKE FOR THIS. TO HEAR ABOUT WHAT I'M GOING TO *DO* TO HER..."
BUT FIRST, LET'S CLEAN THE BLOOD OUT OF YOUR EARS.
DID *I* DO THAT?
I'M SORRY. I GET SO EXCITED SOMETIMES!
SIGH NO, YOUR EARS WON'T STOP BLEEDING. WELL, HERE, I'LL LEAN IN CLOSE AND WHISPER TO MAKE IT EASIER...
THAT DOESN'T HURT, DOES IT?
GOOD. NOW LET ME *TELL* YOU ABOUT HER...

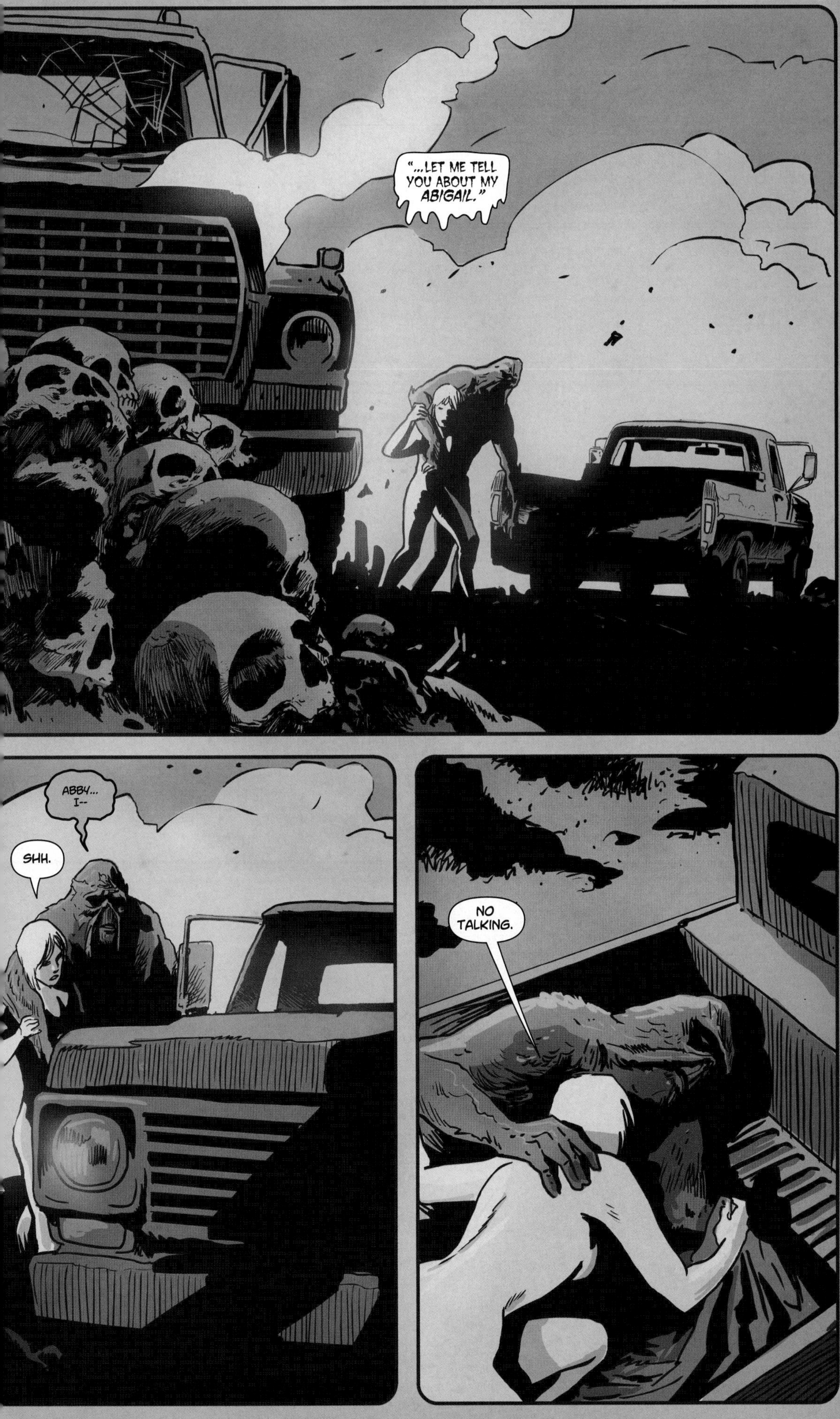
"...LET ME TELL YOU ABOUT MY ABIGAIL."
ABBY... I--
SHH.
NO TALKING.

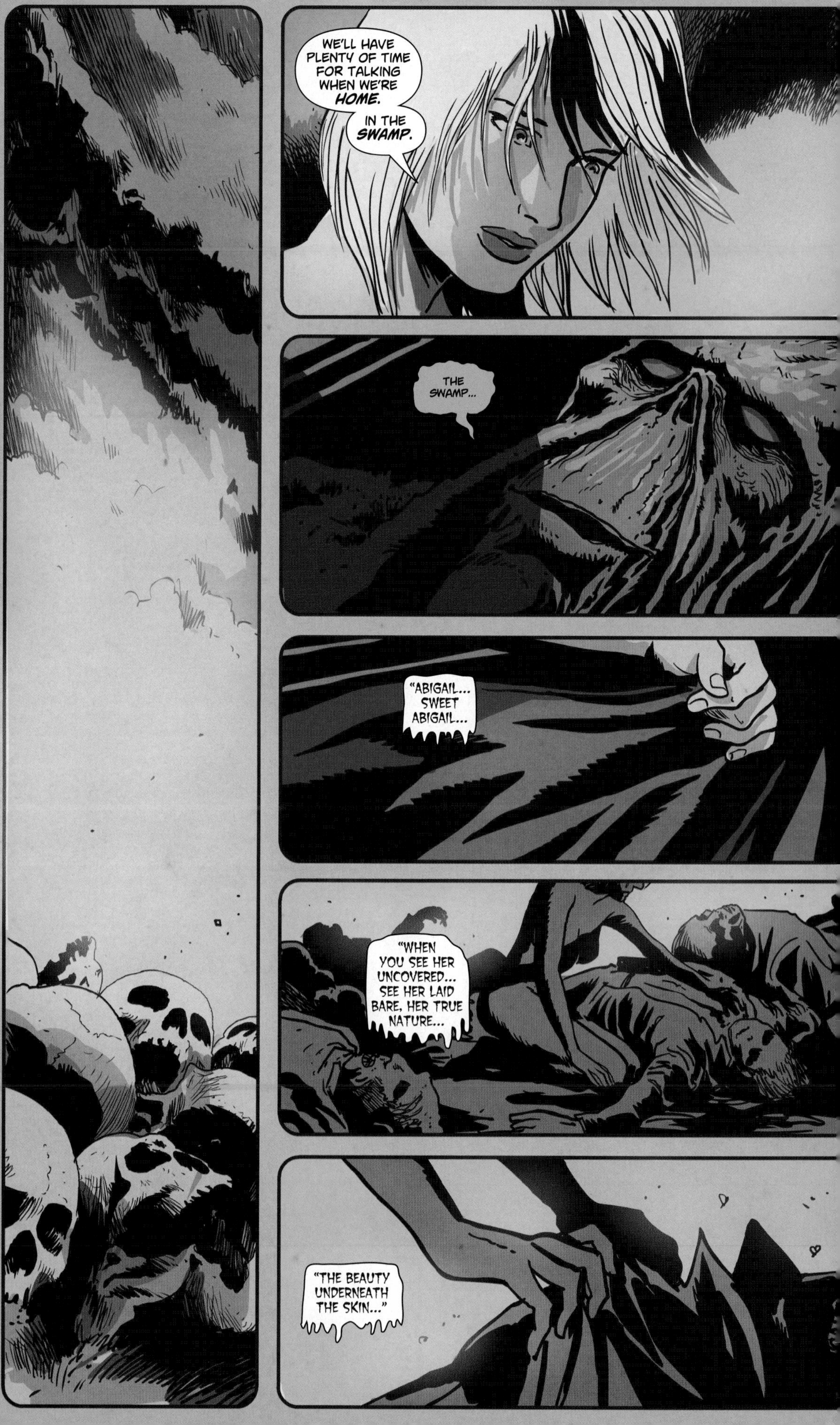

WE'LL HAVE PLENTY OF TIME FOR TALKING WHEN WE'RE HOME.
IN THE SWAMP.
THE SWAMP...
"ABIGAIL... SWEET ABIGAIL...
"WHEN YOU SEE HER UNCOVERED... SEE HER LAID BARE, HER TRUE NATURE...
"THE BEAUTY UNDERNEATH THE SKIN..."

OH NO, DON'T SLIP AWAY YET.
THERE. THAT'S BETTER.
I PROMISE, YOUR PAIN WILL ONLY LAST A LITTLE LONGER. IN JUST A MOMENT, I'M GOING TO BASH YOUR HEAD IN.
BUT FOR NOW, LISTEN TO AN OLD MAN. AND I AM OLD, MY FRIEND...
I WALKED THE EARTH AS A MAN FOR MORE THAN A CENTURY. I SIRED FIFTY CHILDREN, ALL FOR THE ROT.
BUT IN ALL MY TIME, ABOVE THE GROUND AND BENEATH IT...

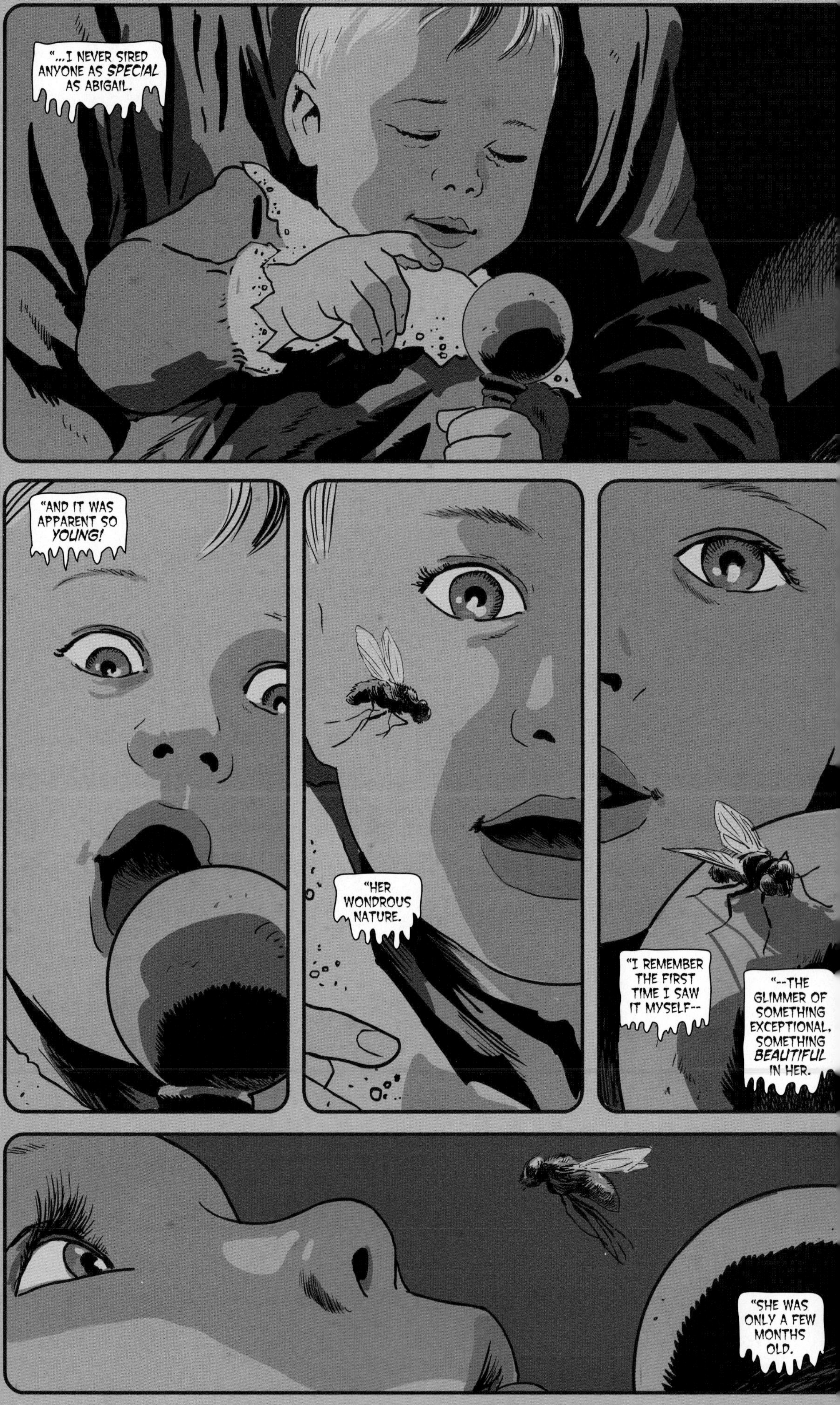
"...I NEVER SIRED ANYONE AS SPECIAL AS ABIGAIL.
"AND IT WAS APPARENT SO YOUNG!
"HER WONDROUS NATURE.
"I REMEMBER THE FIRST TIME I SAW IT MYSELF--
"--THE GLIMMER OF SOMETHING EXCEPTIONAL, SOMETHING BEAUTIFUL IN HER.
"SHE WAS ONLY A FEW MONTHS OLD.

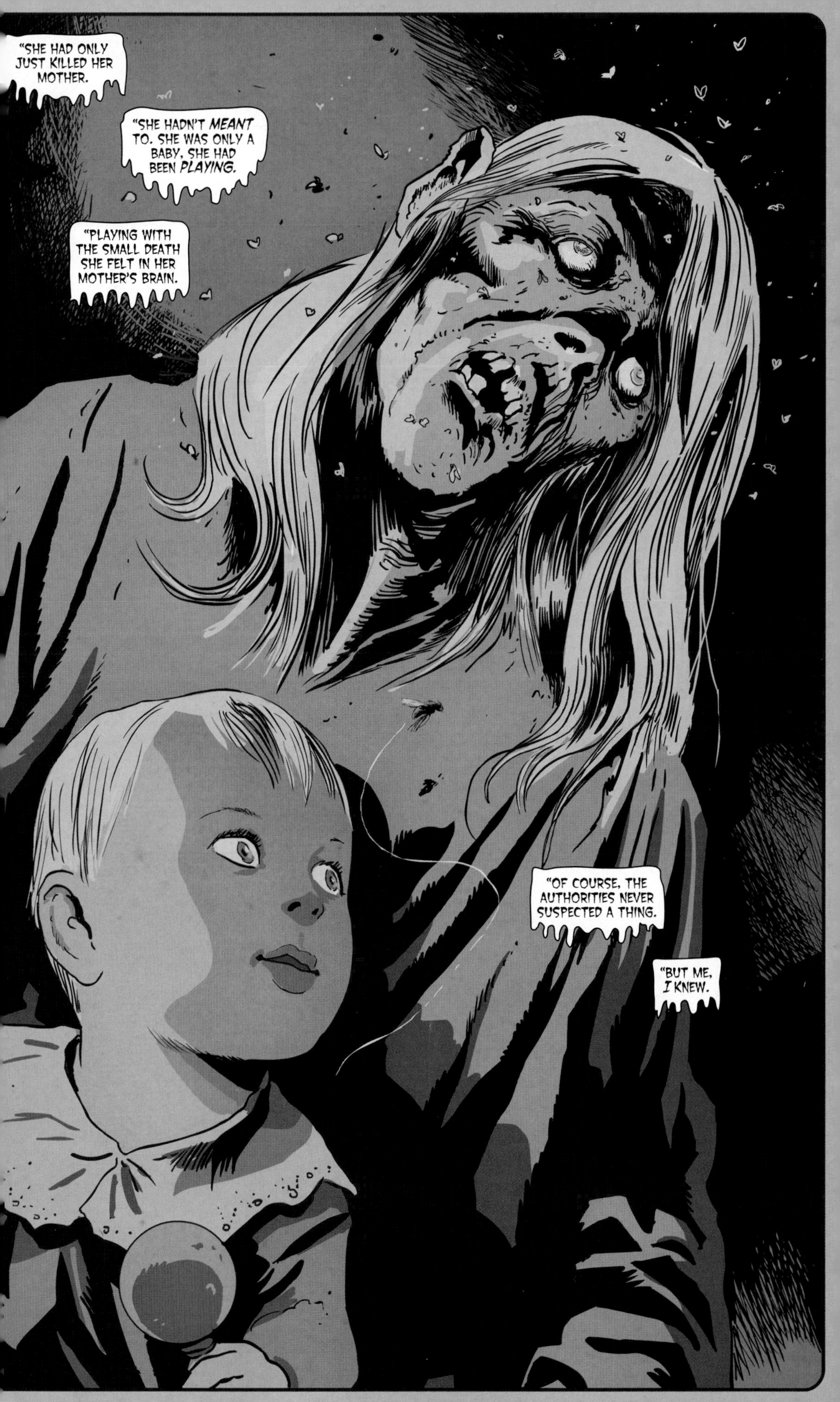
"SHE HAD ONLY JUST KILLED HER MOTHER.
"SHE HADN'T MEANT TO. SHE WAS ONLY A BABY, SHE HAD BEEN PLAYING.
"PLAYING WITH THE SMALL DEATH SHE FELT IN HER MOTHER'S BRAIN.
"OF COURSE, THE AUTHORITIES NEVER SUSPECTED A THING.
"BUT ME, I KNEW.

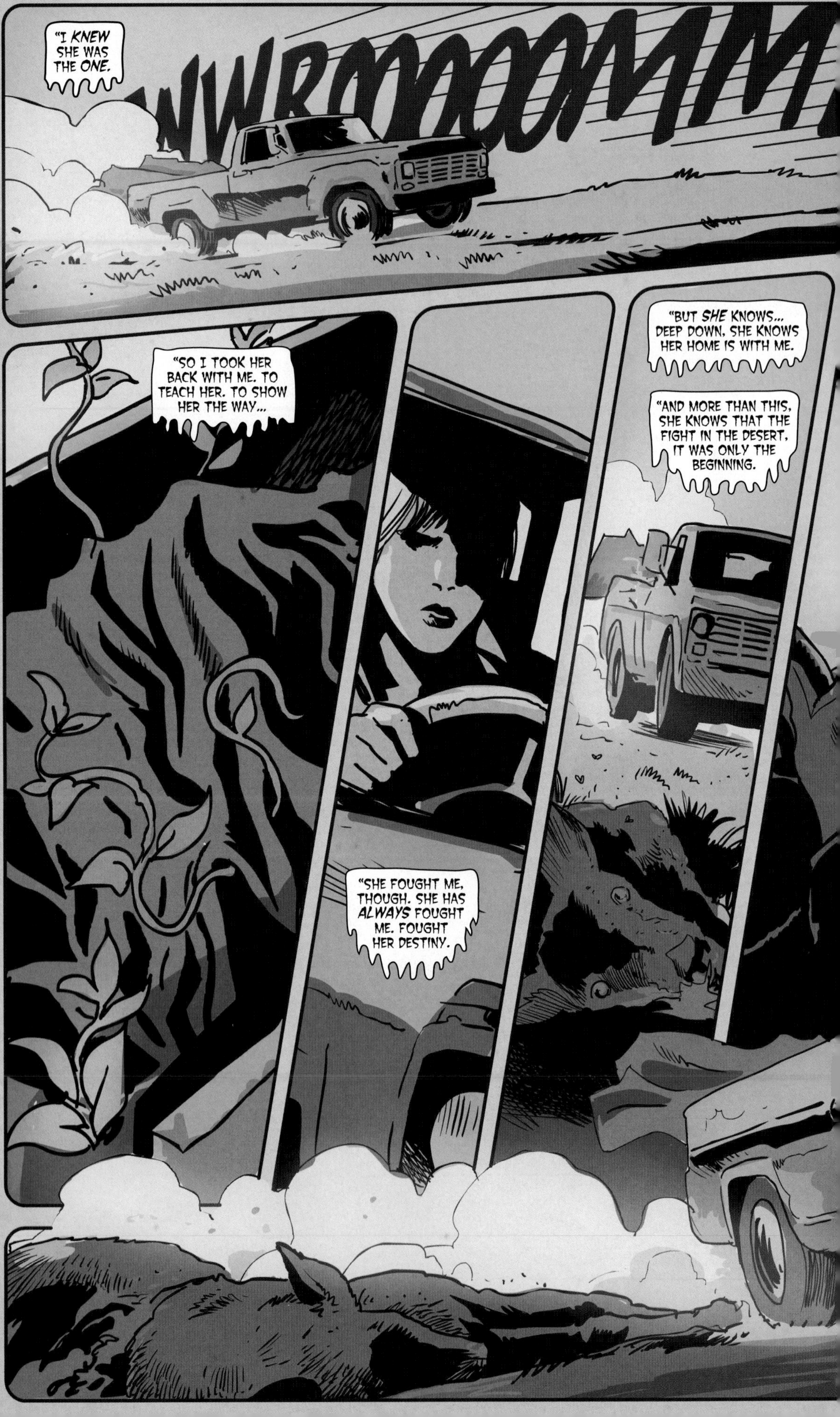
"I KNEW SHE WAS THE ONE.
WWROOOOOMM
"SO I TOOK HER BACK WITH ME. TO TEACH HER. TO SHOW HER THE WAY...
"SHE FOUGHT ME, THOUGH. SHE HAS ALWAYS FOUGHT ME. FOUGHT HER DESTINY.
"BUT SHE KNOWS... DEEP DOWN, SHE KNOWS HER HOME IS WITH ME.
"AND MORE THAN THIS, SHE KNOWS THAT THE FIGHT IN THE DESERT, IT WAS ONLY THE BEGINNING.

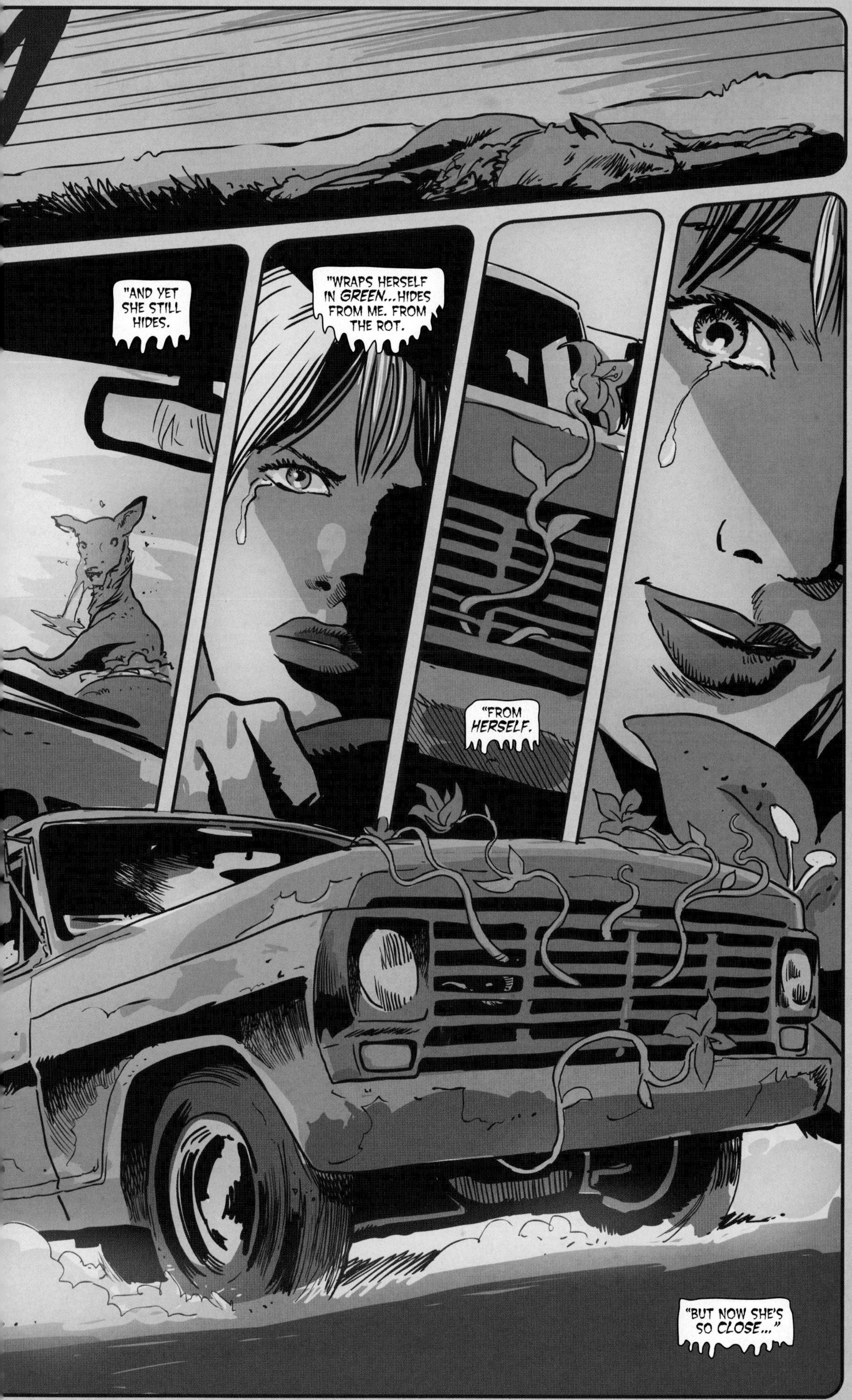
"AND YET SHE STILL HIDES.
"WRAPS HERSELF IN GREEN...HIDES FROM ME. FROM THE ROT.
"FROM HERSELF.
"BUT NOW SHE'S SO CLOSE..."

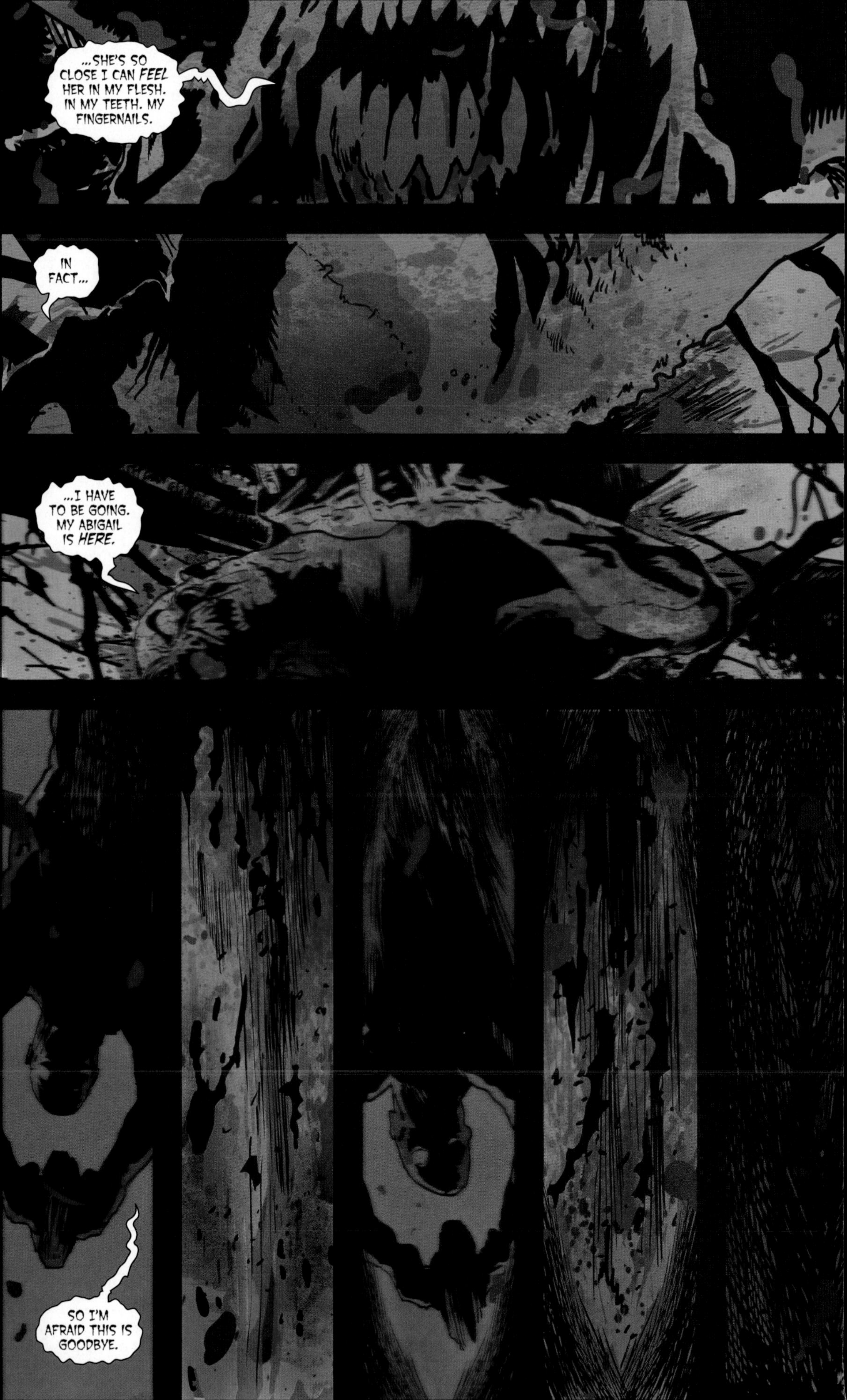
...SHE'S SO CLOSE I CAN *FEEL* HER IN MY FLESH. IN MY TEETH. MY FINGERNAILS.
IN FACT...
...I HAVE TO BE GOING. MY ABIGAIL IS *HERE*.
SO I'M AFRAID THIS IS GOODBYE.

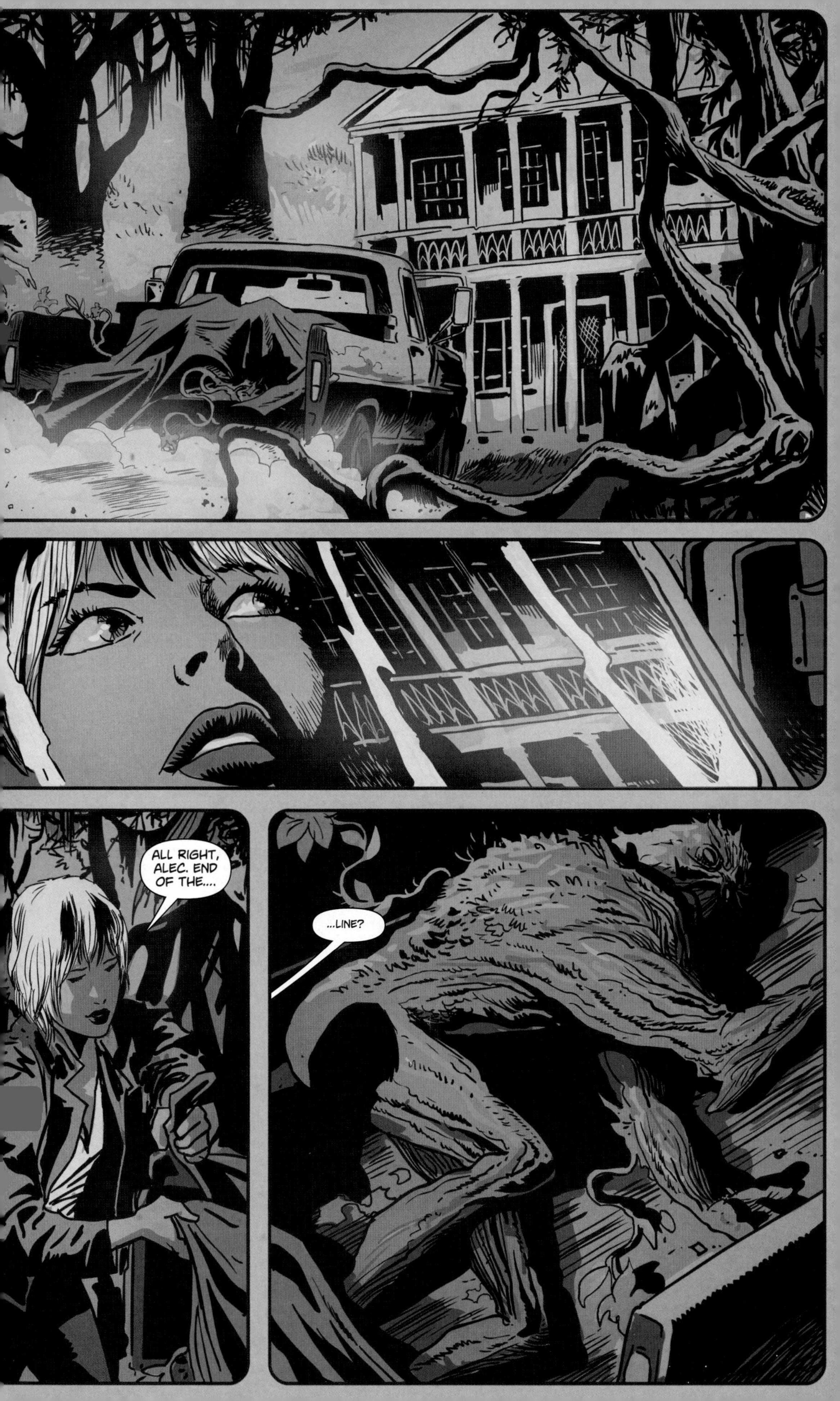
ALL RIGHT, ALEC. END OF THE....
...LINE?

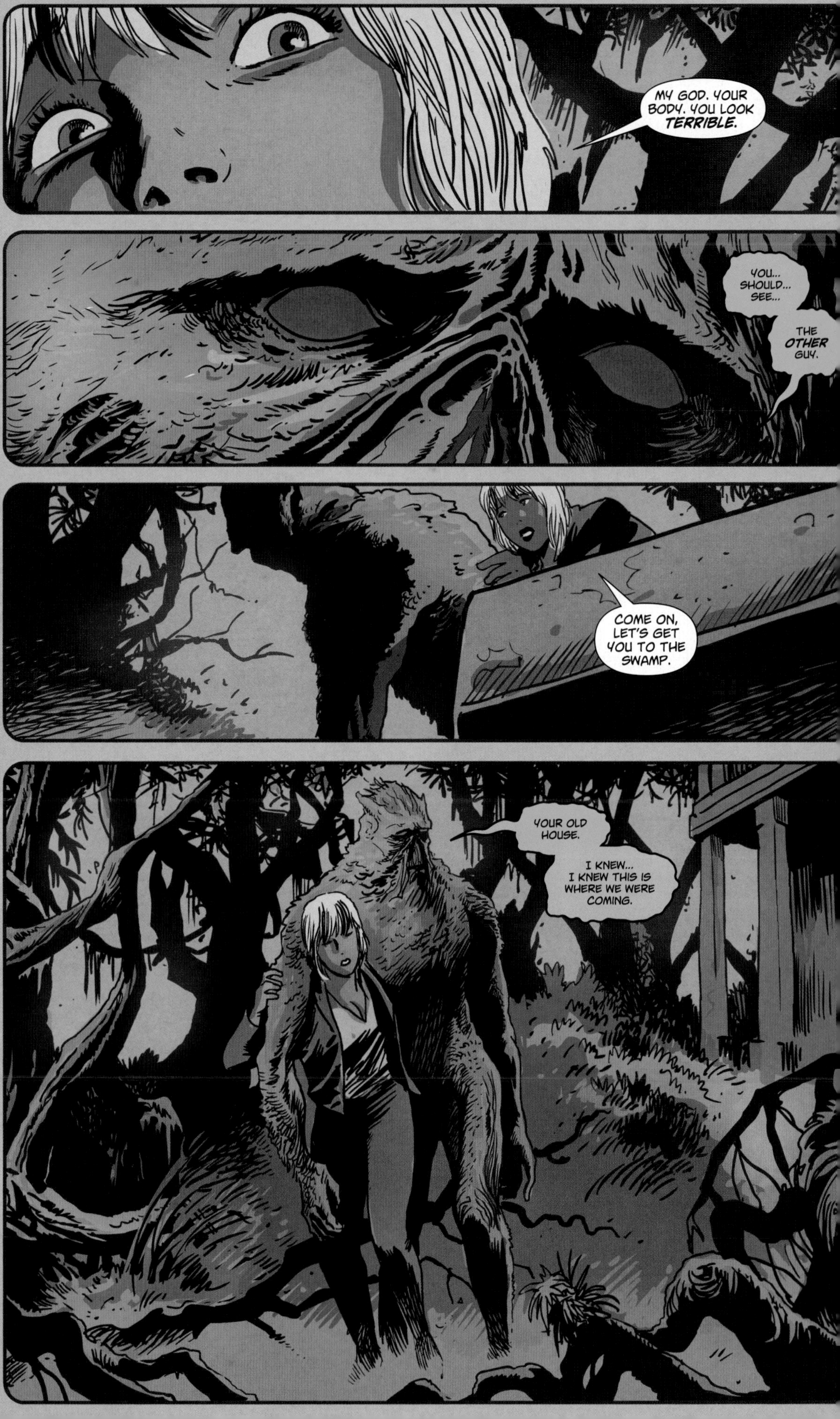
MY GOD. YOUR BODY. YOU LOOK TERRIBLE.
YOU... SHOULD... SEE...
THE OTHER GUY.
COME ON, LET'S GET YOU TO THE SWAMP.
YOUR OLD HOUSE.
I KNEW... I KNEW THIS IS WHERE WE WERE COMING.

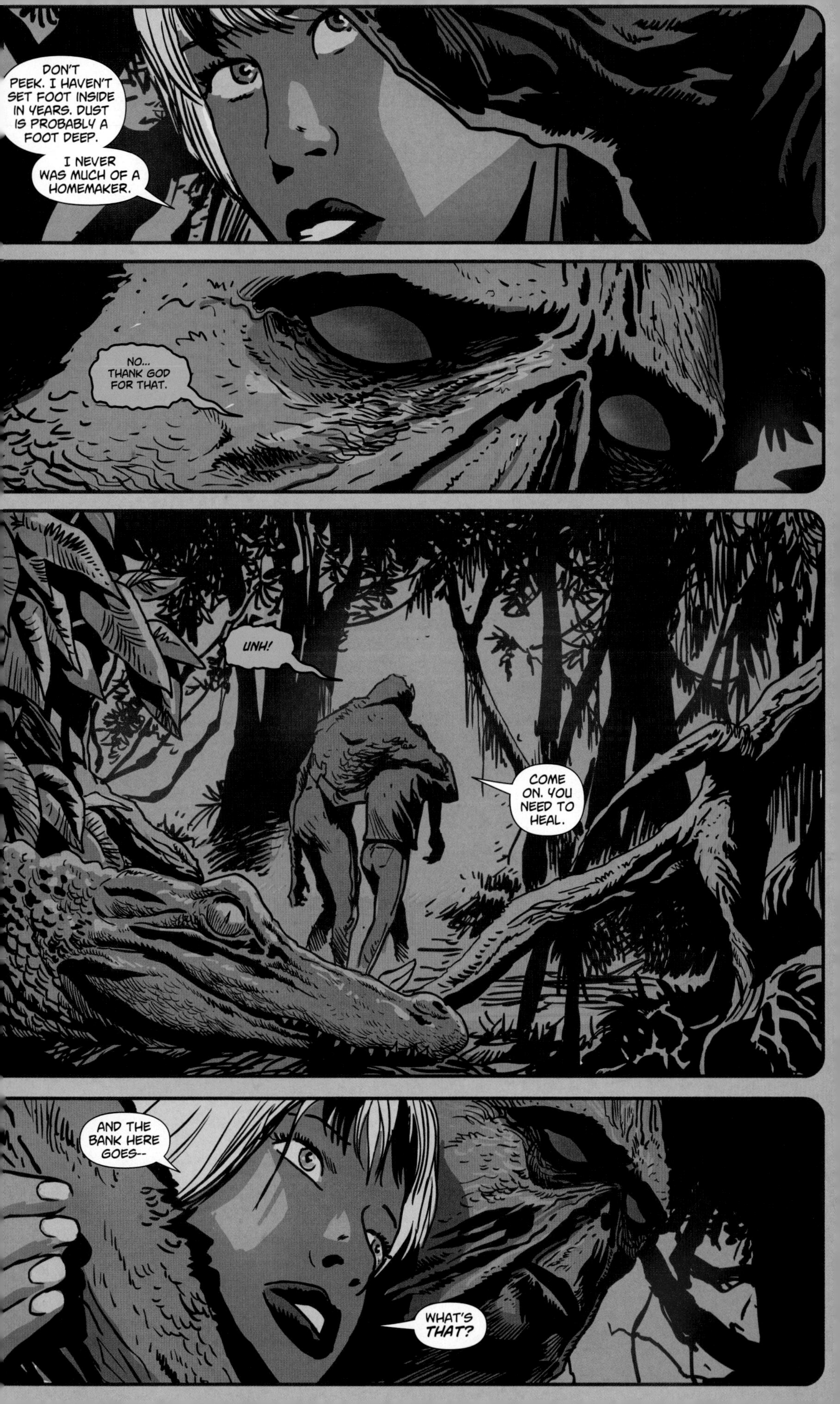
DON'T PEEK. I HAVEN'T SET FOOT INSIDE IN YEARS. DUST IS PROBABLY A FOOT DEEP.
I NEVER WAS MUCH OF A HOMEMAKER.
NO... THANK GOD FOR THAT.
UNH!
COME ON. YOU NEED TO HEAL.
AND THE BANK HERE GOES--
WHAT'S *THAT?*

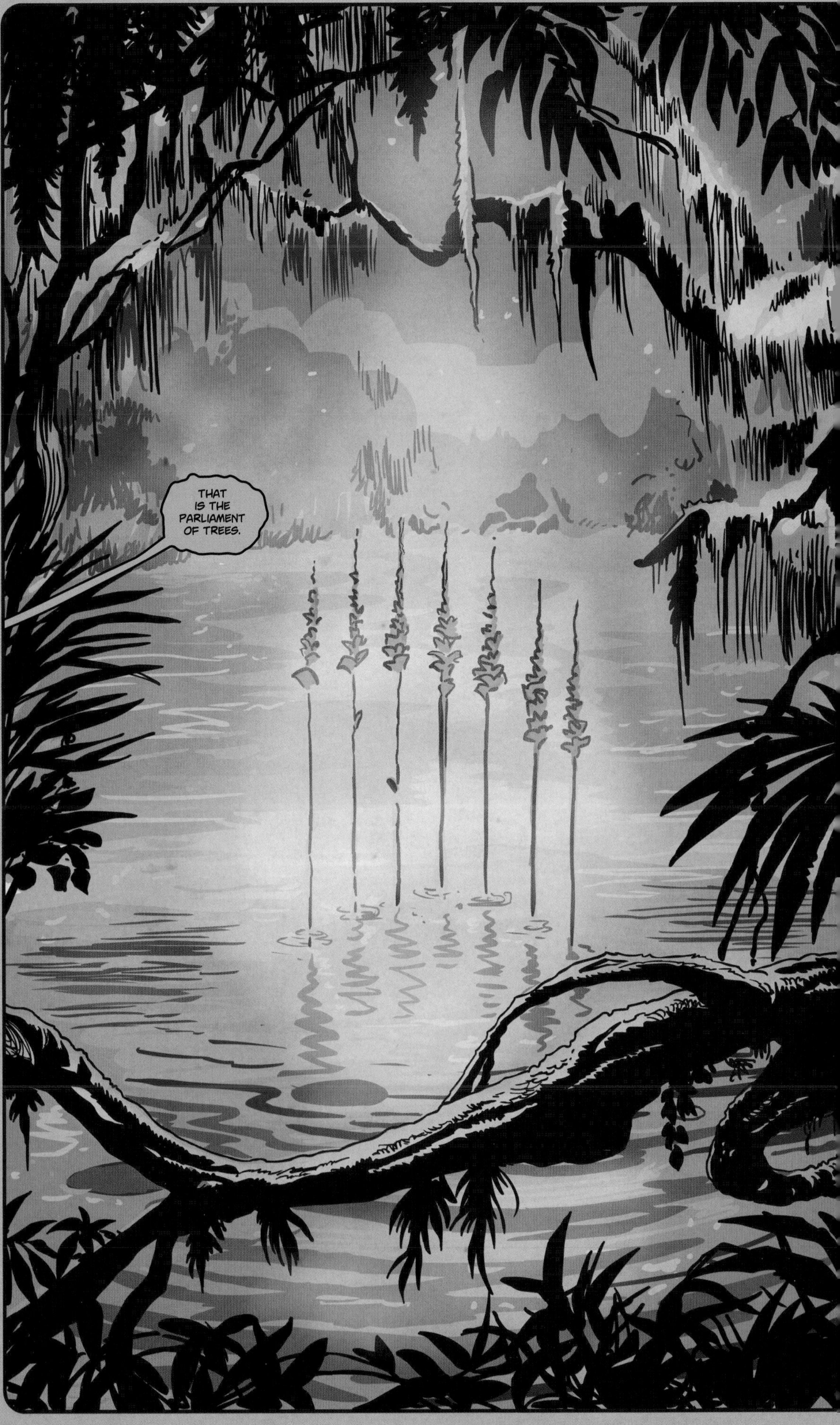
THAT IS THE PARLIAMENT OF TREES.

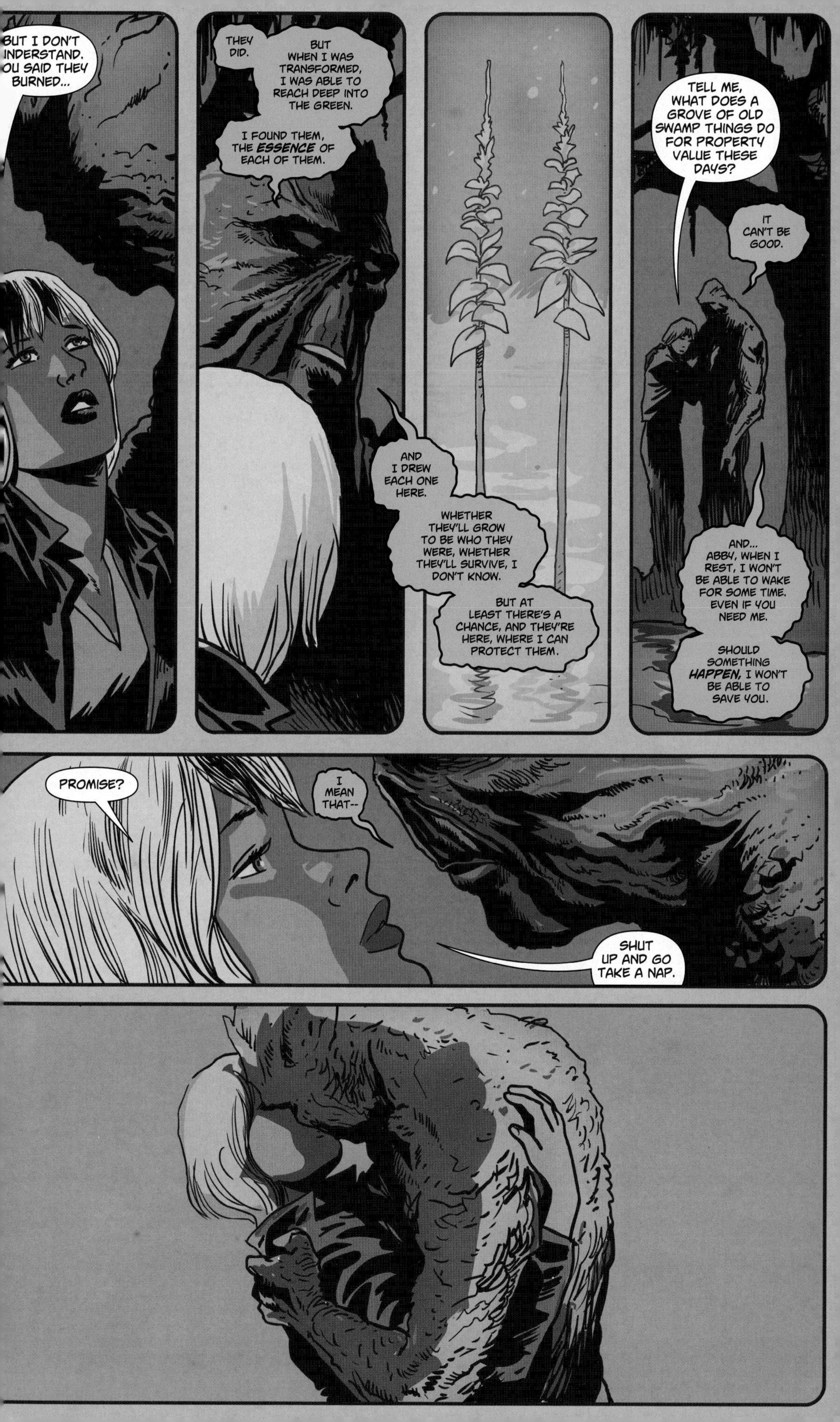
BUT I DON'T
INDERSTAND.
OU SAID THEY
BURNED...
THEY DID.
BUT WHEN I WAS TRANSFORMED, I WAS ABLE TO REACH DEEP INTO THE GREEN.
I FOUND THEM, THE ESSENCE OF EACH OF THEM.
AND I DREW EACH ONE HERE.
WHETHER THEY'LL GROW TO BE WHO THEY WERE, WHETHER THEY'LL SURVIVE, I DON'T KNOW.
BUT AT LEAST THERE'S A CHANCE, AND THEY'RE HERE, WHERE I CAN PROTECT THEM.
TELL ME, WHAT DOES A GROVE OF OLD SWAMP THINGS DO FOR PROPERTY VALUE THESE DAYS?
IT CAN'T BE GOOD.
AND... ABBY, WHEN I REST, I WON'T BE ABLE TO WAKE FOR SOME TIME. EVEN IF YOU NEED ME.
SHOULD SOMETHING HAPPEN, I WON'T BE ABLE TO SAVE YOU.
I MEAN THAT--
PROMISE?
SHUT UP AND GO TAKE A NAP.

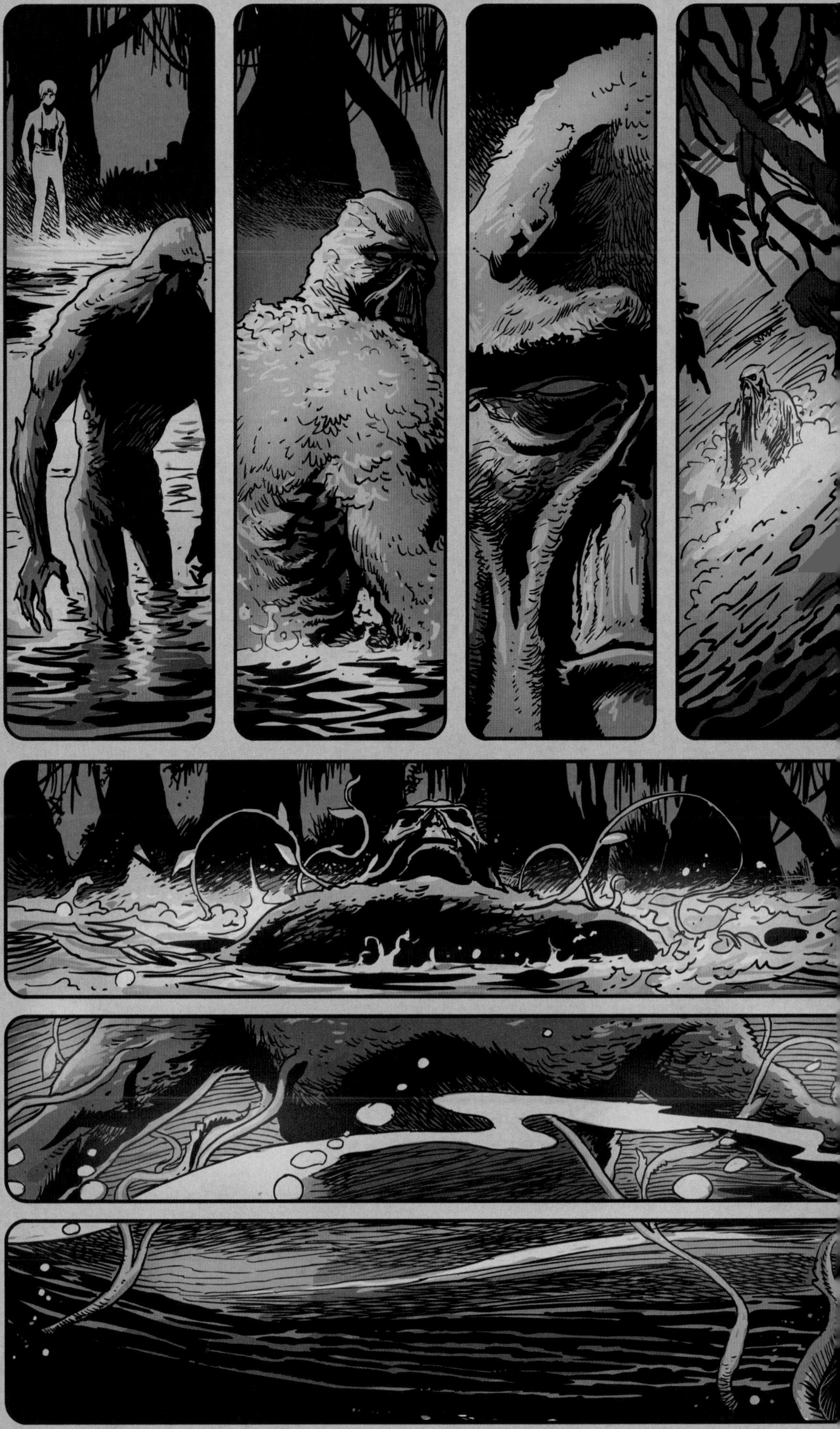

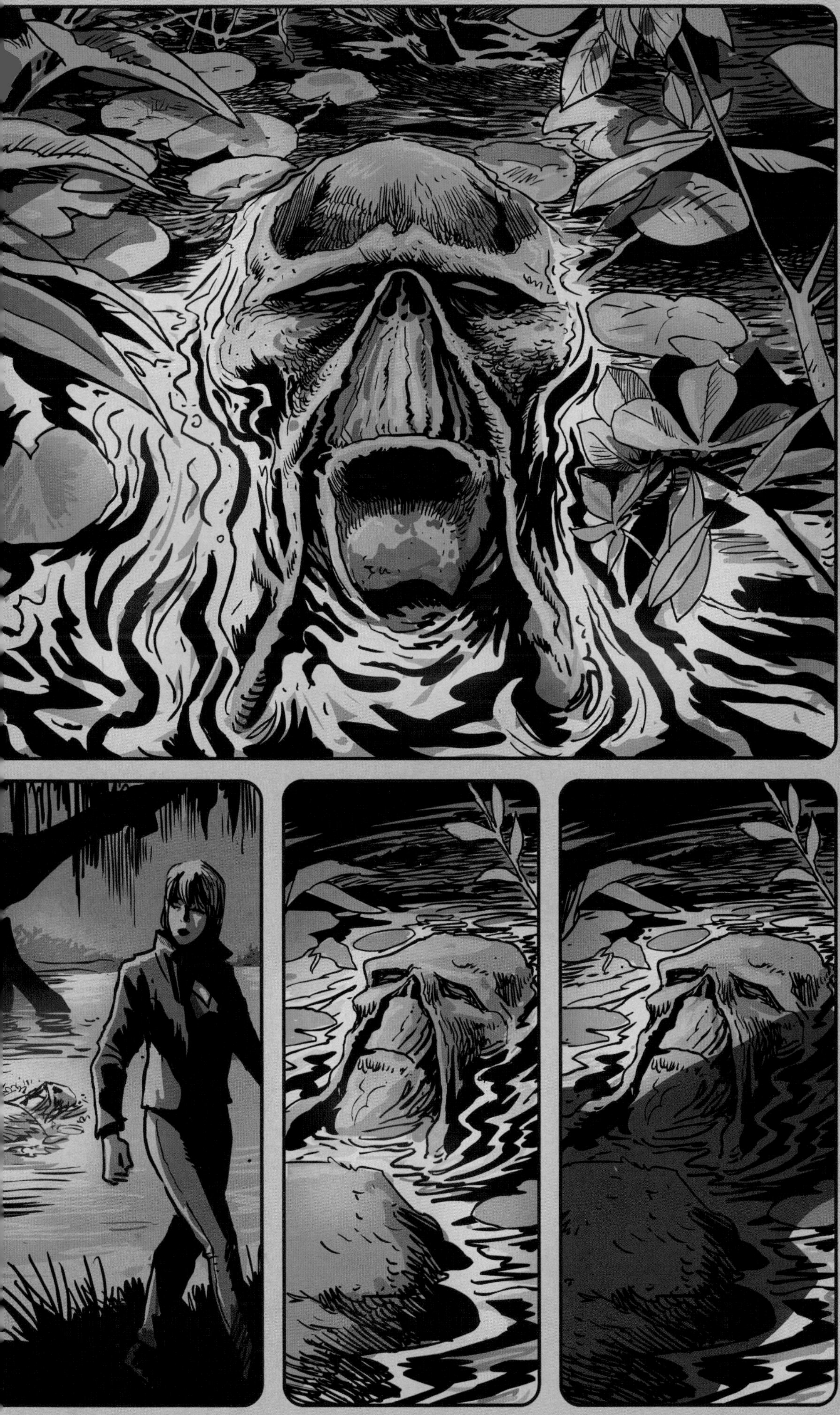

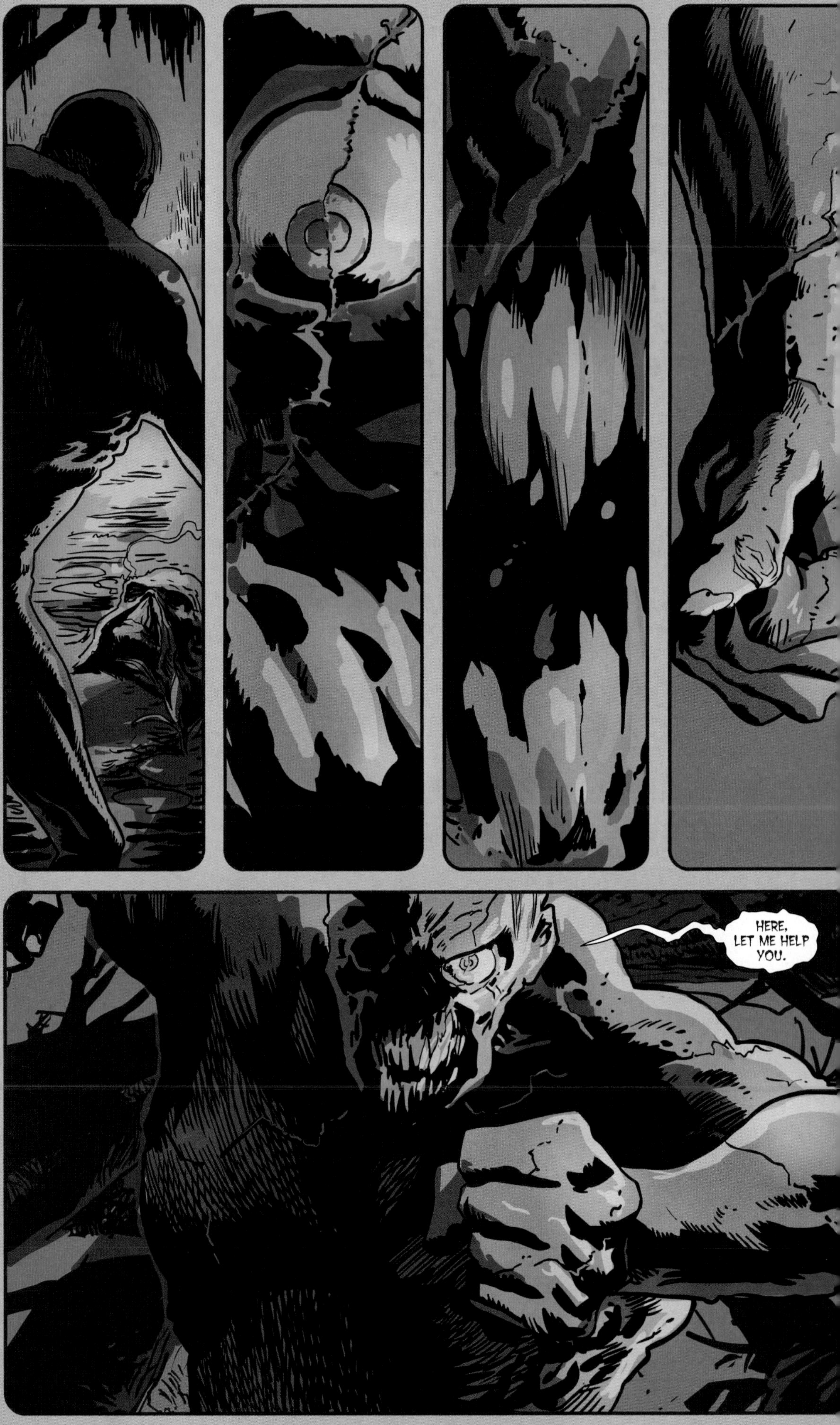
HERE, LET ME HELP YOU.

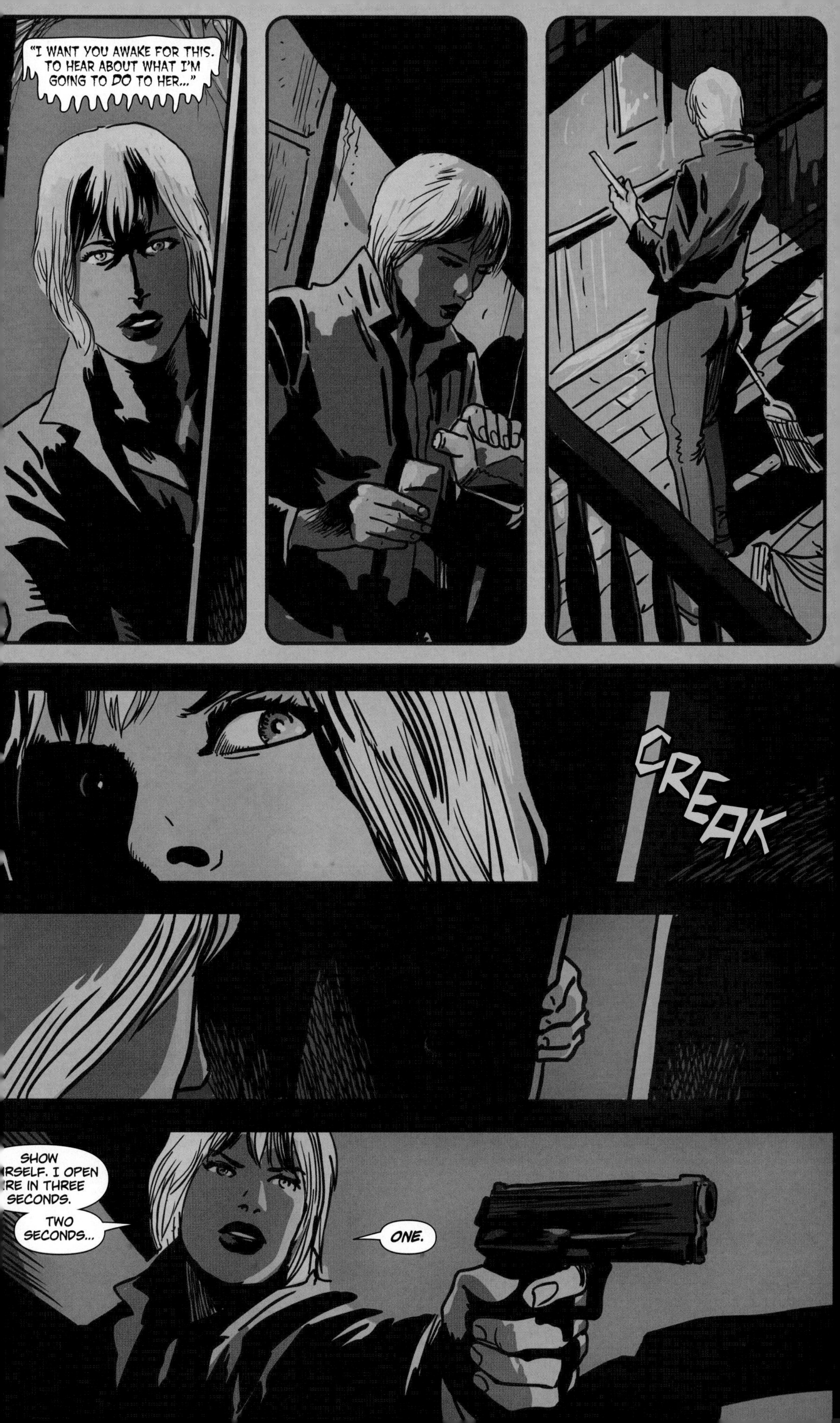
"I WANT YOU AWAKE FOR THIS. TO HEAR ABOUT WHAT I'M GOING TO DO TO HER..."
CREAK
SHOW
RSELF. I OPEN
RE IN THREE
SECONDS.
TWO SECONDS...
ONE.

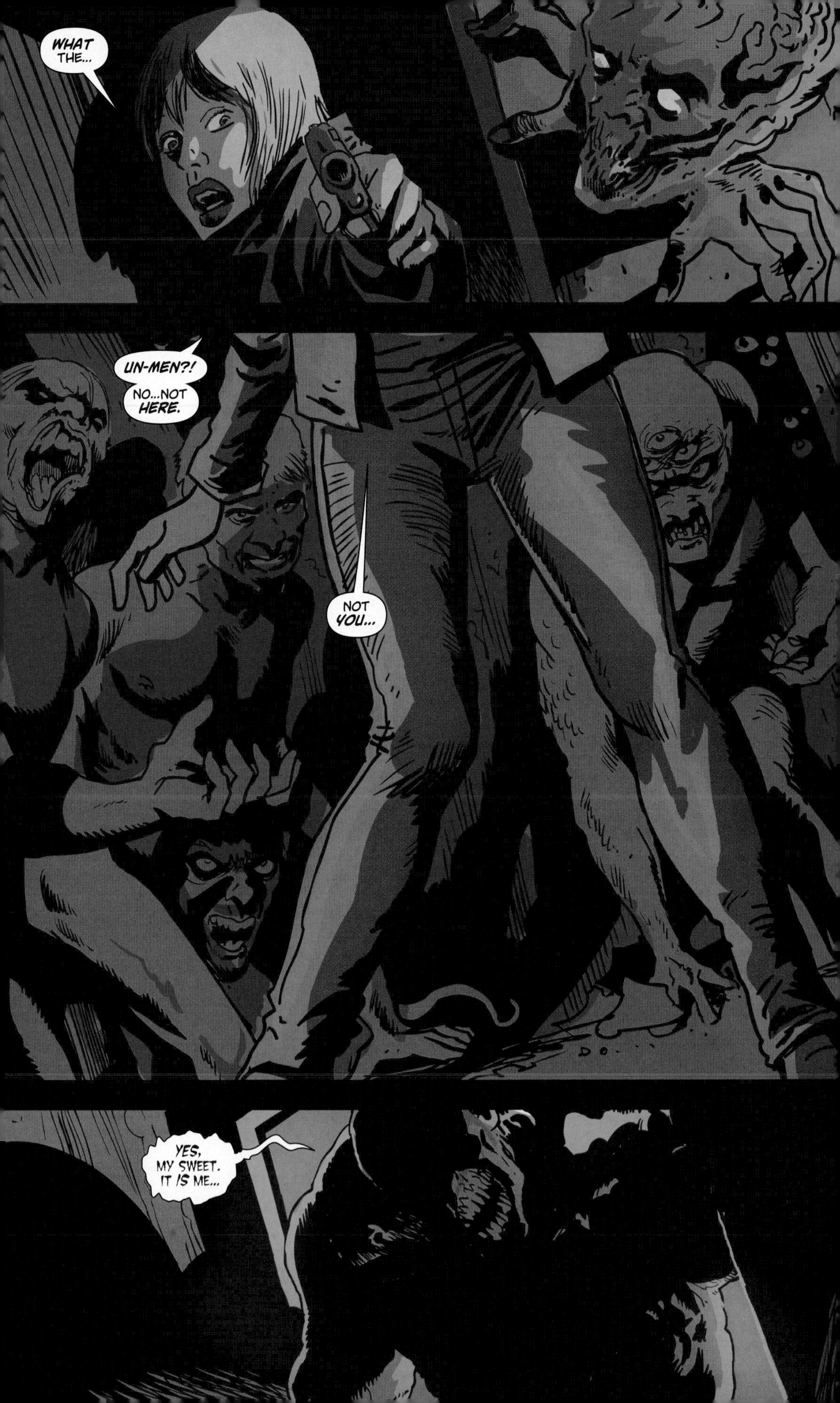

WHAT THE...
UN-MEN?! NO...NOT HERE.
NOT YOU...
YES, MY SWEET. IT IS ME...

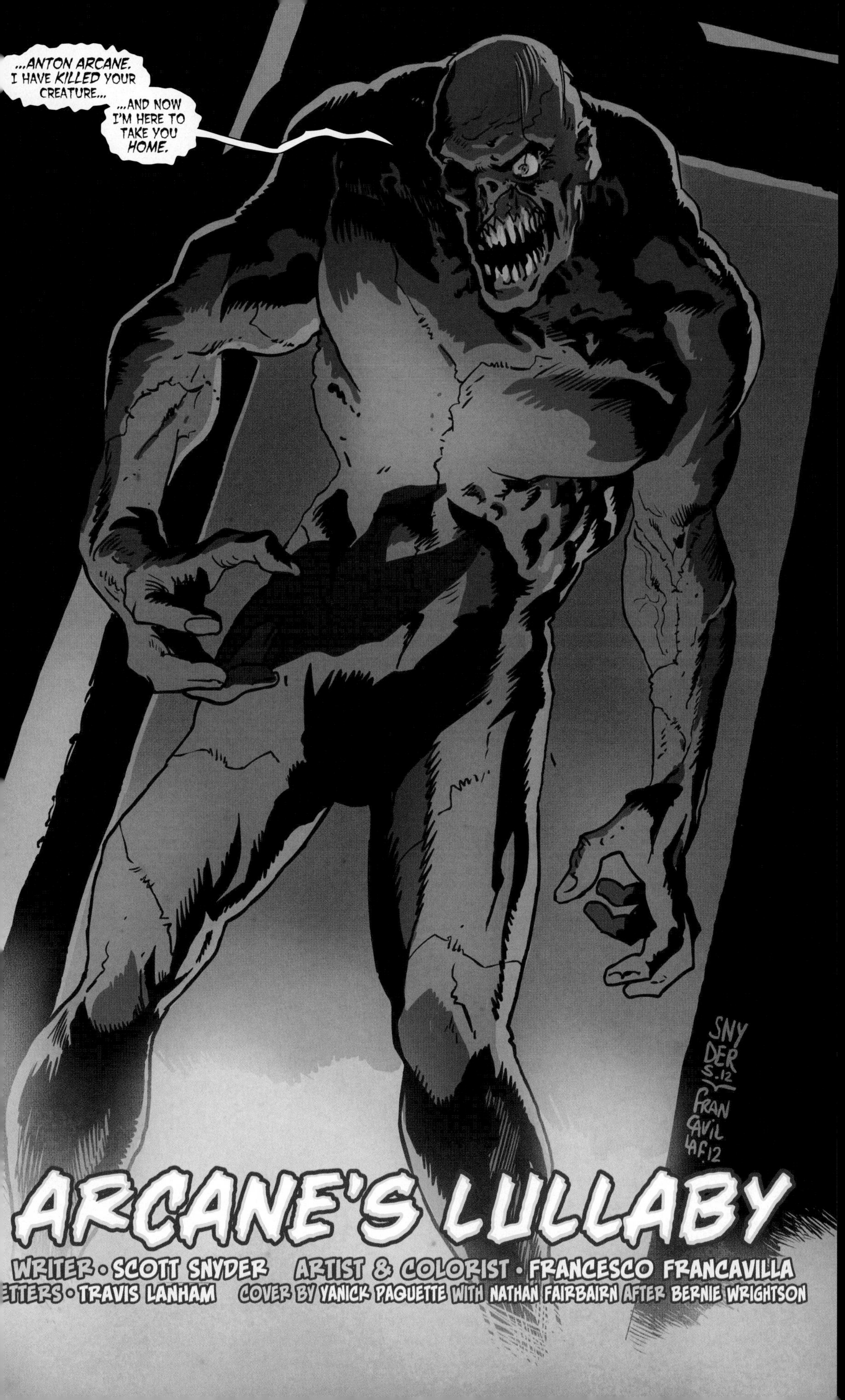
...ANTON ARCANE. I HAVE KILLED YOUR CREATURE...
...AND NOW I'M HERE TO TAKE YOU HOME.
ARCANE'S LULLABY
WRITER • SCOTT SNYDER ARTIST & COLORIST • FRANCESCO FRANCAVILLA
ETTERS • TRAVIS LANHAM COVER BY YANICK PAQUETTE WITH NATHAN FAIRBAIRN AFTER BERNIE WRIGHTSON

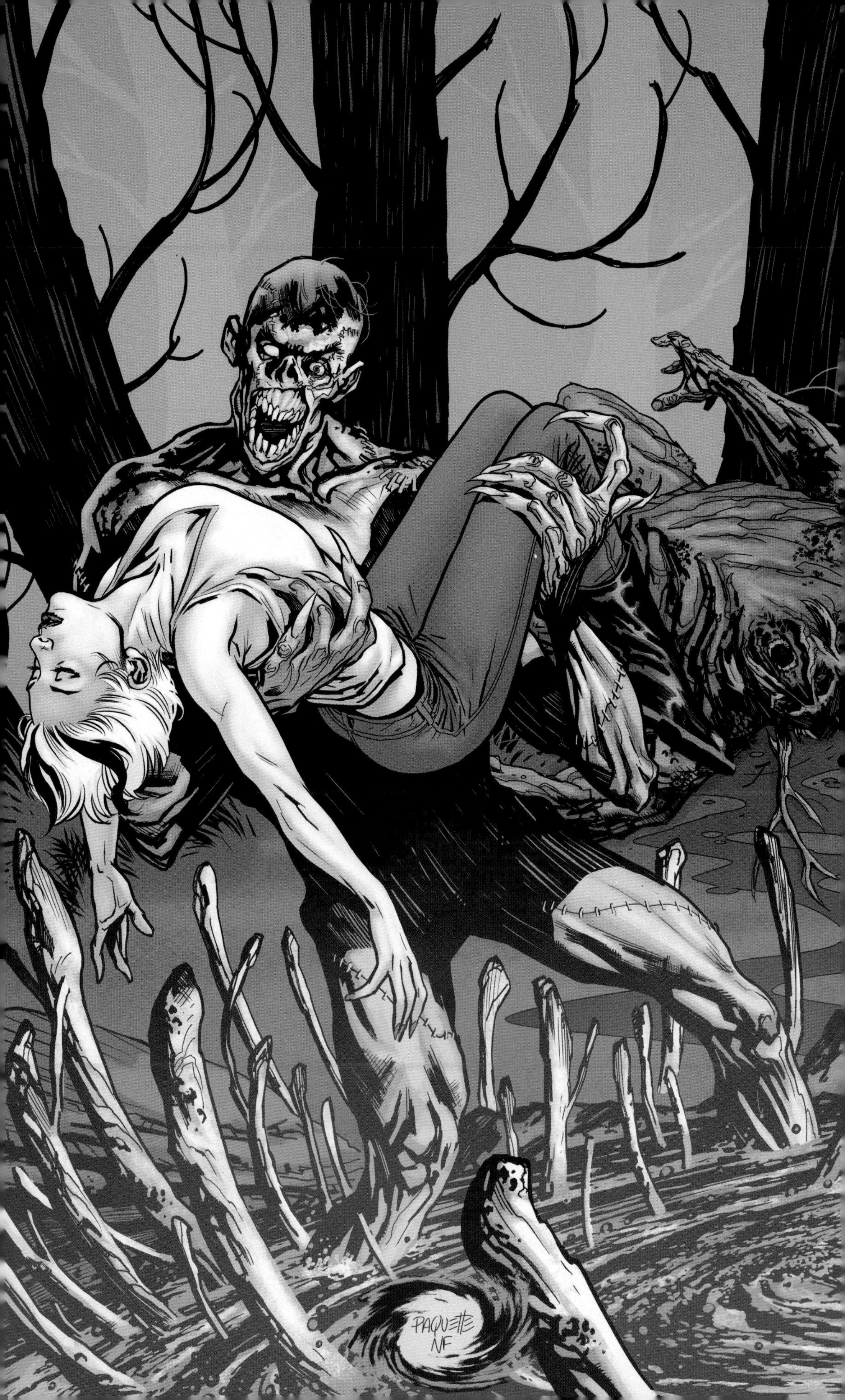
PAQUETTE
NF

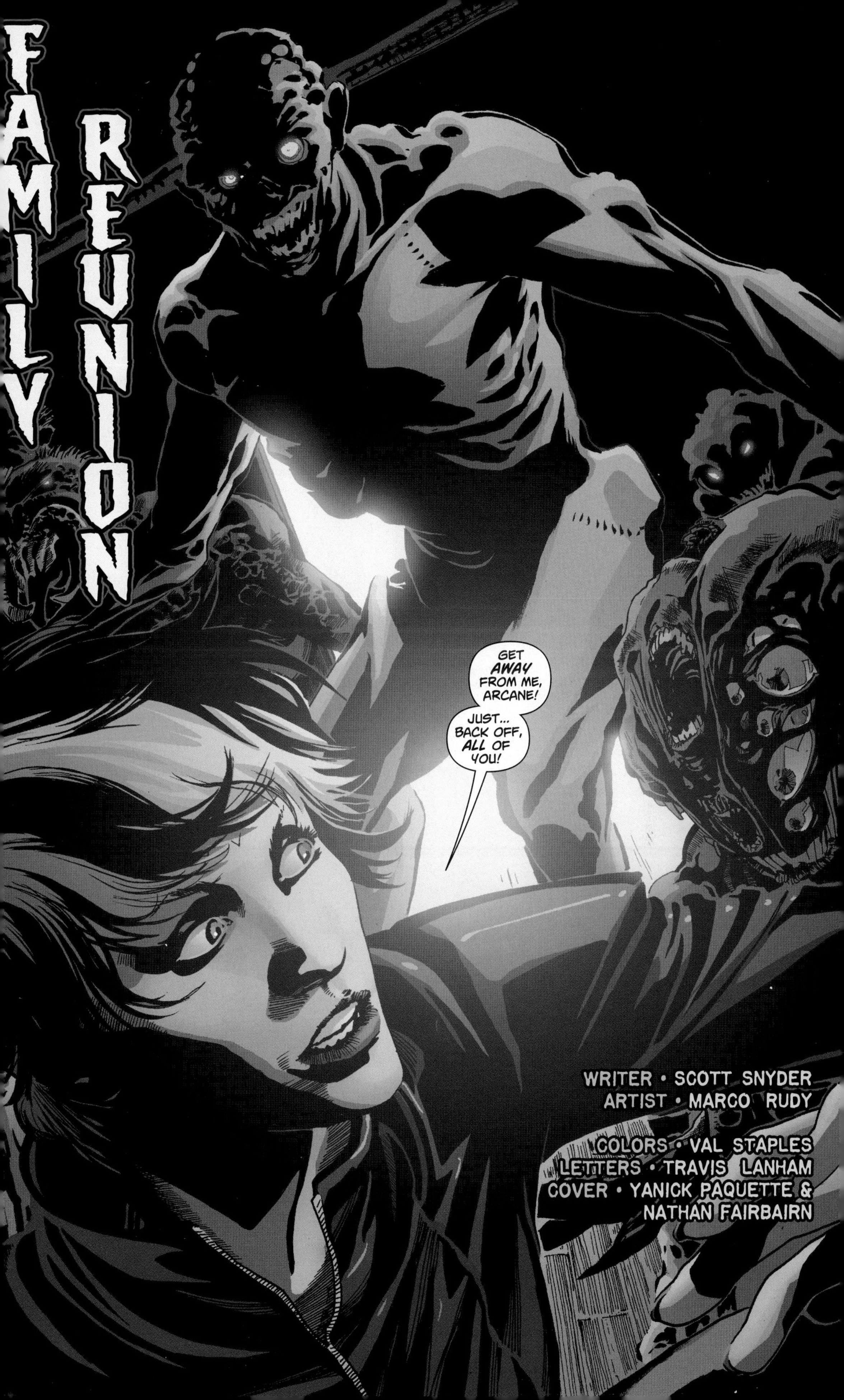
FAMILY REUNION
GET AWAY FROM ME, ARCANE!
JUST... BACK OFF, ALL OF YOU!
WRITER • SCOTT SNYDER
ARTIST • MARCO RUDY
COLORS • VAL STAPLES
LETTERS • TRAVIS LANHAM
COVER • YANICK PAQUETTE & NATHAN FAIRBAIRN

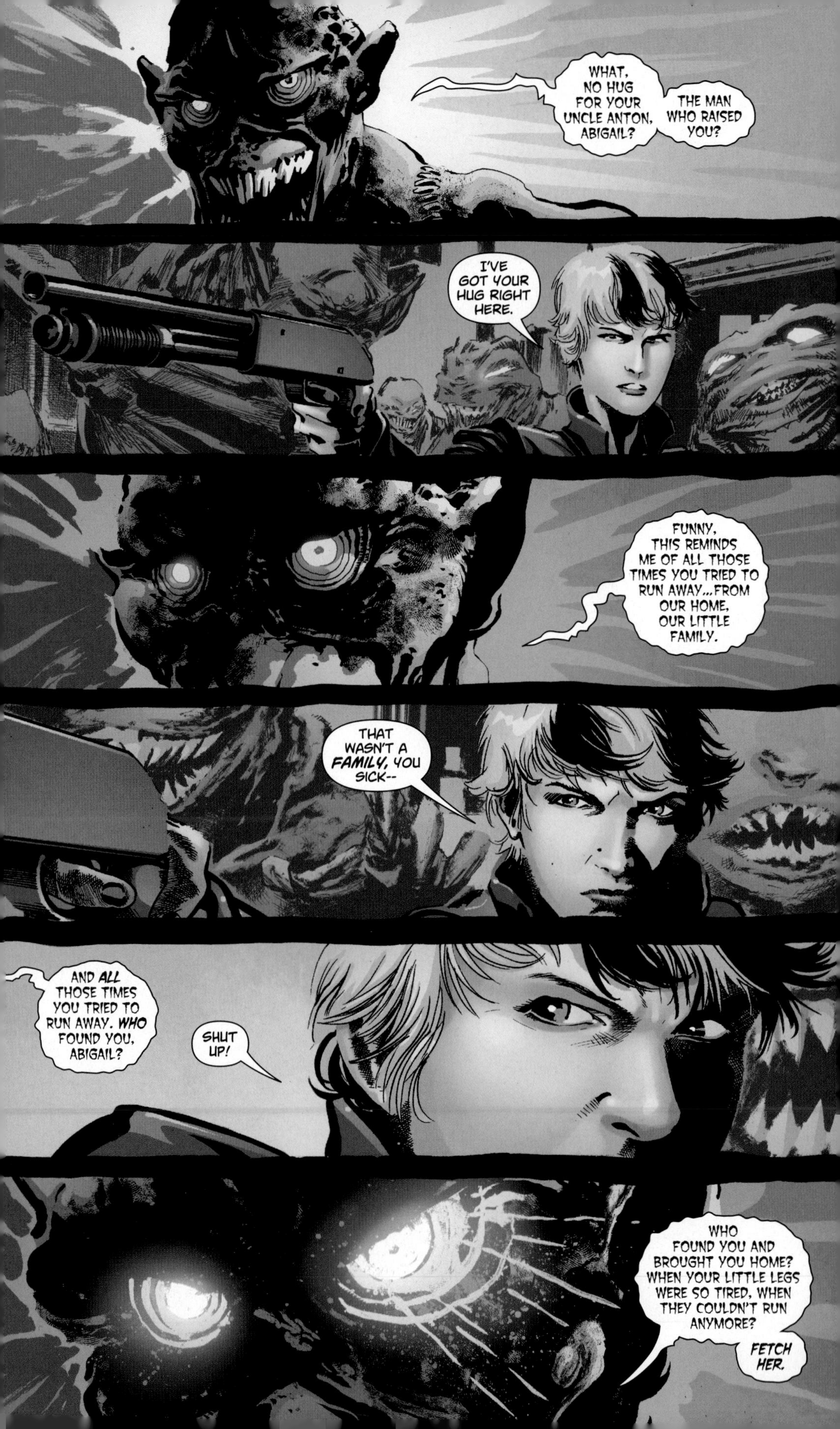
WHAT, NO HUG FOR YOUR UNCLE ANTON, ABIGAIL?
THE MAN WHO RAISED YOU?
I'VE GOT YOUR HUG RIGHT HERE.
FUNNY, THIS REMINDS ME OF ALL THOSE TIMES YOU TRIED TO RUN AWAY...FROM OUR HOME, OUR LITTLE FAMILY.
THAT WASN'T A *FAMILY,* YOU SICK--
AND *ALL* THOSE TIMES YOU TRIED TO RUN AWAY. *WHO* FOUND YOU, ABIGAIL?
SHUT UP!
WHO FOUND YOU AND BROUGHT YOU HOME? WHEN YOUR LITTLE LEGS WERE SO TIRED, WHEN THEY COULDN'T RUN ANYMORE?
FETCH HER.

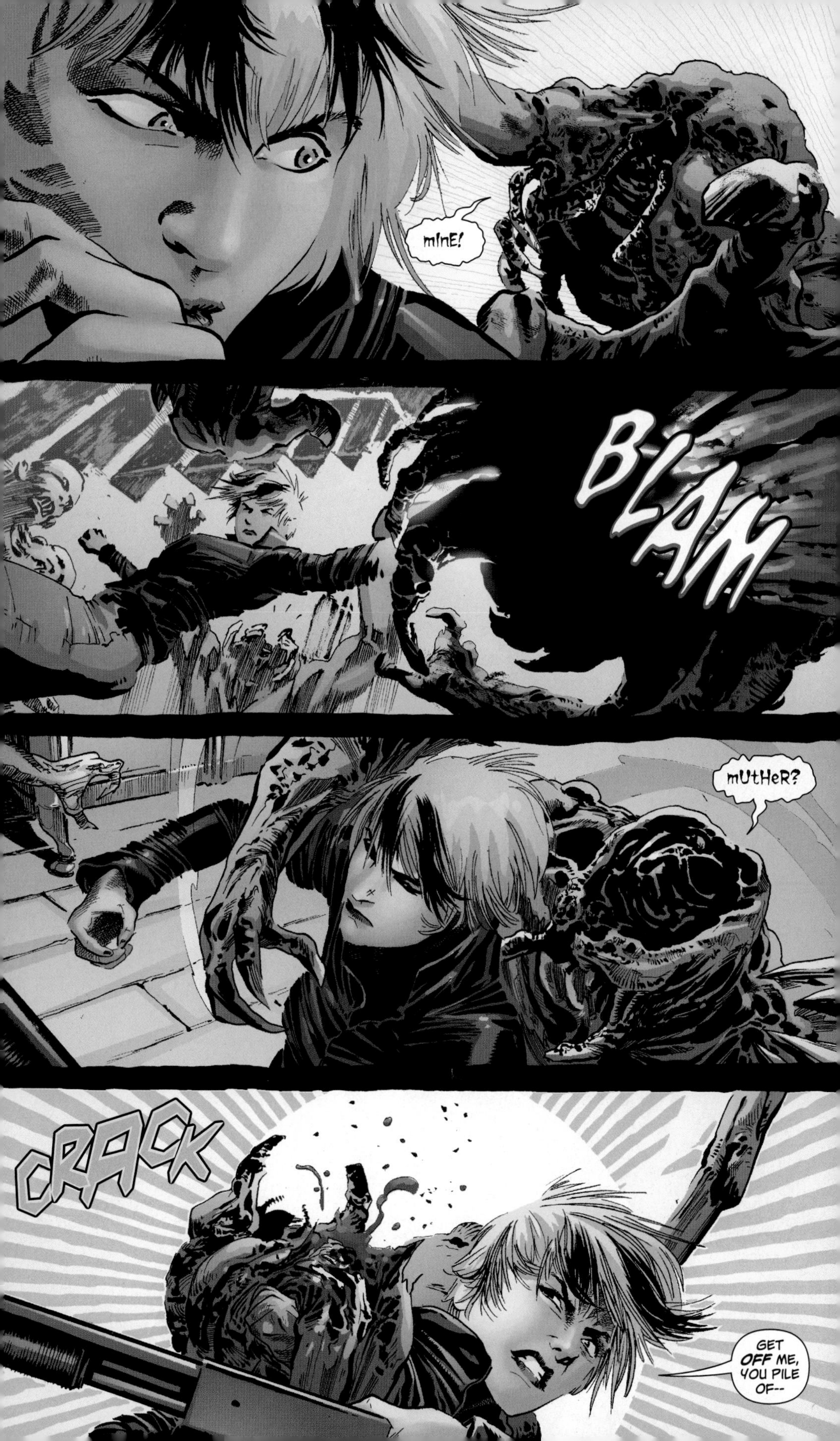
mInE!
BLAM
mUtHeR?
CRACK
GET OFF ME, YOU PILE OF--

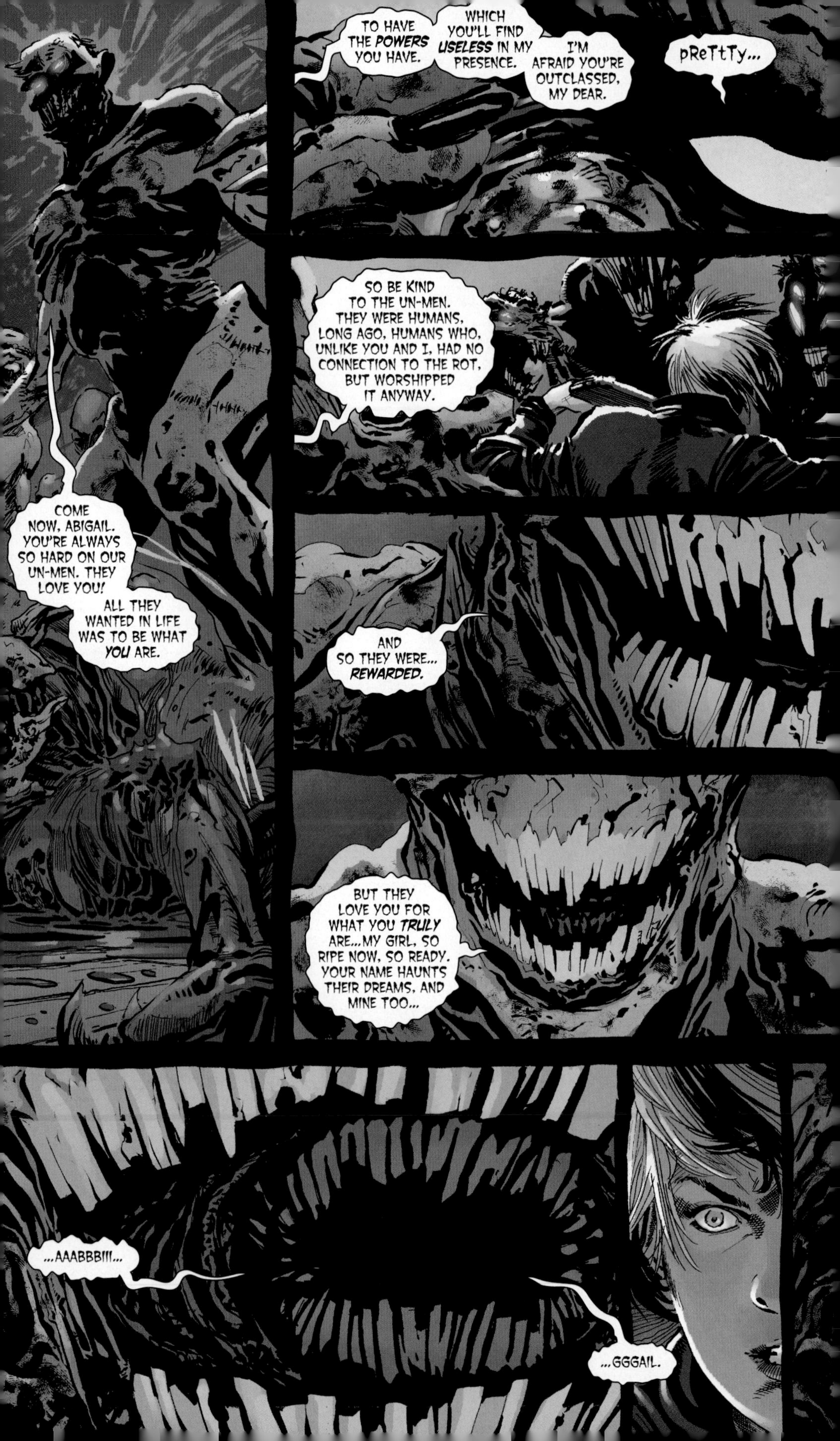
TO HAVE THE POWERS YOU HAVE.
WHICH YOU'LL FIND USELESS IN MY PRESENCE.
I'M AFRAID YOU'RE OUTCLASSED, MY DEAR.
pReTtTy...
COME NOW, ABIGAIL. YOU'RE ALWAYS SO HARD ON OUR UN-MEN. THEY LOVE YOU!
ALL THEY WANTED IN LIFE WAS TO BE WHAT YOU ARE.
SO BE KIND TO THE UN-MEN. THEY WERE HUMANS, LONG AGO, HUMANS WHO, UNLIKE YOU AND I, HAD NO CONNECTION TO THE ROT, BUT WORSHIPPED IT ANYWAY.
AND SO THEY WERE... REWARDED.
BUT THEY LOVE YOU FOR WHAT YOU TRULY ARE...MY GIRL, SO RIPE NOW, SO READY. YOUR NAME HAUNTS THEIR DREAMS, AND MINE TOO...
...AAABBBIII...
...GGGAIL.

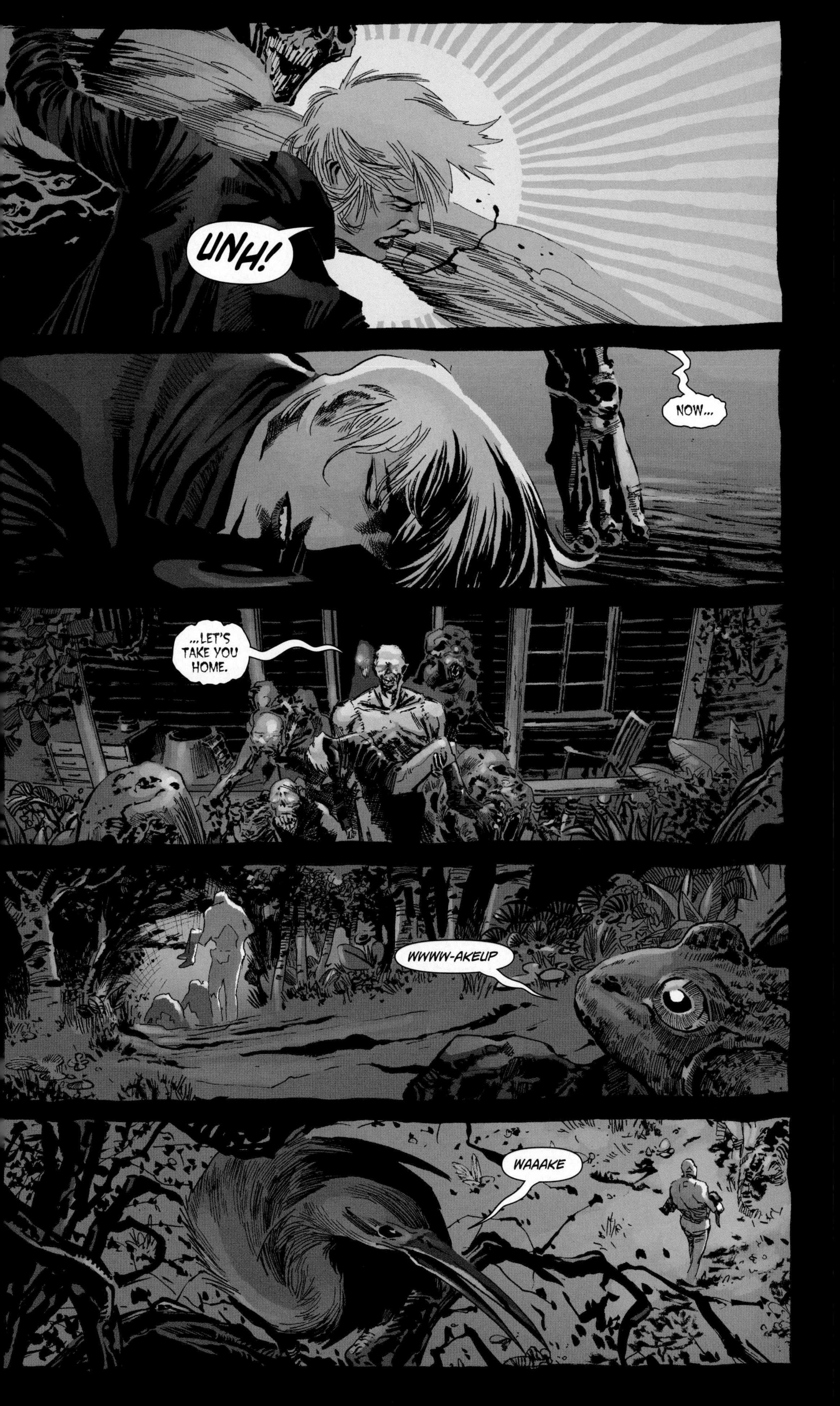
UNH!
NOW...
...LET'S TAKE YOU HOME.
WWWW-AKEUP
WAAAKE

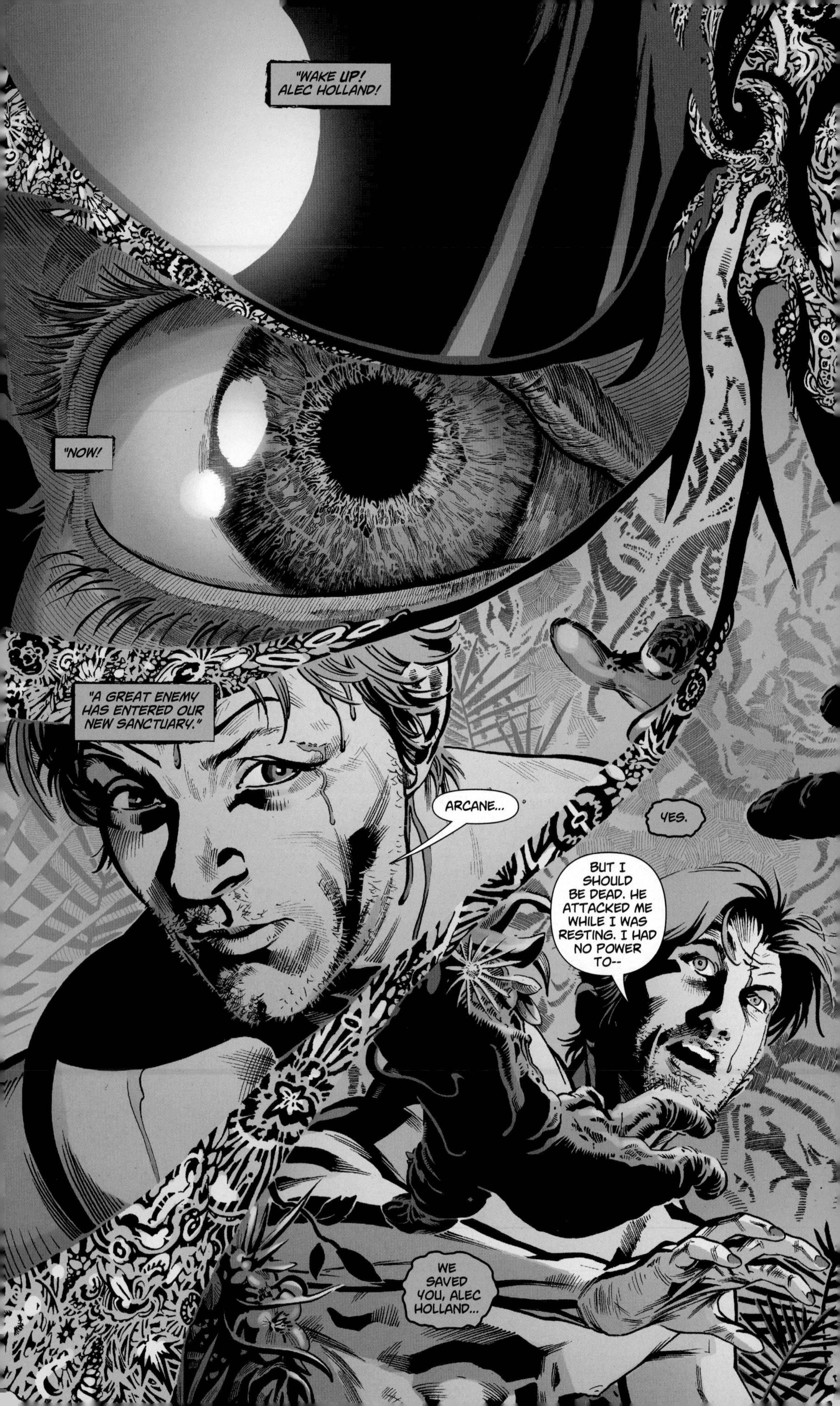
"WAKE UP! ALEC HOLLAND!
"NOW!
"A GREAT ENEMY HAS ENTERED OUR NEW SANCTUARY."
ARCANE...
YES.
BUT I SHOULD BE DEAD. HE ATTACKED ME WHILE I WAS RESTING. I HAD NO POWER TO--
WE SAVED YOU, ALEC HOLLAND...

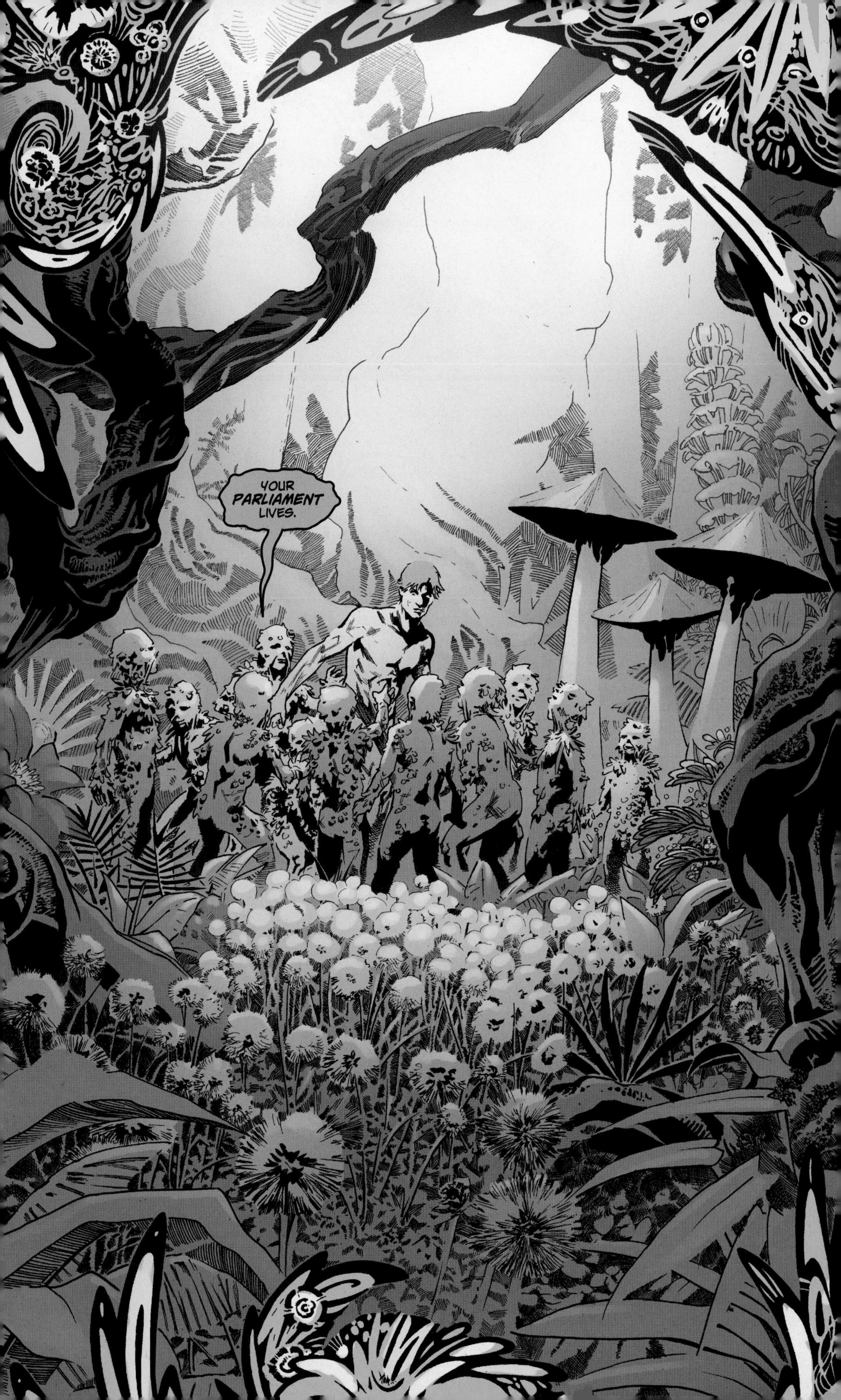
YOUR PARLIAMENT LIVES.

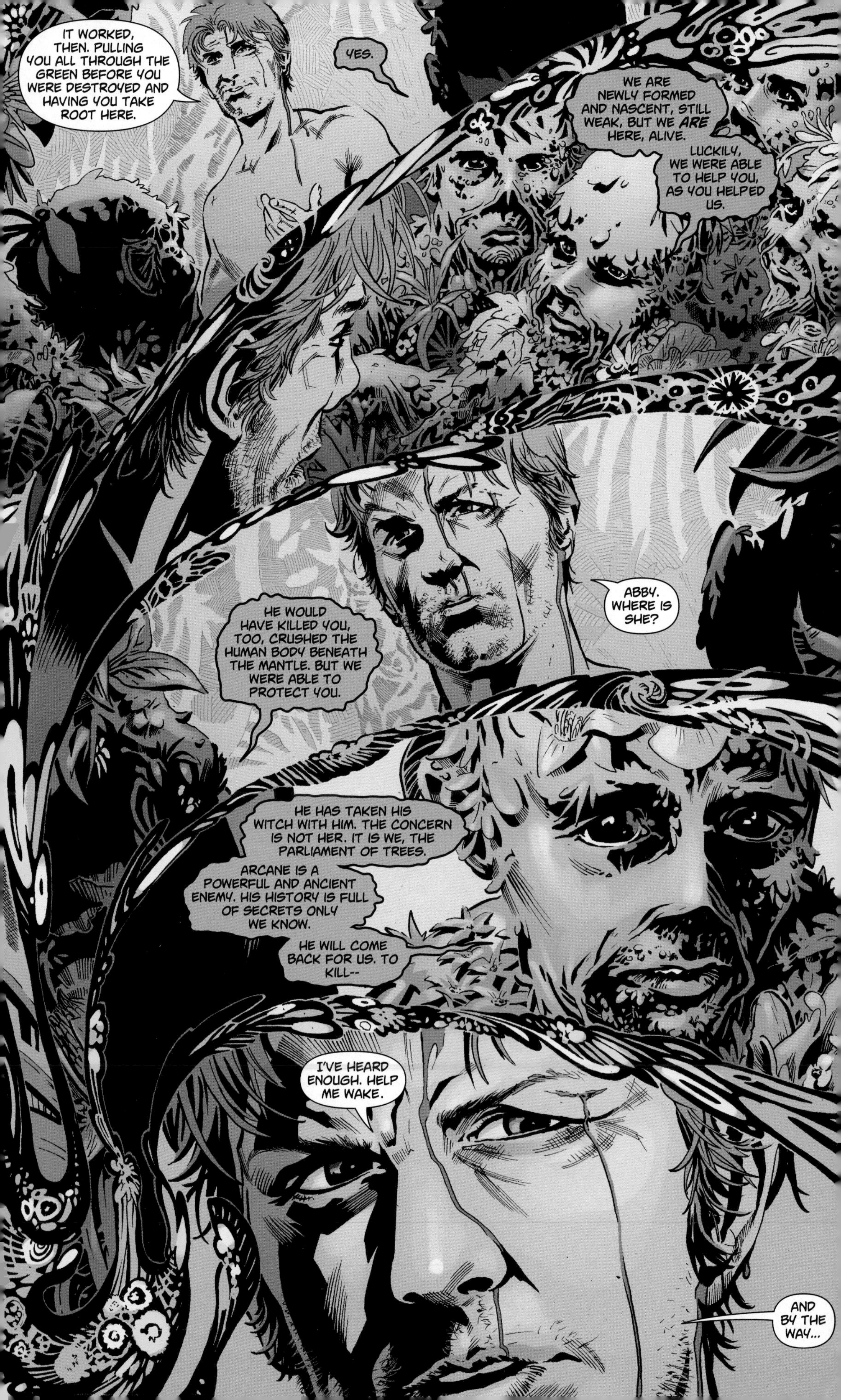

IT WORKED, THEN. PULLING YOU ALL THROUGH THE GREEN BEFORE YOU WERE DESTROYED AND HAVING YOU TAKE ROOT HERE.
YES.
WE ARE NEWLY FORMED AND NASCENT, STILL WEAK, BUT WE *ARE* HERE, ALIVE.
LUCKILY, WE WERE ABLE TO HELP YOU, AS YOU HELPED US.
ABBY. WHERE IS SHE?
HE WOULD HAVE KILLED YOU, TOO, CRUSHED THE HUMAN BODY BENEATH THE MANTLE. BUT WE WERE ABLE TO PROTECT YOU.
HE HAS TAKEN HIS WITCH WITH HIM. THE CONCERN IS NOT HER. IT IS WE, THE PARLIAMENT OF TREES.
ARCANE IS A POWERFUL AND ANCIENT ENEMY. HIS HISTORY IS FULL OF SECRETS ONLY WE KNOW.
HE WILL COME BACK FOR US. TO KILL--
I'VE HEARD ENOUGH. HELP ME WAKE.
AND BY THE WAY...

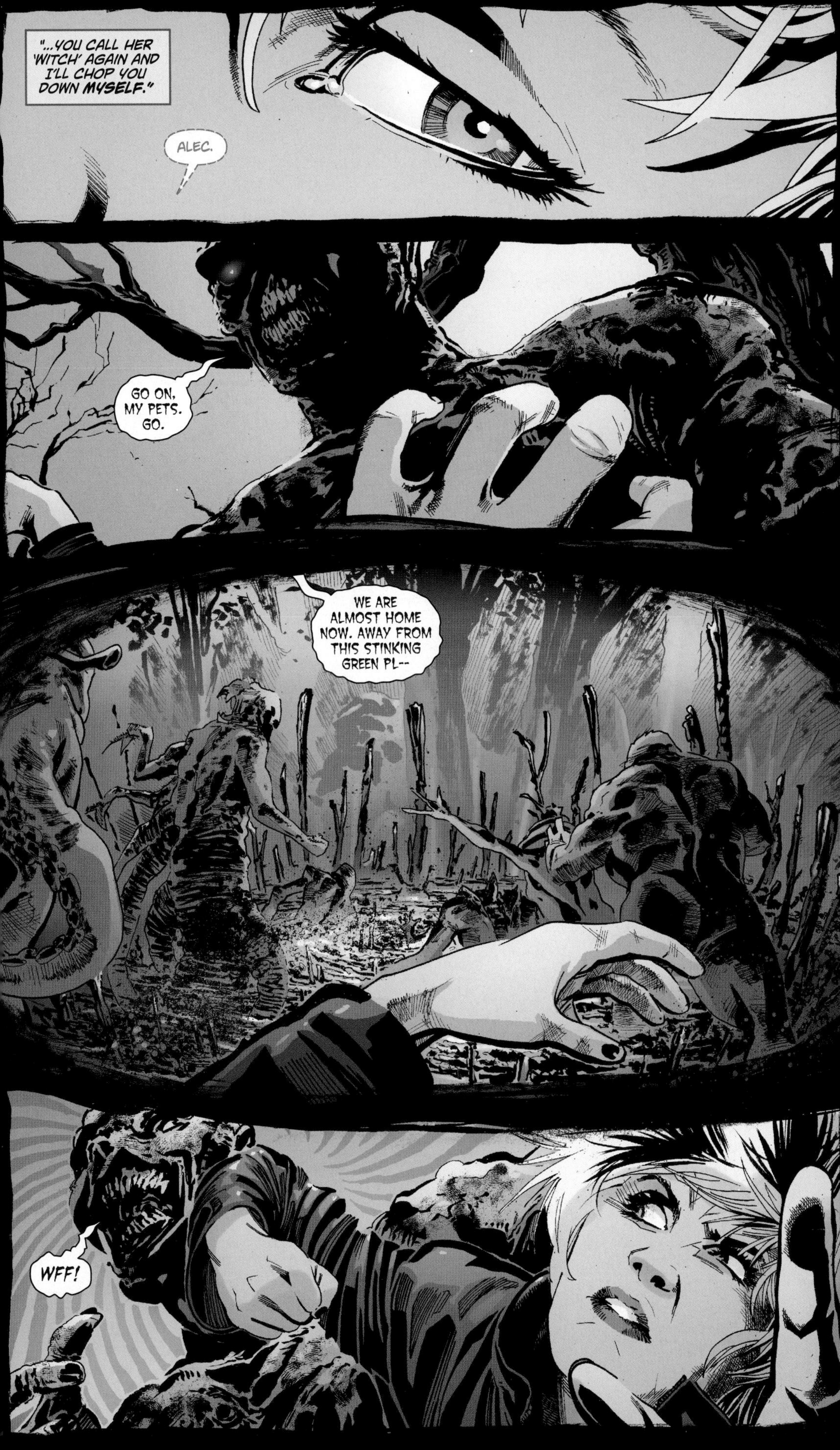
"...YOU CALL HER 'WITCH' AGAIN AND I'LL CHOP YOU DOWN MYSELF."
ALEC.
GO ON, MY PETS. GO.
WE ARE ALMOST HOME NOW. AWAY FROM THIS STINKING GREEN PL--
WFF!

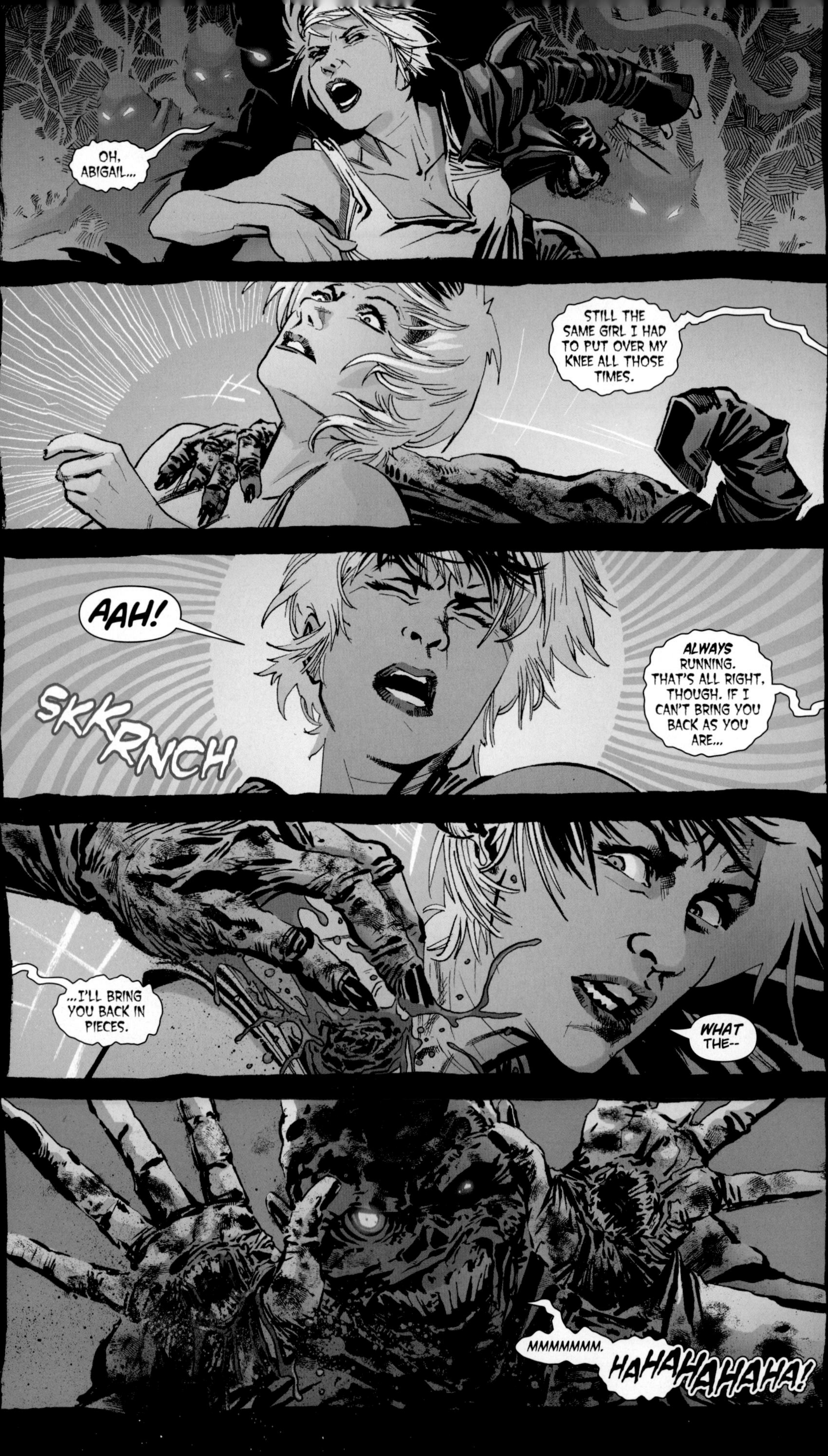
OH, ABIGAIL...
STILL THE SAME GIRL I HAD TO PUT OVER MY KNEE ALL THOSE TIMES.
AAH!
SKKRNCH
ALWAYS RUNNING. THAT'S ALL RIGHT, THOUGH. IF I CAN'T BRING YOU BACK AS YOU ARE...
...I'LL BRING YOU BACK IN PIECES.
WHAT THE--
MMMMMMM. HAHAHAHAHAHA!

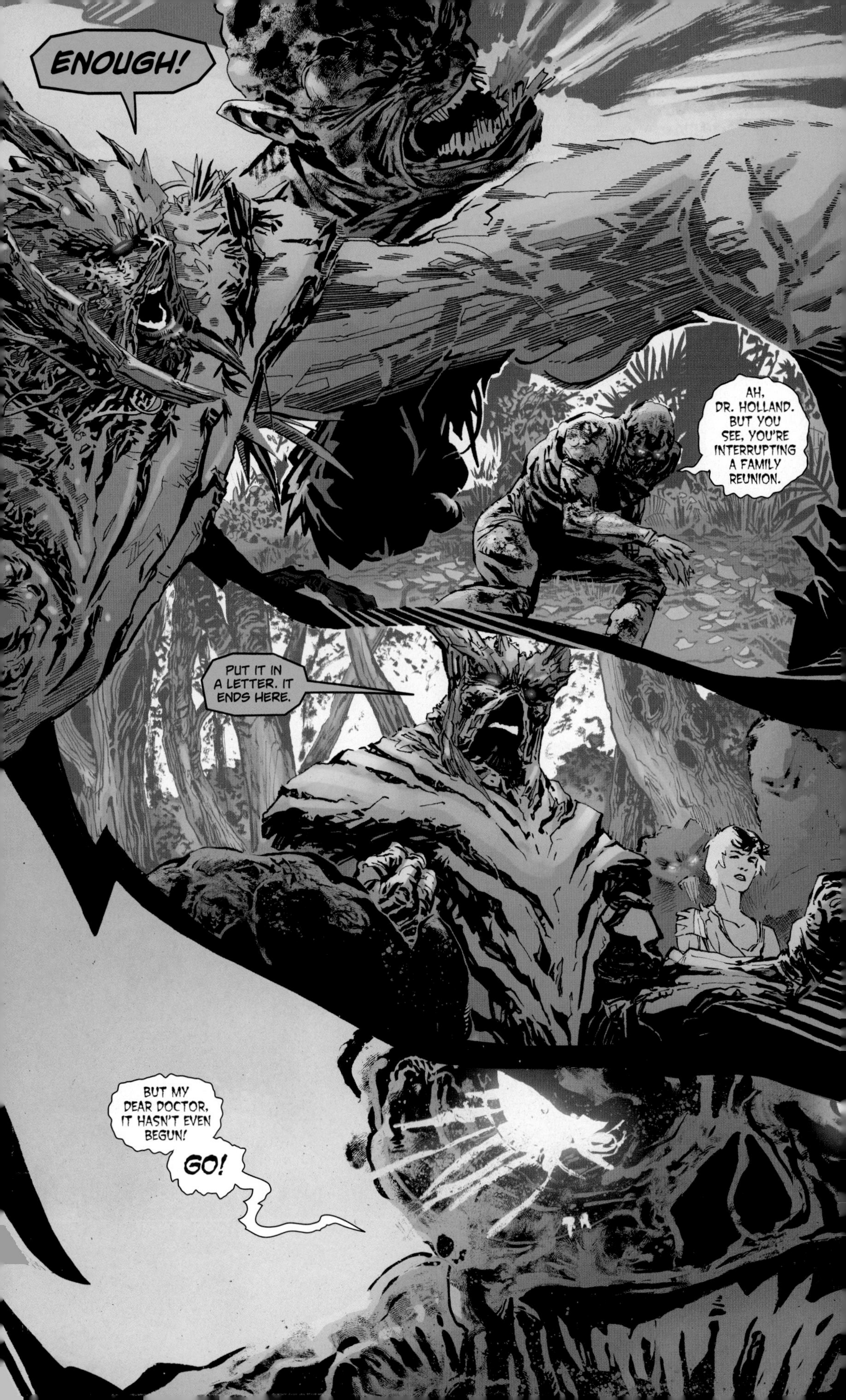
ENOUGH!
AH, DR. HOLLAND. BUT YOU SEE, YOU'RE INTERRUPTING A FAMILY REUNION.
PUT IT IN A LETTER. IT ENDS HERE.
BUT MY DEAR DOCTOR, IT HASN'T EVEN BEGUN!
GO!

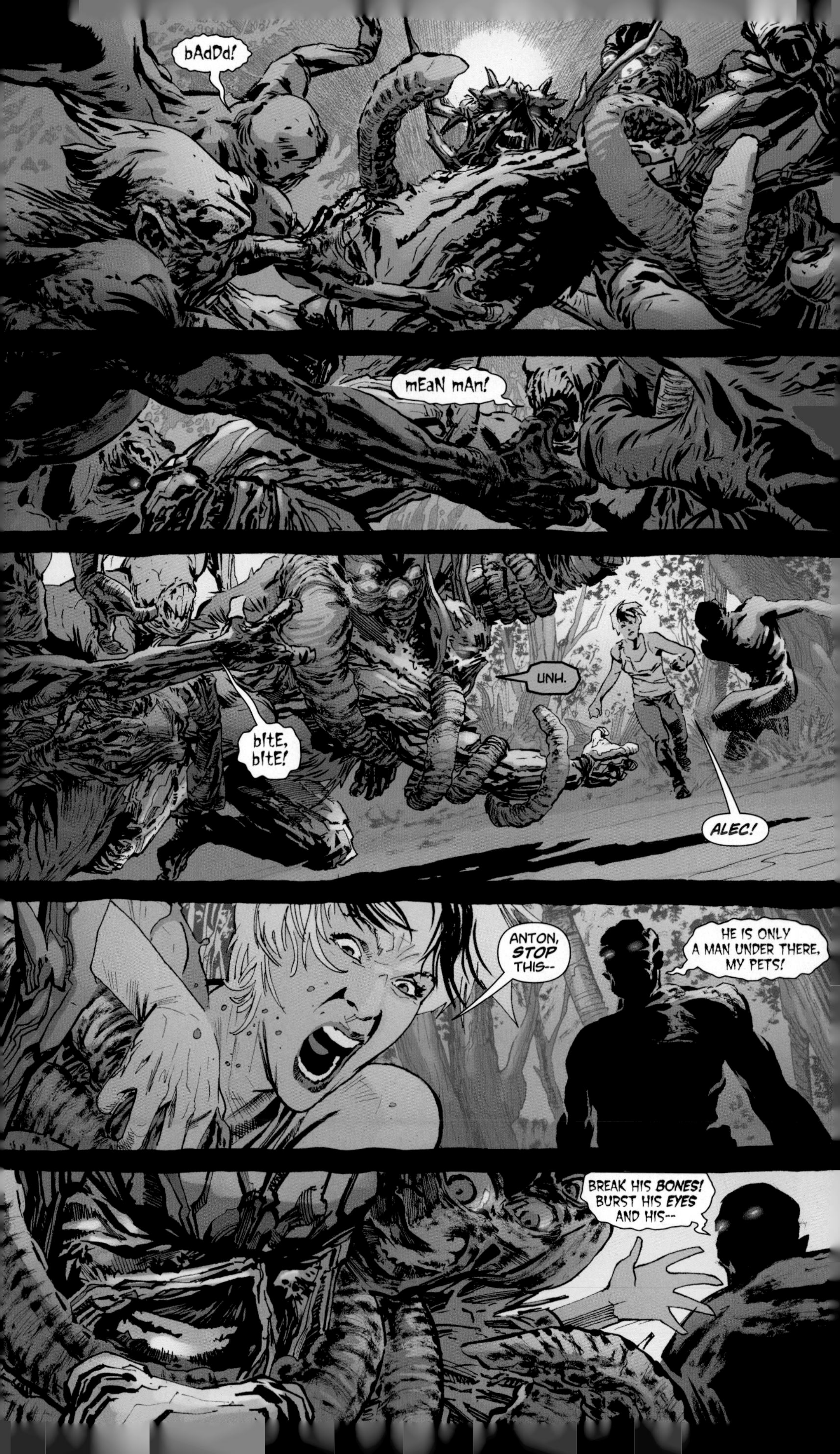
bAdDd!
mEaN mAn!
UNH.
bItE, bItE!
ALEC!
ANTON, STOP THIS--
HE IS ONLY A MAN UNDER THERE, MY PETS!
BREAK HIS BONES! BURST HIS EYES AND HIS--

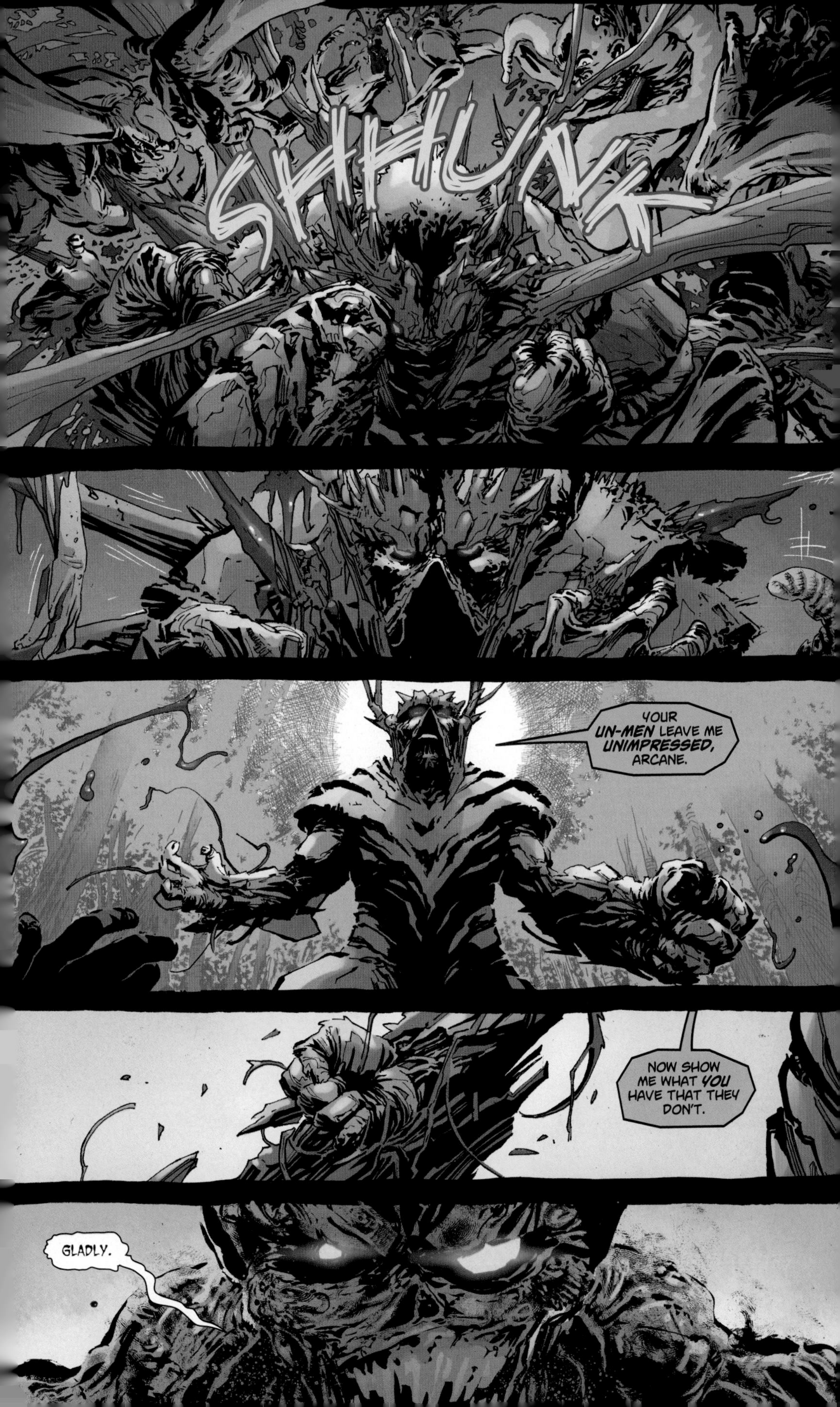
SHHUNK
YOUR UN-MEN LEAVE ME UNIMPRESSED, ARCANE.
NOW SHOW ME WHAT YOU HAVE THAT THEY DON'T.
GLADLY.

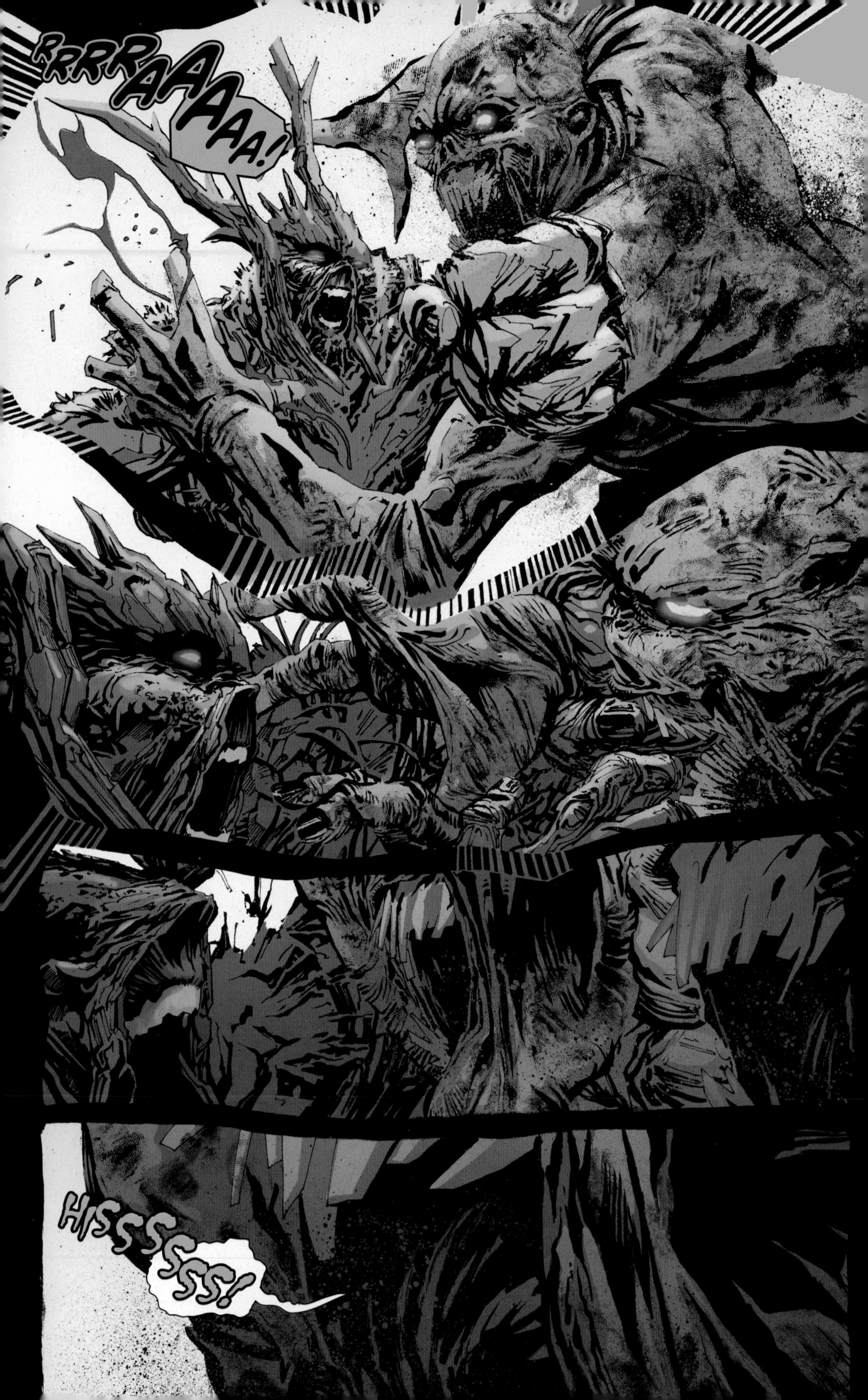
RRRRAAAAAAA!
HISSSSSS!

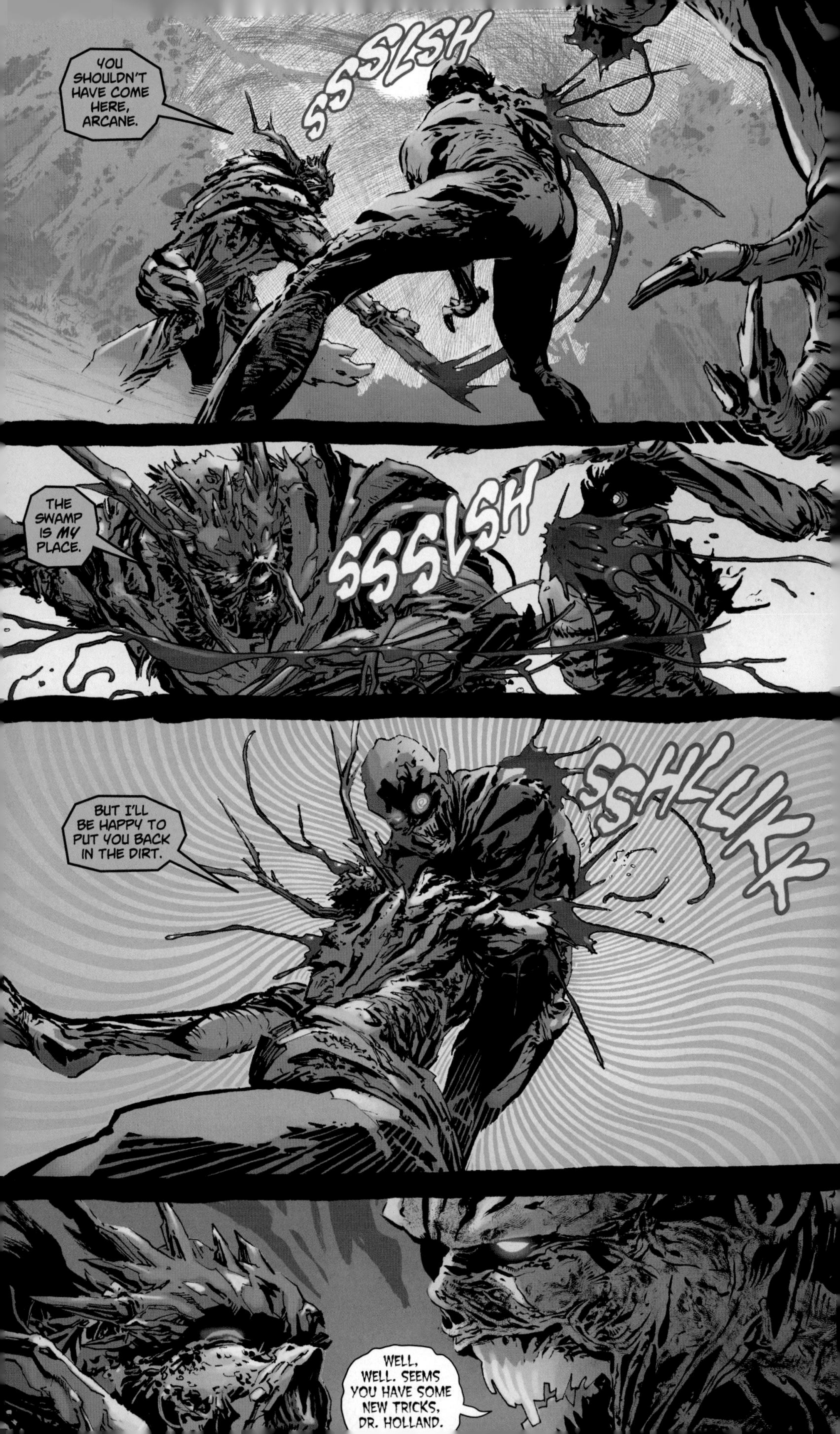
YOU SHOULDN'T HAVE COME HERE, ARCANE.
SSSLSH
THE SWAMP IS MY PLACE.
SSSLSH
BUT I'LL BE HAPPY TO PUT YOU BACK IN THE DIRT.
SSHLUKK
WELL, WELL. SEEMS YOU HAVE SOME NEW TRICKS, DR. HOLLAND.

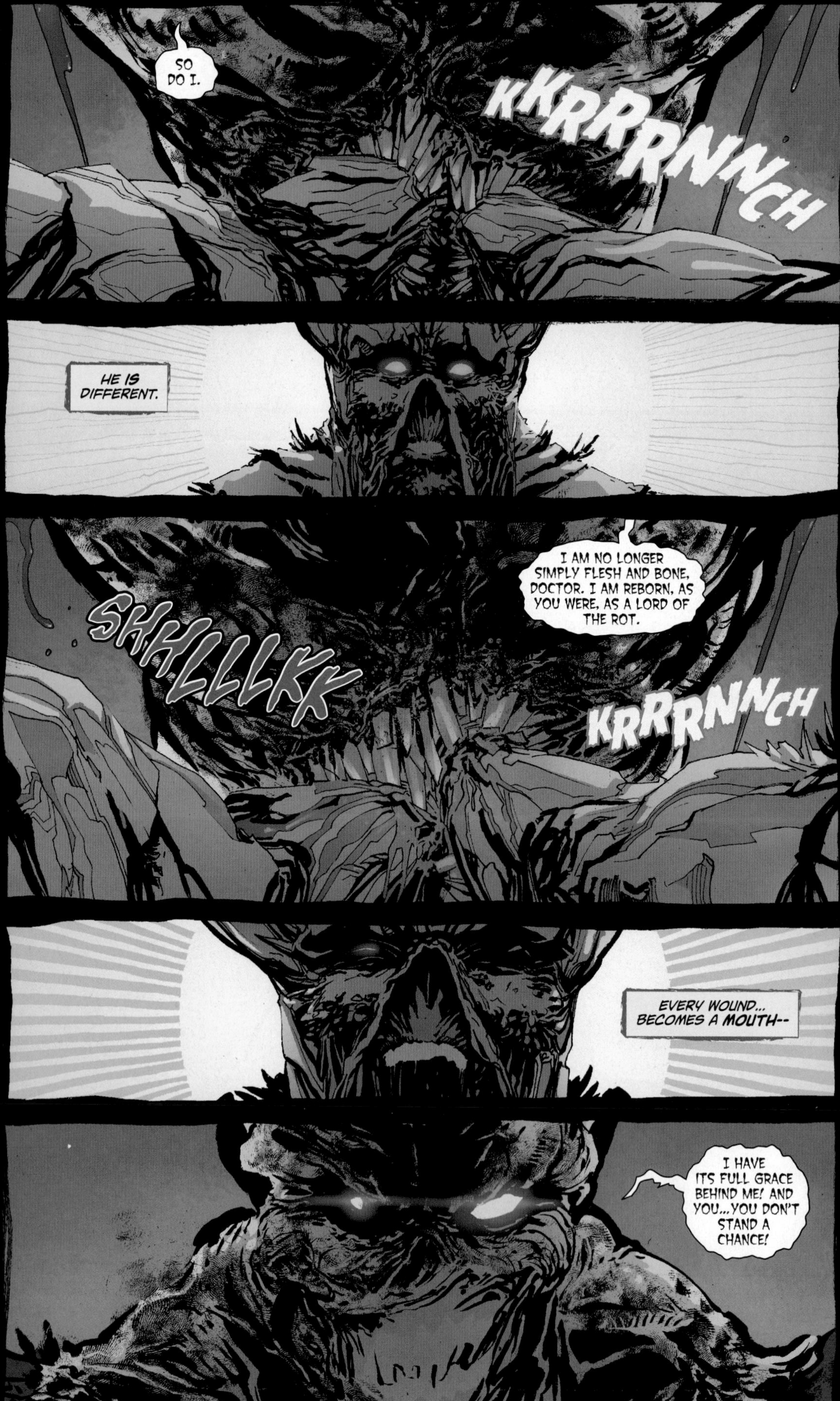
SO DO I.
KKRRRRNNNCH
HE IS DIFFERENT.
I AM NO LONGER SIMPLY FLESH AND BONE, DOCTOR. I AM REBORN, AS YOU WERE, AS A LORD OF THE ROT.
SHHLLLKK
KRRRNNNCH
EVERY WOUND... BECOMES A MOUTH--
I HAVE ITS FULL GRACE BEHIND ME! AND YOU...YOU DON'T STAND A CHANCE!

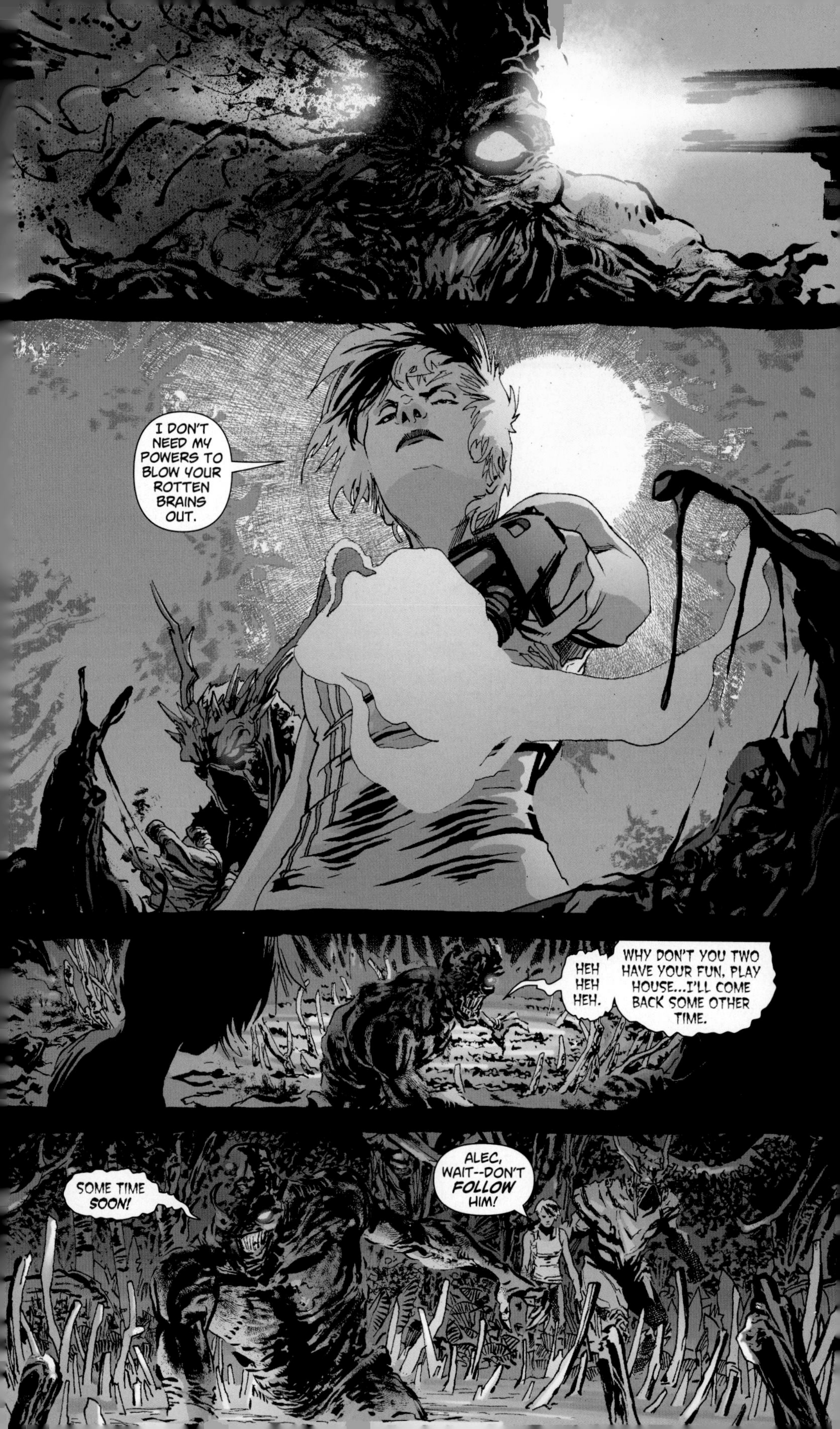
I DON'T NEED MY POWERS TO BLOW YOUR ROTTEN BRAINS OUT.
HEH HEH HEH.
WHY DON'T YOU TWO HAVE YOUR FUN, PLAY HOUSE...I'LL COME BACK SOME OTHER TIME.
SOME TIME SOON!
ALEC, WAIT--DON'T FOLLOW HIM!

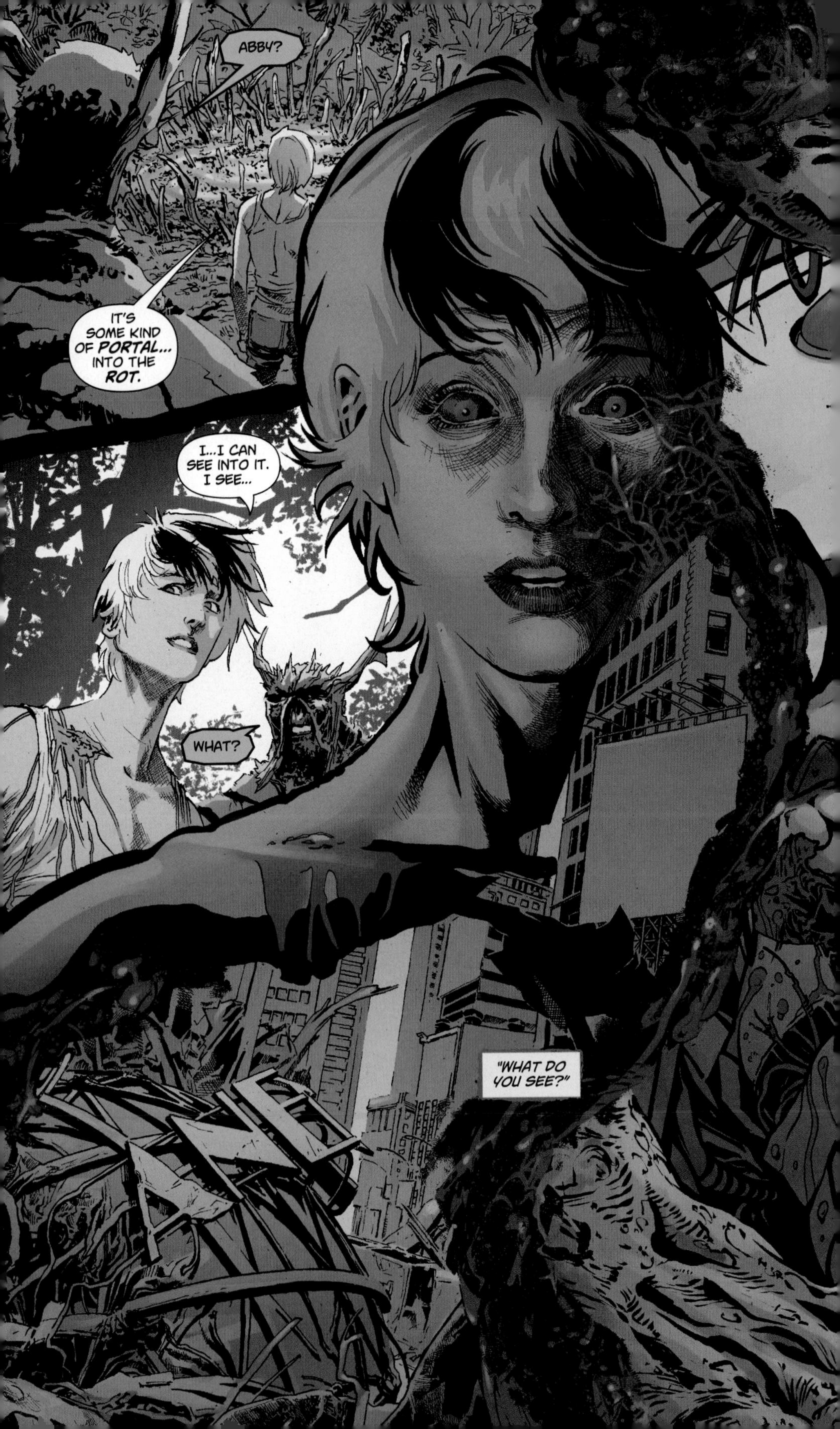
ABBY?
IT'S SOME KIND OF PORTAL... INTO THE ROT.
I...I CAN SEE INTO IT. I SEE...
WHAT?
"WHAT DO YOU SEE?"

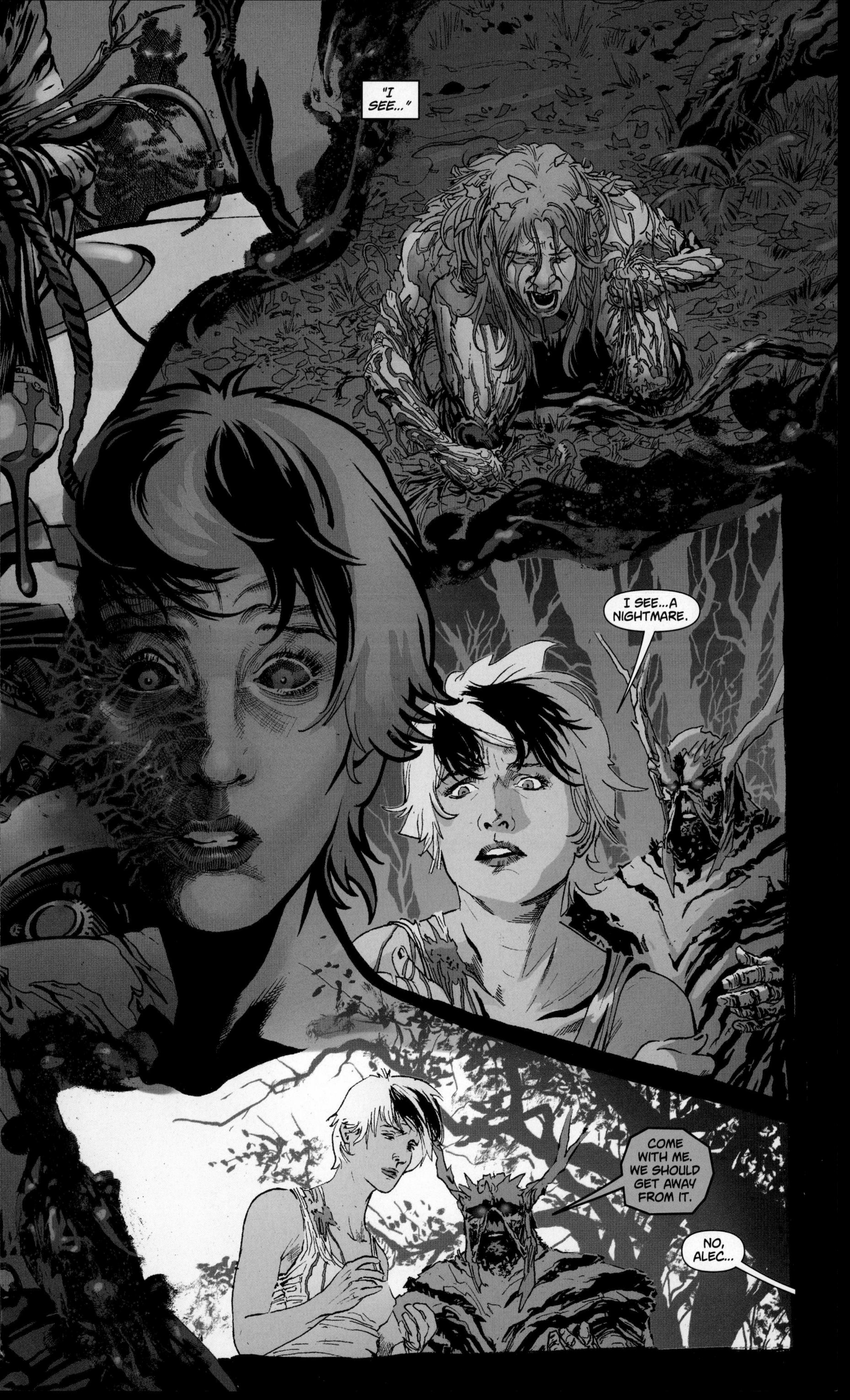
"I SEE..."
I SEE...A NIGHTMARE.
COME WITH ME. WE SHOULD GET AWAY FROM IT.
NO, ALEC...

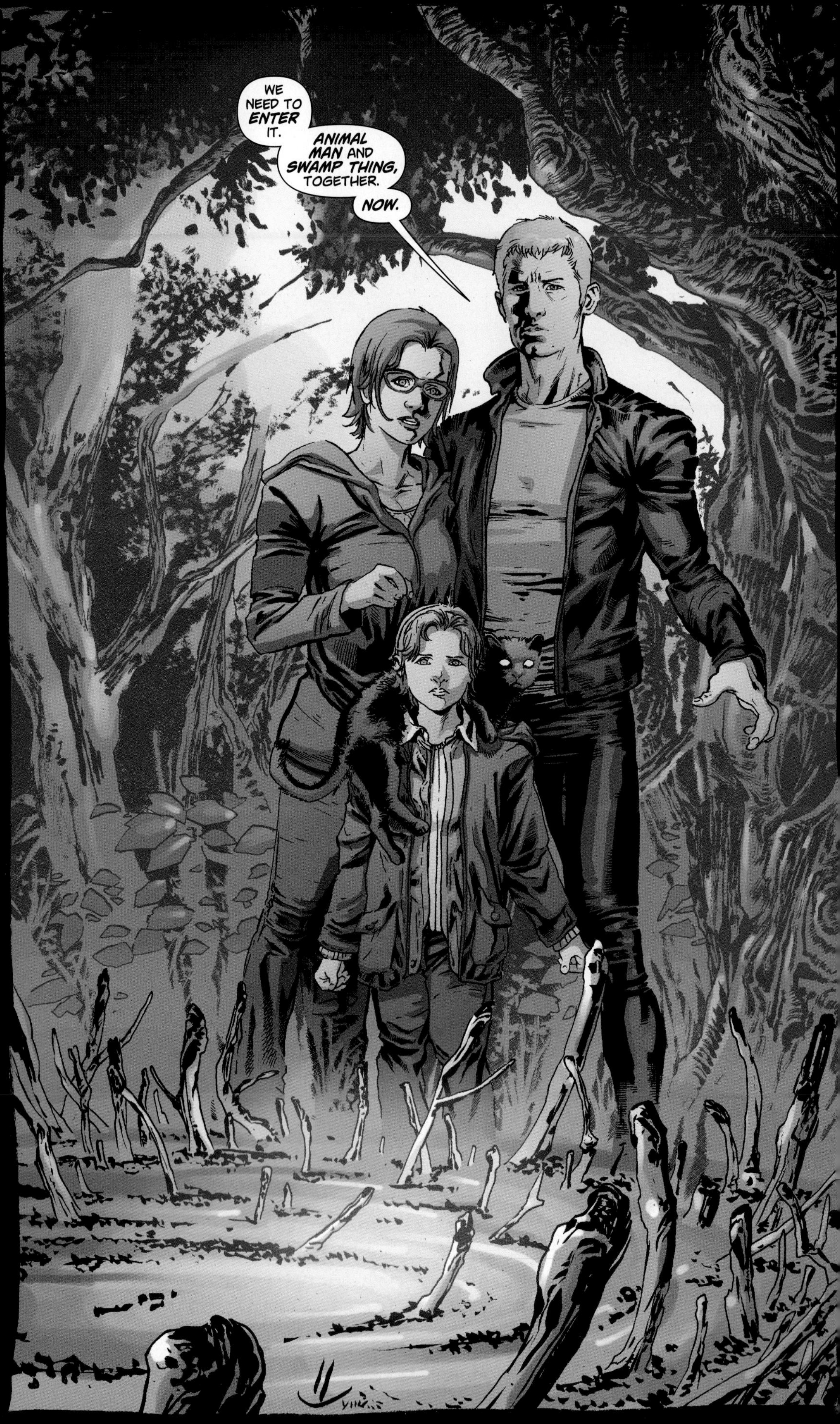
WE NEED TO ENTER IT.
ANIMAL MAN AND SWAMP THING, TOGETHER.
NOW.

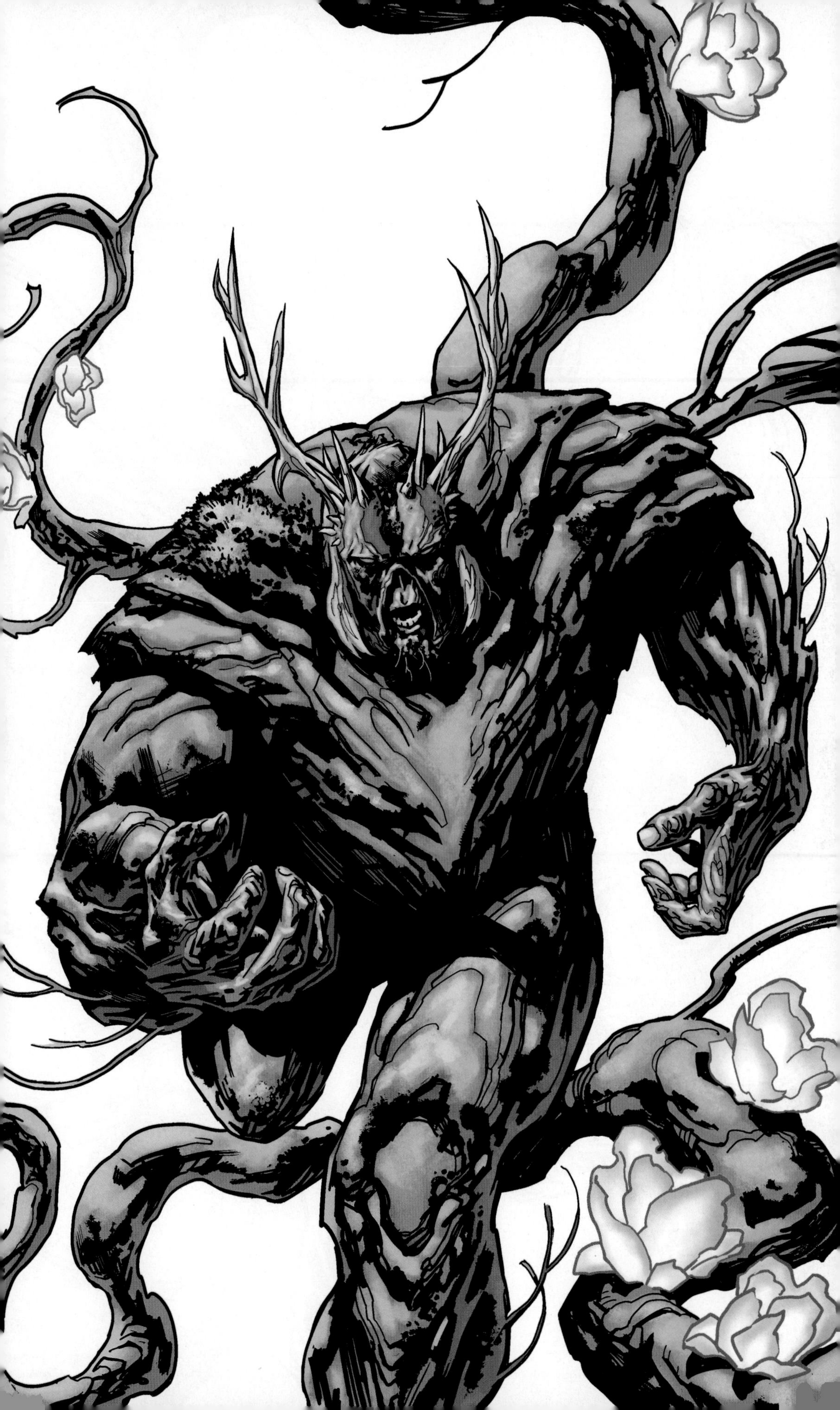

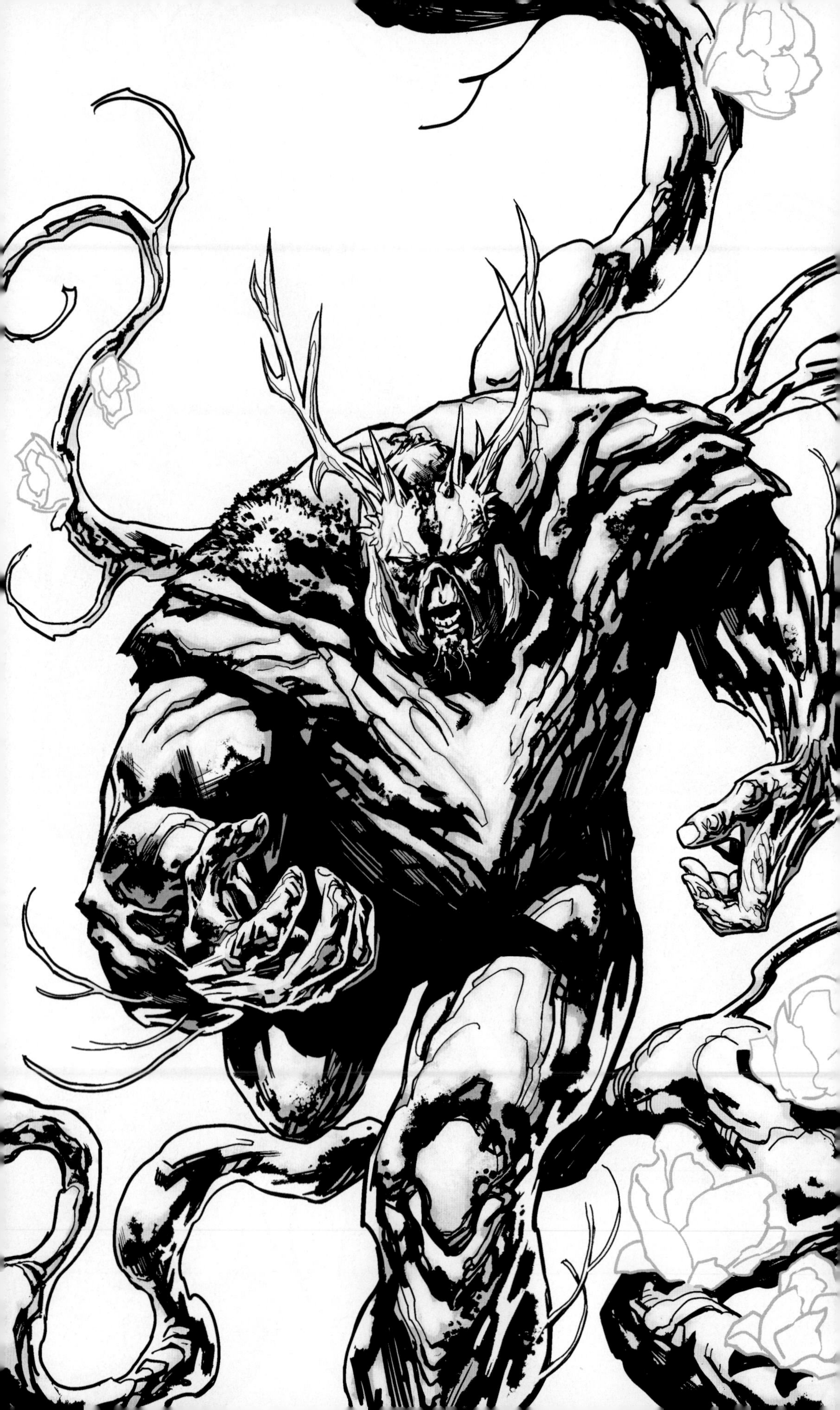

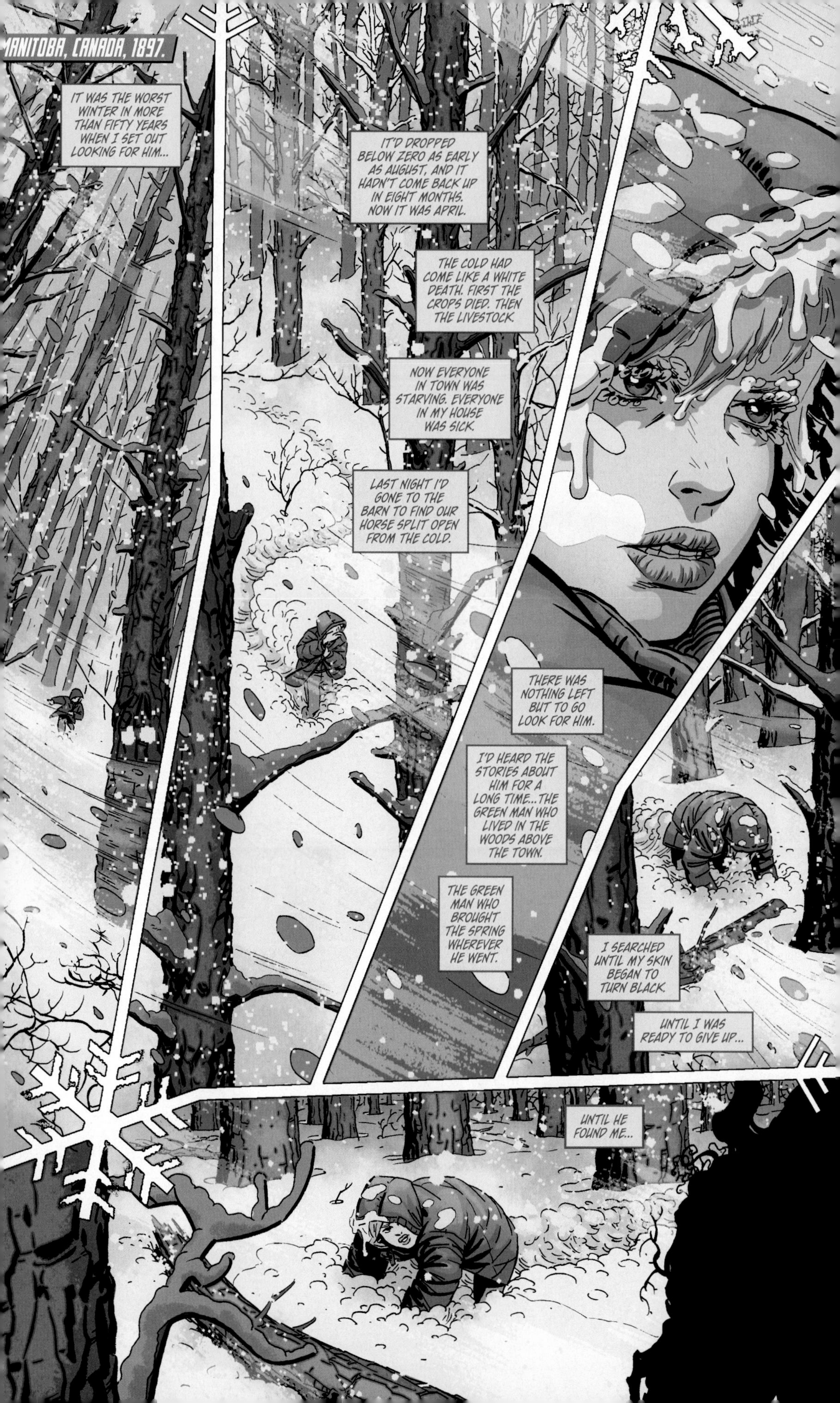
MANITOBA, CANADA, 1897.
IT WAS THE WORST WINTER IN MORE THAN FIFTY YEARS WHEN I SET OUT LOOKING FOR HIM...
IT'D DROPPED BELOW ZERO AS EARLY AS AUGUST, AND IT HADN'T COME BACK UP IN EIGHT MONTHS. NOW IT WAS APRIL.
THE COLD HAD COME LIKE A WHITE DEATH. FIRST THE CROPS DIED. THEN THE LIVESTOCK.
NOW EVERYONE IN TOWN WAS STARVING. EVERYONE IN MY HOUSE WAS SICK.
LAST NIGHT I'D GONE TO THE BARN TO FIND OUR HORSE SPLIT OPEN FROM THE COLD.
THERE WAS NOTHING LEFT BUT TO GO LOOK FOR HIM.
I'D HEARD THE STORIES ABOUT HIM FOR A LONG TIME...THE GREEN MAN WHO LIVED IN THE WOODS ABOVE THE TOWN.
THE GREEN MAN WHO BROUGHT THE SPRING WHEREVER HE WENT.
I SEARCHED UNTIL MY SKIN BEGAN TO TURN BLACK.
UNTIL I WAS READY TO GIVE UP...
UNTIL HE FOUND ME...

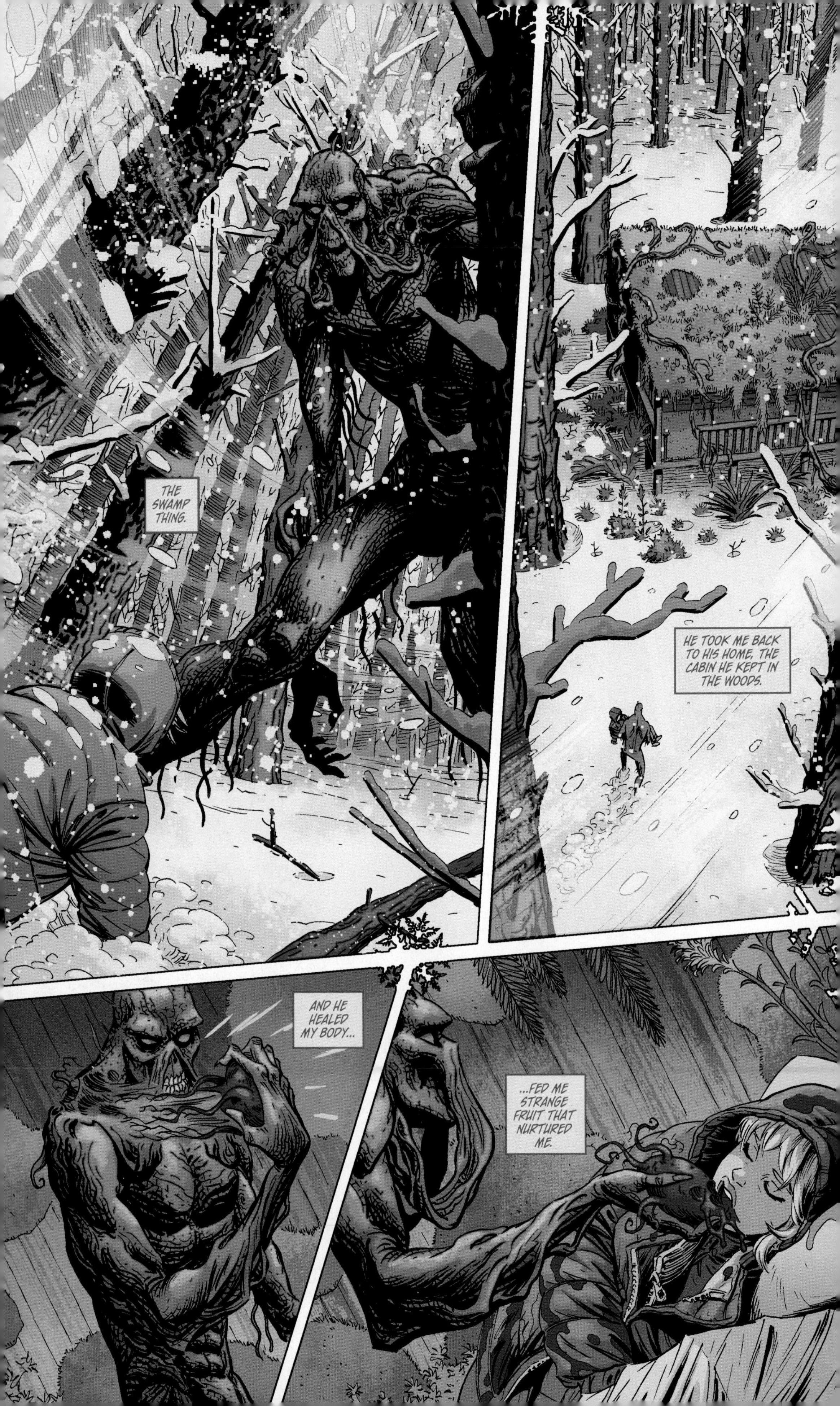
THE SWAMP THING.
HE TOOK ME BACK TO HIS HOME. THE CABIN HE KEPT IN THE WOODS.
AND HE HEALED MY BODY...
...FED ME STRANGE FRUIT THAT NURTURED ME.

WHEN I FINALLY WOKE, HE WAS THERE. RIGHT IN FRONT OF ME.

DO NOT WORRY, LITTLE ONE. YOU ARE SAFE.

THIS COLD...I CAME BECAUSE THE COLD IS KILLING EVERYONE.

I AM SORRY. THE COLD--AND THE DEATH IT BRINGS--HAS GONE ON LONG, BUT IT HAS NOT BROKEN THE NATURAL ORDER QUITE YET.

YOU MUST WAIT JUST A SHORT WHILE LONGER, AND THEN I WILL MAKE A GREAT BLOOM.

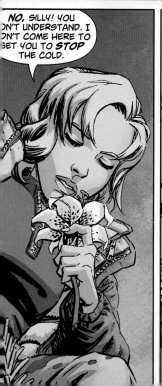

NO, SILLY! YOU DON'T UNDERSTAND. I DIDN'T COME HERE TO GET YOU TO STOP THE COLD.

I NEVER WANT THE COLD TO END!

NEVER WANT IT TO...?

NO... YOU...

YES. ME.

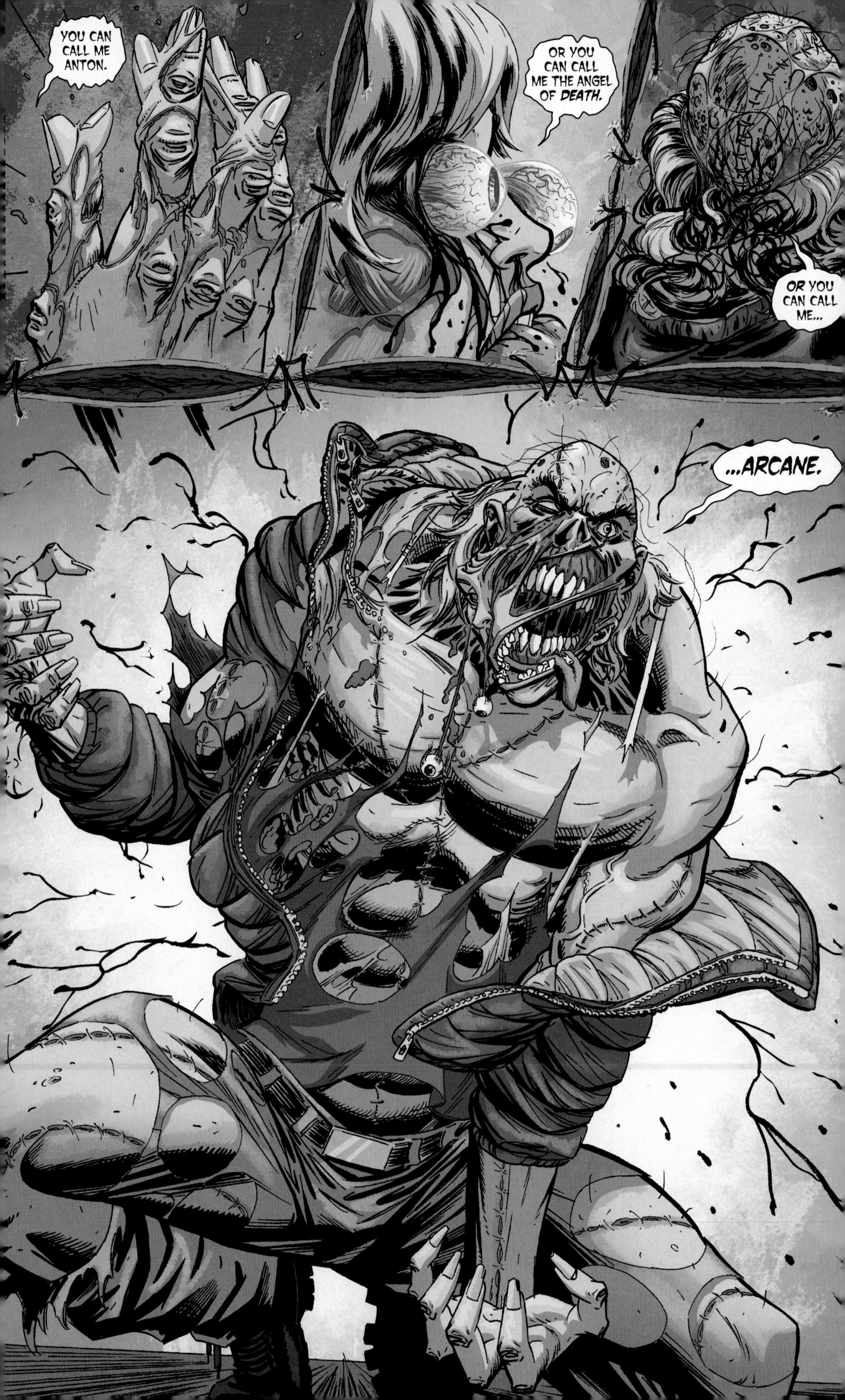
YOU CAN CALL ME ANTON.
OR YOU CAN CALL ME THE ANGEL OF *DEATH*.
OR YOU CAN CALL ME...
...ARCANE.

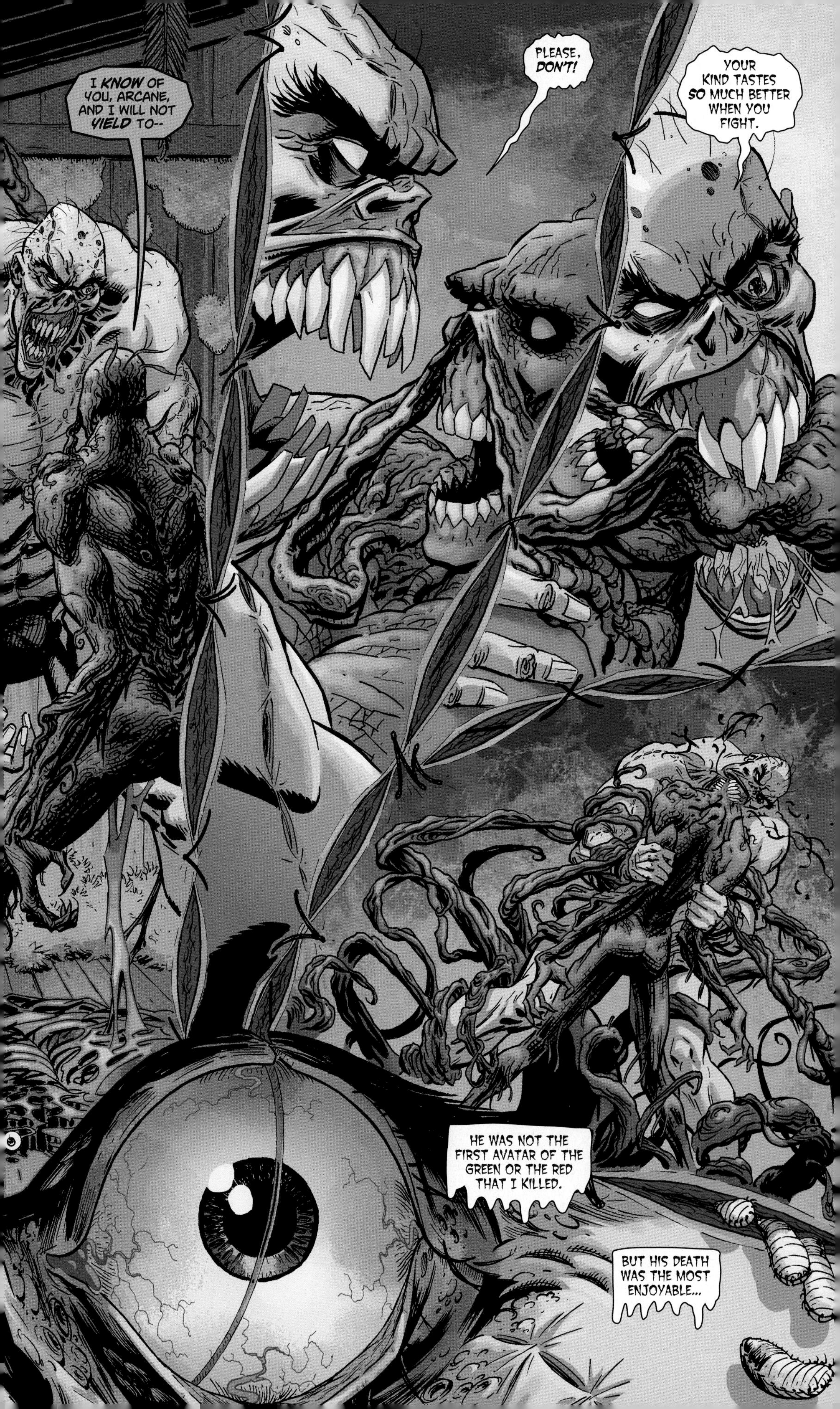
I KNOW OF YOU, ARCANE, AND I WILL NOT YIELD TO--
PLEASE, DON'T!
YOUR KIND TASTES SO MUCH BETTER WHEN YOU FIGHT.
HE WAS NOT THE FIRST AVATAR OF THE GREEN OR THE RED THAT I KILLED.
BUT HIS DEATH WAS THE MOST ENJOYABLE...

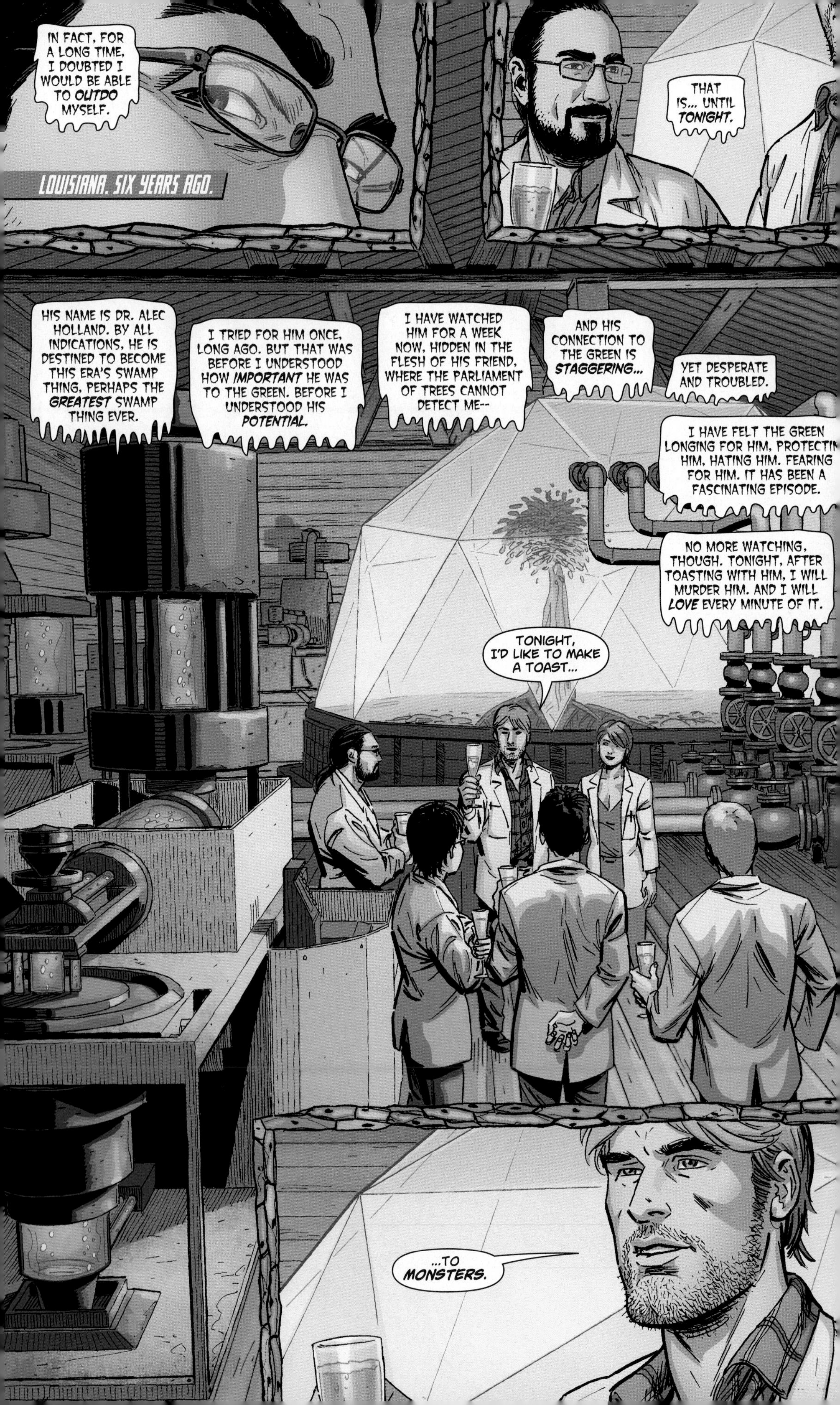
IN FACT, FOR A LONG TIME, I DOUBTED I WOULD BE ABLE TO *OUTDO* MYSELF.
LOUISIANA. SIX YEARS AGO.
THAT IS... UNTIL *TONIGHT.*
HIS NAME IS DR. ALEC HOLLAND. BY ALL INDICATIONS, HE IS DESTINED TO BECOME THIS ERA'S SWAMP THING, PERHAPS THE *GREATEST* SWAMP THING EVER.
I TRIED FOR HIM ONCE, LONG AGO. BUT THAT WAS BEFORE I UNDERSTOOD HOW *IMPORTANT* HE WAS TO THE GREEN. BEFORE I UNDERSTOOD HIS *POTENTIAL.*
I HAVE WATCHED HIM FOR A WEEK NOW, HIDDEN IN THE FLESH OF HIS FRIEND, WHERE THE PARLIAMENT OF TREES CANNOT DETECT ME--
AND HIS CONNECTION TO THE GREEN IS *STAGGERING...*
YET DESPERATE AND TROUBLED.
I HAVE FELT THE GREEN LONGING FOR HIM, PROTECTIN HIM, HATING HIM. FEARING FOR HIM. IT HAS BEEN A FASCINATING EPISODE.
NO MORE WATCHING, THOUGH. TONIGHT, AFTER TOASTING WITH HIM, I WILL MURDER HIM. AND I WILL *LOVE* EVERY MINUTE OF IT.
TONIGHT, I'D LIKE TO MAKE A TOAST...
...TO *MONSTERS.*

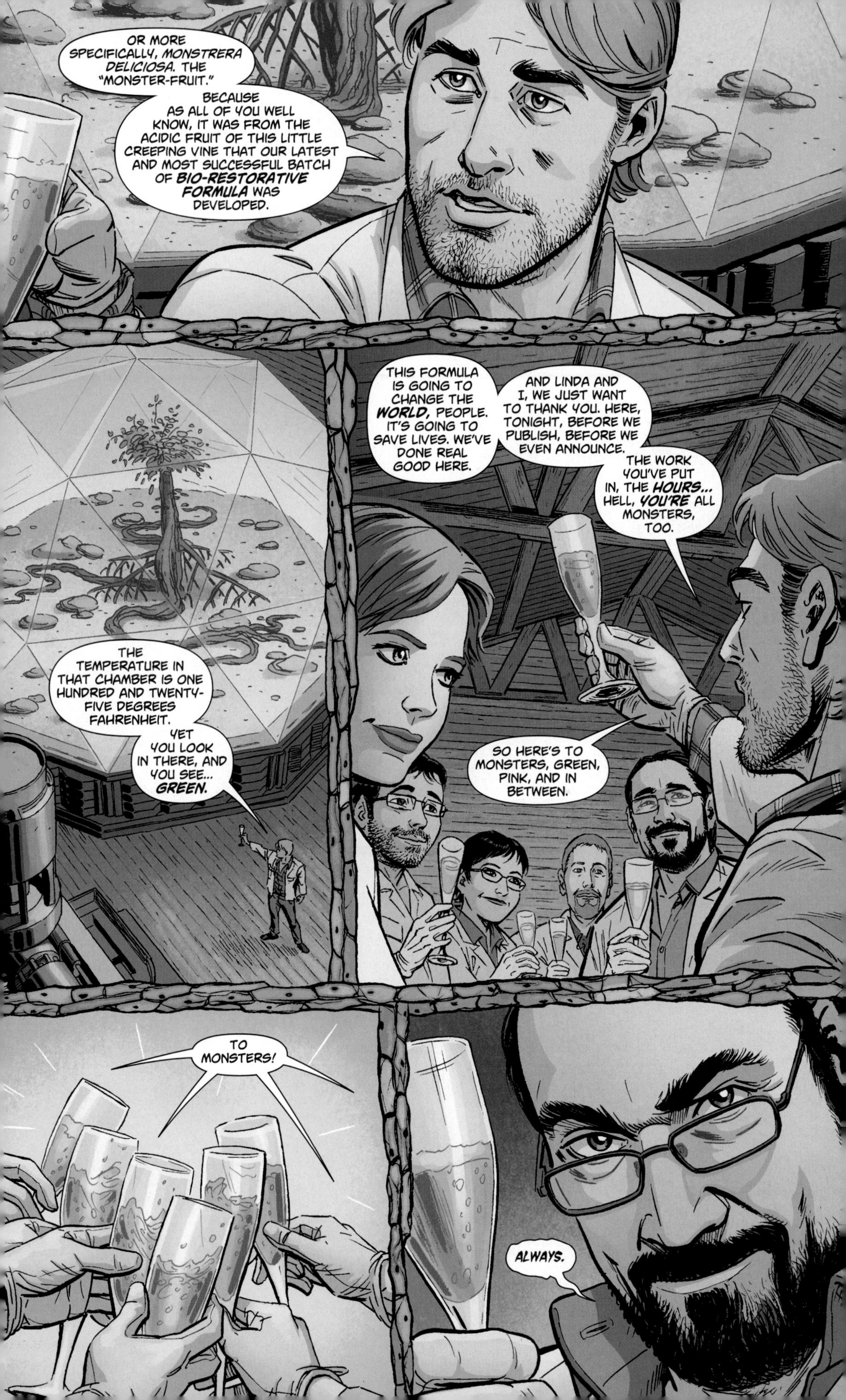
OR MORE SPECIFICALLY, *MONSTRERA DELICIOSA*. THE "MONSTER-FRUIT."
BECAUSE AS ALL OF YOU WELL KNOW, IT WAS FROM THE ACIDIC FRUIT OF THIS LITTLE CREEPING VINE THAT OUR LATEST AND MOST SUCCESSFUL BATCH OF ***BIO-RESTORATIVE FORMULA*** WAS DEVELOPED.
THE TEMPERATURE IN THAT CHAMBER IS ONE HUNDRED AND TWENTY-FIVE DEGREES FAHRENHEIT.
YET YOU LOOK IN THERE, AND YOU SEE... ***GREEN***.
THIS FORMULA IS GOING TO CHANGE THE ***WORLD***, PEOPLE. IT'S GOING TO SAVE LIVES. WE'VE DONE REAL GOOD HERE.
AND LINDA AND I, WE JUST WANT TO THANK YOU. HERE, TONIGHT, BEFORE WE PUBLISH, BEFORE WE EVEN ANNOUNCE.
THE WORK YOU'VE PUT IN, THE ***HOURS...*** HELL, ***YOU'RE*** ALL MONSTERS, TOO.
SO HERE'S TO MONSTERS, GREEN, PINK, AND IN BETWEEN.
TO MONSTERS!
ALWAYS.

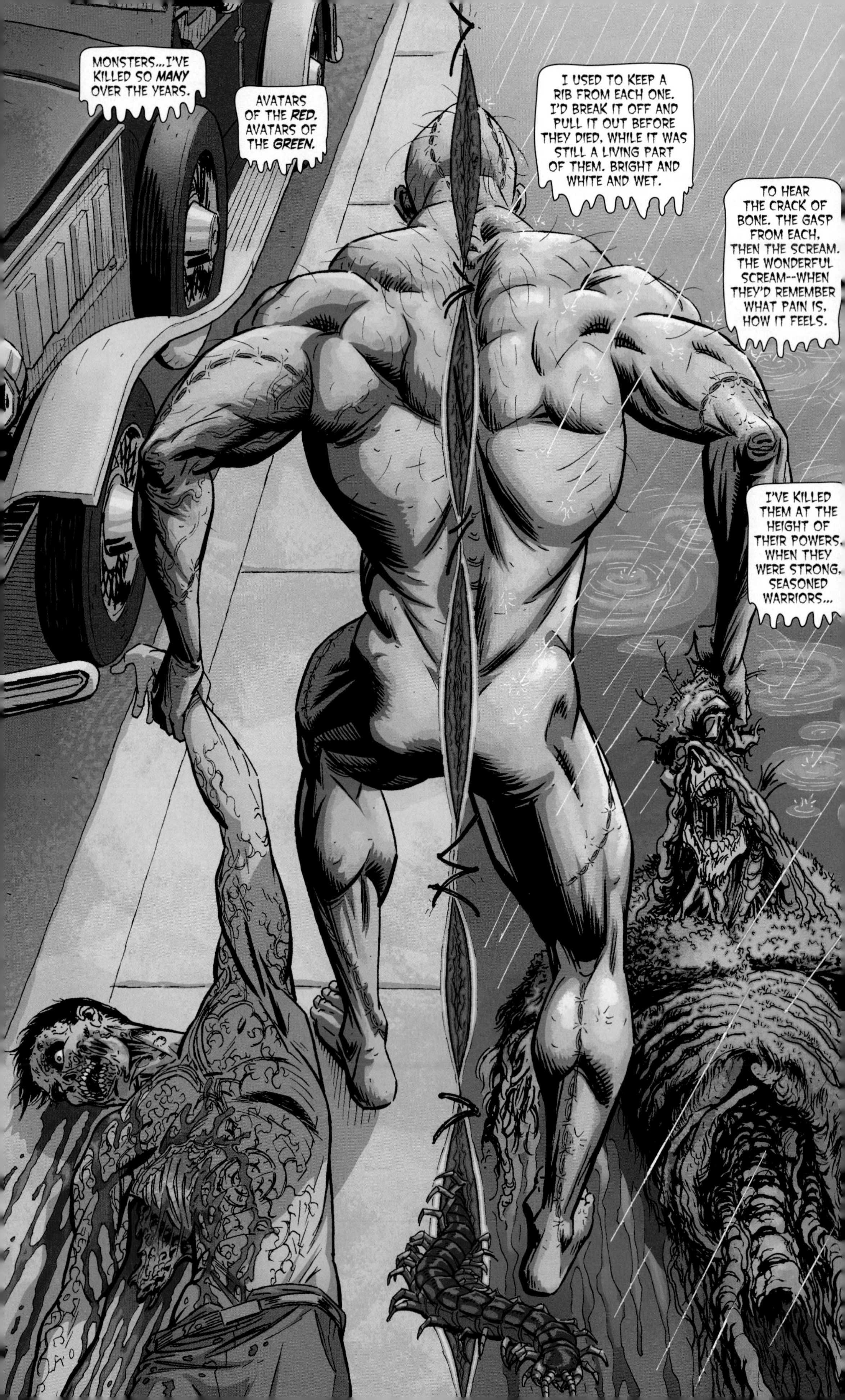
MONSTERS...I'VE KILLED SO *MANY* OVER THE YEARS.
AVATARS OF THE *RED*. AVATARS OF THE *GREEN*.
I USED TO KEEP A RIB FROM EACH ONE. I'D BREAK IT OFF AND PULL IT OUT BEFORE THEY DIED, WHILE IT WAS STILL A LIVING PART OF THEM. BRIGHT AND WHITE AND WET.
TO HEAR THE CRACK OF BONE. THE GASP FROM EACH, THEN THE SCREAM. THE WONDERFUL SCREAM--WHEN THEY'D REMEMBER WHAT PAIN IS. HOW IT FEELS.
I'VE KILLED THEM AT THE HEIGHT OF THEIR POWERS, WHEN THEY WERE STRONG, SEASONED WARRIORS...

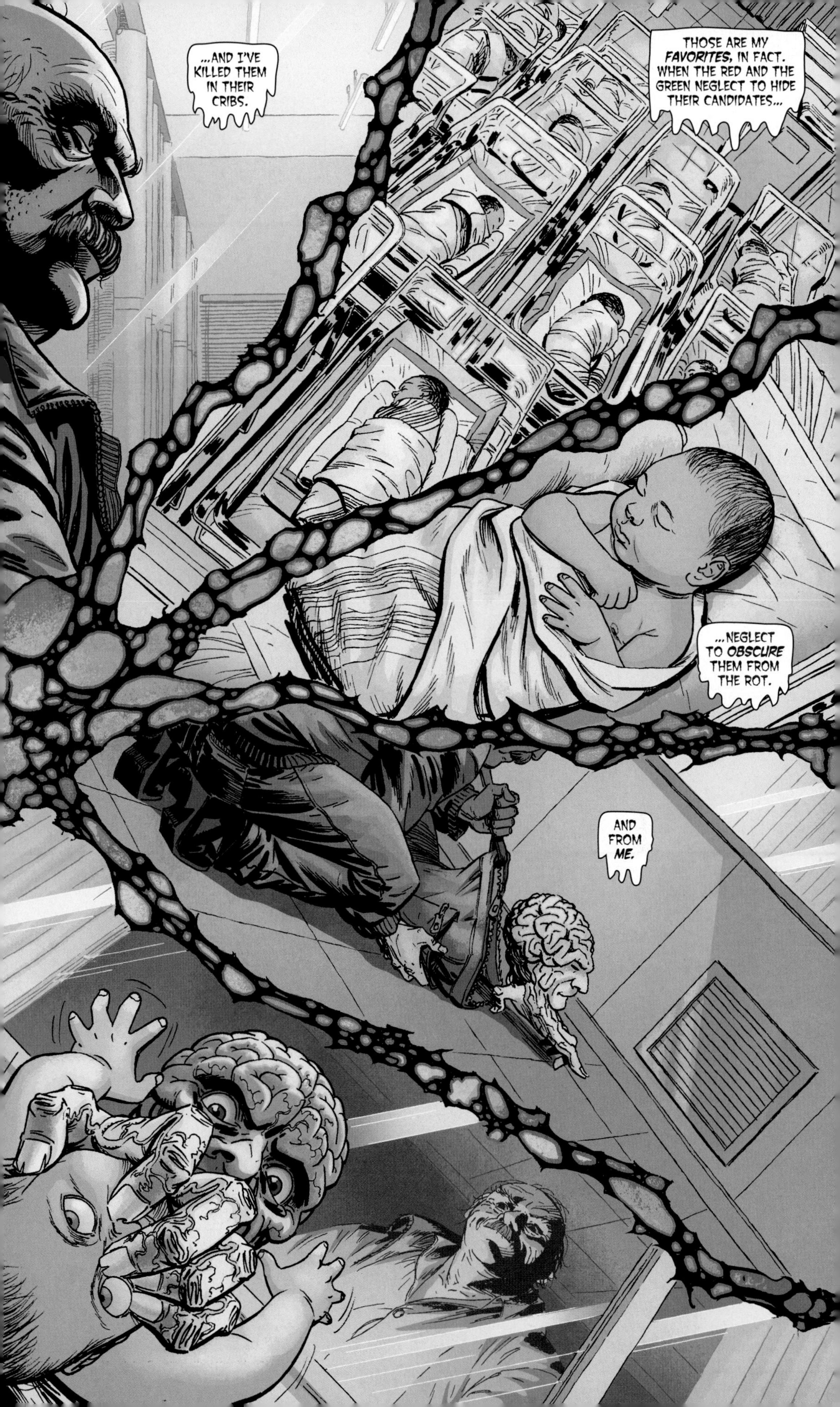

...AND I'VE KILLED THEM IN THEIR CRIBS.
THOSE ARE MY FAVORITES, IN FACT. WHEN THE RED AND THE GREEN NEGLECT TO HIDE THEIR CANDIDATES...
...NEGLECT TO OBSCURE THEM FROM THE ROT.
AND FROM ME.

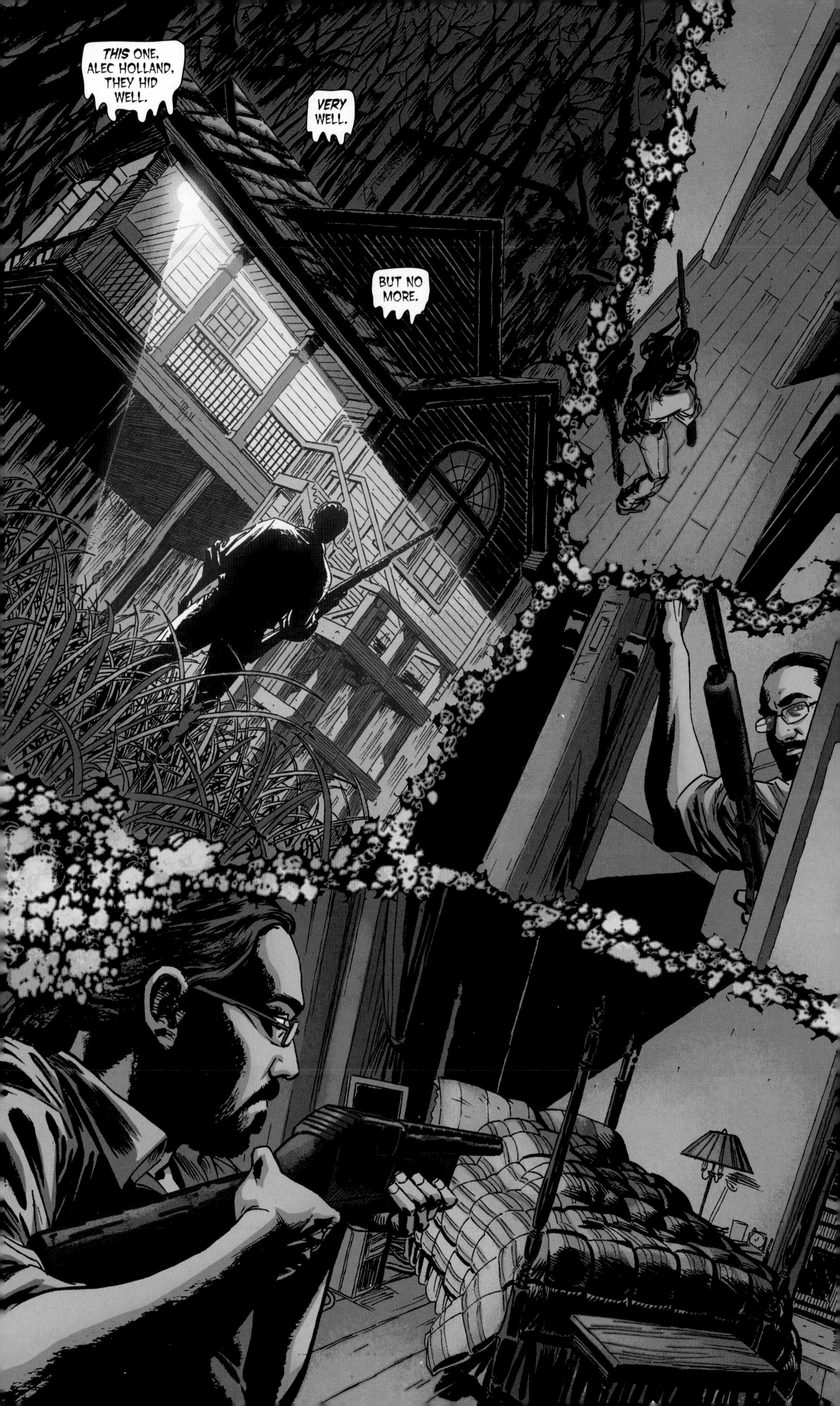
THIS ONE, ALEC HOLLAND, THEY HID WELL.
VERY WELL.
BUT NO MORE.

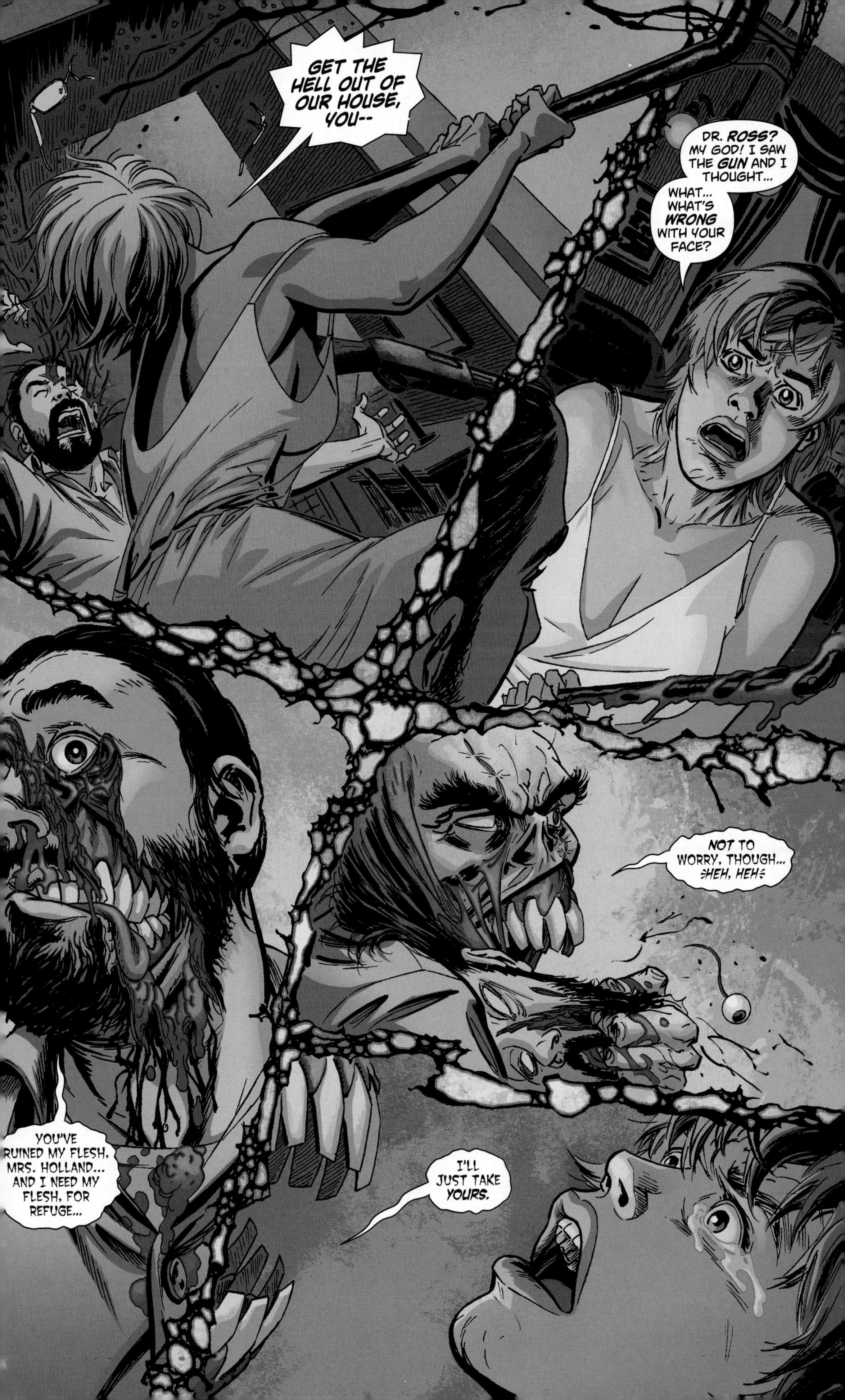
GET THE HELL OUT OF OUR HOUSE, YOU--
DR. ROSS? MY GOD! I SAW THE GUN AND I THOUGHT...
WHAT... WHAT'S WRONG WITH YOUR FACE?
NOT TO WORRY, THOUGH... HEH, HEH
YOU'VE RUINED MY FLESH, MRS. HOLLAND... AND I NEED MY FLESH, FOR REFUGE...
I'LL JUST TAKE YOURS.

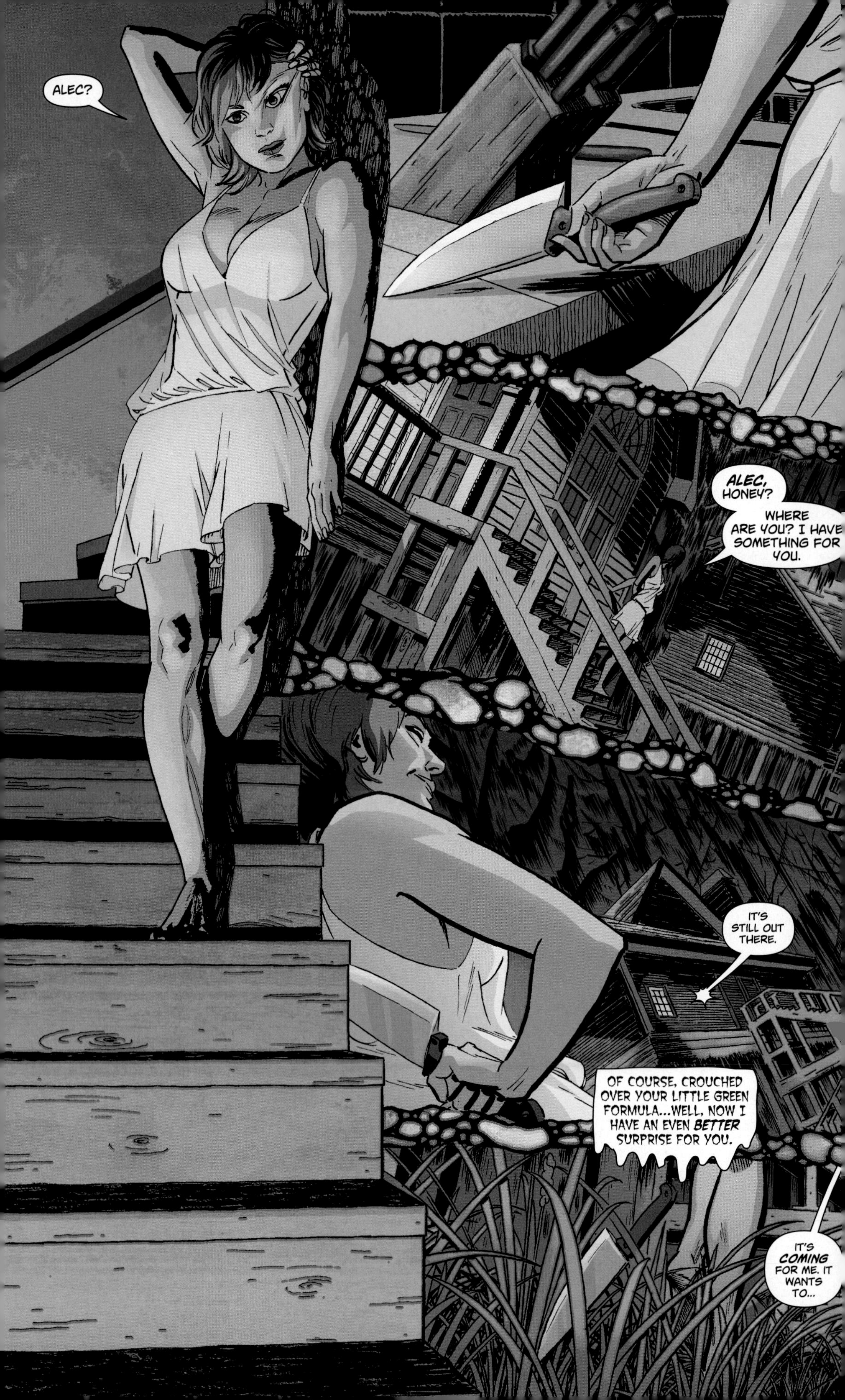
ALEC?
ALEC, HONEY?
WHERE ARE YOU? I HAVE SOMETHING FOR YOU.
IT'S STILL OUT THERE.
OF COURSE, CROUCHED OVER YOUR LITTLE GREEN FORMULA...WELL, NOW I HAVE AN EVEN BETTER SURPRISE FOR YOU.
IT'S COMING FOR ME. IT WANTS TO...

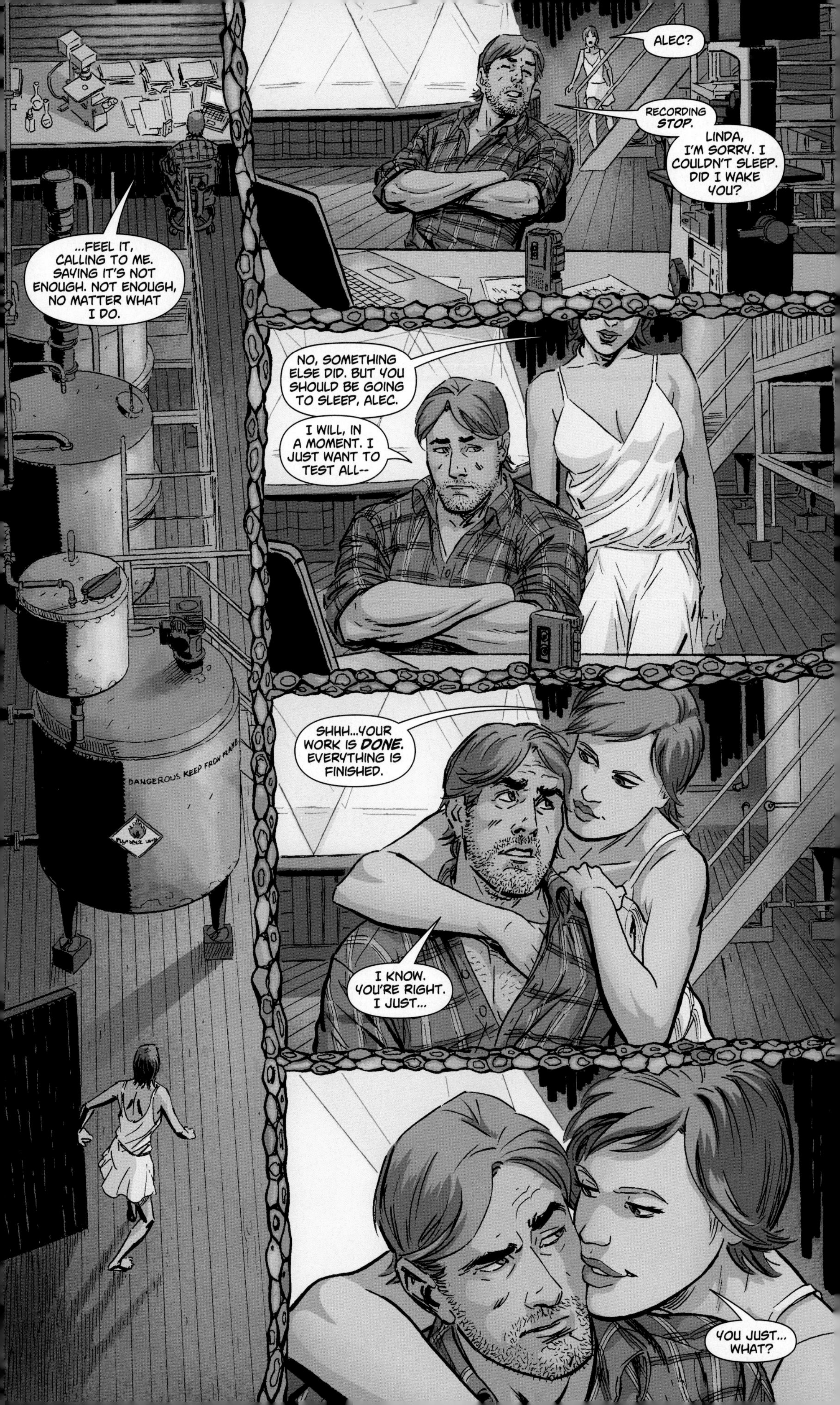
...FEEL IT, CALLING TO ME. SAYING IT'S NOT ENOUGH. NOT ENOUGH, NO MATTER WHAT I DO.
DANGEROUS KEEP FROM FLAME
ALEC?
RECORDING STOP.
LINDA, I'M SORRY. I COULDN'T SLEEP. DID I WAKE YOU?
NO, SOMETHING ELSE DID. BUT YOU SHOULD BE GOING TO SLEEP, ALEC.
I WILL, IN A MOMENT. I JUST WANT TO TEST ALL--
SHHH...YOUR WORK IS DONE. EVERYTHING IS FINISHED.
I KNOW. YOU'RE RIGHT. I JUST...
YOU JUST... WHAT?

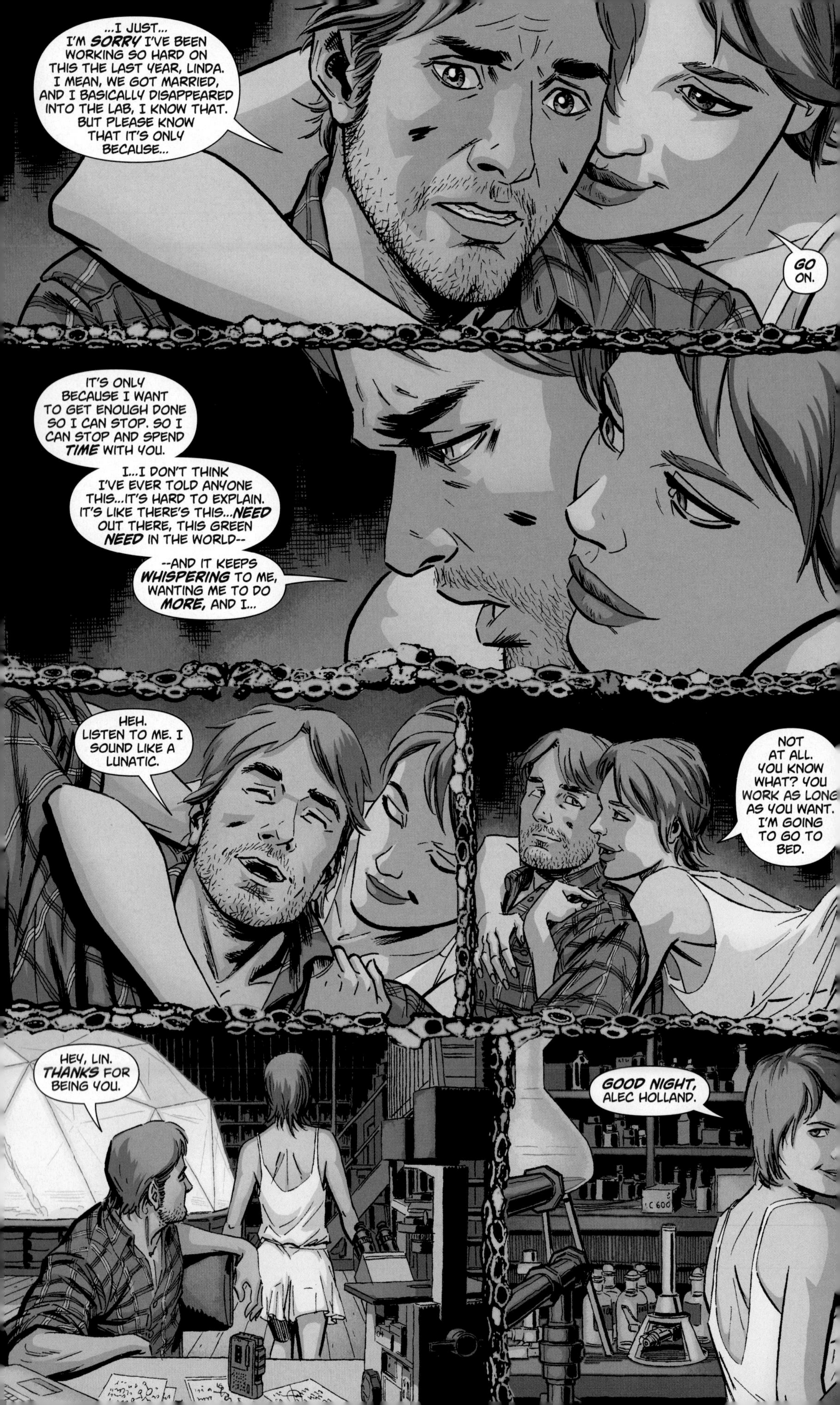
...I JUST... I'M SORRY I'VE BEEN WORKING SO HARD ON THIS THE LAST YEAR, LINDA. I MEAN, WE GOT MARRIED, AND I BASICALLY DISAPPEARED INTO THE LAB, I KNOW THAT. BUT PLEASE KNOW THAT IT'S ONLY BECAUSE...
GO ON.
IT'S ONLY BECAUSE I WANT TO GET ENOUGH DONE SO I CAN STOP. SO I CAN STOP AND SPEND TIME WITH YOU.
I...I DON'T THINK I'VE EVER TOLD ANYONE THIS...IT'S HARD TO EXPLAIN. IT'S LIKE THERE'S THIS...NEED OUT THERE, THIS GREEN NEED IN THE WORLD--
--AND IT KEEPS WHISPERING TO ME, WANTING ME TO DO MORE, AND I...
HEH. LISTEN TO ME. I SOUND LIKE A LUNATIC.
NOT AT ALL. YOU KNOW WHAT? YOU WORK AS LONG AS YOU WANT. I'M GOING TO GO TO BED.
HEY, LIN. THANKS FOR BEING YOU.
GOOD NIGHT, ALEC HOLLAND.

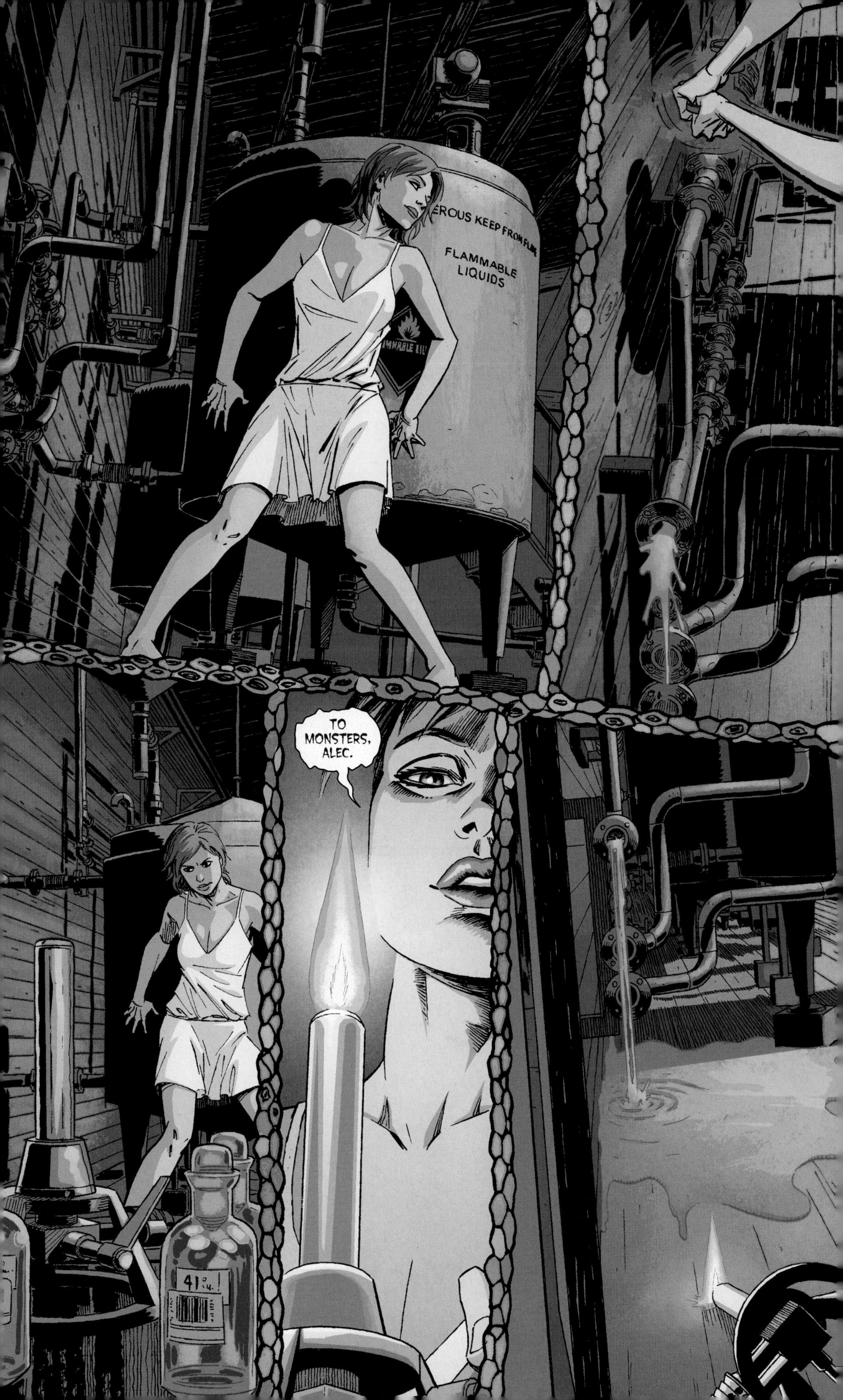

FLAMMABLE LIQUIDS
TO MONSTERS, ALEC.

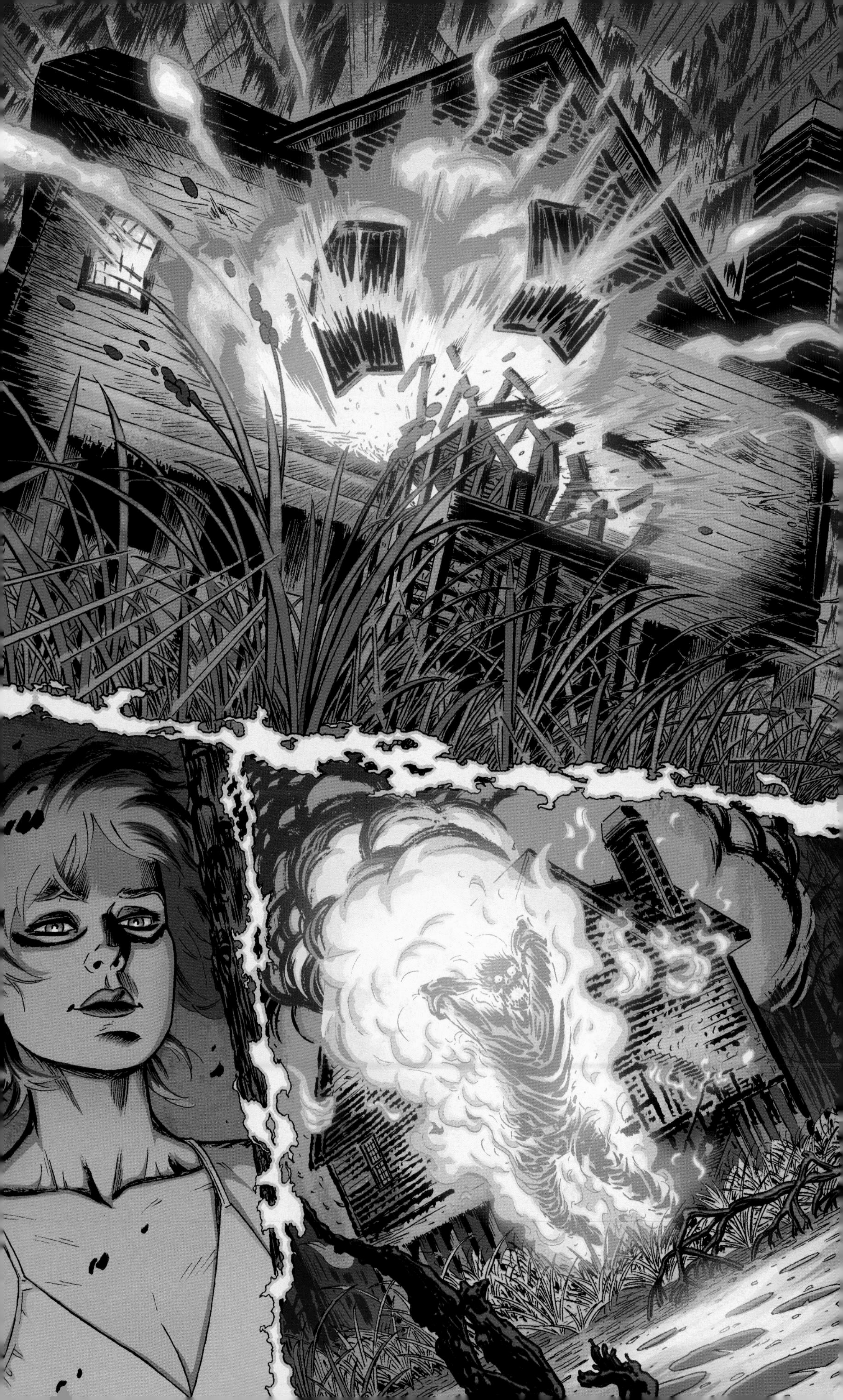

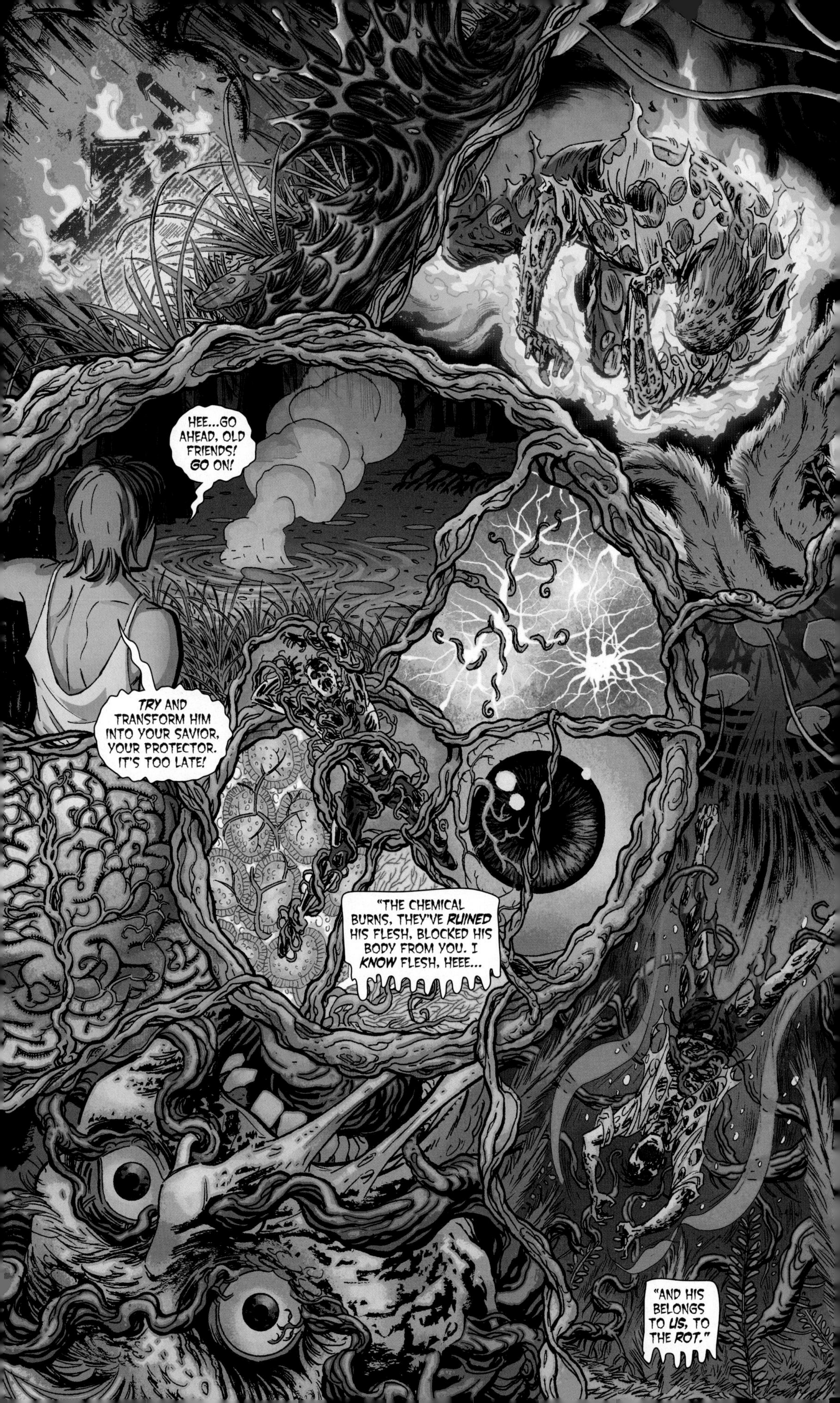
HEE...GO AHEAD, OLD FRIENDS! GO ON!
TRY AND TRANSFORM HIM INTO YOUR SAVIOR, YOUR PROTECTOR. IT'S TOO LATE!
"THE CHEMICAL BURNS, THEY'VE RUINED HIS FLESH, BLOCKED HIS BODY FROM YOU. I KNOW FLESH, HEEE...
"AND HIS BELONGS TO US, TO THE ROT."

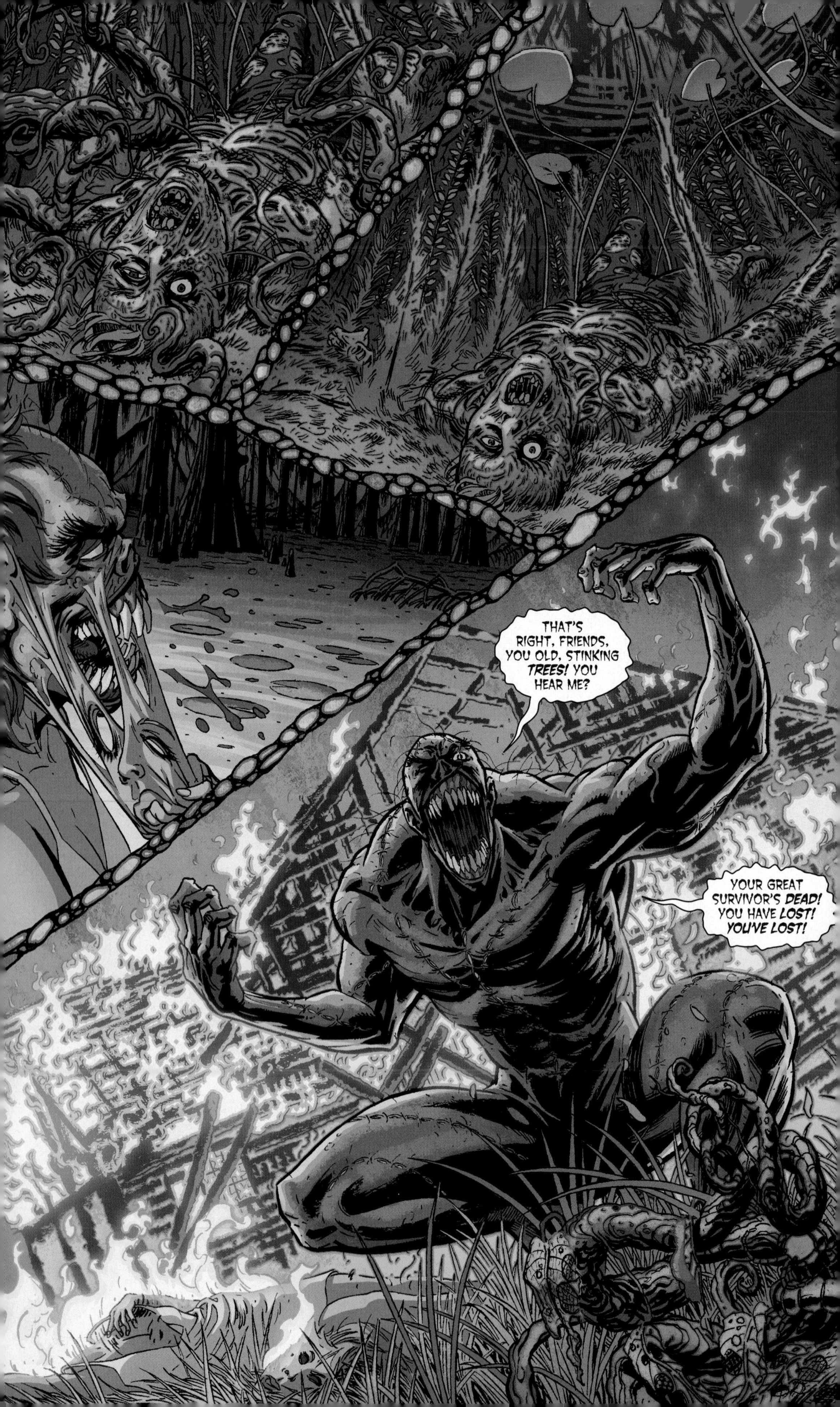
THAT'S RIGHT, FRIENDS, YOU OLD, STINKING *TREES!* YOU HEAR ME?
YOUR GREAT SURVIVOR'S *DEAD!* YOU HAVE *LOST!* *YOU'VE LOST!*

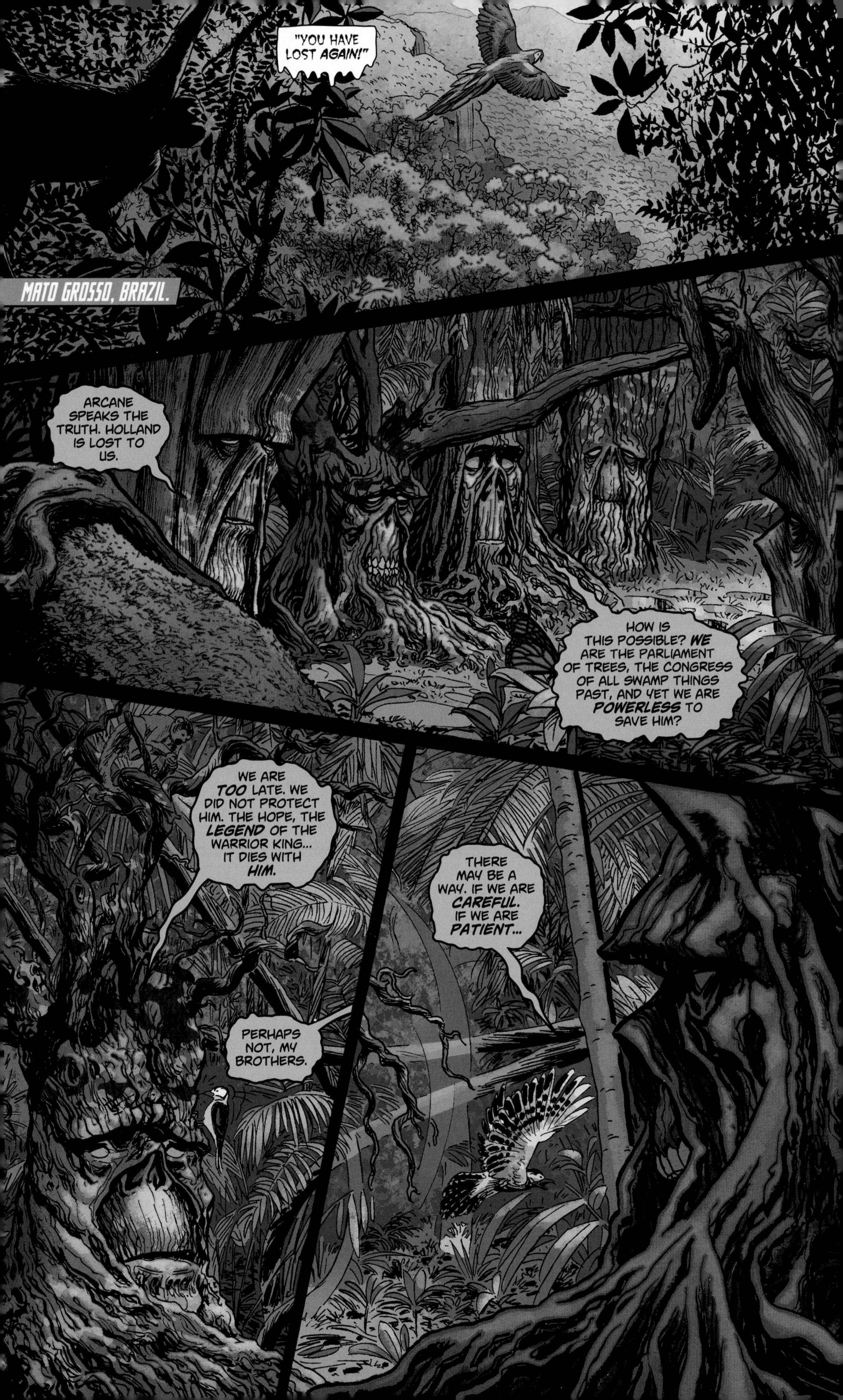
"YOU HAVE LOST AGAIN!"
MATO GROSSO, BRAZIL.
ARCANE SPEAKS THE TRUTH. HOLLAND IS LOST TO US.
HOW IS THIS POSSIBLE? WE ARE THE PARLIAMENT OF TREES, THE CONGRESS OF ALL SWAMP THINGS PAST, AND YET WE ARE POWERLESS TO SAVE HIM?
WE ARE TOO LATE. WE DID NOT PROTECT HIM. THE HOPE, THE LEGEND OF THE WARRIOR KING... IT DIES WITH HIM.
THERE MAY BE A WAY. IF WE ARE CAREFUL. IF WE ARE PATIENT...
PERHAPS NOT, MY BROTHERS.

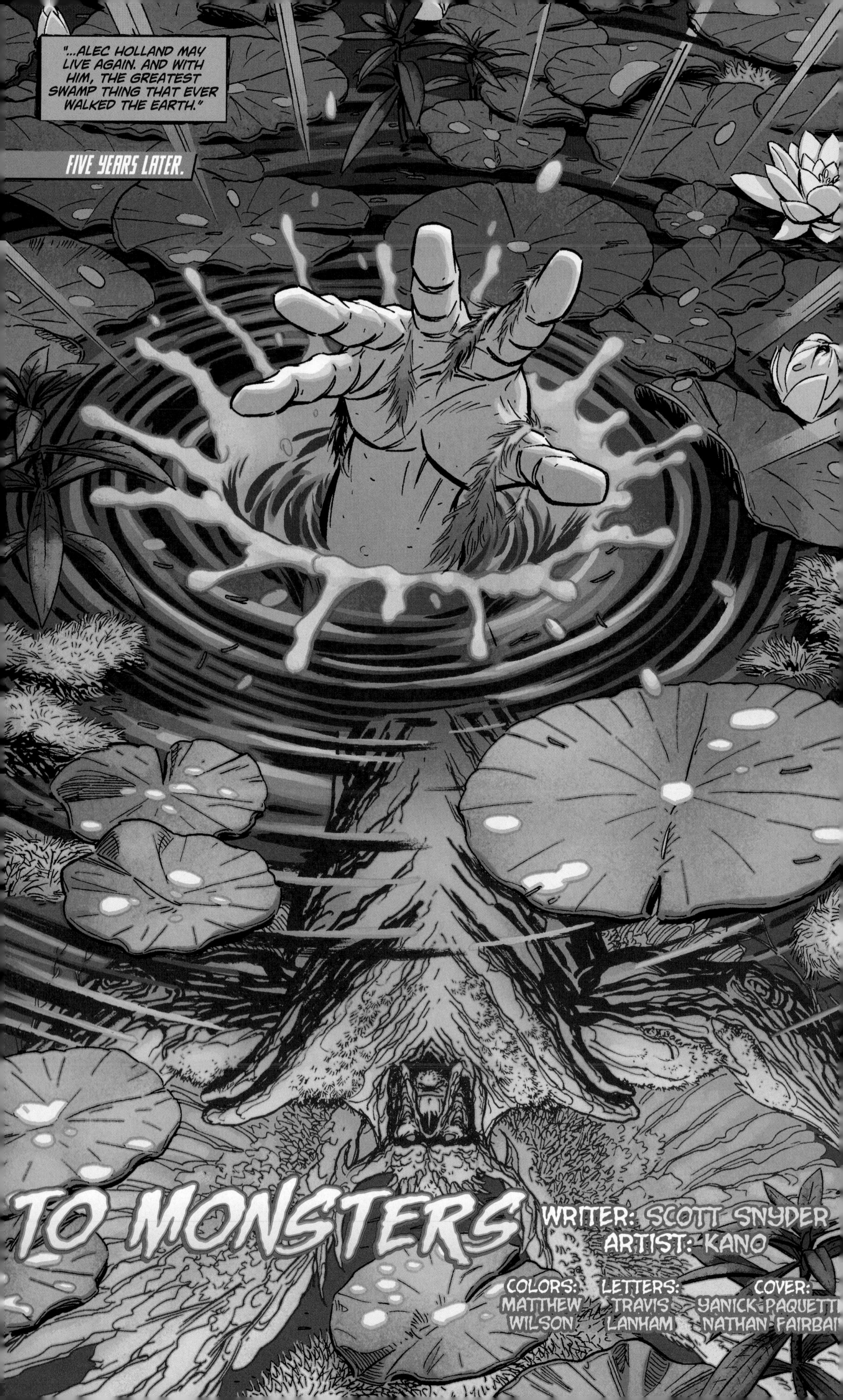

"...ALEC HOLLAND MAY LIVE AGAIN. AND WITH HIM, THE GREATEST SWAMP THING THAT EVER WALKED THE EARTH."
FIVE YEARS LATER.
TO MONSTERS
WRITER: SCOTT SNYDER
ARTIST: KANO
COLORS: MATTHEW WILSON
LETTERS: TRAVIS LANHAM
COVER: YANICK PAQUETTE NATHAN FAIRBAIRN

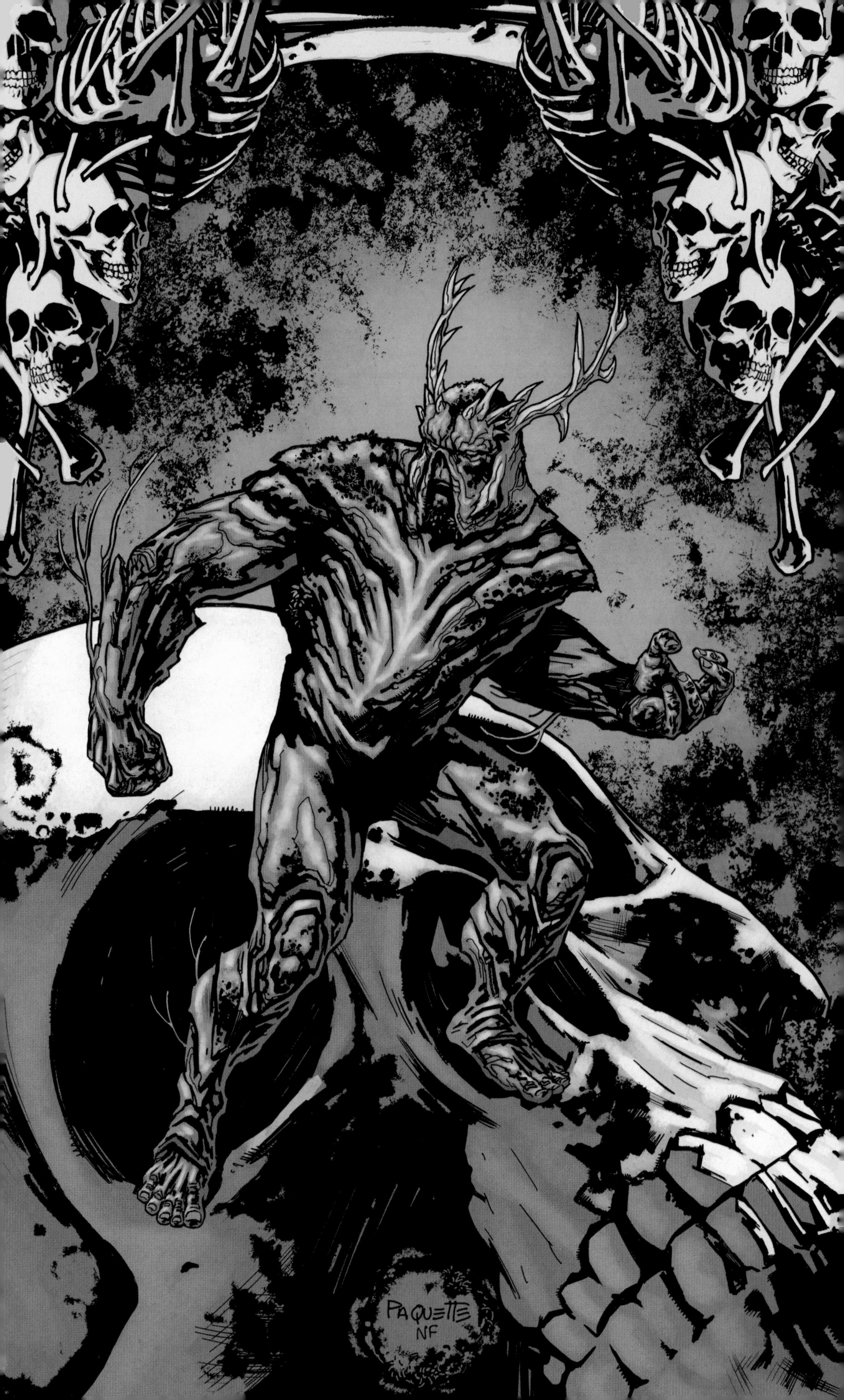
PAQUETTE
NF

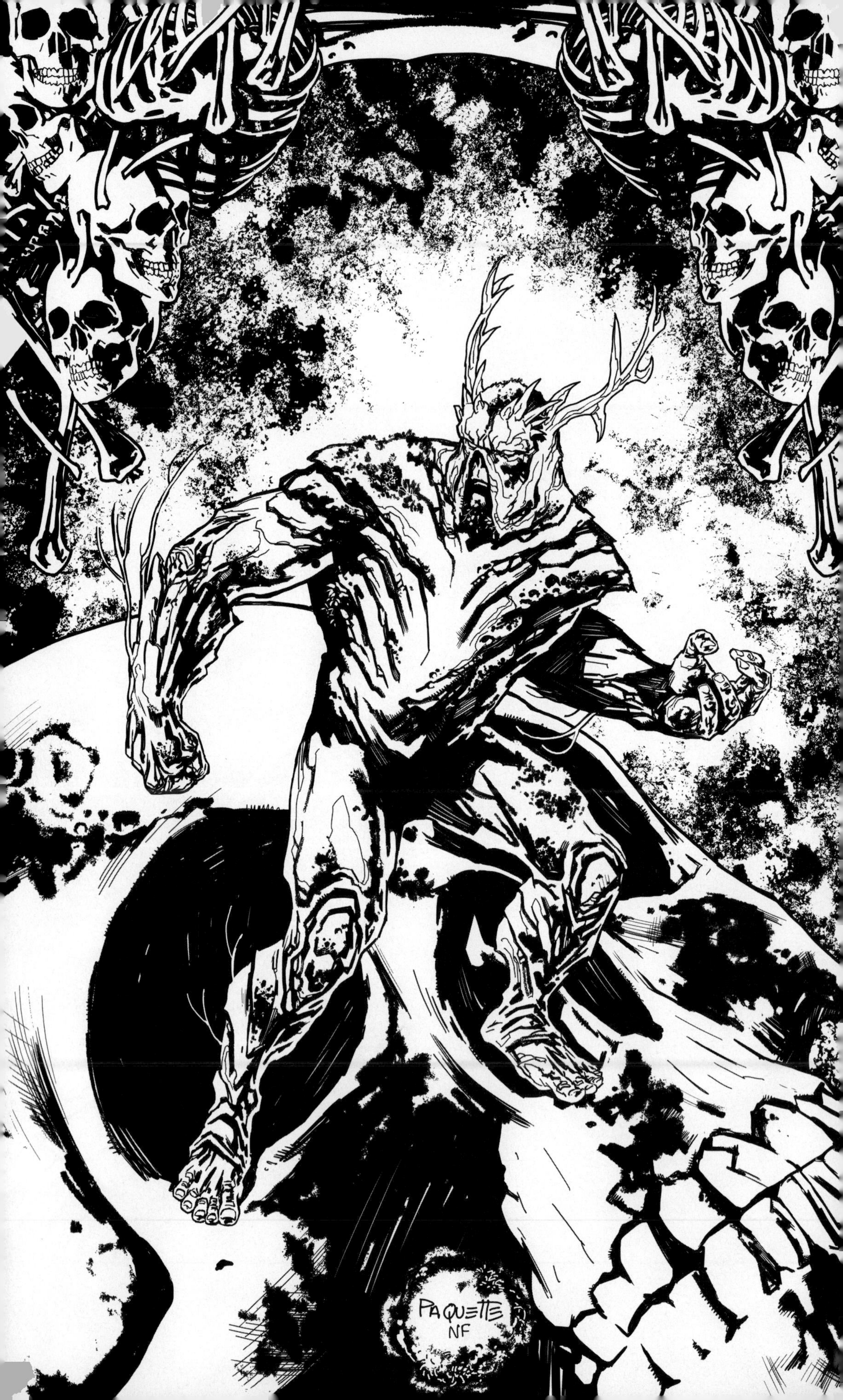
PAQUETTE
NF

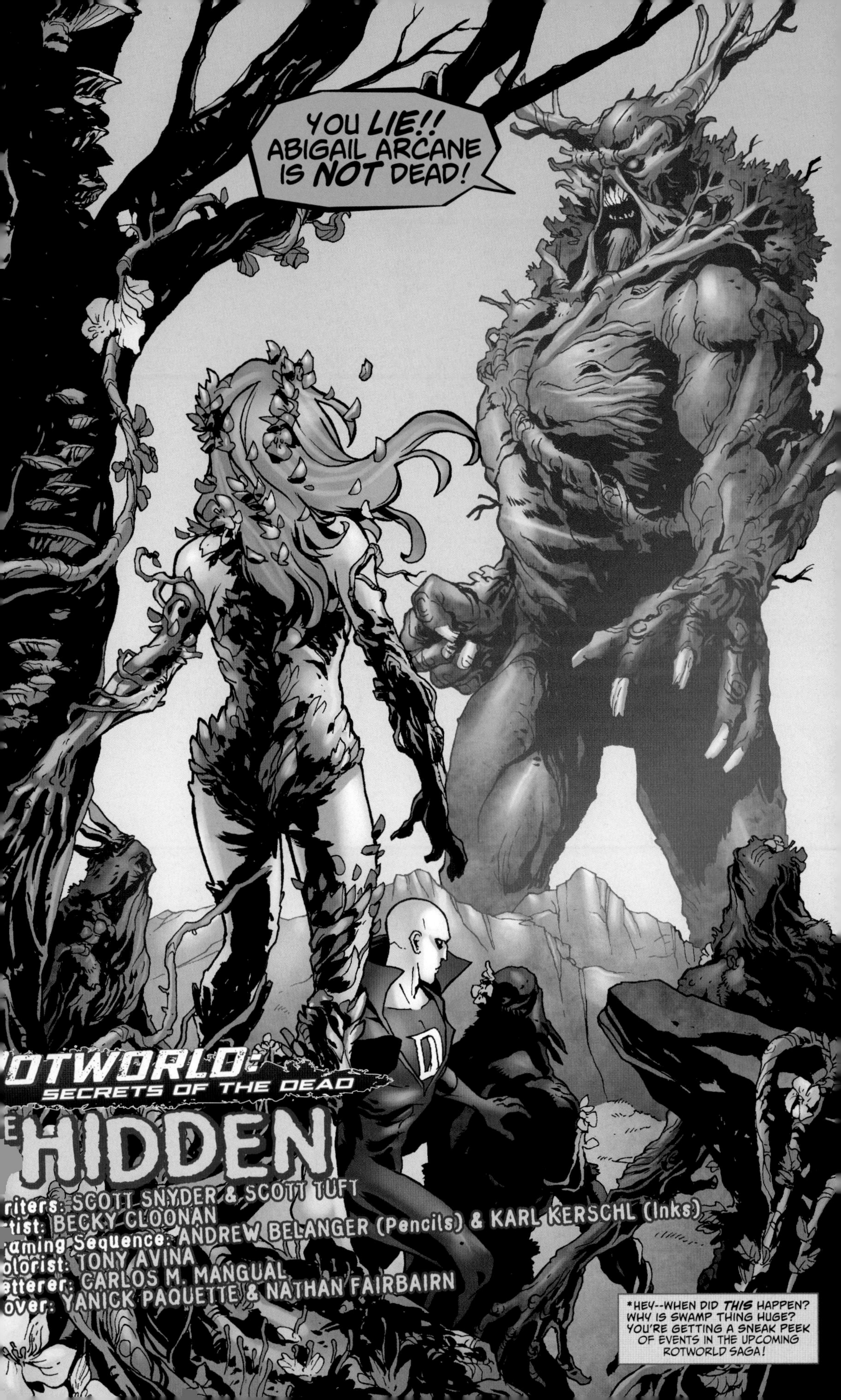

YOU LIE!! ABIGAIL ARCANE IS NOT DEAD!
OTWORLD:
SECRETS OF THE DEAD
E HIDDEN
riters: SCOTT SNYDER & SCOTT TUFT
tist: BECKY CLOONAN
aming Sequence: ANDREW BELANGER (Pencils) & KARL KERSCHL (Inks)
olorist: TONY AVINA
etterer: CARLOS M. MANGUAL
over: YANICK PAQUETTE & NATHAN FAIRBAIRN
*HEY--WHEN DID THIS HAPPEN? WHY IS SWAMP THING HUGE? YOU'RE GETTING A SNEAK PEEK OF EVENTS IN THE UPCOMING ROTWORLD SAGA!

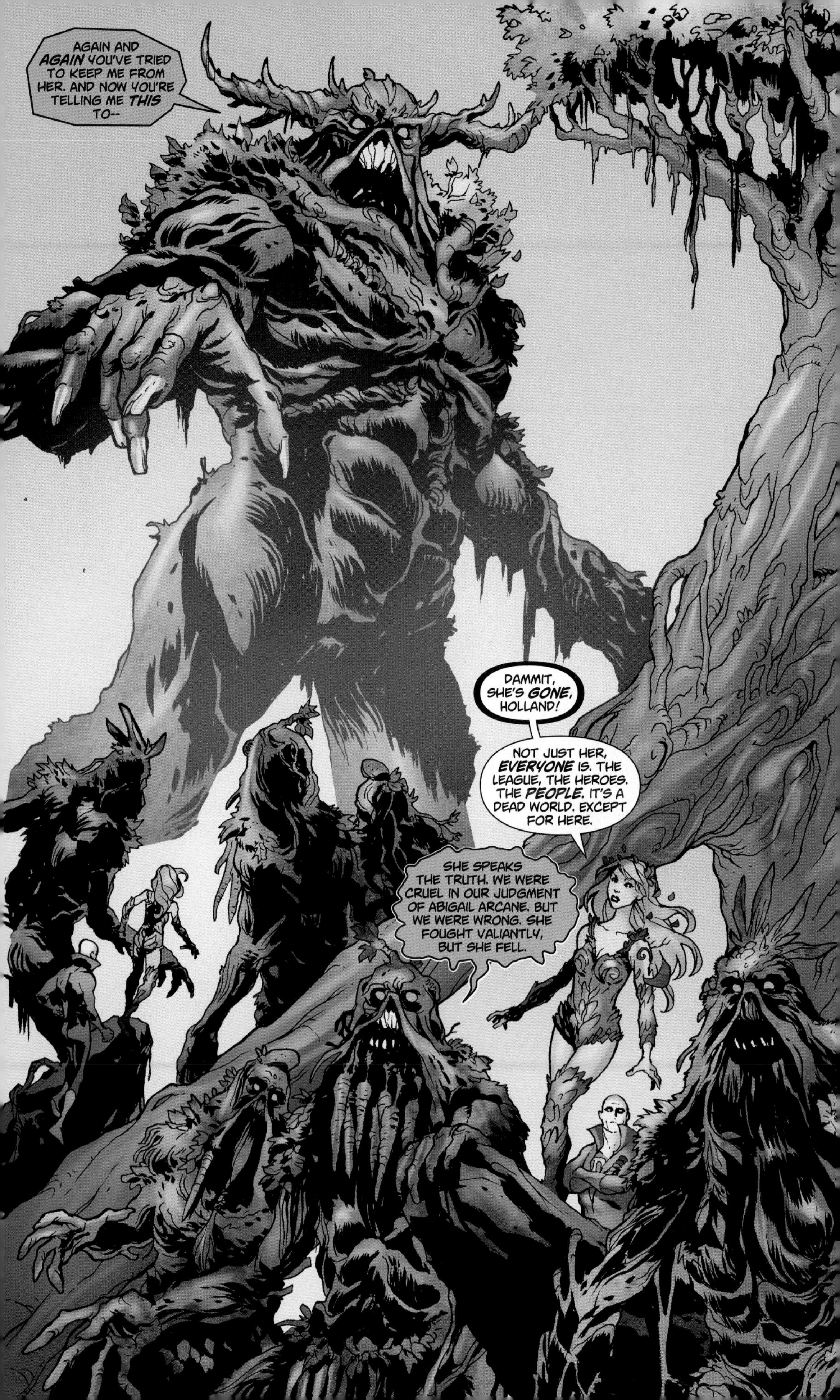
AGAIN AND AGAIN YOU'VE TRIED TO KEEP ME FROM HER. AND NOW YOU'RE TELLING ME THIS TO--
DAMMIT, SHE'S GONE, HOLLAND!
NOT JUST HER, EVERYONE IS. THE LEAGUE, THE HEROES. THE PEOPLE. IT'S A DEAD WORLD. EXCEPT FOR HERE.
SHE SPEAKS THE TRUTH. WE WERE CRUEL IN OUR JUDGMENT OF ABIGAIL ARCANE. BUT WE WERE WRONG. SHE FOUGHT VALIANTLY, BUT SHE FELL.

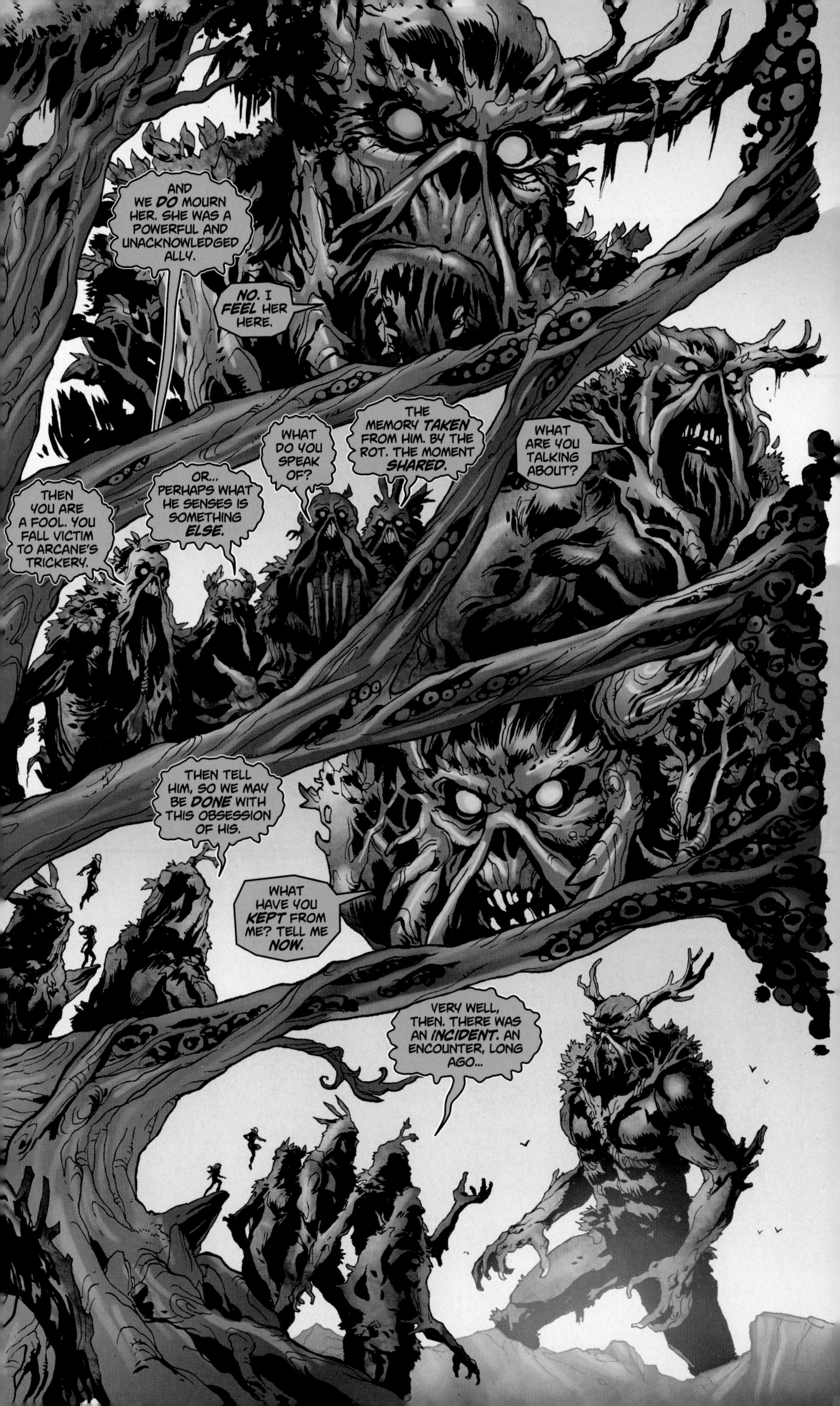

AND WE DO MOURN HER. SHE WAS A POWERFUL AND UNACKNOWLEDGED ALLY.
NO. I FEEL HER HERE.
THEN YOU ARE A FOOL. YOU FALL VICTIM TO ARCANE'S TRICKERY.
OR... PERHAPS WHAT HE SENSES IS SOMETHING ELSE.
WHAT DO YOU SPEAK OF?
THE MEMORY TAKEN FROM HIM. BY THE ROT. THE MOMENT SHARED.
WHAT ARE YOU TALKING ABOUT?
THEN TELL HIM, SO WE MAY BE DONE WITH THIS OBSESSION OF HIS.
WHAT HAVE YOU KEPT FROM ME? TELL ME NOW.
VERY WELL, THEN. THERE WAS AN INCIDENT. AN ENCOUNTER, LONG AGO...

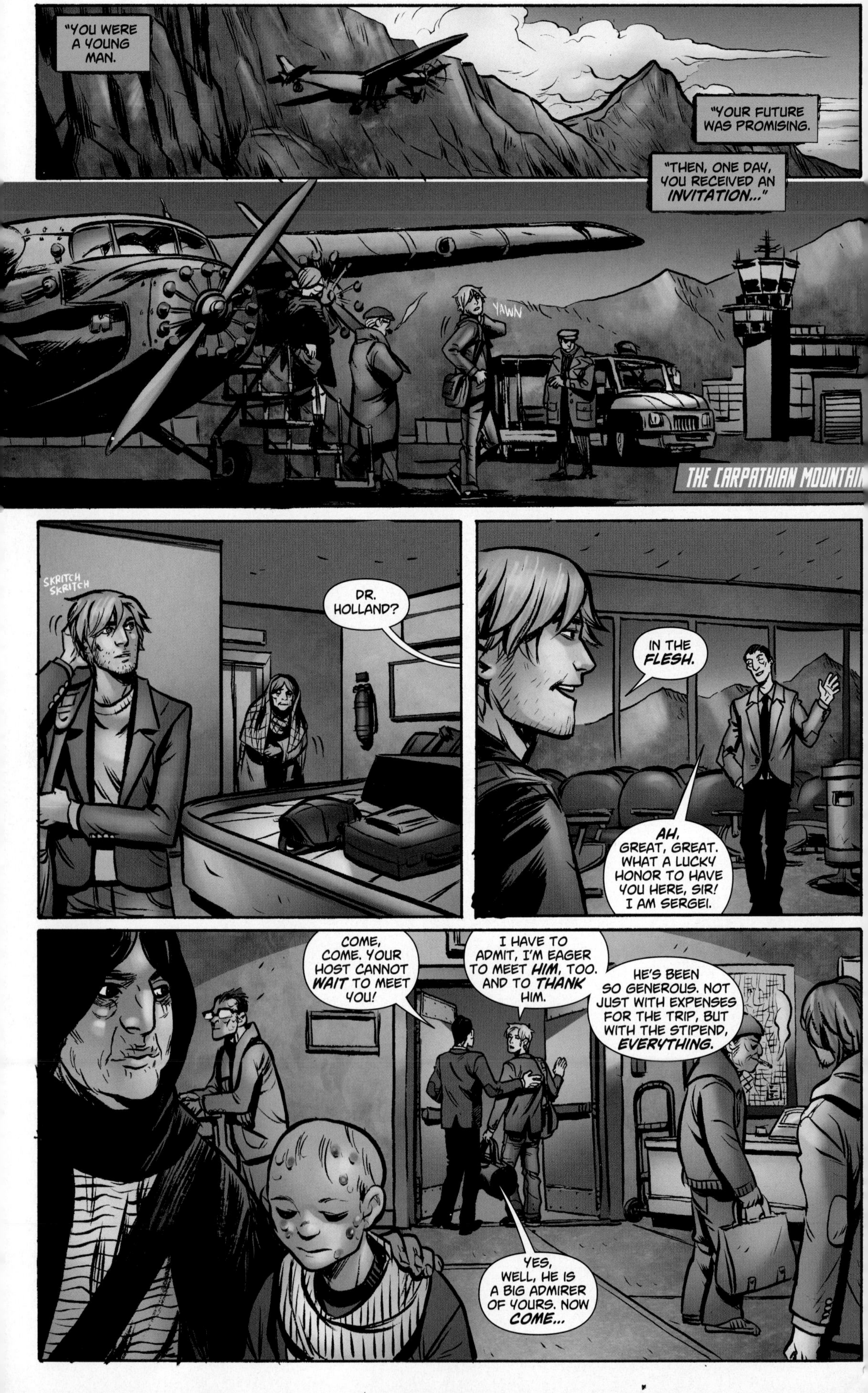
"YOU WERE A YOUNG MAN.
"YOUR FUTURE WAS PROMISING.
"THEN, ONE DAY, YOU RECEIVED AN *INVITATION...*"
YAWN
THE CARPATHIAN MOUNTAI
SKRITCH SKRITCH
DR. HOLLAND?
IN THE *FLESH.*
AH, GREAT, GREAT. WHAT A LUCKY HONOR TO HAVE YOU HERE, SIR! I AM SERGEI.
COME, COME. YOUR HOST CANNOT *WAIT* TO MEET YOU!
I HAVE TO ADMIT, I'M EAGER TO MEET *HIM*, TOO. AND TO *THANK* HIM.
HE'S BEEN SO GENEROUS. NOT JUST WITH EXPENSES FOR THE TRIP, BUT WITH THE STIPEND, *EVERYTHING.*
YES, WELL, HE IS A BIG ADMIRER OF YOURS. NOW *COME...*

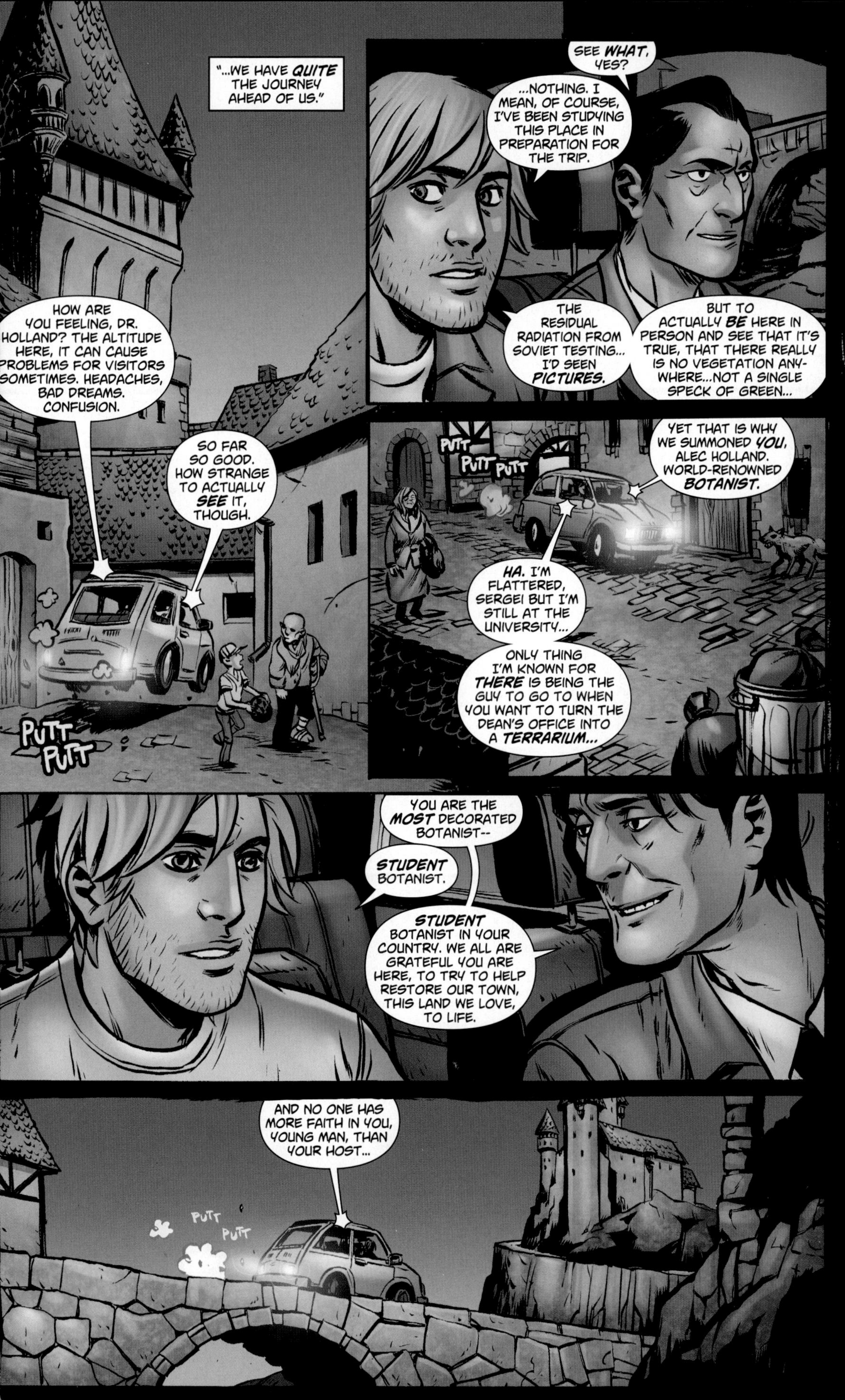
"...WE HAVE QUITE THE JOURNEY AHEAD OF US."
SEE WHAT, YES?
...NOTHING. I MEAN, OF COURSE, I'VE BEEN STUDYING THIS PLACE IN PREPARATION FOR THE TRIP.
THE RESIDUAL RADIATION FROM SOVIET TESTING... I'D SEEN PICTURES.
BUT TO ACTUALLY BE HERE IN PERSON AND SEE THAT IT'S TRUE, THAT THERE REALLY IS NO VEGETATION ANYWHERE...NOT A SINGLE SPECK OF GREEN...
HOW ARE YOU FEELING, DR. HOLLAND? THE ALTITUDE HERE, IT CAN CAUSE PROBLEMS FOR VISITORS SOMETIMES. HEADACHES, BAD DREAMS. CONFUSION.
SO FAR SO GOOD. HOW STRANGE TO ACTUALLY SEE IT, THOUGH.
PUTT PUTT
PUTT PUTT PUTT
YET THAT IS WHY WE SUMMONED YOU, ALEC HOLLAND. WORLD-RENOWNED BOTANIST.
HA. I'M FLATTERED, SERGEI BUT I'M STILL AT THE UNIVERSITY...
ONLY THING I'M KNOWN FOR THERE IS BEING THE GUY TO GO TO WHEN YOU WANT TO TURN THE DEAN'S OFFICE INTO A TERRARIUM...
YOU ARE THE MOST DECORATED BOTANIST--
STUDENT BOTANIST.
STUDENT BOTANIST IN YOUR COUNTRY. WE ALL ARE GRATEFUL YOU ARE HERE, TO TRY TO HELP RESTORE OUR TOWN, THIS LAND WE LOVE, TO LIFE.
AND NO ONE HAS MORE FAITH IN YOU, YOUNG MAN, THAN YOUR HOST...
PUTT PUTT

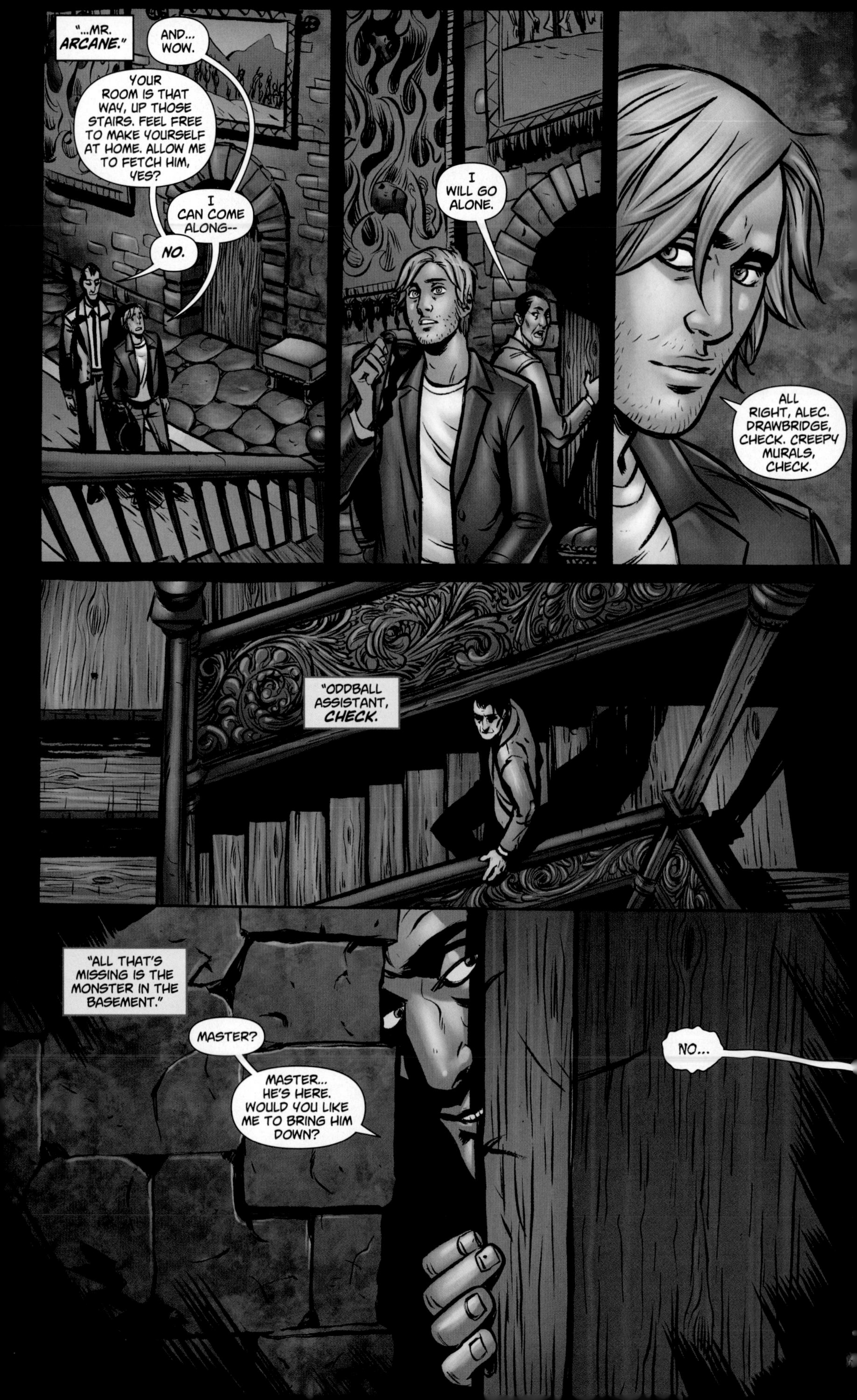
"...MR. ARCANE."
AND... WOW.
YOUR ROOM IS THAT WAY, UP THOSE STAIRS. FEEL FREE TO MAKE YOURSELF AT HOME. ALLOW ME TO FETCH HIM, YES?
I CAN COME ALONG--
NO.
I WILL GO ALONE.
ALL RIGHT, ALEC. DRAWBRIDGE, CHECK. CREEPY MURALS, CHECK.
"ODDBALL ASSISTANT, CHECK.
"ALL THAT'S MISSING IS THE MONSTER IN THE BASEMENT."
MASTER?
MASTER... HE'S HERE. WOULD YOU LIKE ME TO BRING HIM DOWN?
NO...

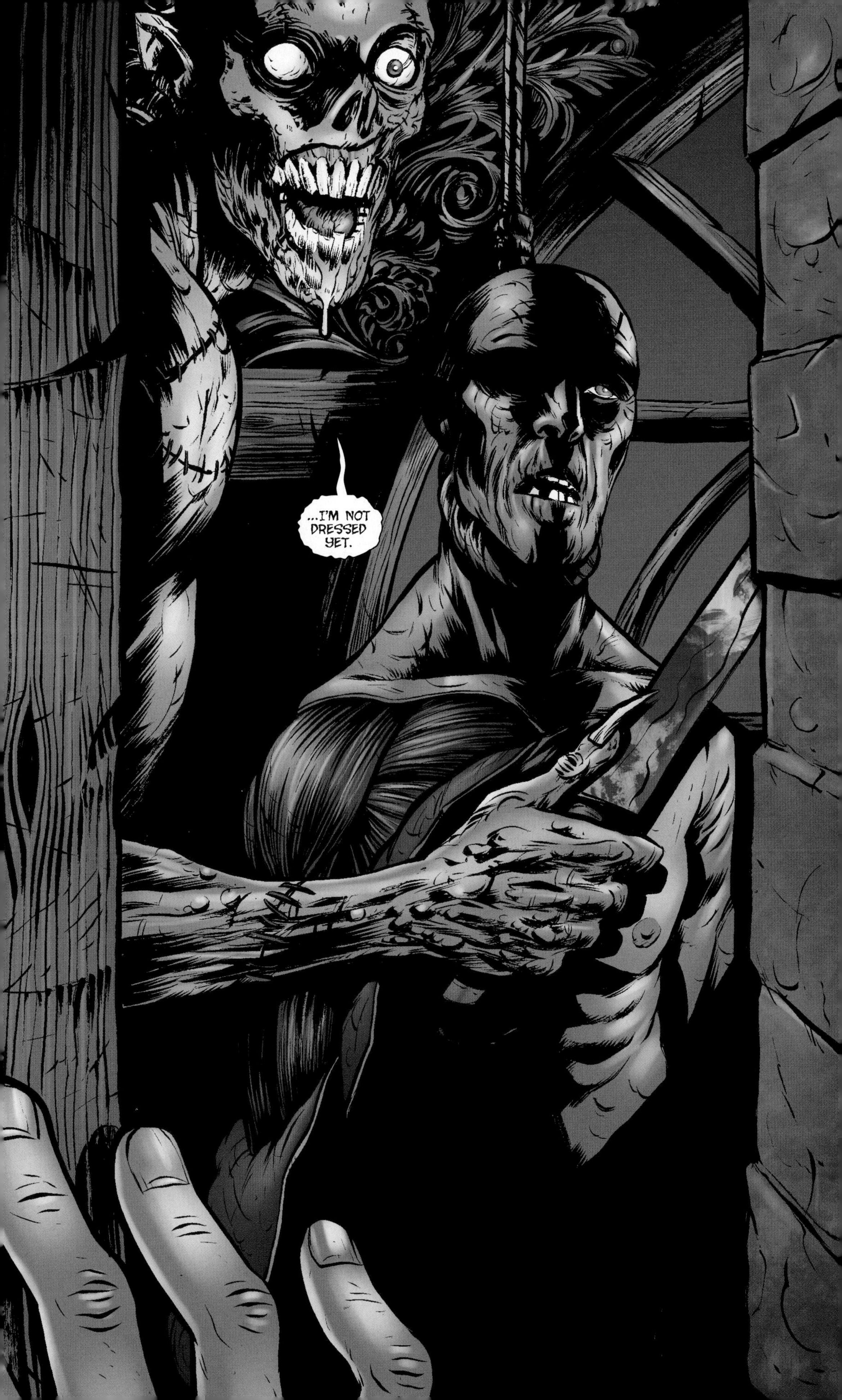
...I'M NOT DRESSED YET.

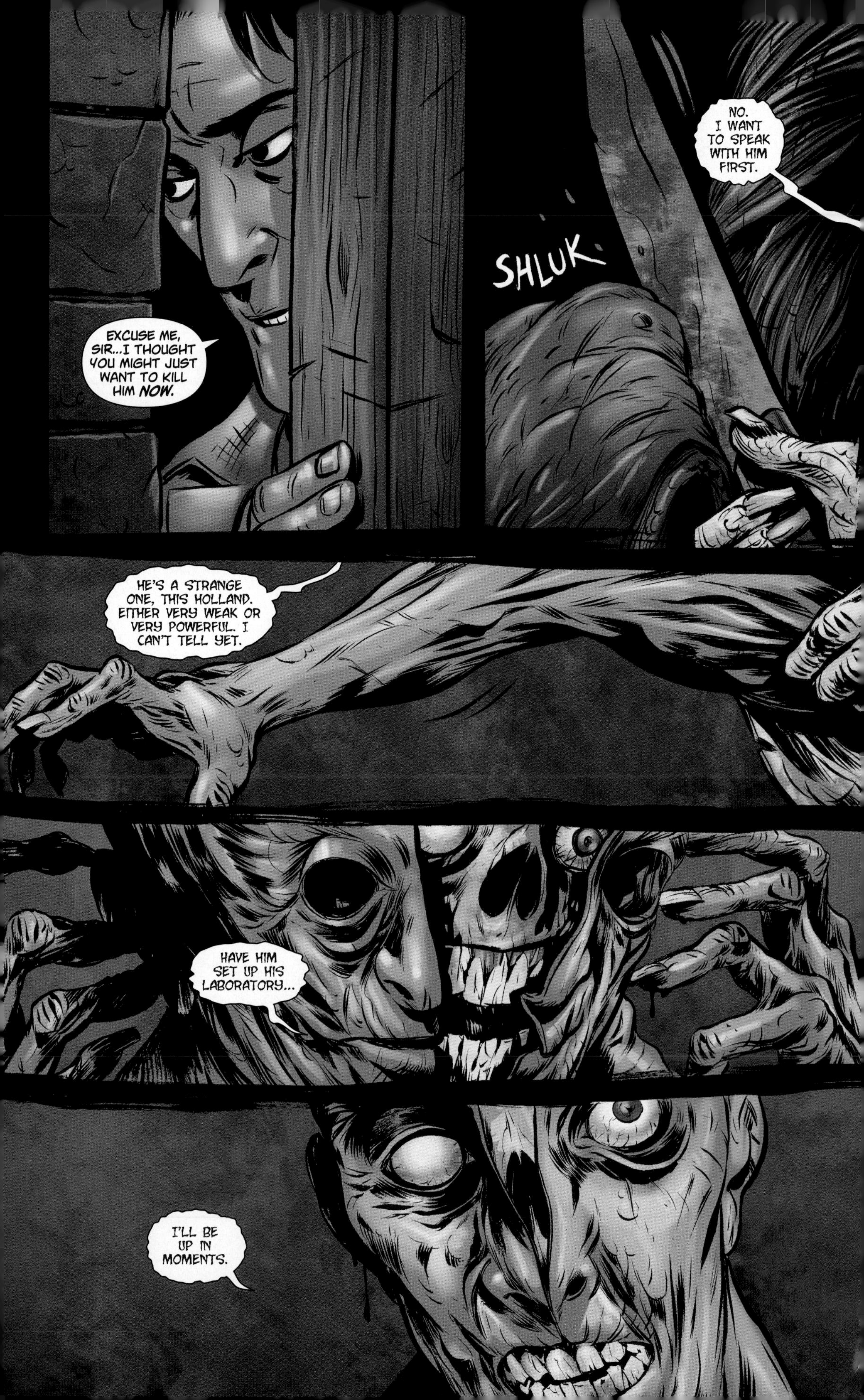
EXCUSE ME, SIR...I THOUGHT YOU MIGHT JUST WANT TO KILL HIM *NOW*.
NO. I WANT TO SPEAK WITH HIM FIRST.
SHLUK
HE'S A STRANGE ONE, THIS HOLLAND. EITHER VERY WEAK OR VERY POWERFUL. I CAN'T TELL YET.
HAVE HIM SET UP HIS LABORATORY...
I'LL BE UP IN MOMENTS.

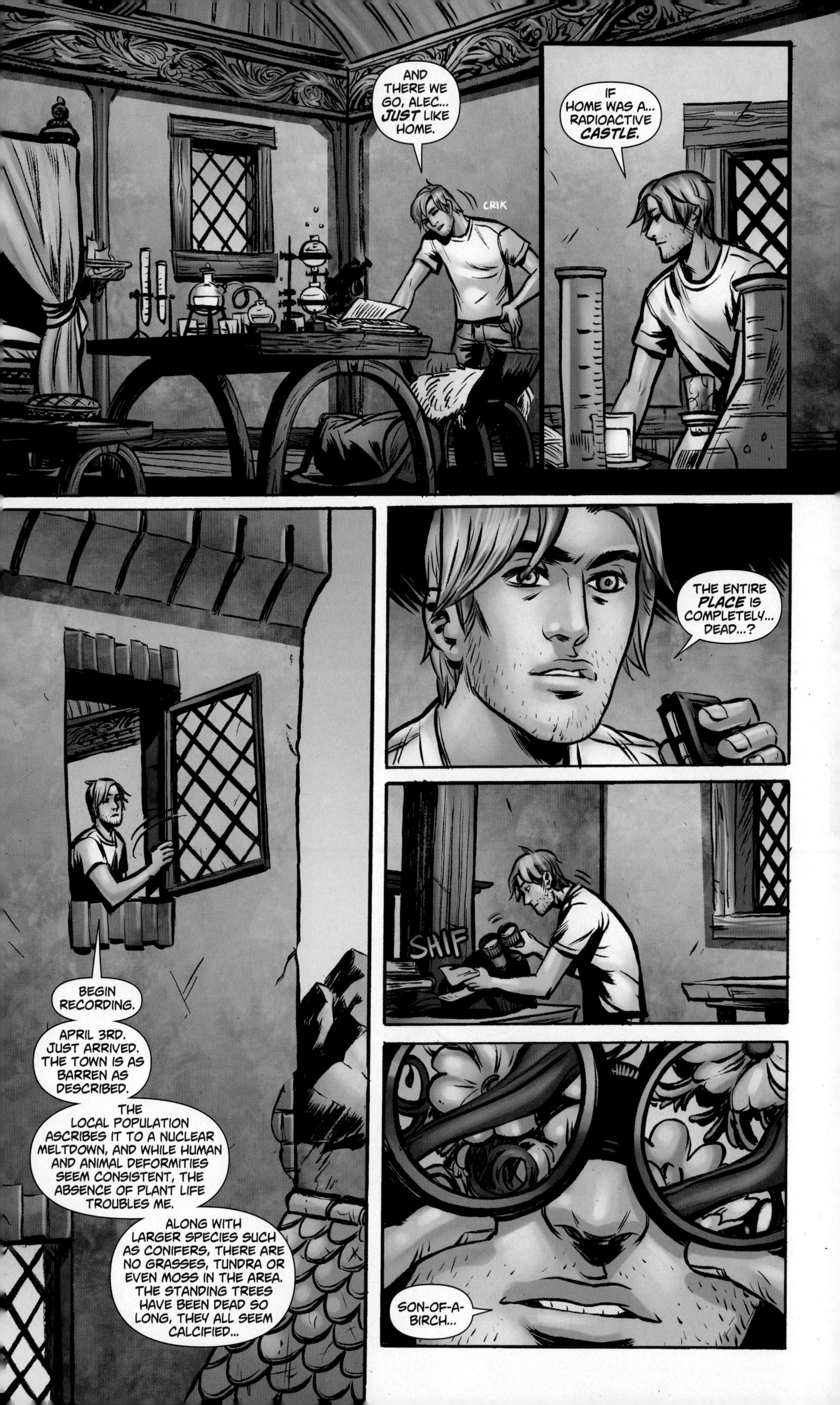
AND THERE WE GO, ALEC... JUST LIKE HOME.
CRIK
IF HOME WAS A... RADIOACTIVE CASTLE.
THE ENTIRE PLACE IS COMPLETELY... DEAD...?
BEGIN RECORDING.
APRIL 3RD. JUST ARRIVED. THE TOWN IS AS BARREN AS DESCRIBED.
THE LOCAL POPULATION ASCRIBES IT TO A NUCLEAR MELTDOWN, AND WHILE HUMAN AND ANIMAL DEFORMITIES SEEM CONSISTENT, THE ABSENCE OF PLANT LIFE TROUBLES ME.
ALONG WITH LARGER SPECIES SUCH AS CONIFERS, THERE ARE NO GRASSES, TUNDRA OR EVEN MOSS IN THE AREA. THE STANDING TREES HAVE BEEN DEAD SO LONG, THEY ALL SEEM CALCIFIED...
SHIF
SON-OF-A-BIRCH...

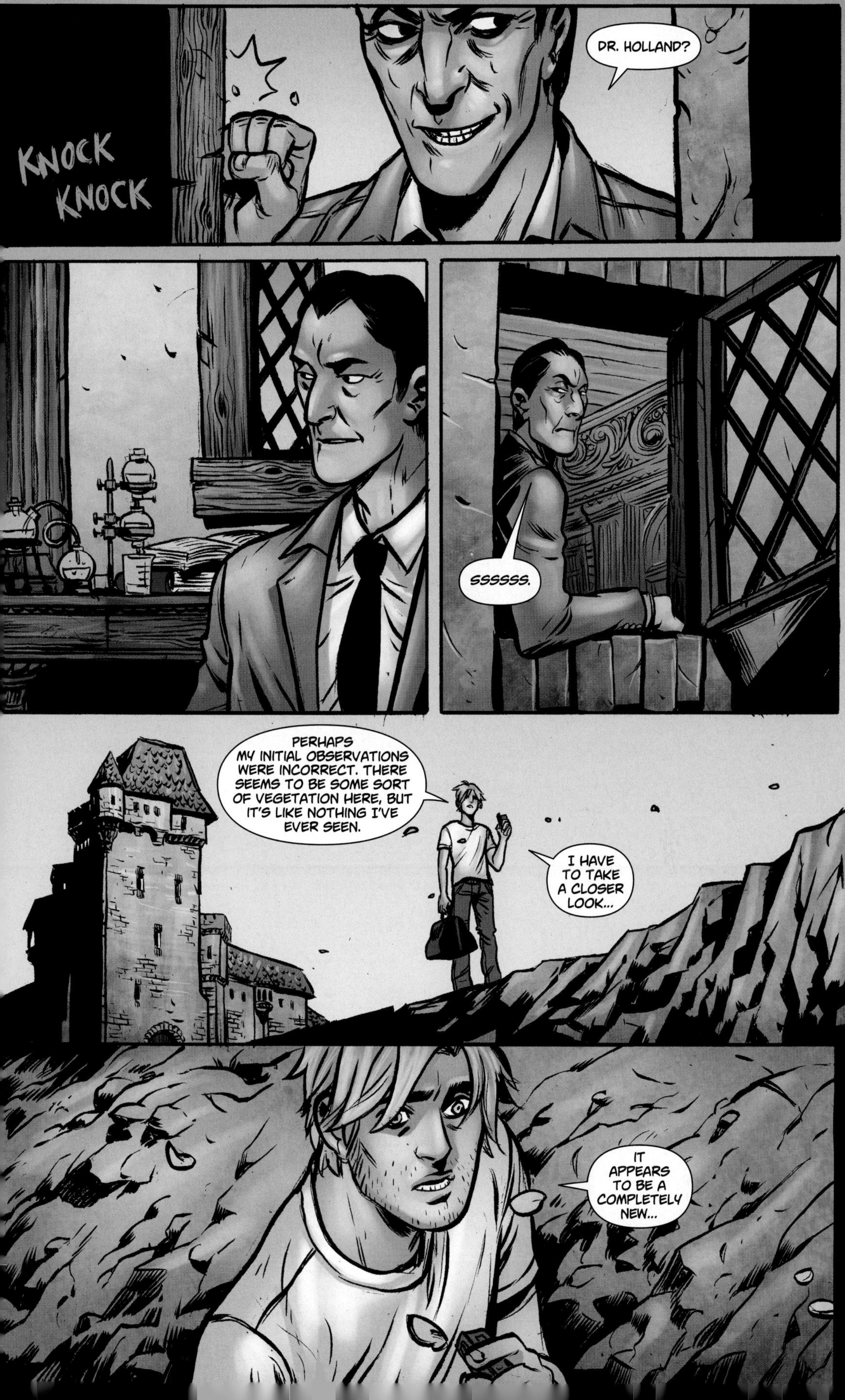
DR. HOLLAND?
KNOCK KNOCK
SSSSSS.
PERHAPS MY INITIAL OBSERVATIONS WERE INCORRECT. THERE SEEMS TO BE SOME SORT OF VEGETATION HERE, BUT IT'S LIKE NOTHING I'VE EVER SEEN.
I HAVE TO TAKE A CLOSER LOOK...
IT APPEARS TO BE A COMPLETELY NEW...

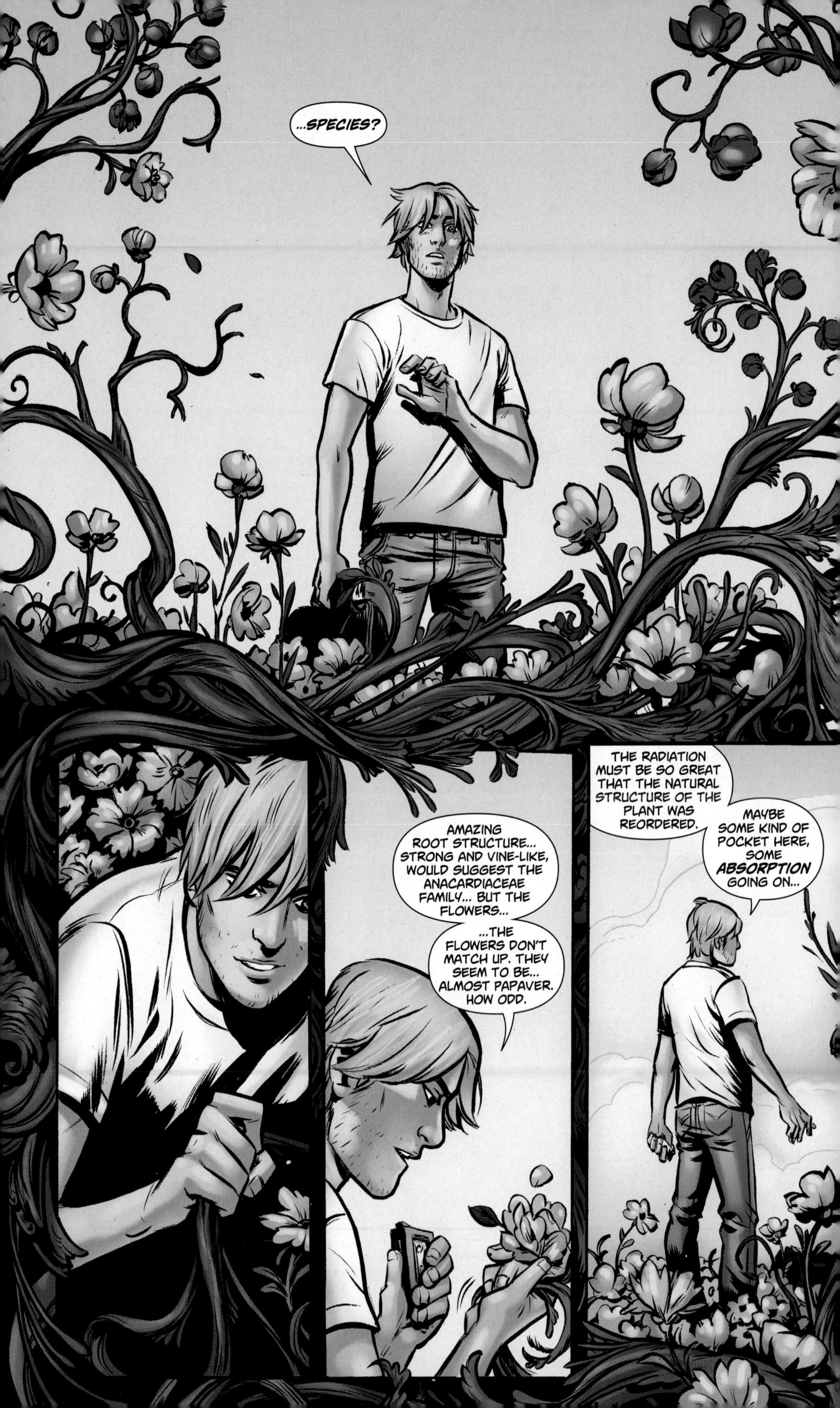
...SPECIES?
AMAZING ROOT STRUCTURE... STRONG AND VINE-LIKE, WOULD SUGGEST THE ANACARDIACEAE FAMILY... BUT THE FLOWERS...
...THE FLOWERS DON'T MATCH UP. THEY SEEM TO BE... ALMOST PAPAVER. HOW ODD.
THE RADIATION MUST BE SO GREAT THAT THE NATURAL STRUCTURE OF THE PLANT WAS REORDERED.
MAYBE SOME KIND OF POCKET HERE, SOME ABSORPTION GOING ON...

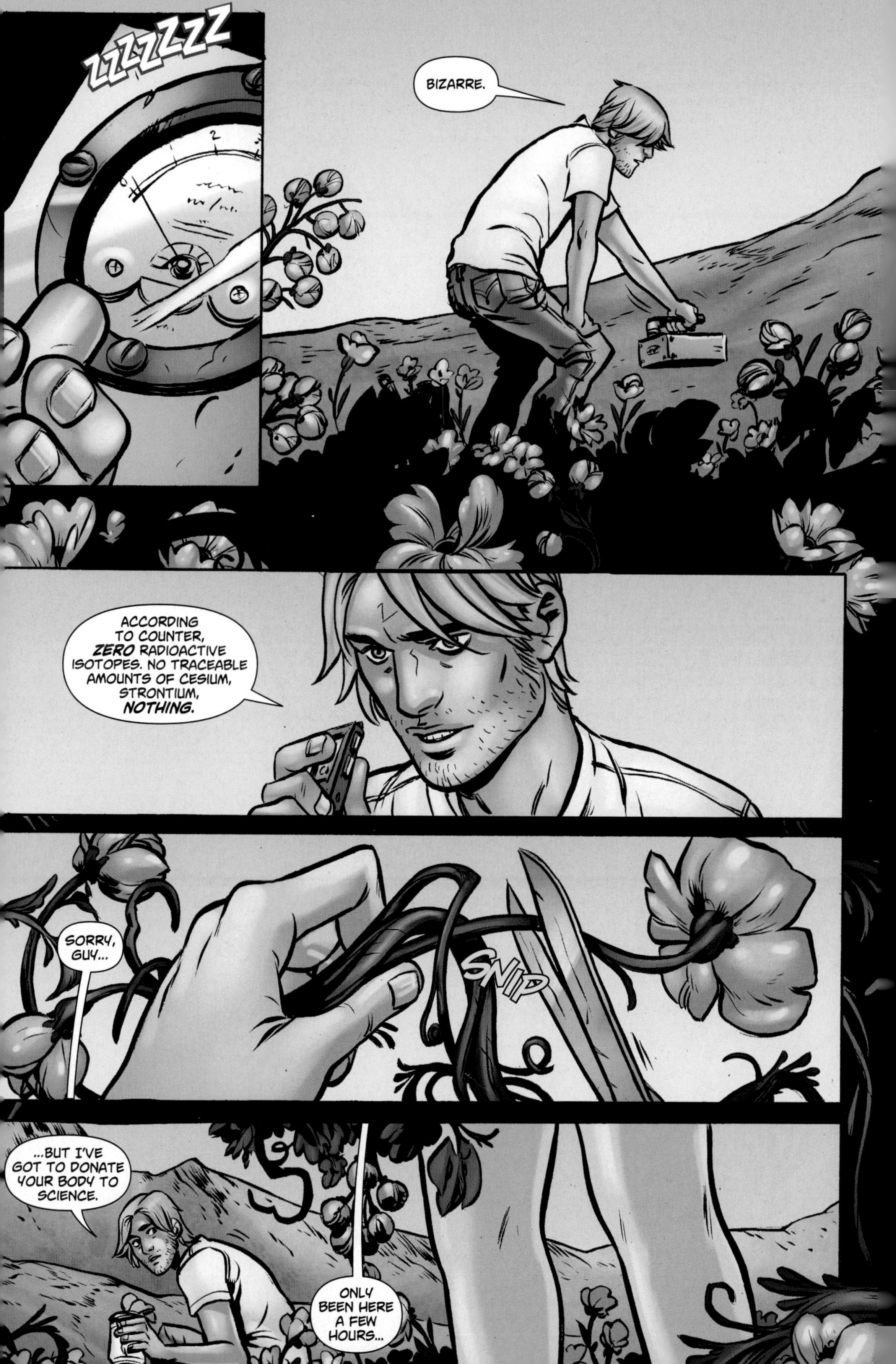
ZZZZZZZ
BIZARRE.
ACCORDING TO COUNTER, ZERO RADIOACTIVE ISOTOPES. NO TRACEABLE AMOUNTS OF CESIUM, STRONTIUM, NOTHING.
SORRY, GUY...
SNIP
...BUT I'VE GOT TO DONATE YOUR BODY TO SCIENCE.
ONLY BEEN HERE A FEW HOURS...

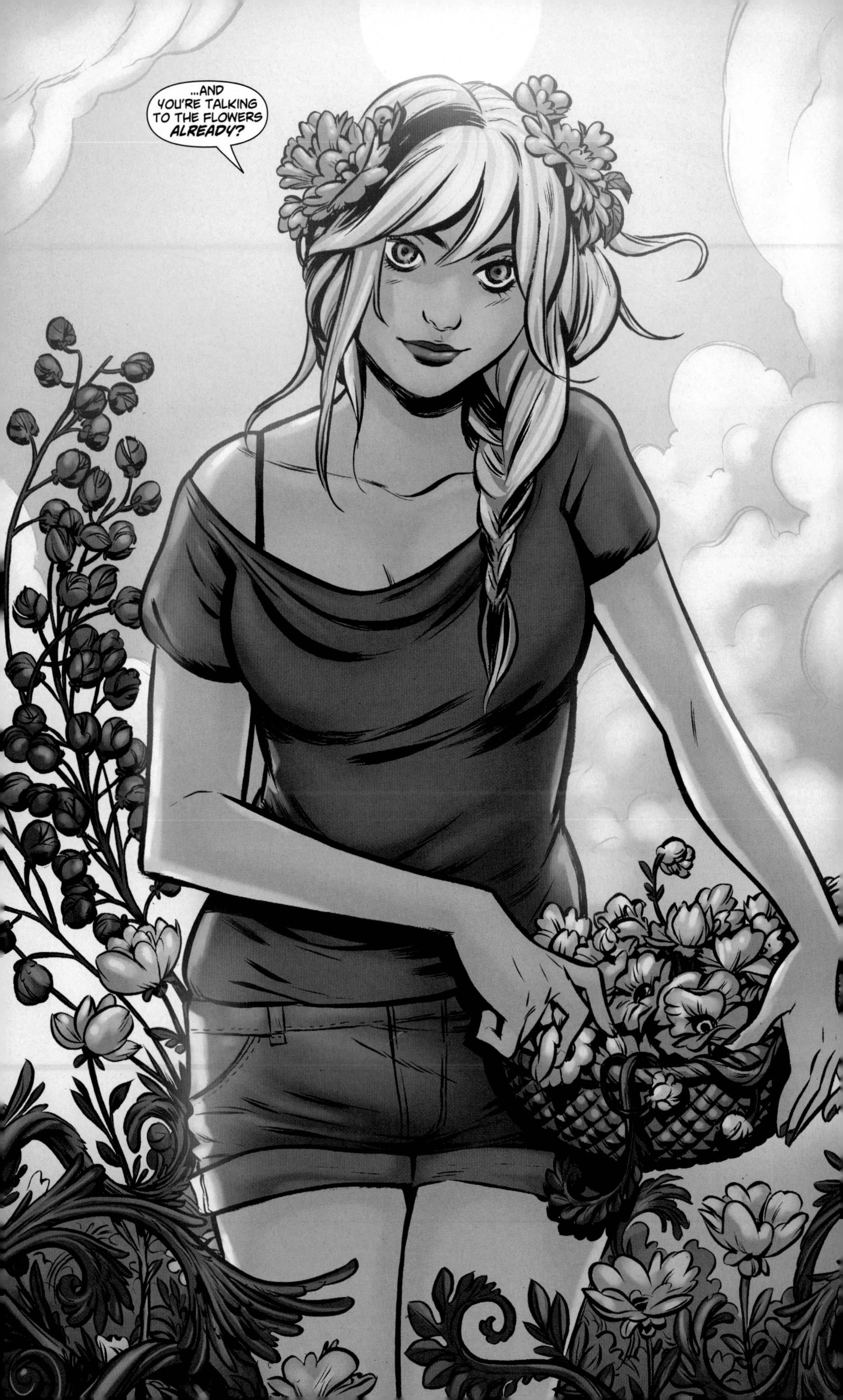
...AND YOU'RE TALKING TO THE FLOWERS *ALREADY?*

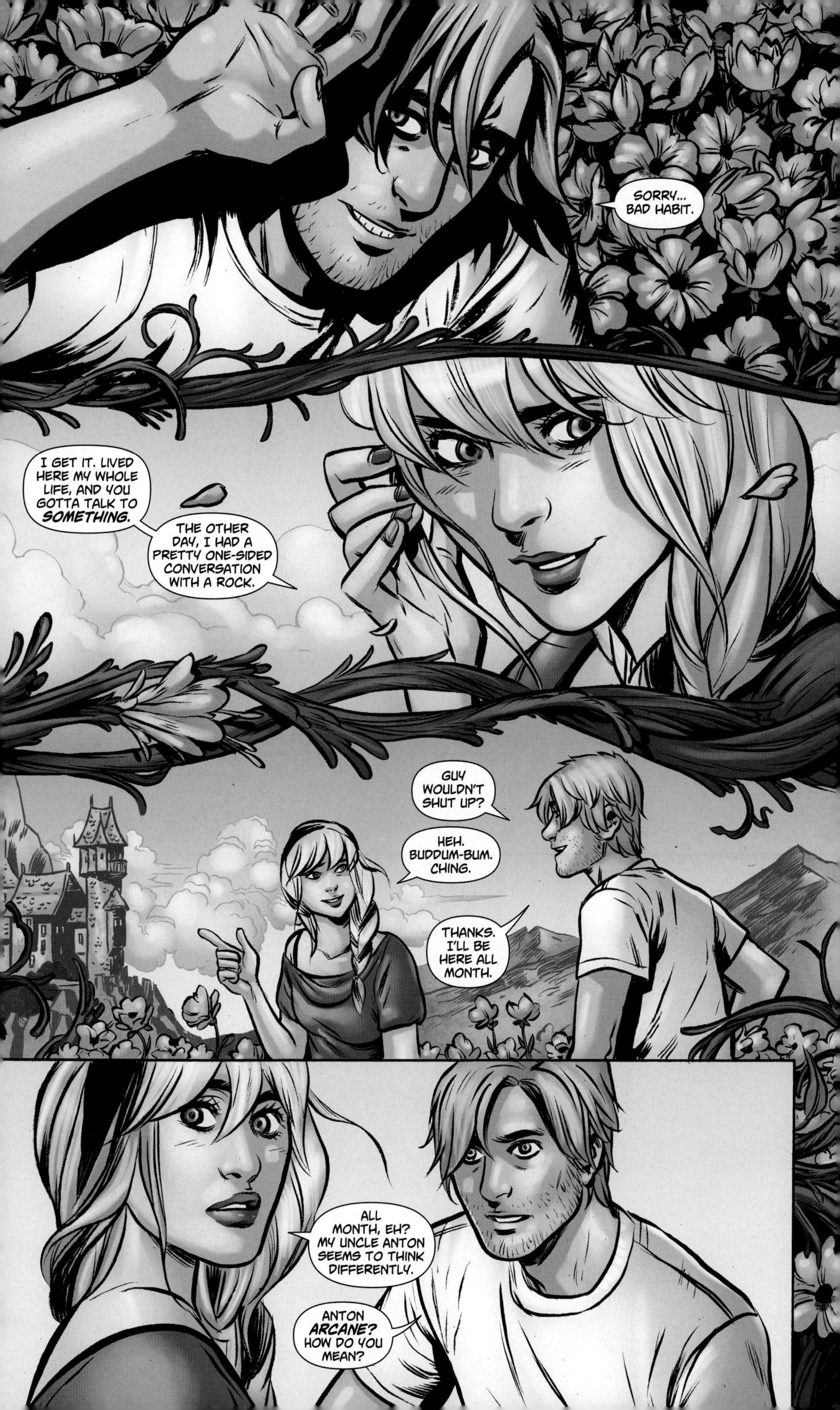

SORRY... BAD HABIT.
I GET IT. LIVED HERE MY WHOLE LIFE, AND YOU GOTTA TALK TO **SOMETHING**.
THE OTHER DAY, I HAD A PRETTY ONE-SIDED CONVERSATION WITH A ROCK.
GUY WOULDN'T SHUT UP?
HEH. BUDDUM-BUM. CHING.
THANKS. I'LL BE HERE ALL MONTH.
ALL MONTH, EH? MY UNCLE ANTON SEEMS TO THINK DIFFERENTLY.
ANTON **ARCANE?** HOW DO YOU MEAN?

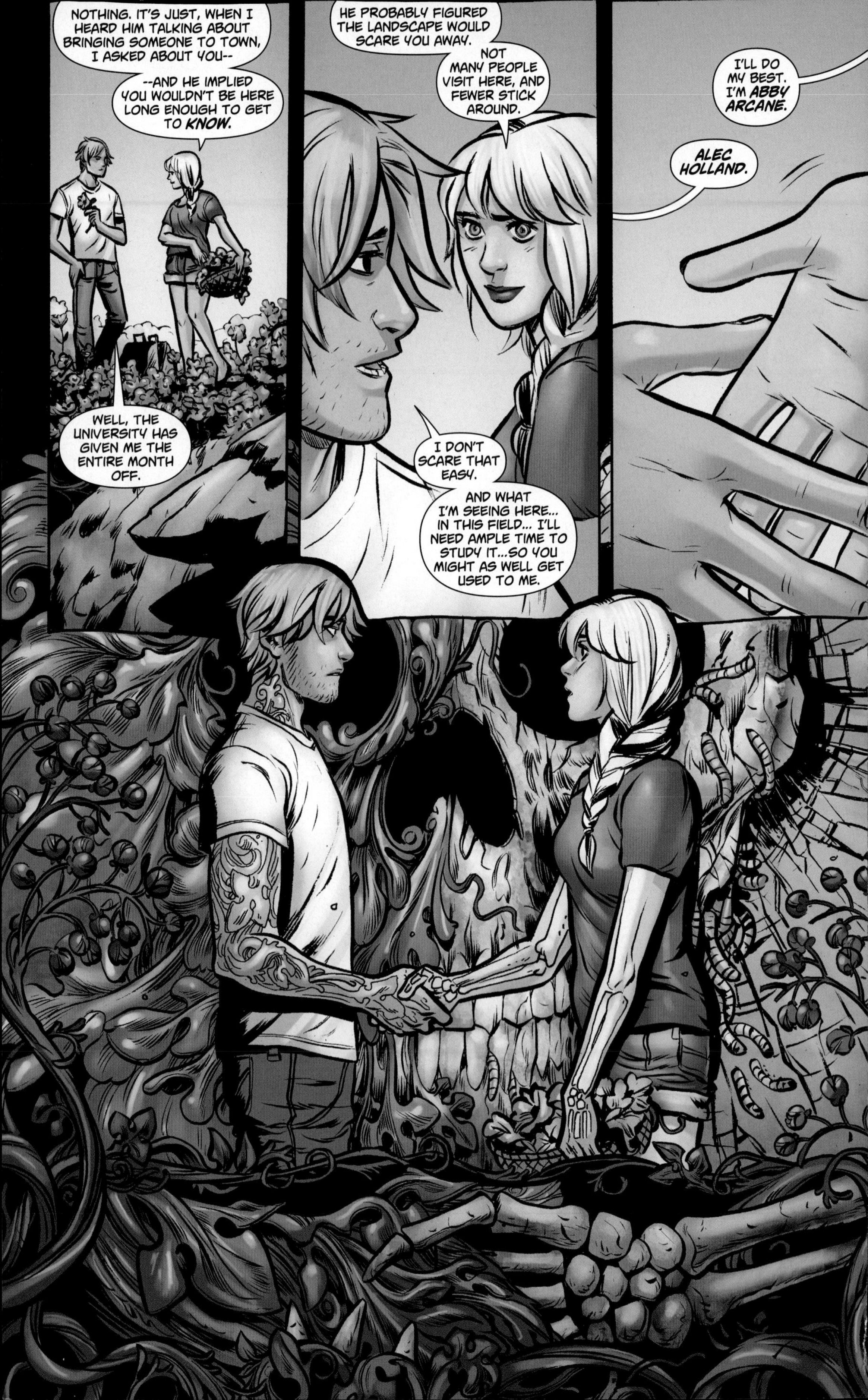

NOTHING. IT'S JUST, WHEN I HEARD HIM TALKING ABOUT BRINGING SOMEONE TO TOWN, I ASKED ABOUT YOU--
--AND HE IMPLIED YOU WOULDN'T BE HERE LONG ENOUGH TO GET TO KNOW.
WELL, THE UNIVERSITY HAS GIVEN ME THE ENTIRE MONTH OFF.
HE PROBABLY FIGURED THE LANDSCAPE WOULD SCARE YOU AWAY.
NOT MANY PEOPLE VISIT HERE, AND FEWER STICK AROUND.
I DON'T SCARE THAT EASY.
AND WHAT I'M SEEING HERE... IN THIS FIELD... I'LL NEED AMPLE TIME TO STUDY IT...SO YOU MIGHT AS WELL GET USED TO ME.
I'LL DO MY BEST. I'M ABBY ARCANE.
ALEC HOLLAND.

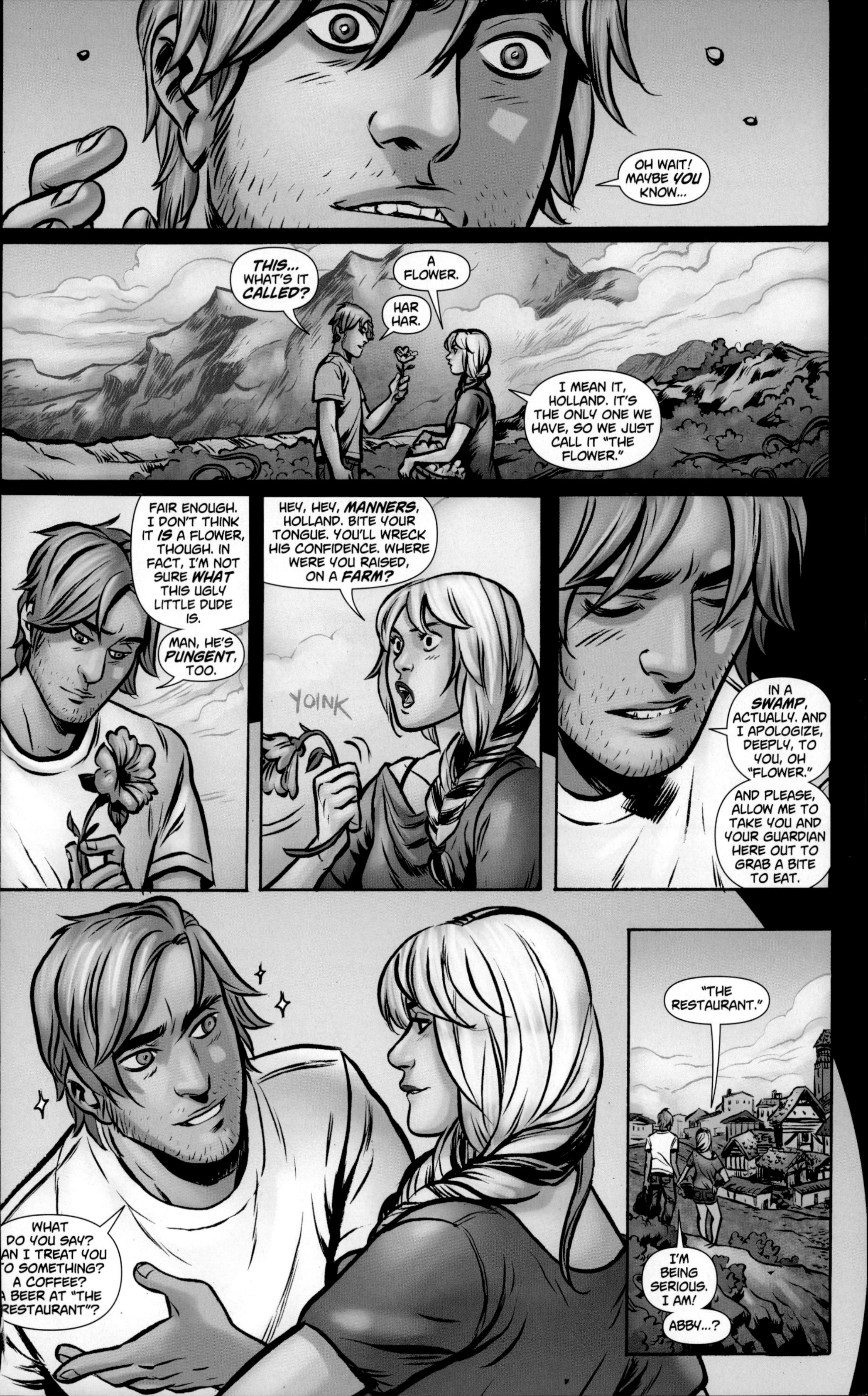
OH WAIT! MAYBE YOU KNOW...
THIS... WHAT'S IT CALLED?
A FLOWER.
HAR HAR.
I MEAN IT, HOLLAND. IT'S THE ONLY ONE WE HAVE, SO WE JUST CALL IT "THE FLOWER."
FAIR ENOUGH. I DON'T THINK IT IS A FLOWER, THOUGH. IN FACT, I'M NOT SURE WHAT THIS UGLY LITTLE DUDE IS.
MAN, HE'S PUNGENT, TOO.
HEY, HEY, MANNERS, HOLLAND. BITE YOUR TONGUE. YOU'LL WRECK HIS CONFIDENCE. WHERE WERE YOU RAISED, ON A FARM?
YOINK
IN A SWAMP, ACTUALLY. AND I APOLOGIZE, DEEPLY, TO YOU, OH "FLOWER."
AND PLEASE, ALLOW ME TO TAKE YOU AND YOUR GUARDIAN HERE OUT TO GRAB A BITE TO EAT.
WHAT DO YOU SAY? AN I TREAT YOU TO SOMETHING? A COFFEE? A BEER AT "THE RESTAURANT"?
"THE RESTAURANT."
I'M BEING SERIOUS. I AM!
ABBY...?

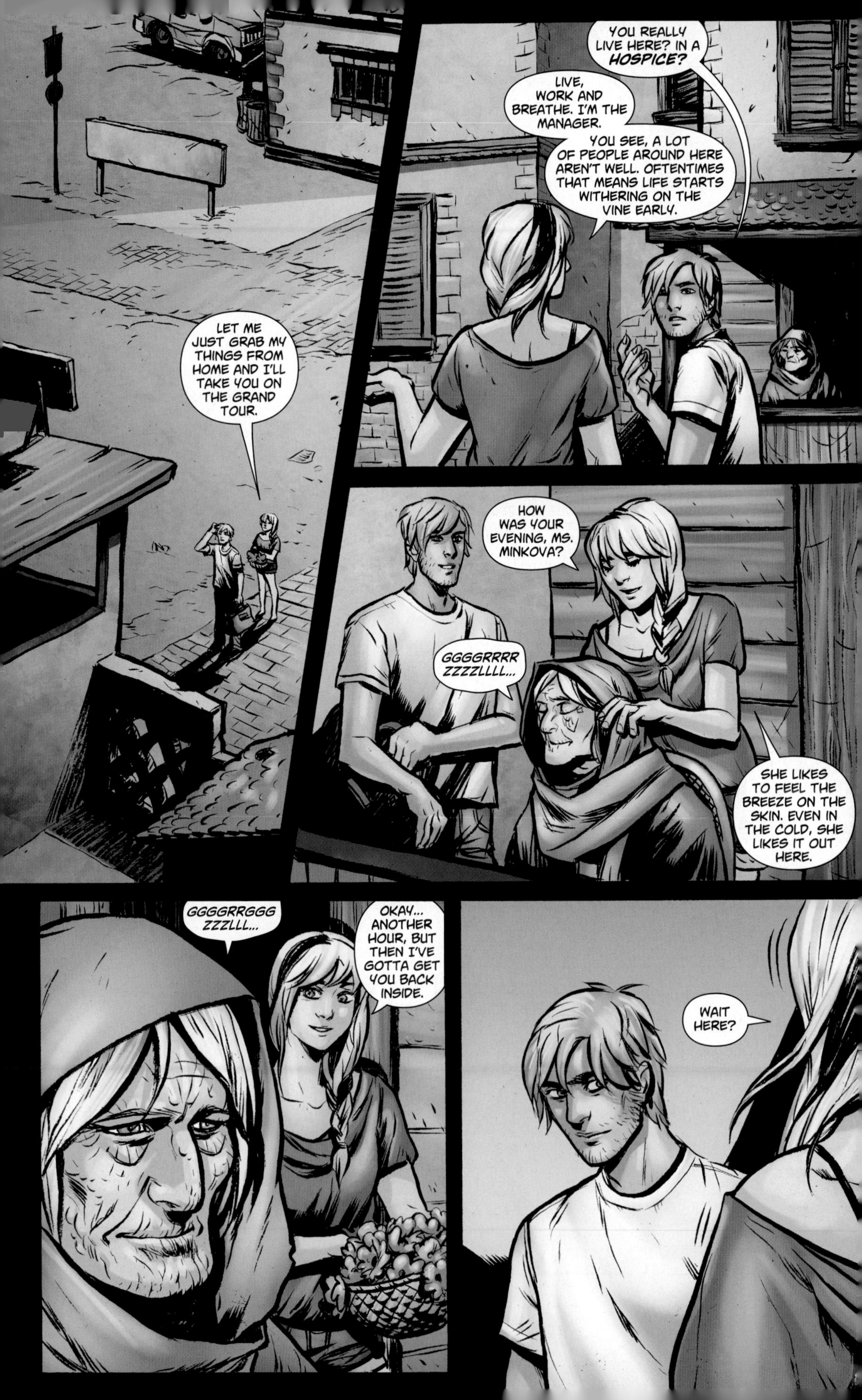
LET ME JUST GRAB MY THINGS FROM HOME AND I'LL TAKE YOU ON THE GRAND TOUR.
YOU REALLY LIVE HERE? IN A HOSPICE?
LIVE, WORK AND BREATHE. I'M THE MANAGER.
YOU SEE, A LOT OF PEOPLE AROUND HERE AREN'T WELL. OFTENTIMES THAT MEANS LIFE STARTS WITHERING ON THE VINE EARLY.
HOW WAS YOUR EVENING, MS. MINKOVA?
GGGGRRRR ZZZZLLLL...
SHE LIKES TO FEEL THE BREEZE ON THE SKIN. EVEN IN THE COLD, SHE LIKES IT OUT HERE.
GGGGRRGGG ZZZLLL...
OKAY... ANOTHER HOUR, BUT THEN I'VE GOTTA GET YOU BACK INSIDE.
WAIT HERE?

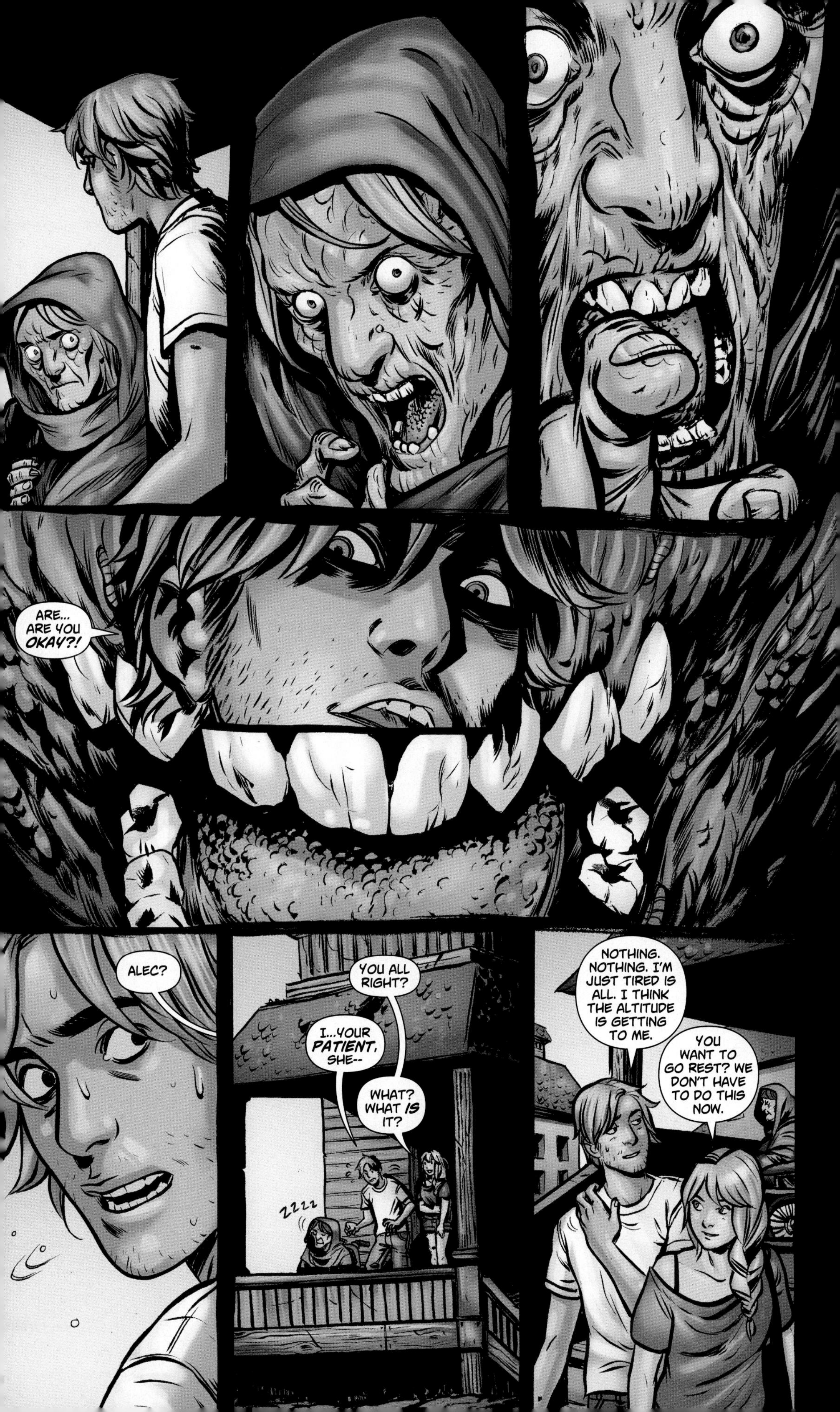
ARE... ARE YOU OKAY?!
ALEC?
YOU ALL RIGHT?
I...YOUR PATIENT, SHE--
WHAT? WHAT IS IT?
ZZZZ
NOTHING. NOTHING. I'M JUST TIRED IS ALL. I THINK THE ALTITUDE IS GETTING TO ME.
YOU WANT TO GO REST? WE DON'T HAVE TO DO THIS NOW.

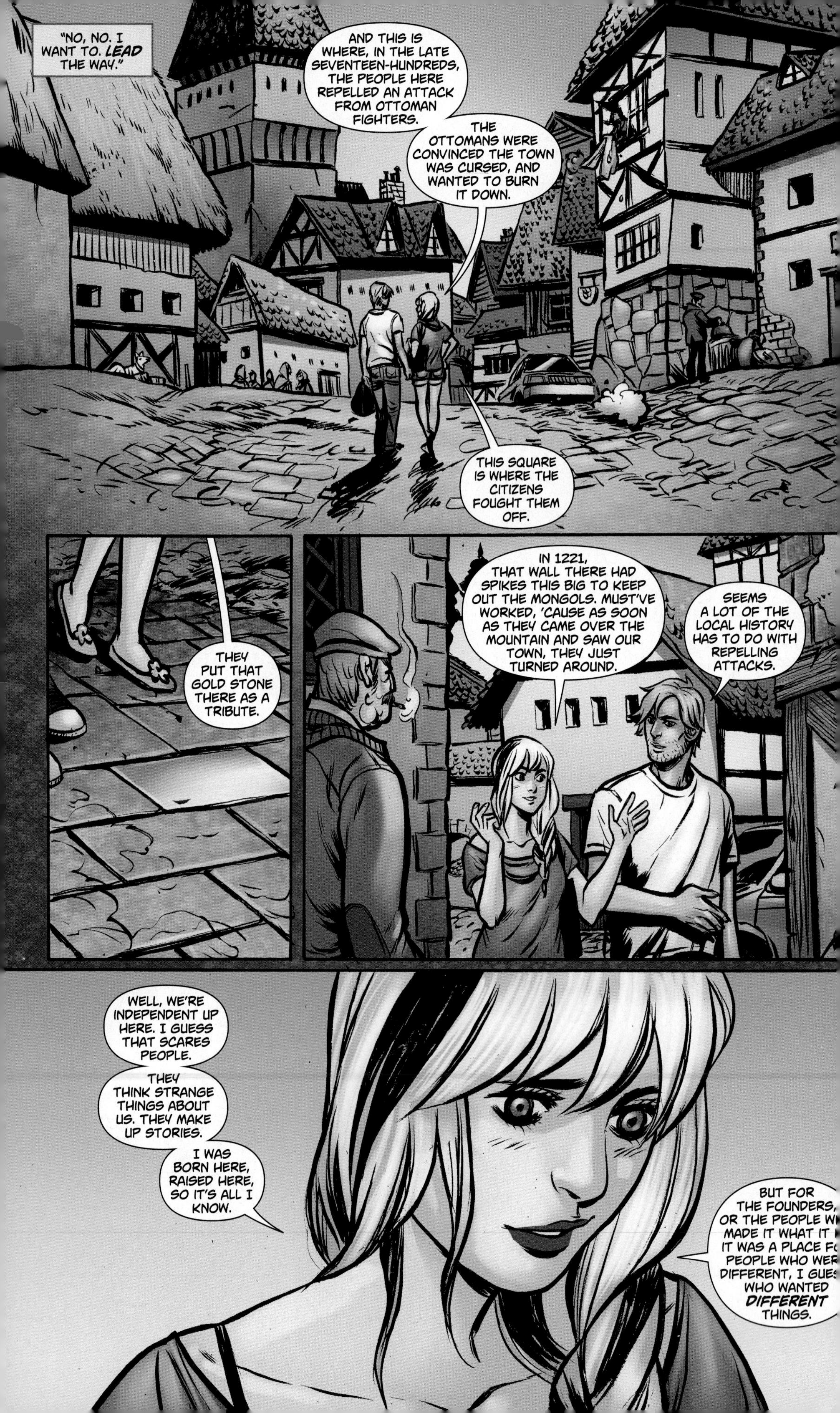
"NO, NO. I WANT TO. LEAD THE WAY."
AND THIS IS WHERE, IN THE LATE SEVENTEEN-HUNDREDS, THE PEOPLE HERE REPELLED AN ATTACK FROM OTTOMAN FIGHTERS.
THE OTTOMANS WERE CONVINCED THE TOWN WAS CURSED, AND WANTED TO BURN IT DOWN.
THIS SQUARE IS WHERE THE CITIZENS FOUGHT THEM OFF.
THEY PUT THAT GOLD STONE THERE AS A TRIBUTE.
IN 1221, THAT WALL THERE HAD SPIKES THIS BIG TO KEEP OUT THE MONGOLS. MUST'VE WORKED, 'CAUSE AS SOON AS THEY CAME OVER THE MOUNTAIN AND SAW OUR TOWN, THEY JUST TURNED AROUND.
SEEMS A LOT OF THE LOCAL HISTORY HAS TO DO WITH REPELLING ATTACKS.
WELL, WE'RE INDEPENDENT UP HERE. I GUESS THAT SCARES PEOPLE.
THEY THINK STRANGE THINGS ABOUT US. THEY MAKE UP STORIES.
I WAS BORN HERE, RAISED HERE, SO IT'S ALL I KNOW.
BUT FOR THE FOUNDERS, OR THE PEOPLE W MADE IT WHAT IT IT WAS A PLACE F PEOPLE WHO WER DIFFERENT, I GUES WHO WANTED DIFFERENT THINGS.

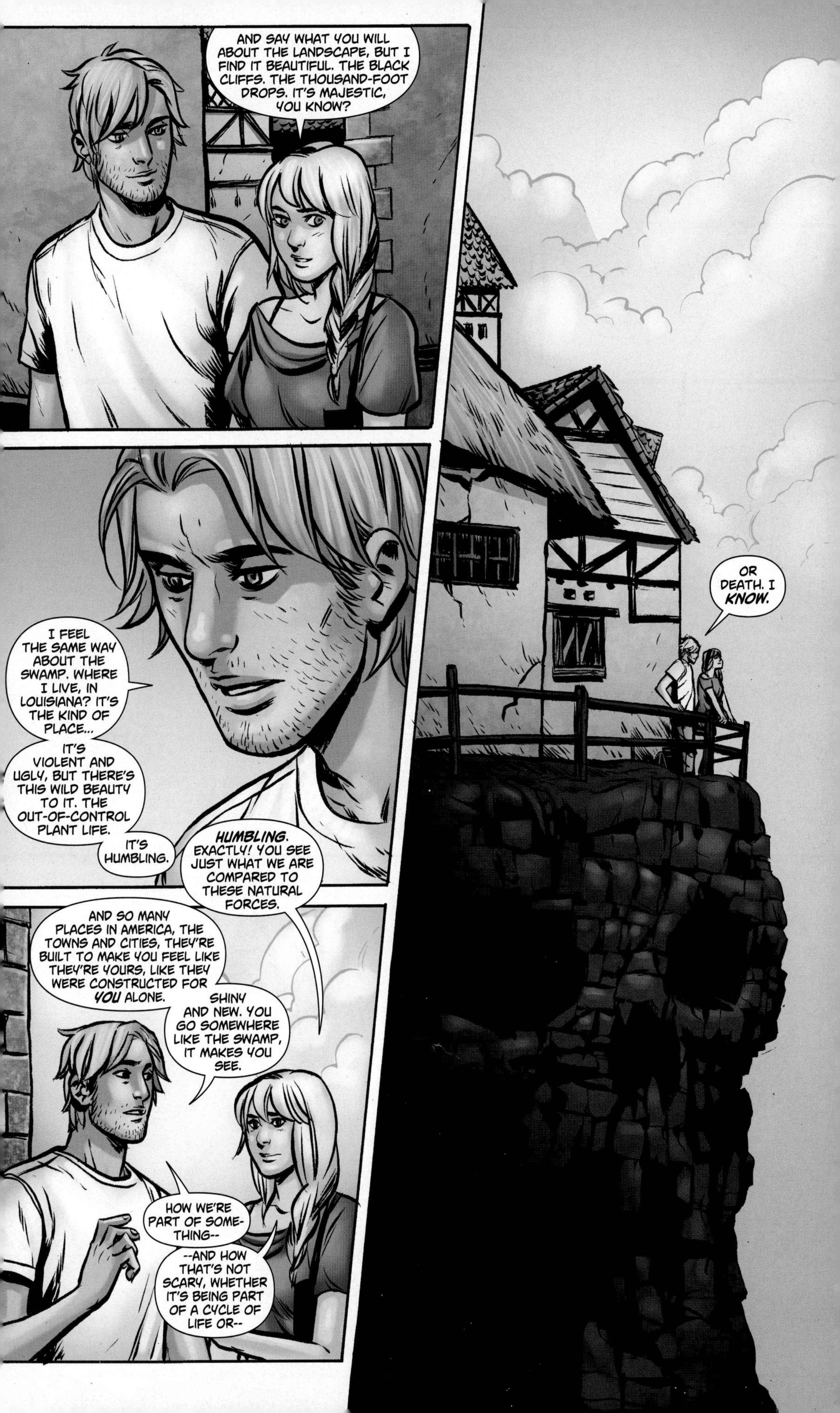
AND SAY WHAT YOU WILL ABOUT THE LANDSCAPE, BUT I FIND IT BEAUTIFUL. THE BLACK CLIFFS. THE THOUSAND-FOOT DROPS. IT'S MAJESTIC, YOU KNOW?
I FEEL THE SAME WAY ABOUT THE SWAMP. WHERE I LIVE, IN LOUISIANA? IT'S THE KIND OF PLACE...
IT'S VIOLENT AND UGLY, BUT THERE'S THIS WILD BEAUTY TO IT. THE OUT-OF-CONTROL PLANT LIFE.
IT'S HUMBLING.
HUMBLING. EXACTLY! YOU SEE JUST WHAT WE ARE COMPARED TO THESE NATURAL FORCES.
AND SO MANY PLACES IN AMERICA, THE TOWNS AND CITIES, THEY'RE BUILT TO MAKE YOU FEEL LIKE THEY'RE YOURS, LIKE THEY WERE CONSTRUCTED FOR *YOU* ALONE.
SHINY AND NEW. YOU GO SOMEWHERE LIKE THE SWAMP, IT MAKES YOU SEE.
HOW WE'RE PART OF SOME-THING--
--AND HOW THAT'S NOT SCARY, WHETHER IT'S BEING PART OF A CYCLE OF LIFE OR--
OR DEATH. I *KNOW*.

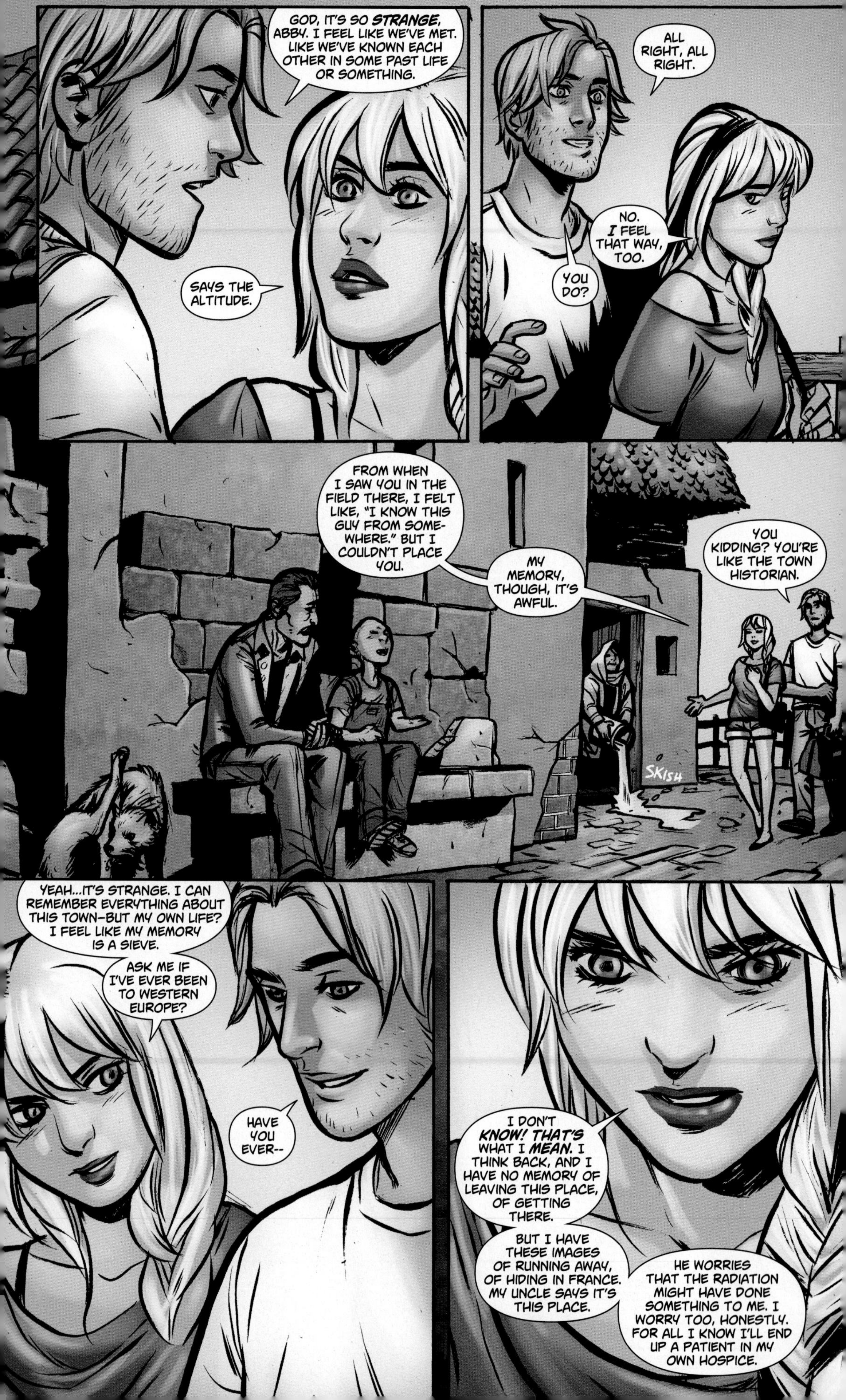
GOD, IT'S SO STRANGE, ABBY. I FEEL LIKE WE'VE MET. LIKE WE'VE KNOWN EACH OTHER IN SOME PAST LIFE OR SOMETHING.
SAYS THE ALTITUDE.
ALL RIGHT, ALL RIGHT.
NO. I FEEL THAT WAY, TOO.
YOU DO?
FROM WHEN I SAW YOU IN THE FIELD THERE, I FELT LIKE, "I KNOW THIS GUY FROM SOMEWHERE." BUT I COULDN'T PLACE YOU.
MY MEMORY, THOUGH, IT'S AWFUL.
YOU KIDDING? YOU'RE LIKE THE TOWN HISTORIAN.
SKIS4
YEAH...IT'S STRANGE. I CAN REMEMBER EVERYTHING ABOUT THIS TOWN--BUT MY OWN LIFE? I FEEL LIKE MY MEMORY IS A SIEVE.
ASK ME IF I'VE EVER BEEN TO WESTERN EUROPE?
HAVE YOU EVER--
I DON'T KNOW! THAT'S WHAT I MEAN. I THINK BACK, AND I HAVE NO MEMORY OF LEAVING THIS PLACE, OF GETTING THERE.
BUT I HAVE THESE IMAGES OF RUNNING AWAY, OF HIDING IN FRANCE. MY UNCLE SAYS IT'S THIS PLACE.
HE WORRIES THAT THE RADIATION MIGHT HAVE DONE SOMETHING TO ME. I WORRY TOO, HONESTLY. FOR ALL I KNOW I'LL END UP A PATIENT IN MY OWN HOSPICE.

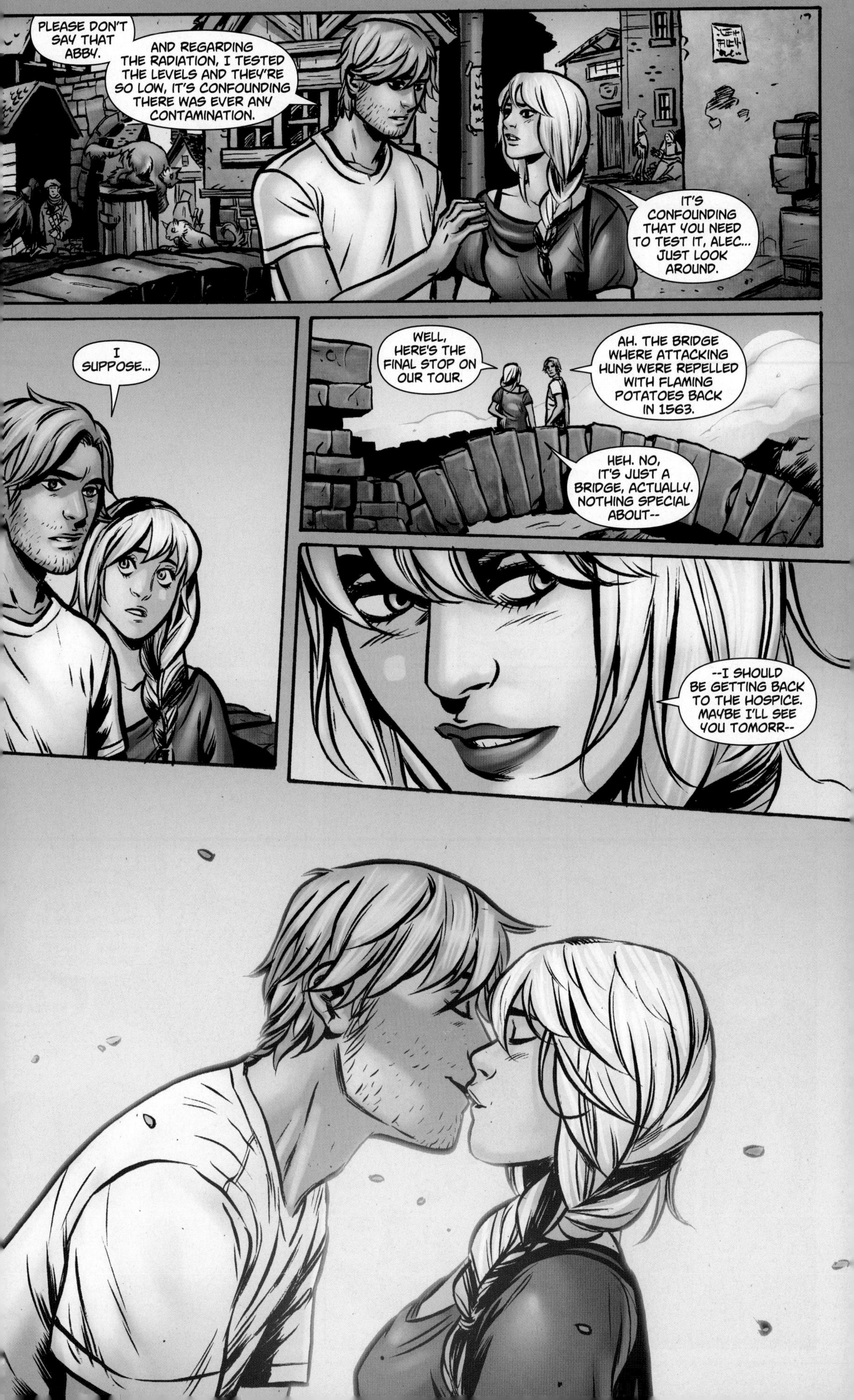
PLEASE DON'T SAY THAT ABBY.
AND REGARDING THE RADIATION, I TESTED THE LEVELS AND THEY'RE SO LOW, IT'S CONFOUNDING THERE WAS EVER ANY CONTAMINATION.
IT'S CONFOUNDING THAT YOU NEED TO TEST IT, ALEC... JUST LOOK AROUND.
I SUPPOSE...
WELL, HERE'S THE FINAL STOP ON OUR TOUR.
AH. THE BRIDGE WHERE ATTACKING HUNS WERE REPELLED WITH FLAMING POTATOES BACK IN 1563.
HEH. NO, IT'S JUST A BRIDGE, ACTUALLY. NOTHING SPECIAL ABOUT--
--I SHOULD BE GETTING BACK TO THE HOSPICE. MAYBE I'LL SEE YOU TOMORR--

...OW... WOW! YOU'RE DEFINITELY THE BEST KISSER IN TOWN.

HAVING ALL MY TEETH PROBABLY DOESN'T HURT.

I'D LIKE TO SEE THE SWAMP WHERE YOU LIVE. MAYBE EAT SOME CRAWFISH GUMBO. WRESTLE AN ALLIGATOR.

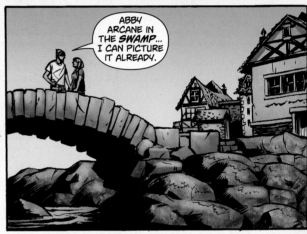

ABBY ARCANE IN THE *SWAMP*... I CAN PICTURE IT ALREADY.

OR BETTER YET, MAYBE WE CAN BRING A LITTLE OF THE SWAMP *HERE*.

HOW'S THAT?

IT'S CALLED FOXGLOVE.

IT'S ONE OF THE MOST RESILIENT FLOWERS ON EARTH. IT CAN GROW JUST ABOUT ANYWHERE. I BROUGHT A LOT OF IT.

SHIF

SO... ASSUMING YOU REMEMBER ME IN THE MORNING, CAN I TAKE YOU TO BREAKFAST?

IF I REMEMBER...

WELL...

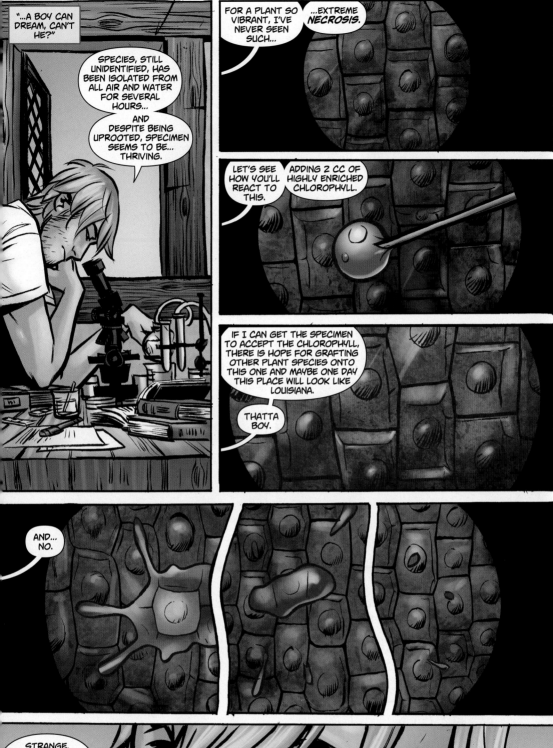

"...A BOY CAN DREAM, CAN'T HE?"

SPECIES, STILL UNIDENTIFIED, HAS BEEN ISOLATED FROM ALL AIR AND WATER FOR SEVERAL HOURS...

AND DESPITE BEING UPROOTED, SPECIMEN SEEMS TO BE... THRIVING.

FOR A PLANT SO VIBRANT, I'VE NEVER SEEN SUCH...

...EXTREME *NECROSIS*.

LET'S SEE HOW YOU'LL REACT TO THIS.

ADDING 2 CC OF HIGHLY ENRICHED CHLOROPHYLL.

IF I CAN GET THE SPECIMEN TO ACCEPT THE CHLOROPHYLL, THERE IS HOPE FOR GRAFTING OTHER PLANT SPECIES ONTO THIS ONE AND MAYBE ONE DAY THIS PLACE WILL LOOK LIKE LOUISIANA.

THATTA BOY.

AND... NO.

STRANGE. THE CELLS FEND OFF CHLOROPHYLL LIKE IT'S A DISEASE. WHAT THE HELL IS THIS PLANT?

MAYBE IT'S NOT A *PLANT*.

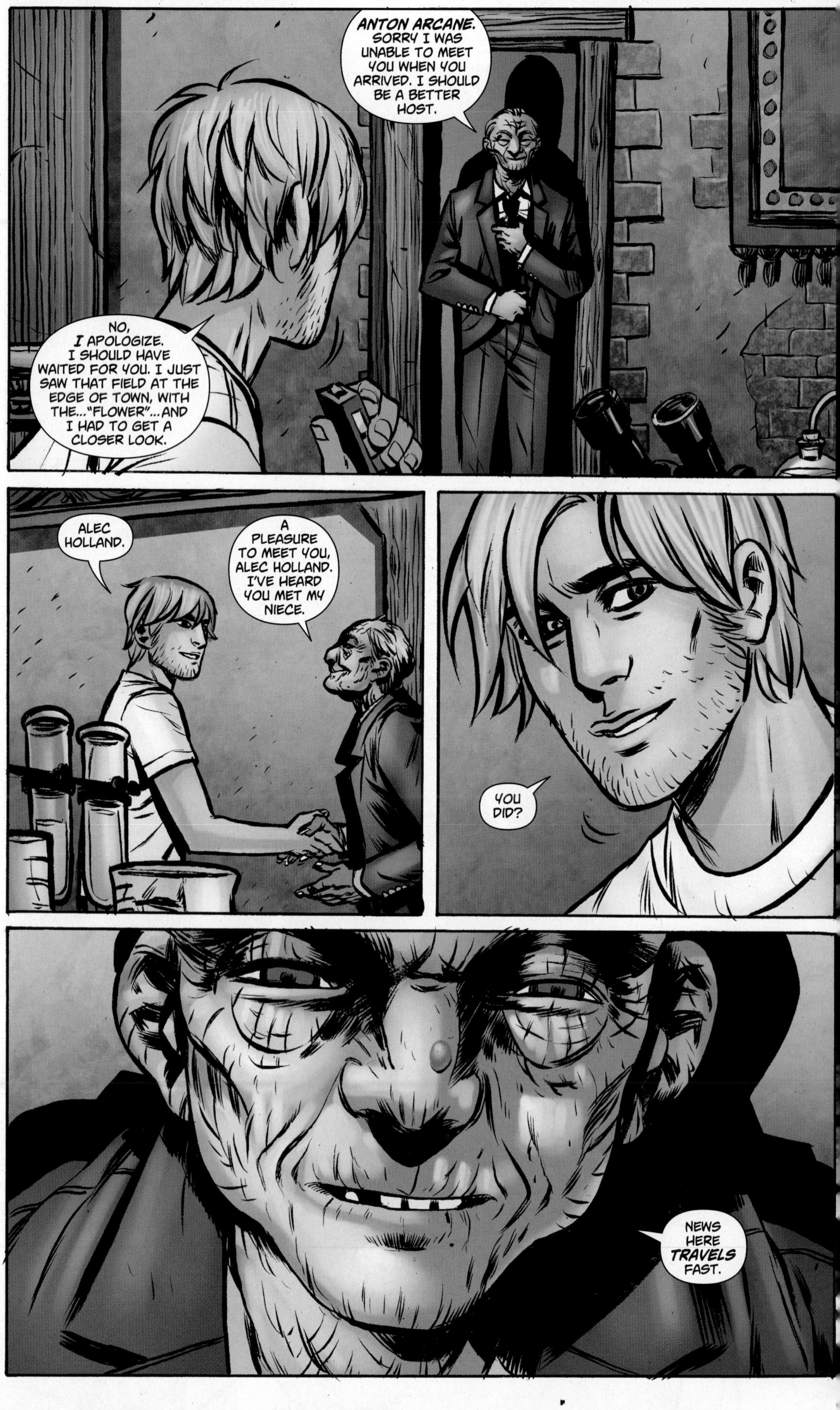
ANTON ARCANE. SORRY I WAS UNABLE TO MEET YOU WHEN YOU ARRIVED. I SHOULD BE A BETTER HOST.
NO, I APOLOGIZE. I SHOULD HAVE WAITED FOR YOU. I JUST SAW THAT FIELD AT THE EDGE OF TOWN, WITH THE..."FLOWER"...AND I HAD TO GET A CLOSER LOOK.
ALEC HOLLAND.
A PLEASURE TO MEET YOU, ALEC HOLLAND. I'VE HEARD YOU MET MY NIECE.
YOU DID?
NEWS HERE TRAVELS FAST.

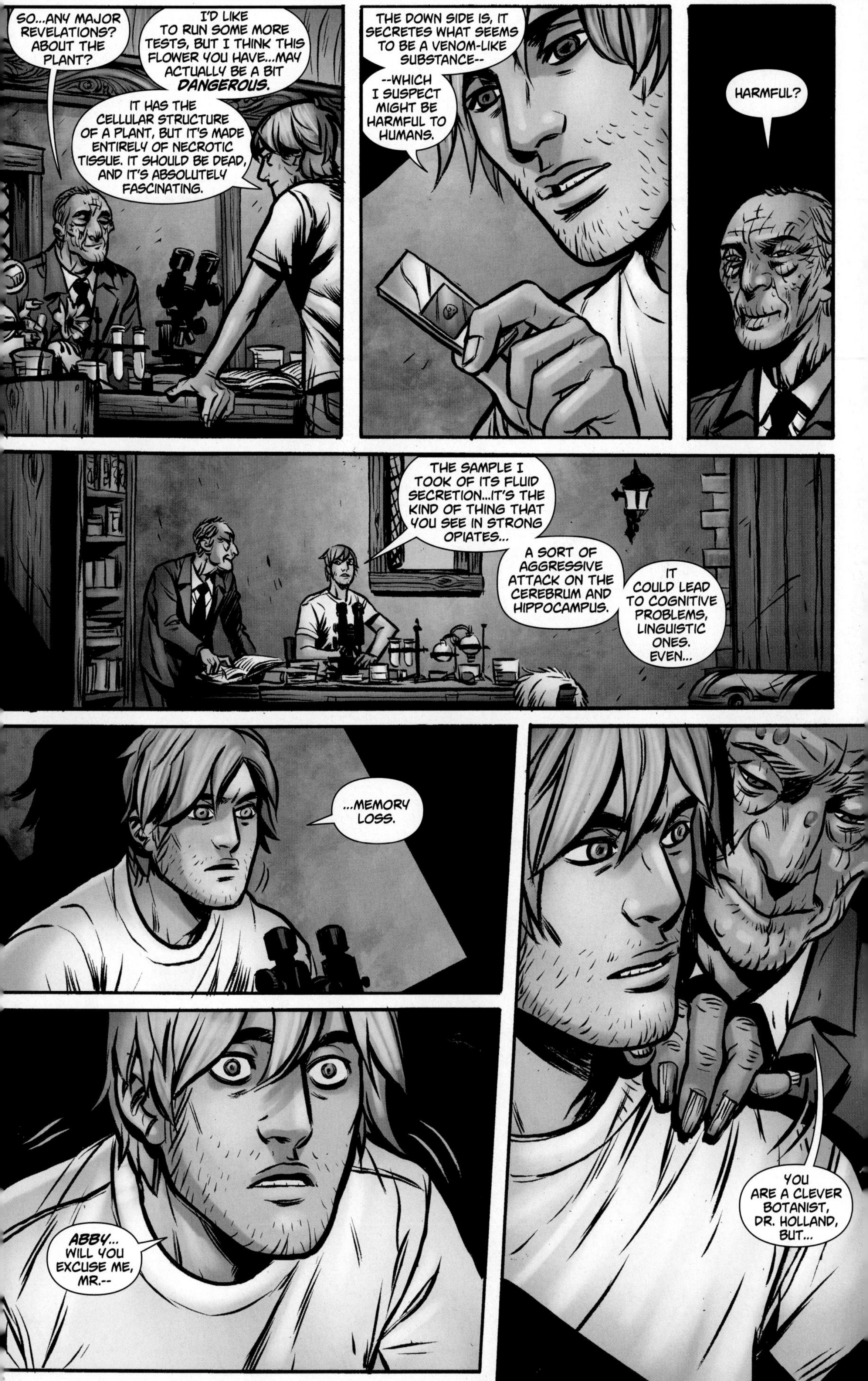
SO...ANY MAJOR REVELATIONS? ABOUT THE PLANT?
I'D LIKE TO RUN SOME MORE TESTS, BUT I THINK THIS FLOWER YOU HAVE...MAY ACTUALLY BE A BIT **DANGEROUS.**
IT HAS THE CELLULAR STRUCTURE OF A PLANT, BUT IT'S MADE ENTIRELY OF NECROTIC TISSUE. IT SHOULD BE DEAD, AND IT'S ABSOLUTELY FASCINATING.
THE DOWN SIDE IS, IT SECRETES WHAT SEEMS TO BE A VENOM-LIKE SUBSTANCE--
--WHICH I SUSPECT MIGHT BE HARMFUL TO HUMANS.
HARMFUL?
THE SAMPLE I TOOK OF ITS FLUID SECRETION...IT'S THE KIND OF THING THAT YOU SEE IN STRONG OPIATES...
A SORT OF AGGRESSIVE ATTACK ON THE CEREBRUM AND HIPPOCAMPUS.
IT COULD LEAD TO COGNITIVE PROBLEMS, LINGUISTIC ONES. EVEN...
...MEMORY LOSS.
ABBY... WILL YOU EXCUSE ME, MR.--
YOU ARE A CLEVER BOTANIST, DR. HOLLAND, BUT...

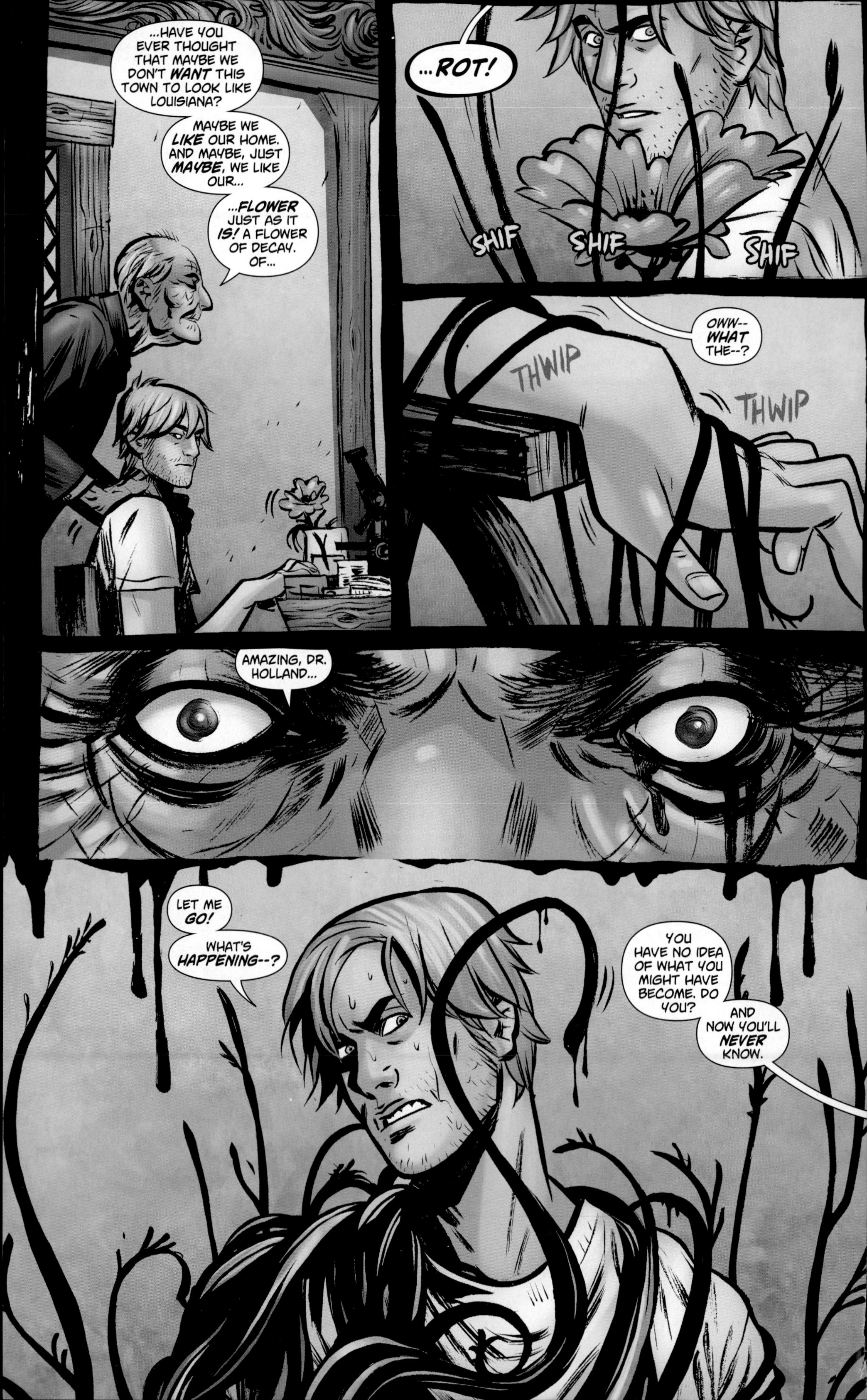
...HAVE YOU EVER THOUGHT THAT MAYBE WE DON'T WANT THIS TOWN TO LOOK LIKE LOUISIANA?
MAYBE WE LIKE OUR HOME. AND MAYBE, JUST MAYBE, WE LIKE OUR...
...FLOWER JUST AS IT IS! A FLOWER OF DECAY. OF...
...ROT!
SHIF
SHIF
SHIF
OWW--WHAT THE--?
THWIP
THWIP
AMAZING, DR. HOLLAND...
LET ME GO!
WHAT'S HAPPENING--?
YOU HAVE NO IDEA OF WHAT YOU MIGHT HAVE BECOME. DO YOU?
AND NOW YOU'LL NEVER KNOW.

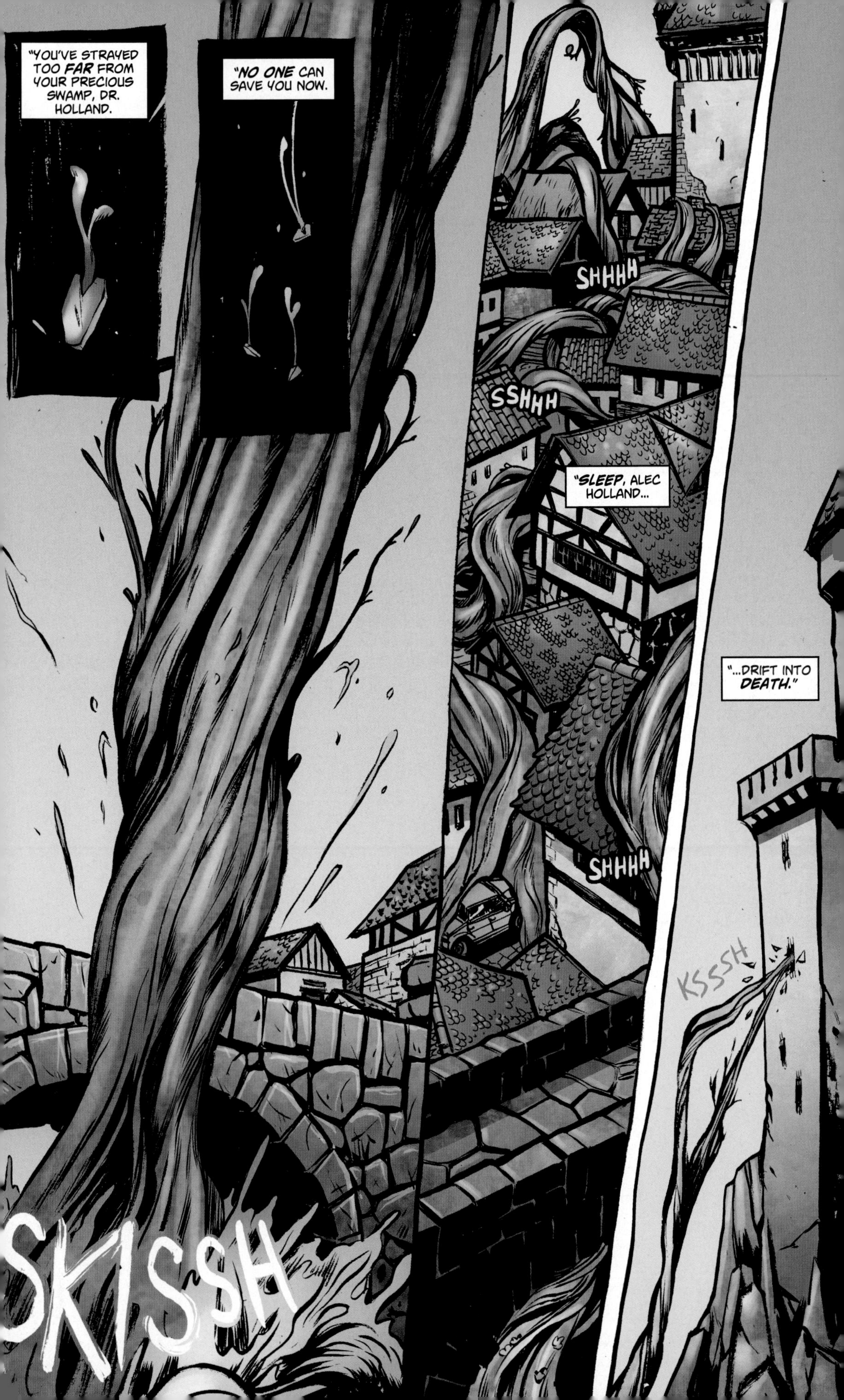
"YOU'VE STRAYED TOO FAR FROM YOUR PRECIOUS SWAMP, DR. HOLLAND.
"NO ONE CAN SAVE YOU NOW.
SHHHH
SSHHH
"SLEEP, ALEC HOLLAND...
SHHHH
"...DRIFT INTO DEATH."
KSSSH
SKISSH

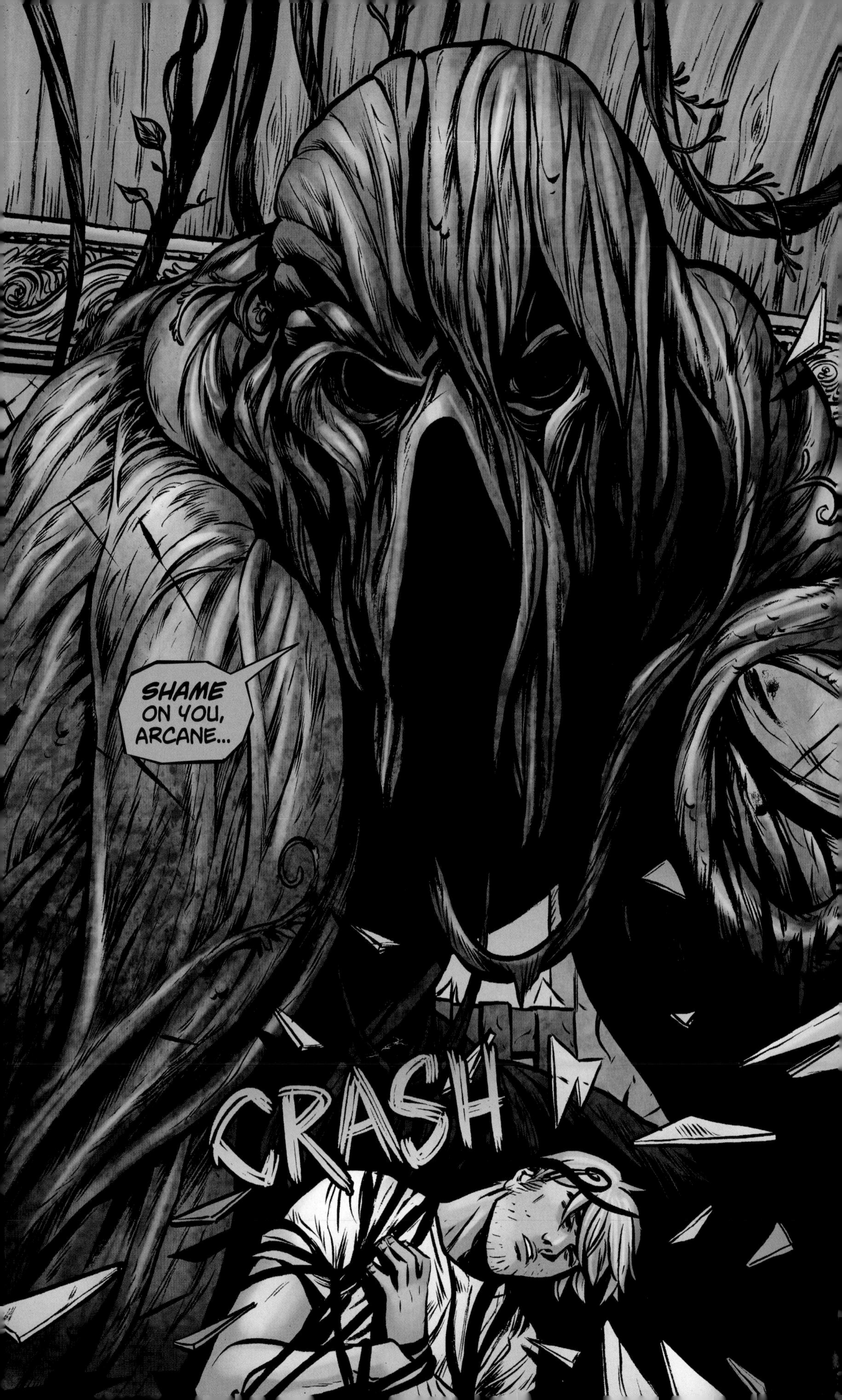
SHAME ON YOU, ARCANE...
CRASH

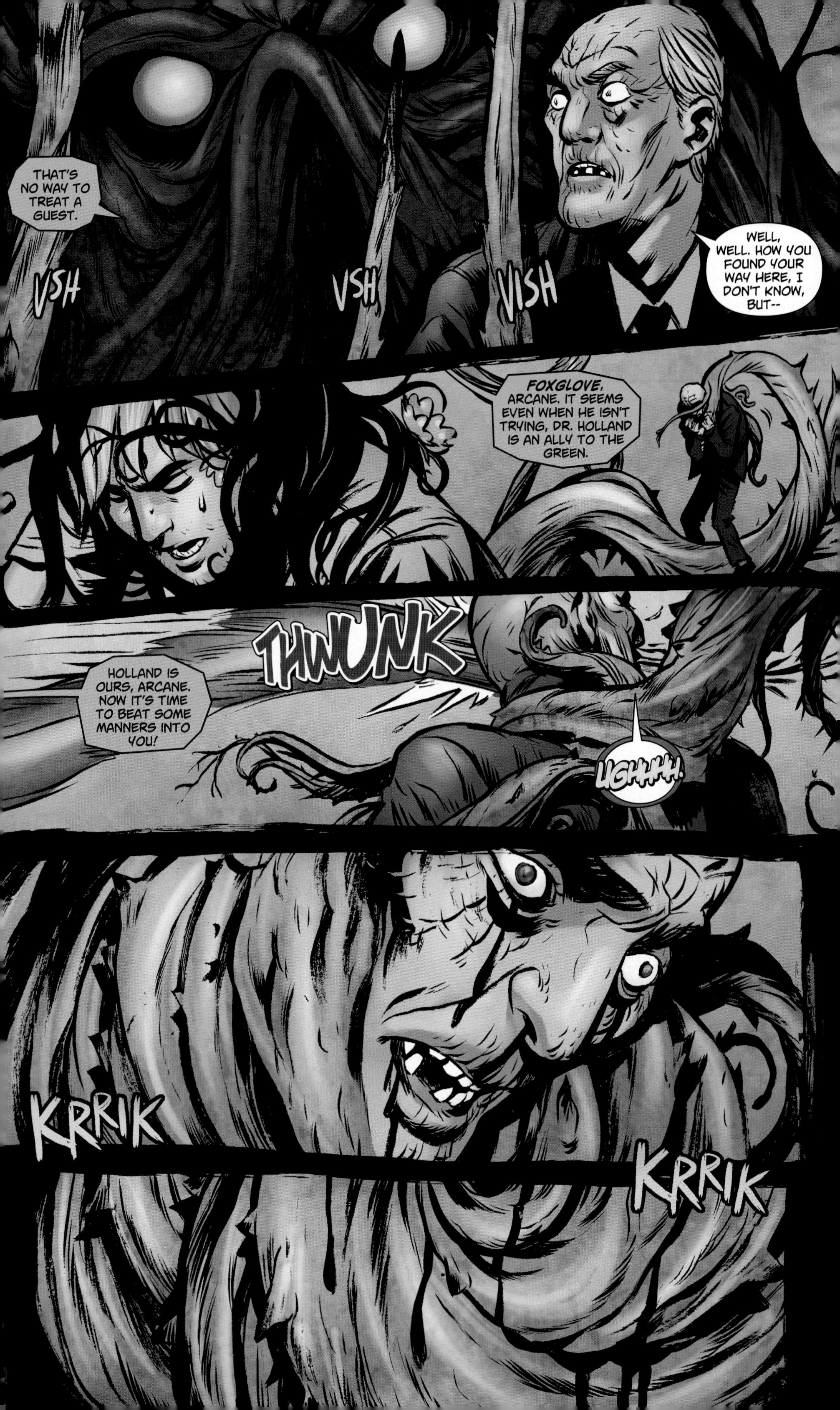
THAT'S NO WAY TO TREAT A GUEST.
WELL, WELL. HOW YOU FOUND YOUR WAY HERE, I DON'T KNOW, BUT--
VSH
VSH
VISH
FOXGLOVE, ARCANE. IT SEEMS EVEN WHEN HE ISN'T TRYING, DR. HOLLAND IS AN ALLY TO THE GREEN.
THWUNK
HOLLAND IS OURS, ARCANE. NOW IT'S TIME TO BEAT SOME MANNERS INTO YOU!
UGHHHH.
KRRIK
KRRIK

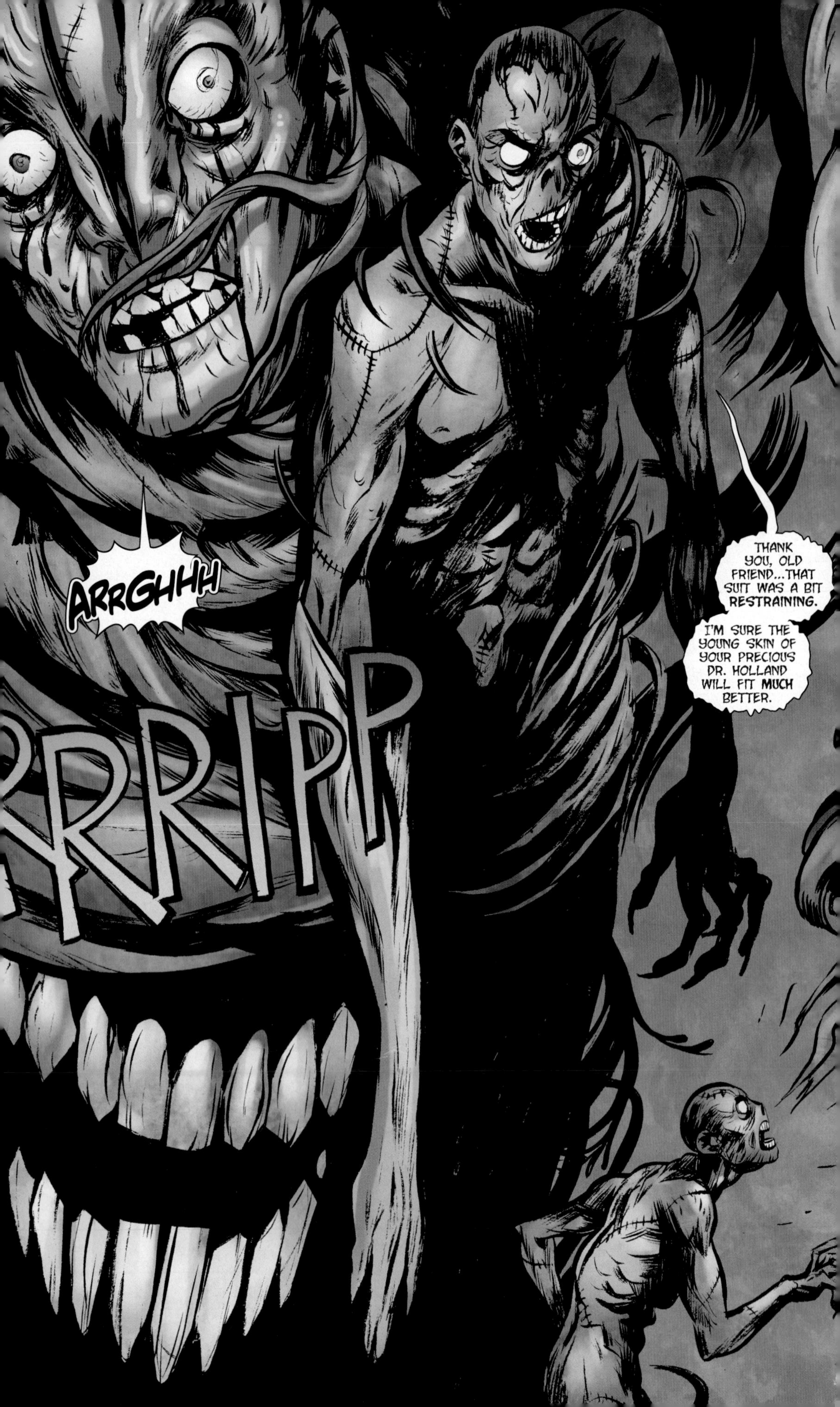
ARRGHHH
RRRIPP
THANK YOU, OLD FRIEND...THAT SUIT WAS A BIT RESTRAINING.
I'M SURE THE YOUNG SKIN OF YOUR PRECIOUS DR. HOLLAND WILL FIT MUCH BETTER.

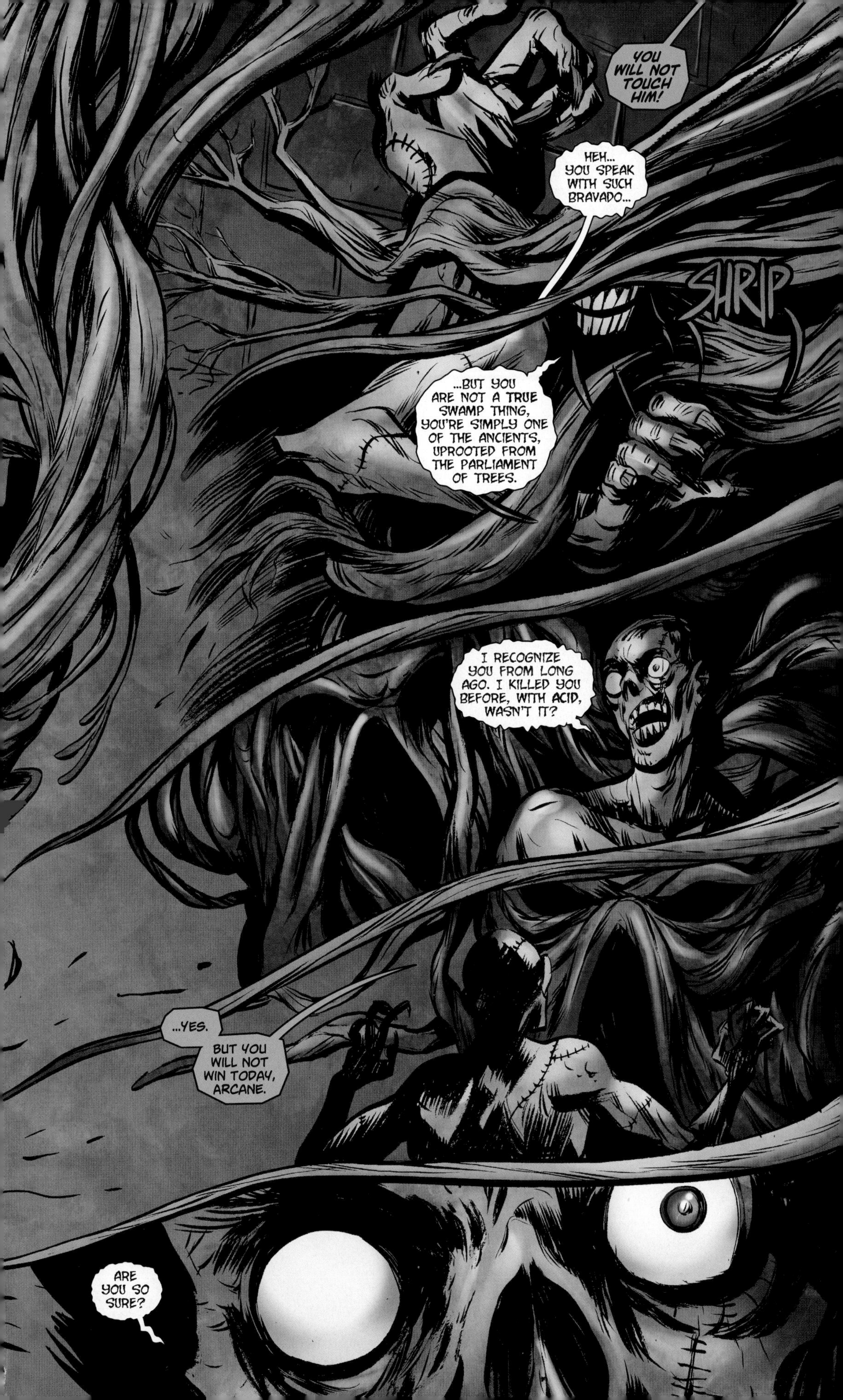
YOU WILL NOT TOUCH HIM!
HEH... YOU SPEAK WITH SUCH BRAVADO...
SHRIP
...BUT YOU ARE NOT A TRUE SWAMP THING, YOU'RE SIMPLY ONE OF THE ANCIENTS, UPROOTED FROM THE PARLIAMENT OF TREES.
I RECOGNIZE YOU FROM LONG AGO. I KILLED YOU BEFORE, WITH ACID, WASN'T IT?
...YES.
BUT YOU WILL NOT WIN TODAY, ARCANE.
ARE YOU SO SURE?

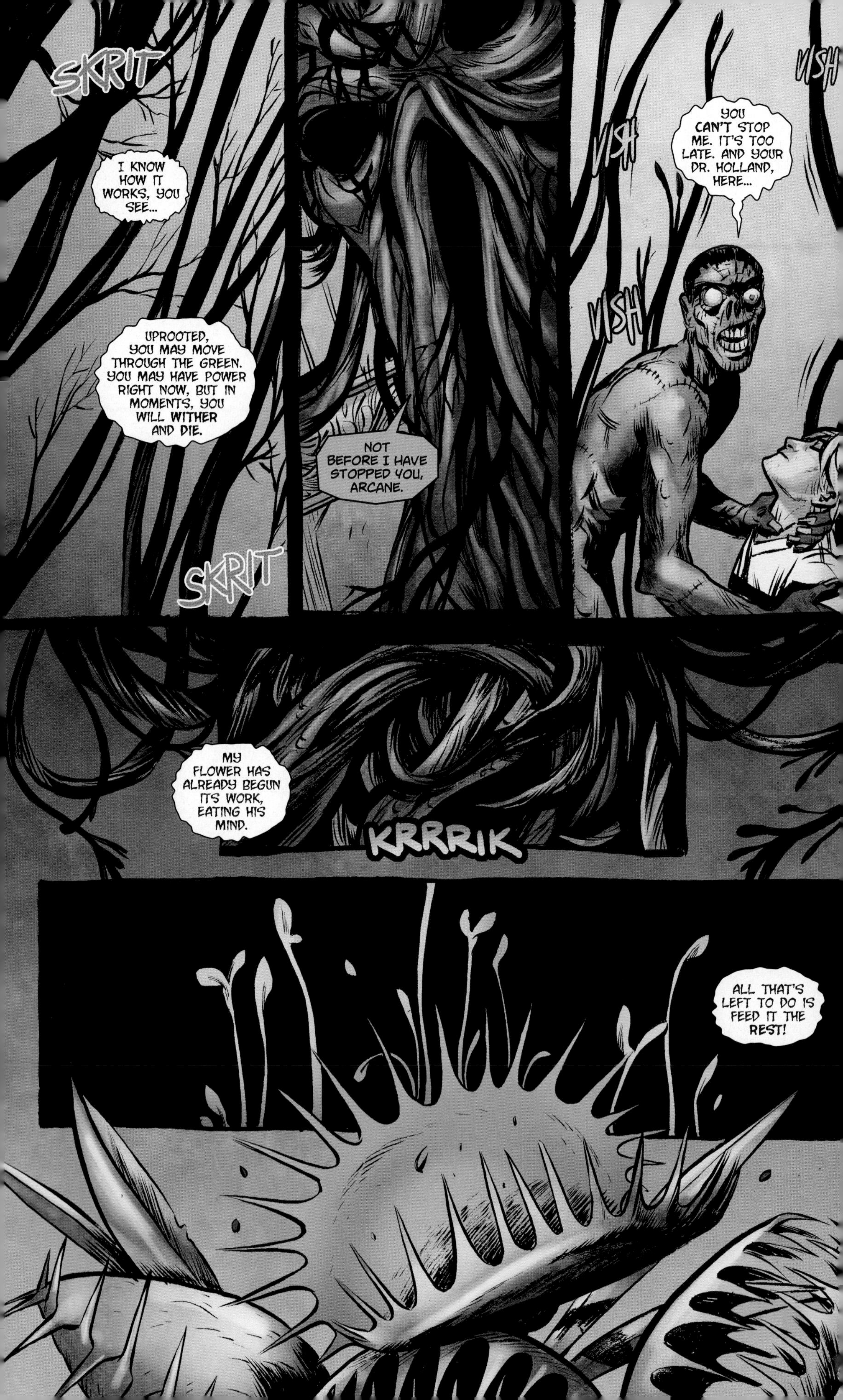
SKRIT
I KNOW HOW IT WORKS, YOU SEE...
UPROOTED, YOU MAY MOVE THROUGH THE GREEN. YOU MAY HAVE POWER RIGHT NOW, BUT IN MOMENTS, YOU WILL WITHER AND DIE.
SKRIT
NOT BEFORE I HAVE STOPPED YOU, ARCANE.
VISH
VISH
YOU CAN'T STOP ME. IT'S TOO LATE. AND YOUR DR. HOLLAND, HERE...
VISH
MY FLOWER HAS ALREADY BEGUN ITS WORK, EATING HIS MIND.
KRRRIK
ALL THAT'S LEFT TO DO IS FEED IT THE REST!

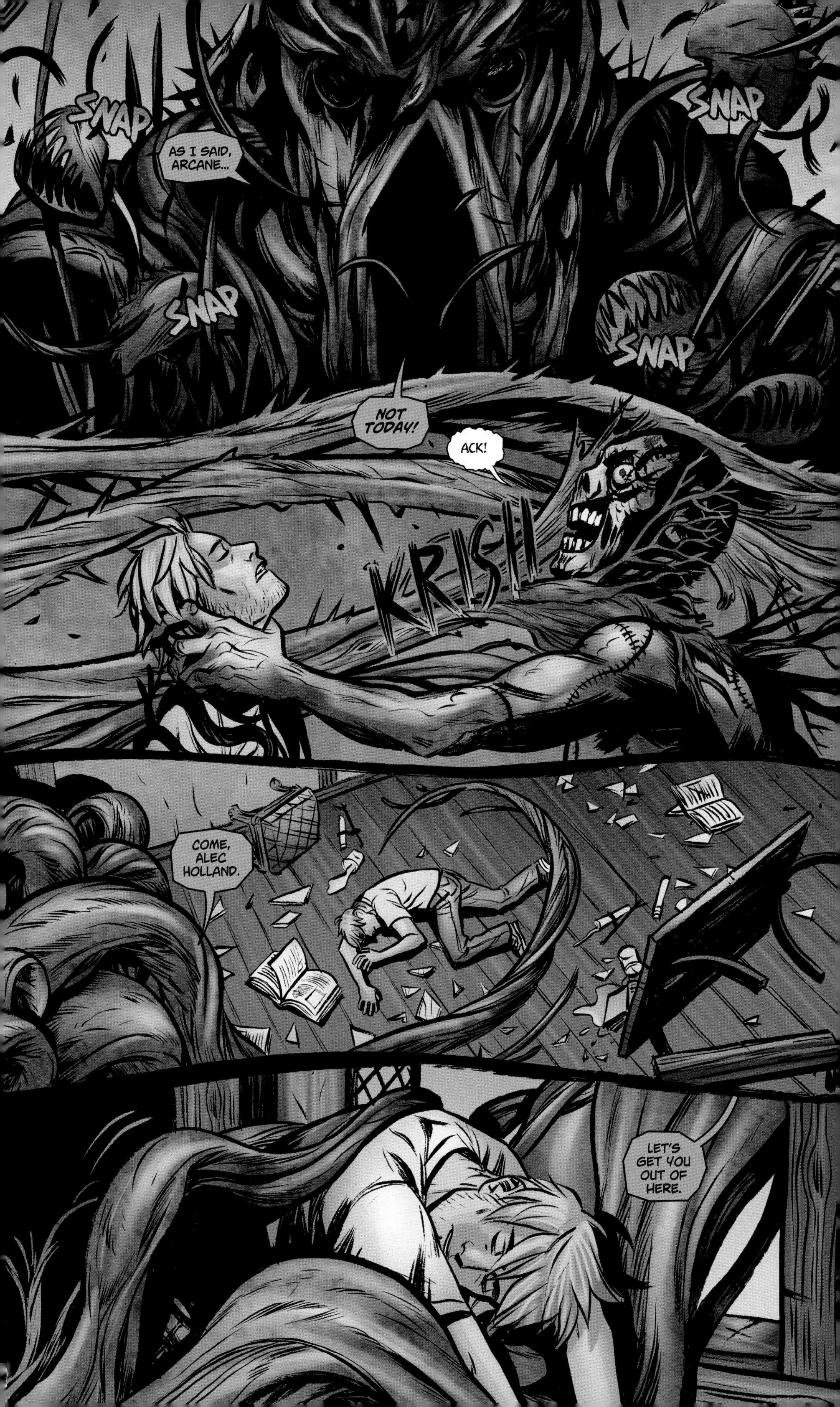
SNAP
AS I SAID, ARCANE...
SNAP
SNAP
SNAP
NOT TODAY!
ACK!
KRISH
COME, ALEC HOLLAND.
LET'S GET YOU OUT OF HERE.

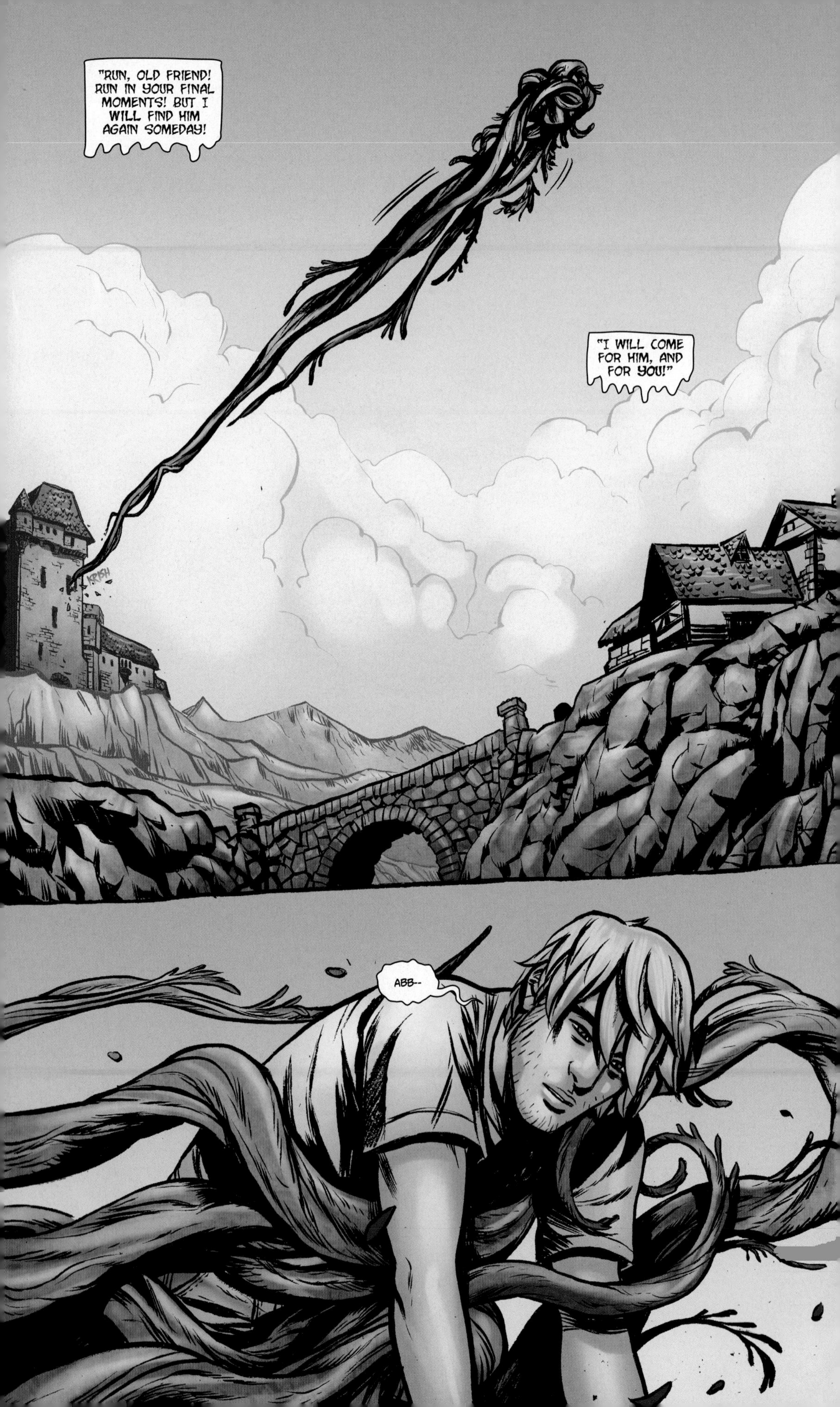
"RUN, OLD FRIEND! RUN IN YOUR FINAL MOMENTS! BUT I WILL FIND HIM AGAIN SOMEDAY!
"I WILL COME FOR HIM, AND FOR YOU!"
KRISH
ABB--

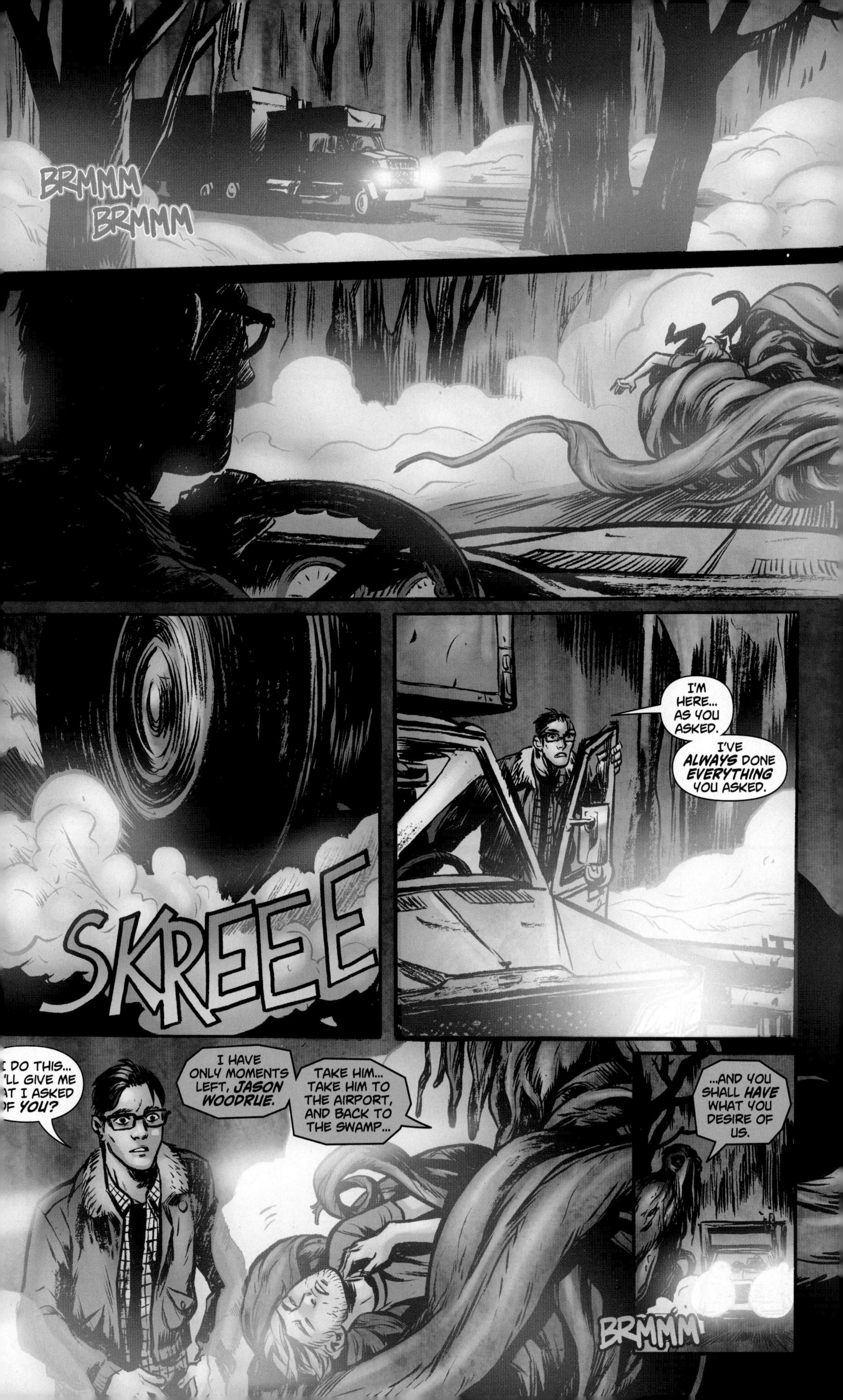
BRMMM BRMMM
SKREEE
I'M HERE... AS YOU ASKED.
I'VE ALWAYS DONE EVERYTHING YOU ASKED.
I DO THIS... 'LL GIVE ME AT I ASKED OF YOU?
I HAVE ONLY MOMENTS LEFT, JASON WOODRUE.
TAKE HIM... TAKE HIM TO THE AIRPORT, AND BACK TO THE SWAMP...
...AND YOU SHALL HAVE WHAT YOU DESIRE OF US.
BRMMM

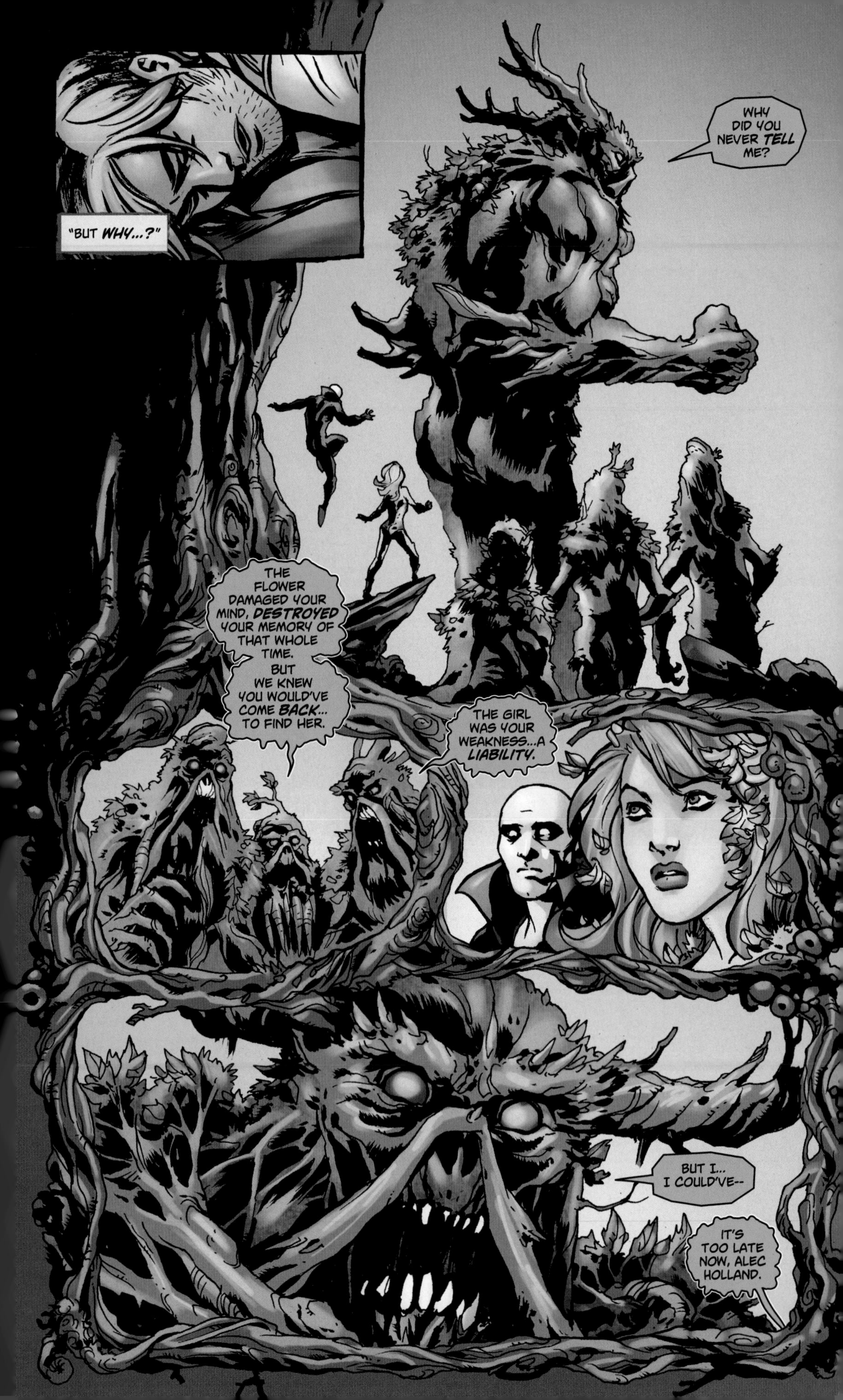

"BUT WHY...?"
WHY DID YOU NEVER TELL ME?
THE FLOWER DAMAGED YOUR MIND, DESTROYED YOUR MEMORY OF THAT WHOLE TIME.
BUT WE KNEW YOU WOULD'VE COME BACK... TO FIND HER.
THE GIRL WAS YOUR WEAKNESS...A LIABILITY.
BUT I... I COULD'VE--
IT'S TOO LATE NOW, ALEC HOLLAND.

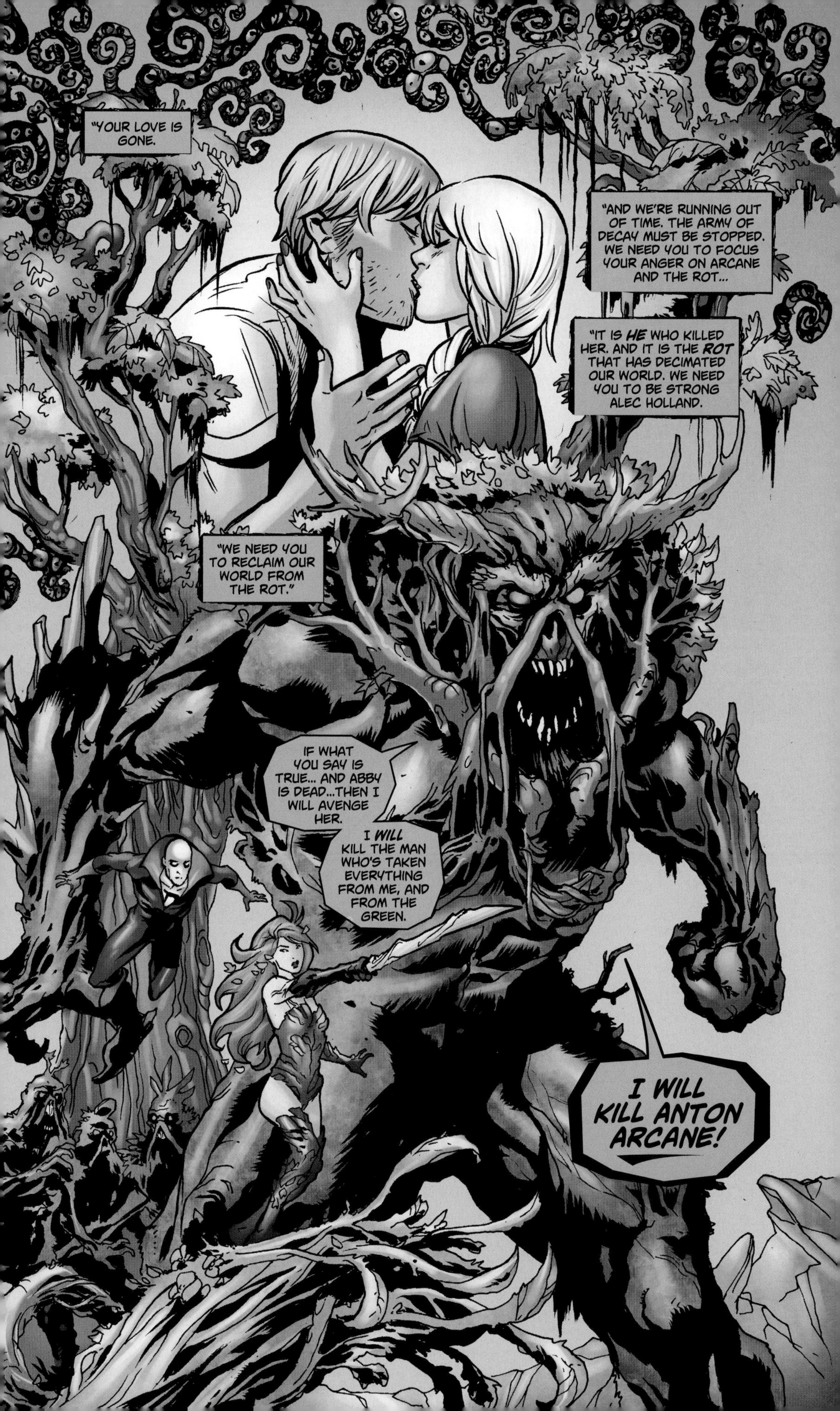
"YOUR LOVE IS GONE.
"AND WE'RE RUNNING OUT OF TIME. THE ARMY OF DECAY MUST BE STOPPED. WE NEED YOU TO FOCUS YOUR ANGER ON ARCANE AND THE ROT...
"IT IS HE WHO KILLED HER. AND IT IS THE ROT THAT HAS DECIMATED OUR WORLD. WE NEED YOU TO BE STRONG ALEC HOLLAND.
"WE NEED YOU TO RECLAIM OUR WORLD FROM THE ROT."
IF WHAT YOU SAY IS TRUE... AND ABBY IS DEAD...THEN I WILL AVENGE HER.
I WILL KILL THE MAN WHO'S TAKEN EVERYTHING FROM ME, AND FROM THE GREEN.
I WILL KILL ANTON ARCANE!

SWAMP THING
SKETCHES BY YANICK PAQUETTE

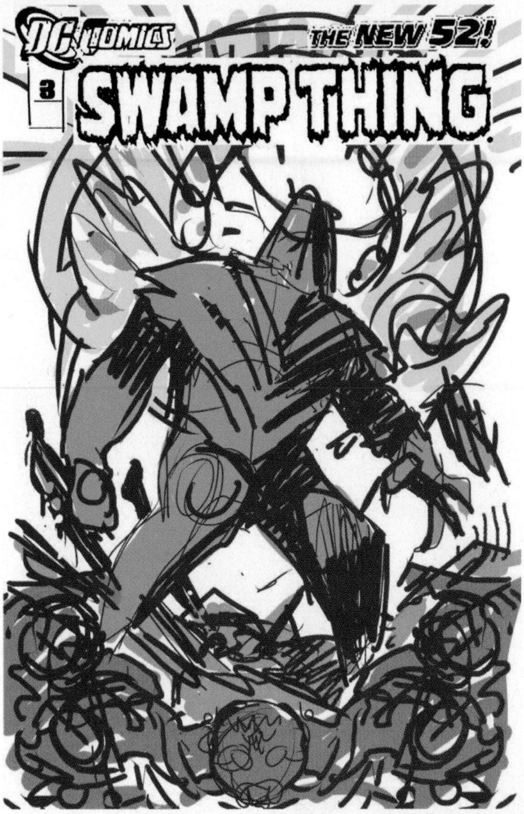
DC COMICS
THE NEW 52!
8
SWAMP THING

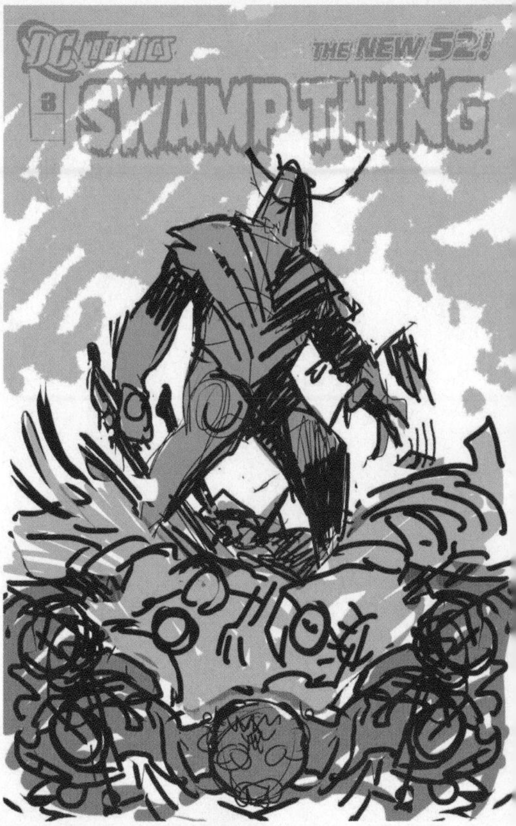
DC COMICS
THE NEW 52!
8
SWAMP THING

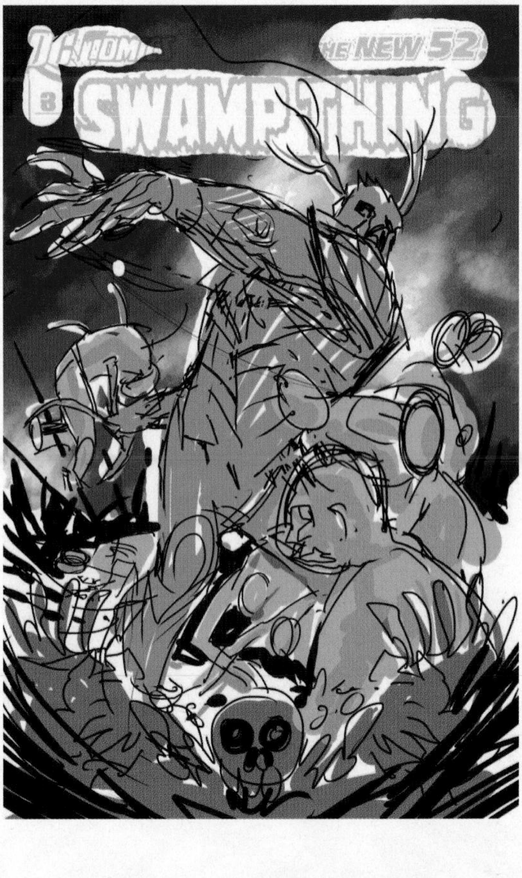
THE NEW 52!
8
SWAMP THING

Sketches for issue #8 cover

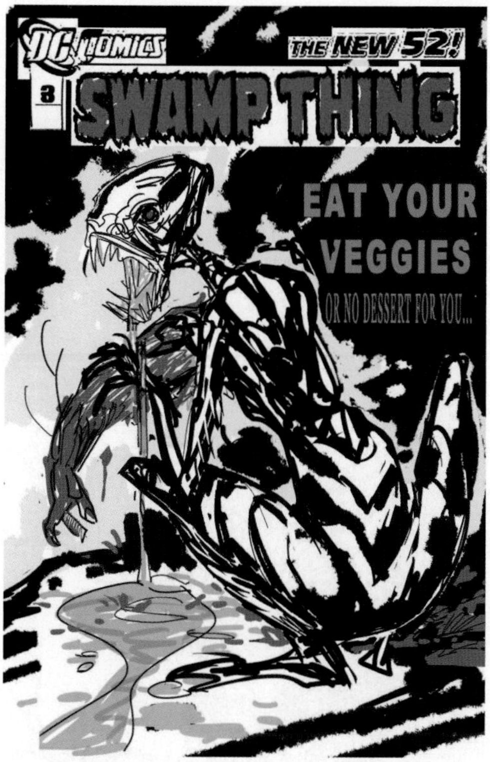
DC COMICS
THE NEW 52!
8
SWAMP THING
EAT YOUR
VEGGIES
OR NO DESSERT FOR YOU...

Sketch for issue #9 cover

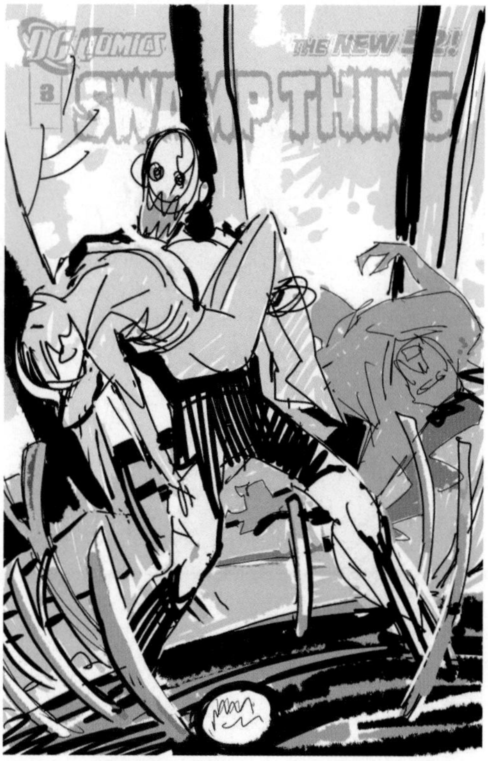
DC COMICS
THE NEW 52!
8
SWAMP THING

Sketch for issue #11 cover

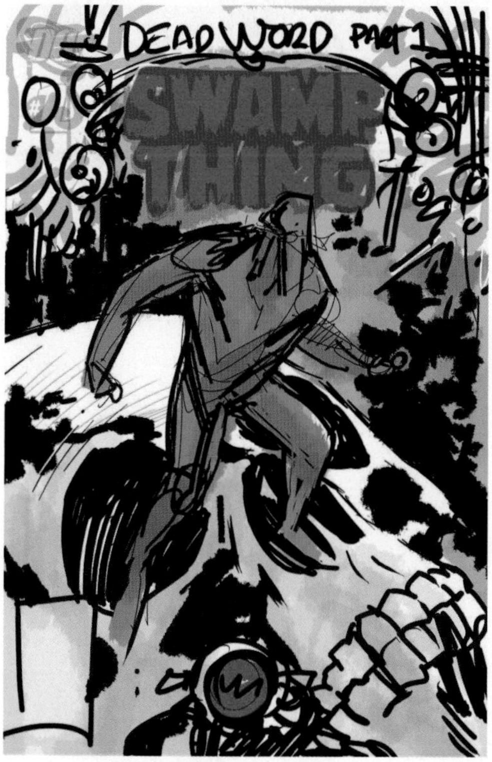
DEAD WORLD PART 1
SWAMP
THING

Sketch for Annual #1 cover

♪ = CHARGE!

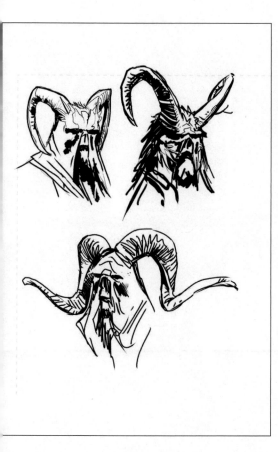

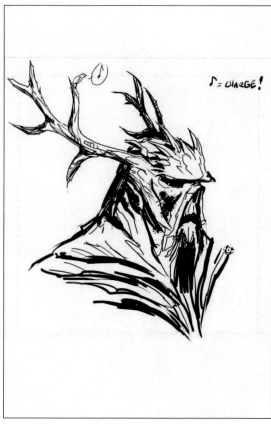

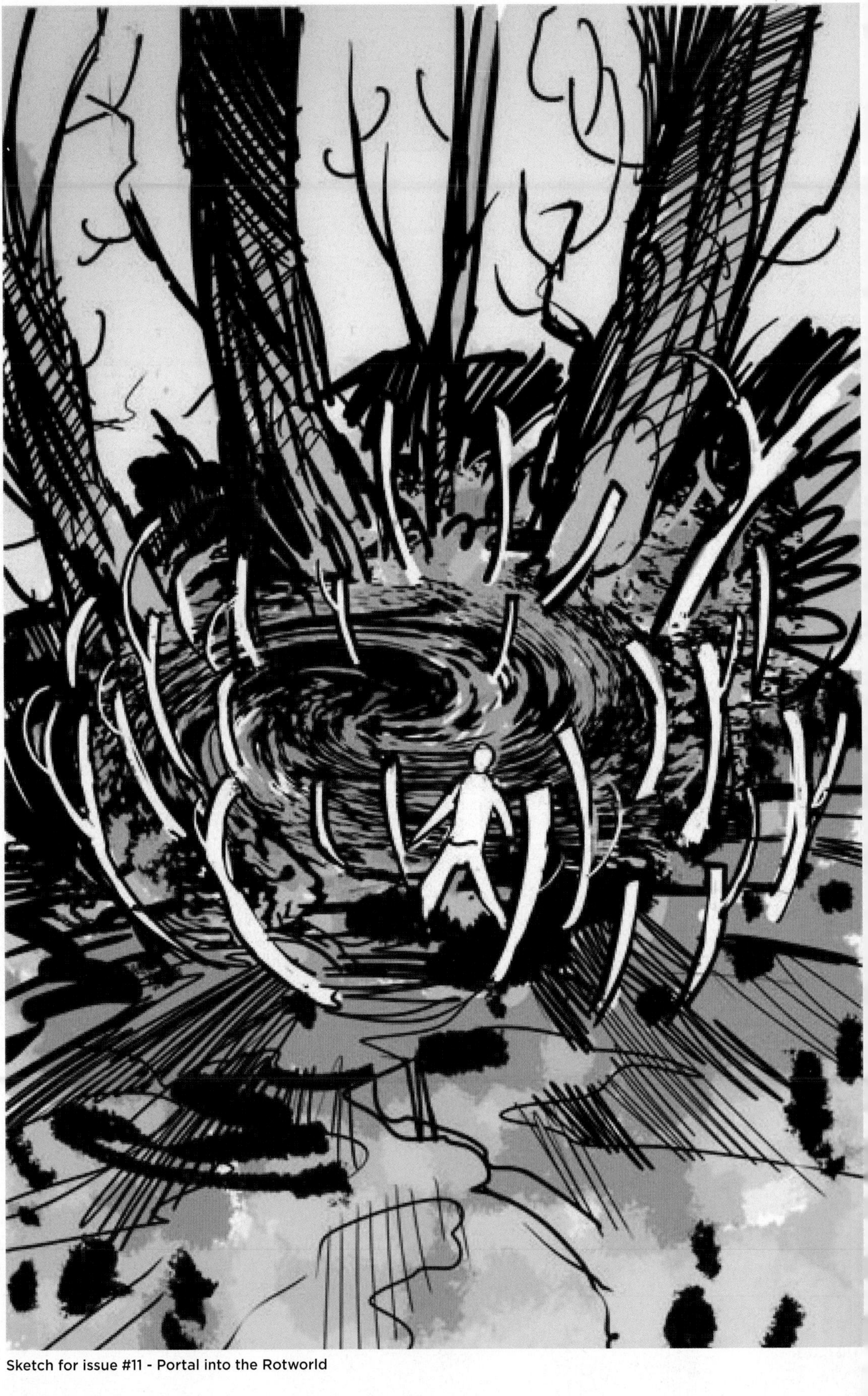

Sketch for issue #11 - Portal into the Rotworld